THE BARBOUR
COLLECTION
OF CONNECTICUT TOWN
VITAL RECORDS

THE BARBOUR COLLECTION

OF CONNECTICUT TOWN

VITAL RECORDS

BARKHAMSTED 1779–1854
BERLIN 1785–1850
BETHANY 1832–1853
BETHLEHEM 1787–1851
BLOOMFIELD 1835–1853
BOZRAH 1786–1850

Compiled by

Lorraine Cook White

INTRODUCTION

As early as 1640 the Connecticut Court of Election ordered all magistrates to keep a record of the marriages they performed. In 1644 the registration of births and marriages became the official responsibility of town clerks and registrars, with deaths added to their duties in 1650. From 1660 until the close of the Revolutionary War these vital records of birth, marriage, and death were generally well kept, but then for a period of about two generations until the mid-nineteenth century, the faithful recording of vital records declined in some towns.

General Lucius Barnes Barbour was the Connecticut Examiner of Public Records from 1911 to 1934 and in that capacity directed a project in which the vital records kept by the towns up to about 1850 were copied and abstracted. Barbour previously had directed the publication of the Bolton and Vernon vital records for the Connecticut Historical Society. For this new project he hired several individuals who were experienced in copying old records and familiar with the old script.

Barbour presented the completed transcriptions of town vital records to the Connecticut State Library where the information was typed onto printed forms. The form sheets were then cut, producing twelve small slips from each sheet. The slips for most towns were then alphabetized and the information was then typed a second time on large sheets of rag paper, which were subsequently bound into separate volumes for each town. The slips for all towns were then interfiled, forming a statewide alphabetized slip index for most surviving town vital records.

The dates of coverage vary from town to town, and of course the records of some towns are more complete than others. There are many cases in which an entry may appear two or three times, apparently because that entry was entered by one or more persons. Altogether the entire Barbour Collection--one of the great genealogical manuscript collections and one of the last to be published--covers 137 towns and comprises 14,333 typed pages.

TABLE OF CONTENTS

ABBREVIATIONS

ae.------------age
b. ------------born, both
bd.------------buried
B. G.---------Burying Ground
d. ------------died, day, or daughter
decd.---------deceased
f.--------------father
h.--------------hour
J. P.-----------Justice of Peace
m.-------------married or month
res.------------resident
s.--------------son
st.-------------stillborn
w. -----------wife
wid.----------widow
wk.-----------week
y. ------------year

THE BARBOUR
COLLECTION
OF CONNECTICUT TOWN
VITAL RECORDS

BARKHAMSTED VITAL RECORDS
1779 - 1854

1

ALVORD, ALFORD, (cont.)

Zora, s. Arba & Eunice, b. Aug. 15, 1795   116

ANDREWS, ANDRUES, ANDRUS, ANDRUSS, Anne, d. Benjamin &

Annice, b. May 3, 1793   23

Archebald, s. Benjamin & Annice, b, Nov. 29, 1788   23

Benjamin, m. Annice **CASE,** Oct. 29, 1784   23

Charles, married, d. Mar. 15, 1855, ae 74   212

Erastus, m. Anna **HART,** [   ], 1826, by Saul Clark   189

Fanny, of Barkhamsted, m. Edward **SEAMOR,** of New Hartford, Feb.
6, 1834, by Rev. William R. Gould   202

Frederick, m. Julia **MERRITT,** Jan. 28, 1830, by Asa Bushnell, L. M.
P.   192

Hannah M., b. Barkhamsted, res. Simsbury, wid., d. June 5, 1859, ae 40   214

Rebecca, m. Caleb **HOUGH,** Nov. 27, 1777   62

Reubin, s. Benjamin & Annice, b. Apr. 2, 1786   23

Reuben, of Cheshire, m. Nancy **MUNSON,** of New Hartford, Oct. 15,
1828, by Saul Clark   191

Roswell, mechanic, res. Barkhamsted, m. Henriette H. **EGGLESTON,**
ae 20, b. Barkhamsted, Nov. 12, 1848, by [   ]   230

Sylvester, s. Benjamin & Annice, b. Apr. 2, 1791   23

Tracy, of Canton, m. Hannah **MOSES,** of Barkhamsted, Aug. 27, 1823,
by Saul Clark   188

Willard, m. Jerusha **BARBER,** b. of Barkhamsted, Dec. 21, 1828, by
John Merrell, J. P.   128

ATWATER, Clara, married, d. July 27, 1861, ae 52   215

Josiah H., m. Mahala **CASE,** b. of Barkhamsted, Sept. 12, 1843, by
Reuben S. Hazen   212

Josiah W., m. Fanny **BLANNOT,** b. of Barkhamsted, Jan. 10, 1837, by
Rev. William R. Gould   208

Sarah L., m. Martin **RUST,** b. of Barkhamsted, Sept. 4, 1838, by Rev.
William R. Gould   208

ATWELL, Mary M., b. Colchester, married, d. Jan. 19 , 1863, ae 65   216

AUSTIN, Annice, d. William & Sarah, b. Nov. 10, 1776   11

Annice, m. Aaron **HART,** Dec. 3, 1795   99

Hyla, ae 20, b. Colebrook, m. Beecher **GOODWIN,** farmer, ae 24, b.
New Hartford, res. same, Feb. 9, 1849   230

Hyler, m. Beecher A. **GOODWIN,** of Farmington, Feb. 21, 1850, by
Rev. George B. Atwell   221

James, m. Hannah **WILDER,** Dec. 9, 1779   5

Levi, s. William & Sara, b. Feb. 1, 1772   11

Lucinda, d. James & Hannah, b. Aug. 7, 1783   5

Mabel, d. James & Hannah, b. Jan. 6, 1782   5

Molly, d. James & Hannah, b. Oct. 3, 1780   5

Sara, d. William & Sara, b. Nov. 29, 1774   11

Sara, m. Jonathan **WILDER,** Apr. 1, 1779   6

Sylvia, ae 24, b. Granvill, m. James M. **RAU,** farmer, ae 26, res.
Colebrook, Mar. 4, 1849   230

Tahpenes, m. Thomas **WILDER,** [   ]   5

Page

AUSTIN, (cont.)

William, Jr., m. Sara **FISH**, Aug. 23, 1771   11

William, Jr., d. May 8, 1778, ae 30 y.   11

William, s. James & Hannah, b. Feb. 6, 1785   5

AVERY, Ichabod, married, d. Oct. 22, 1859, ae 52   214

Ichabod Austin, of Barkhamsted, m. Lucy Ann **AVERY**, of Groton, Oct. 24, 1830, by Rev. Cyrus Yale   195

Lucy Ann, of Groton, m. Ichabod Austin **AVERY**, of Barkhamsted, Oct. 24, 1830, by Rev. Cyrus Yale   195

Sophronia, of Barkhamsted, m. Herman **HOLCOMB**, of New Hartford, Nov. 27, 1828, by Cyrus Yale   126

BACON, Eunice, m. Eber **WEED**, Mar. 22, 1793   104

BAKER, Emerson, b. Sailsbury, res. Barkhamsted, d. [   ], ae 18 m.   234

Emily L., of Colebrook, m. Hiram **POND**, of Colebrook, Apr. 3, 1851, by Rev. Luther H. Barber, of Hitchcockville   224

BALDWIN, Almon, of New Marlborough, Mass., m. Amanda **MESSENGER**, of Barkhamsted, Sept. [   ], 1822, by Saul Clark   187

Chauncey, of Winsted, m. Rumah **PIKE**, of Barkhamsted, Sept. 1, 1828, by Saul Clark   191

Jane, m. Martin V. **HULBERT**, b. of Barkhamsted, Mar. 4, 1848, by George B. Atwell   219

BANNING, BANNIN, Abigail, m. Gabril **CASE**, June 24, 1783   16

Hannah, m. Joseph **WILLCOCKS**, Jr., Dec. [   ], 1784   56

BARBER. BARBOUR, Abiram, s. Ephraim & Sarah, b. Mar. 1, 1796   54

Alexander. s. Ezekiel & Elizabeth, b. Sept. 3, 1780   3

Alvin, s. Ephraim & Sarah, b. Apr. 24, 1789   54

Anna, w. Naham B., d. May 16, 1819   141

Betsey, housewife, b. Canton, res. Barkhamsted, d. Sept. 28, 1847, ae 53   228

Bidkah, s. David & Deborah, b. Apr. 19, 1782   15

Candace, d. Jacob & Patience, b. Sept. 30 , 1779   114

Dan, s. Jacob & Patience, b. Dec. 18, 1781   114

David, s. David & Deborah, b. July 2, 1778   15

David, married, d. Feb. 11, 1858, ae 80   213

Deborah, d. David & Deborah, b. Oct. 30, 1773   15

Dilly, d. Jacob & Patience, b. Feb. 21, 1784   114

Elijah Willslow, b. Sept. 22, 1813   141

Ephraim, Jr., s. Ephraim & Sarah, b. Nov. 11, 1781   54

Ezekiel, m. Elizabeth **GODARD**, Jan. 15, 1779   3

Gaylord, of Canton, m. Catherine **HAYDEN**, of Barkhamsted, May 8, 1850 , by Luther H. Barber   223

Gaylord, farmer, ae 26, b. Canton, res. same, m. Catherine **HAYDEN**, ae 25, b. Barkhamsted, res. same, May 8, 1850, by Luther Barber   233

George, farmer, ae 25, b. Barkhamsted, res. same, m. Orpha **CASE**, ae 20, b. Barkhamsted, res. same, Feb. [   ], 1850, by William Goodwin   233

Gideon, s. Zimri & Thanks, b. May 15, 1803   131

Grove, d. Oct. 26, 1848, ae 3   231

Hannah, d. Ephraim & Sarah, b. Dec. 17, 1785   54

Page

BARBER, BARBOUR, (cont.)

Heman H., of Columbus, Ind., m. Francis E. **MERRELL,** of
Barkhamsted, Oct. 23, 1845, by Reubin S. Hough ... 216

Henry, s. Zimri & Thanks, b. Sept. 3, 1805 ... 131

Jacob, m. Patience **LAWRENCE,** Jan. 24, 1765 ... 114

James, s. Jacob & Patience, b. Feb. 16, 1768 ... 114

Jason, s. Zimri & Thanks, b. May 4, 1798 ... 131

Jerusha, m. Willard **ANDRUS,** b. of Barkhamsted, Dec. 21, 1828, by
John Merrell, J. P. ... 128

Laraney, d. Ezekiel & Elizabeth, b. Oct. 7, 1783 ... 3

Lucy, d. Zimri & Thanks, b. Dec. 26, 1791 ... 131

Marcy, d. Jacob & Patience, b. Oct. 11, 1787 ... 114

Naham Corrin, b. May 24, 1810 ... 141

Nashti, d. Zimri & Thanks, b. Jan. 24, 1794 ... 131

Patience Tabitha, d. Jacob & Patience, b. Mar. 17, 1770 ... 114

Patience Talitha, m. Roger **MOSES,** Feb. 9, 1792 ... 117

Peter, s. Jacob & Patience, b. Mar. 6, 1775 ... 114

Phebe Maria, of Canton, m. James H. **COE,** of Colebrook, May 10,
1846, by Rev. Luther H. Barber, of Hitchcockville ... 216

Rhoda, of Barkhamsted, m. Andrew **INGRAHAM,** of Bristol, June 6,
1838, by Rev. Isaac Jones, of Hitchcockville ... 206

Rozilla, d. Ephraim & Sarah, b. Oct. 7, 1792 ... 54

Salmon, farmer, ae 47, b. Canton, res. Barkhamsted, m. Ann
RICHARDSON, ae 44, b. Barkhamsted, res. same, Apr. 7, 1850,
by Rev. Mr. Leadbetter ... 233

Sarah Drake, d. Ephraim & Sarah, b. Dec. 1, 1783 ... 54

Seth, m. Darcos **HOWD,** Dec. 20, 1796 ... 96

Susanna, d. Jacob & Patience, b. Jan. 9, 1777 ... 114

Thanks, d. Zimri & Thanks, b. Sept. 18, 1789 ... 131

Thomas, s. Jacob & Patience, b. Apr. 13, 1773 ... 114

Thomas, s. Rosetta **CASE** b. Jan. 13, 1781 ... 54

Violet, d. Zimri & Thanks, b. Jan. 12, 1796 ... 131

Zimri, s. Jacob & Patience, b. Mar. 24, 1766 ... 114

Zimri, m. Thanks **WILLCOX,** [   ] ... 131

Zimri A., s. Zimri & Thanks, b. Feb. 1, 1787 ... 131

BARKER, Caty, m. Eli **FORSTER,** Dec. 19, 1793 ... 82

BARNES, BARNS, Anson E., of Barkhamsted, m. Polly M. **CASTLE,** of
Winchester, Mar, 30, 1851, by Rev. Luther H. Barber, of
Hitchcockville ... 223

Charles M., of New Hartford, m. Lamantia **HARGER,** of Barkhamsted,
Nov. 20 , [   ], at the house of Oliver Phelps, by James Beach ... 15

Dwight, b. Winchester, single, d. Mar. 27, 1856, ae 22 ... 212

Emily, m. Reuben **RICE,** Aug. 17, 1824, by Eli Barnet, Elder ... 30

John J. C., m. Clarissa **HINKLEY,** b. of Barkhamsted, Nov. 23, 1834,
by Joshua Hudson ... 200

Levi, married, d. Jan. 30, 1863, ae 70 ... 216

Martha, Mrs., m. Allen **DRAKE,** Nov. 27, 1834, by Anson Wheeler, J.
P. ... 200

Page

BARRETT,BARRET,Jason, b. New Hartford, wid., d. Mar. 20 , 1854, ae 38   211
  Jason, d. [   ]   231
  Marcus D. T., s. Jason M., farmer, b. Apr. [ ], 1850   232
  William R., farmer, ae 36, b. New Hartford, res. Barkhamsted, m. Julia
    H. MARSH, ae 25, b. New Hartford, Apr. 30, 1850 , by Ira
    Pettebone   233
BASSETT, BASSET, Christopher, m. Julia PHELPS, Mar. 15, 1805   137
  Hiram, twin with Homer, s. Christopher & Julia, b. Dec. 15, 1807   137
  Homer, twin with Hiram, s. Christopher & Julia, b. Dec. 15, 1807   137
  Miriah*, d. Christopher & Julia, b. Mar. 17, 1806 *(Surname crossed
    out)   137
BEACH,BEECH,Abigail, m. Isaiah I. TUTTLE,Oct. 24, 1824,by Saul Clark   188
  Charlotte, d. Samuel & Desire, b. Nov. 28, 1787   63
  David, m. Elizabeth JONES, Dec. 2, 1804   136
  Elizabeth, d. David & Elizabeth, b. Nov. 2, 1805   136
  Fanny, of Hartland, m. Salmon C. TIFFANY, of Barkhamsted, Jan. 1,
    1854, by Luther H. Barber   239
  Miles, s. Samuel & Desire, b. Sept. 30, 1791   63
  Oliver, of Granby, m. Rosanna ALLEN, of Barkhamsted, Jan. 22, 1849,
    by Rev. A. B. Pulling   219
  Oliver, farmer, ae 71, b. Milford, res. Granby, m. Rosannah ALLEN, ae
    54, b. Barkhamsted, Feb. [ ], 1849   230
  Samuel, m. Desire CASE, Oct. [ ], 1783   63
  Samuel, m. Desire CASE, [   ] *   *(Entry erased)   58
  Samuel, s. Samuel & Desire, b. Feb. 7, 1784   63
BEANON (?), Harriet, of Granby, m. Francis H. MATHEWS, of
    Southington, June 29 , 1851, by Rev. A. B. Pulling   221
BECKLEY, J[ ], farmer, ae 40 & L[   ], ae 35, had d. [ ], b. June 16,
    1850   232
BEECHER, Amos, b. Wolcott, res. Barkhamsted, d. [ ], ae 76   231
  Eliza J., of Barkhamsted, m. William S. WATSON, of Norfolk, Oct. 11,
    1853, by Rev. George B. Atwell   241
  Julia L., m. Lyman HART, Feb. 5, 1837, by Asa Bushnell   203
  Sally, of Wolcott, m. James MARTIN, of Barkhamsted, May 15, 1828,
    by Rev. James Beach, of Winsted   182
BEERS, Comfort, m. Samuel CROSS, Nov. 21, 1826, by John Merrell, J. P.   178
  Luanna, m. Japhet J. CASE, b. of Barkhamsted, Apr. 27, 1834, by Rev.
    William R. Gould   201
  Lydia, b. Granby, married, d. Oct. 24, 1854, ae 37   211
  Susan, of Barkhamsted, m. John W. VINING, of Granby, Dec. 31,
    1826, by John Merrell, J. P.   178
BELDEN, Benaja, m. Orpha MANCHESTER, Dec. 7, 1839, by J. W.
    Alvord   209
  Henry B., of Sandisfield, Mass., m. Mary KNIGHT, of Colebrook, Aug.
    30, 1853, by Rev. Luther H. Barber, of Hitchockville   238
  Mary Ann, b. Pleasant Valley, single, d. Oct. 6, 1865, ae 22   219
BEMAN, Austria S., of Granby, m. Albert HAYES, of Barkhamsted, Mar.
    15, 1840, by Leister Loomis, J. P.   209

BLANNOT, BLONNET, (cont.)

Mary, m. George **GAINS**, b. of Barkhamsted, Nov. 26, 1829, by Amasa
  Jerome   147

BLISS, Abijah, of Barkhamsted, m. Maria **CASE**, of Canton, Oct. 28, 1844,   214
  by Rev. Reuben S. Hazen

Agnes, d. Gad & Cloe **(ADAMS)**, b. Dec. 18, 1789   93

Cloe, d. Gad & Cloe, b. Jan. 3, 1785   93

Cloe, m. Luther **RICE**, Dec. 8, 1803   24

Corintha, d. Gad & Cloe, b. Sept. 9, 1801   93

Daniel, s. Gad & Cloe, b. Oct. 15, 1804   93

Daniel, m. Betsey **CASE**, Dec. 21, 1826, by Saul Clark   189

Gad, m. Cloe **ADAMS**, Dec. 11, 1783   93

Linus, m. Ruth **CASE**, Dec. 6, 1821, by Saul Clark   186

Lorinda, m. Jerome **HAYES**, b. of Barkhamsted, Mar. 19, 1850, by
  Rev. A. B. Pulling   220

Lorinda, ae 22, m. Jerome **HAYES**, farmer, ae 27, b. Barkhamsted, res.
  Granby, Mar. 19, 1850, by Rev. Mr. Pulling   233

Lucy, d. Gad & Cloe, b. May 29, 1796   93

Phebe, d. Gad & Cloe, b. Oct. 23, 1787   93

Ruth, married, d. Mar. 31, 1860, ae 59   214

Sibbell, d. Gad & Cloe, b. Aug. 3, 1793   93

Zenus, s. Gad & Cloe, b. July 8, 1798   93

BODWELL, Elliott D., of Collinsville, m. Martha C. **ROBINSON**, of
  Hitchcockville, May 1, 1853, by Rev. L. S. Weed. Witnesses
  Emory M. Davis & Charlott A. Davis   240

BONNY, Elisabeth, m. Abijah **PHELPS**, Mar. 14, 1815   156

BRACE, Ruth, b. Feb. 16, 1743; m. Moses **SHEPARD**, Aug. 23, 1763   6

BRAINARD, Enoch W., ae 24, b. N. H., res. Collinsville, m. Julia A. **CASE**,
  ae 21, b. Barkhamsted, Sept. 5, 1847, by P. Tatro   227

Enoch W., of Collinsville, m. Julia M. **CASE**, of Barkhamsted, Sept. 8,
  1847, by Rev. Peter Tabro   217

BRIGHT, Mary, of Colebrook, m. Henry W. **SAGE**, of Norfolk, Apr. 9,
  1848, by Luther H. Barber   218

BRISTOL, Abigail, d. David & Lois, b. Sept. 13, 1772   92

Adna, s. David & Lois, b. Aug. 29, 1778   92

David, m. Lois **HART**, May 30, 1771   92

David, s. David & Lois, b. Jan. 29, 1776   92

David, m. Hannah **WILLEY**, Jan. 20, 1795   129

David Benedict, s. David & Hannah, b. Aug. 17, 1795   129

Ery, s. David & Lois, b. May 22, 1782   92

Fanny Charlotte, d. Hope, b. May 20, 1827   129

Hannah, d. David & Hannah, b. Sept. 16, 1797   129

Hope, d. David & Hannah, b. Mar. 21, 1806   129

Hope, had d. Fanny Charlotte, b. May 20, 1827   129

Lois, d. David & Lois, b. Apr. 11, 1784   92

Lois, m. Aaron **MUNSON**, Nov. 13, 1827, by John Merrell, J. P. 181

Loisa, d. David & Hannah, b. July 2, 1803   129

Lot, s. David & Hannah, b. May 11, 1801   129

BRISTOL, (cont.)

Mary Hart, d. David & Lois, b. Mar. 15, 1774   92

Namah, of Barkhamsted, m. Asahel EDGERTON, of Granby, May 28,
  1828, by John Merrell, J. P.   184

Sarah, d. David & Lois,˙b. May 28, 1780   92

Sena, d. David & Lois, b. Apr. 2, 1787; d. May 20, 1789, ae 2 y. 18 d.   129

Sina, d. David & Hannah. b. [   ] 4, 1800 ; d. May 10, 1800   112

BROCKWAY, Abigail, m. Isaac JONES, [   ]

BROMHAM, John, m. 1849   (see under BENHAM

BROWN, Helen M., of Winchester, m. Virgil J. DAVID, of Troy, N. Y.,
  Aug. 7, 1846, by Rev. Luther H. Barber, of Hitchcockville   216

Lodiathe, wid. d. Mar. 3, 1865, ae 94   219

Martha C., ae 34, b. Colebrook, m. Charles HOTCHKISS, farmer, res.
  Colebrook, Dec. 24, 1848   230

Orren, of Bristol, m. Jane DOWD, of Barkhamsted, Apr. 8, 1844, by
  Rev. Reuben S. Hazen   213

Rebecca, m. Seth BISHOP, Jr., Sept. 26, 1831, by Anson Wheeler, J. P.   196

BULL, Washburn T., b. Kent, res. Barkhamsted, d. Apr. [   ], 1851, ae 34   237

BULLER, John H., infant, d. July 12, 1855   212

BUMPUS, Lydia, m. Ebenezer HUDSON, Jan. 1, 1783   22

BUMSELL, Martha L., ae 24, b. Barkhemsted, m. Henry MARSH, farmer,
  ae 30, b. New Hartford, res. same, June 1, 1851, by Rev. Hugh
  Gibson   236

BUNNELL, Sarah, b. Oxford, wid., d. Mar. 23, 1856, ae 94   212

BURNET, James E., b. Barkhamsted, d. Sept. 4, 1854, ae 2   211

BURNHAM, Ann R., of Winchester, m. Hosea HULBERT, of Sandisfield,
  Mass., May 12, 1844, by Luther H. Barber   214

BURR, Charlotte, m. Erasmus N. RANSOM, Jan. 28, 1840, at Winsted   105

BURROWS, Lucy, m. Lyman ROCKWELL, Oct. 3, 1837, in
  Hitchcockville, by Rev. Isaac Jones   204

BURWELL, Abigail, b. Milford, married, d. July 13, 1864, ae 81   218

Dora, single, d. Mar. 29, 1863, ae 17   217

Flora, m. Lemuel H. HURLBERT, b. of Barkhamsted, July 15, 1840,
  by Rev. David Stocking   209

Harriet Ella, d. Markes, farmer, ae 50, & Harriet, ae 41, b. Apr. 31,
  [sic], 1848   226

Isabella, b. Great Barrington, Mass., d. July 21, 1864, ae 10 m.   218

John W., b. Milford, wid., d. Aug. 4, 1864, ae 88   218

Julia, m. Robert FANCHER, May 29, 1828, by Saul Clark   190

Laura, of Barkhamsted, m. William S. MALLERY, of New Haven,
  Nov. 20, 1836, by Rev. William R. Gould   208

Marcus, m. Harriet SQUIRE, Jan. 28, 1824, by Saul Clark   188

Martha M., m. Elija TIFFANY, b. of Barkhamsted, Sept. 20, 1829, by
  Amasa Jerome   140

Whitman, m. Mrs. Mayry WHITING, Nov. 27, 1827, by Saul Clark   190

BUSHNELL, BUSHALL, Hiram, of West Hartland, m. Bulia CASE, of
  Barkhamsted, Feb. 8, 1837, by Rev. Richard Hayter   203

Liviny B., s. Hiram & Bulah, b. Feb. 10, 1850   232

BARKHAMSTED VITAL RECORDS 11

Page

CASE, (cont.)

Adah, m. Samuel PINE, b. of Barkhamsted, July 4, 1838, by Rev.

William R. Gould 208

Adah E., d. Rufus & Susan, b. Sept. 14, 1817 179

Ada M., b. Bloomfield, single, d. Mar. 4, 1863, ae 9 217

Adelisa M., m. Watson GIDDINGS, Jan. 6, 1853, by Rev. Augustus B.

Collins 225

Adnah, b. Barkhamsted, m. William SLADE, farmer, b. Barkhamsted, res.

Affy, d. Oliver & Amy, b. July 27, 1801 119

Alanson, s. Ashbel & Mary, b. June 11, 1807 145

Alanson, farmer, ae 40, b. Barkhamsted, res. Hartland, m. Alcene

HERRICK, ae 35, b. Hartland, Mar. 18, 1851, by [ ] 236

Altha, d. Manna & Abigael, b. Oct. 24, 1808 138

Amelia, of Barkhamsted, m. Munson HITCHCOCK, of Hartland, Mar.

19, 1822, by Saul Clark 186

Amerett, d. Humphrey & Freelove, b. July 23, 1807 83

Amos, m. Elizabeth WARD, Dec. 17, 1767 25

Amos, s. Amos & Elizabeth, b. Dec. 3, 1770 25

Amy, m. Oliver CASE, Nov. 10, 1791 119

Amy, d. Oliver & Amy, b. Sept. 21, 1792 119

Amy, of Barkhamsted, m. Lucius GILBERT, of Tolland, Mass., Feb. 2,

1834, by Rev. William R. Gould 202

Amy Fanny, d. Titus & Amy, b. Oct. 14, 1811 106

Andrew, s. Andrew & Rhoda, b. Oct. 25, 1777 17

Annice, m. Benjamin ANDREWS, Oct. 29, 1784 23

Aphia, of Barkhamsted, m. Harvey CURTIS, of Farmington, June 24,

1834, by Rev. William R. Gould 203

Ashbel, m. Mary FRAZUR, July 19, 1801 145

Aurelia, of Barkhamsted, m. Oliver CASE, of Canton, Jan. 10 , 1833, by

Rev. Edwin E. Griswold 197

Austin, s. Manna & Abigail, b. Nov. 19, 1820 138

Austin, farmer, b. Barkhamsted, res. same, d. Jan. 9, 1848, ae 19 228

Betsy, d. Giles & Polly, b. Jan. 23, 1800 113

Betsey, m. Daniel BLISS, Dec. 21, 1826, by Saul Clark 189

Bula, d. Zabad & Sarah, b. Apr. 1, 1803 100

Beulah, m. Ralph JOHNSON, Jan. 24, 1827, by Saul Clark 189

Bulia, of Barkhamsted, m. Hiram BUSHNELL, of West Hartland, Feb. 8,

1837, by Rev. Richard Hayter 203

Bulah M., d. Rufus & Susan, b. Feb. 4, 1819 179

Candace, d. Abner & Hannah, b. Oct. 2, 1777 45

Candace, d. Eliphalet & Rachel, b. Aug. 8, 1802 132

Catura, m. Robert CASE, Jr., Sept. 20, 1825, by Samuel Munson, J. P. 176

Cestus, of Canton, m. Rhoda PIKE, of Barkhamsted, Dec. 28, 1826, by

Saul Clark 189

Charles, d. Jan. 20, 1857, ae 3 212

Charlotte, d. Ozias & Lucy, b. Jan. 10, 1792 67

Charlotte, d. Humphrey & Freelove, b. Sept. 3, 1794 83

Page

CASE, (cont.)

Page

CASE, (cont.)

Julia A., ae 21, b. Barkhamsted, m. Enock W. BRAINARD, ae 24, b. N.
H., res. Collinsville, Sept. 5, 1847, by P. Tatro — 227

Julia A., b. Canton, married, d. Jan. 9, 1858, ae 34 — 213

Julia M., of Barkhamsted, m. Enoch W. BRAINARD, of Collinsville,
Sept. 8, 1847, by Rev. Peter Tabro — 217

Julina, m. Julius WEED, May 2, 1837, by Rev. William R. Gould — 208

Laura, of Barkhamsted, m. Wait RICE, of Canton, Oct. 11, 1835, by
Leister Loomis, J. P. — 201

Levi, s. Titus & Amy, b. Dec. 1, 1803 — 106

Levi, m. Lutia FARNAM, May 11, 1824, by Gershom Pierce — 166

Levi P., b. Simsbury, res. Hartland, d. Jan. [ ], 1850, ae 50 — 234

Lois, single, d. May 7, 1861, ae 76 — 215

Lotey, d. Gabril & Abigail, b. Aug. 16, 1788 — 16

Louisa, b. Hartland, married, d. Apr. 8, 1864, ae 44 — 218

Loviah, d. Titus & Amy, b. Oct. 5, 1792 — 106

Lovisa, m. Solon CASE, b. of Barkhamsted, Feb. 5, 1850, by Rev. Asa
Bushnell, Jr. — 220

Lovisa, ae 18, m. Solon CASE, farmer, ae 22, b. Barkhamsted, res. same,
Feb. 5, 1850, by Asa Bushnell, Jr. — 233

Lucien, of Hudson, O., m. Lucia H. LYMAN, of Barkhamsted, Oct. 24,
1854, by Luther H. Barber — 239

Lucy, d. Eliphelet & Rachel, b. Mar. 15, 1797 — 132

Lucyetty Christiany, d. Fisher & Lucy, b. Mar. 14, 1809 — 124

Lue, d. Ozias & Lucy, b. Oct. 7, 1785 — 67

Lura, of Barkhamsted, m. Wait RICE, of Canton, Sept. 18, 1836, by
Leister Loomis, J. P. — 201

Lydia, d. Oct. 11, 1847, ae 66 — 228

Mahalath, d. Titus & Amy, b. Feb. 20, 1806 — 106

Mahala, m. Josiah H. ATWATER, b. of Barkhamsted, Sept. 12, 1843, by
Reuben S. Hazen — 212

Manne, s. Humphrey & Freelove, b. Nov. 9, 1786 — 83

Manna, m. Abigail PHELPS, Nov. 25, 1807 — 138

Maranda, d. Manna & Abigail, b. Oct. 9, 1822 — 138

Marcia, m. Luman PEASE, July 4, 1854, by P. T. Holley — 240

Maria, of Canton, m. Abijah BLISS, of Barkhamsted, Oct. 28, 1844, by
Rev. Reuben S. Hazen — 214

Mariah, b. Granby, res. Barkhamsted, d. May [ ], 1849, ae 41 — •231

Mary, d. Andrew & Rhoda, b. Jan. 28, 1772 — 17

Mary, d. Manna & Abigail, b. Dec. 12, 1814 — 138

Mary, ae 21, b. Canton, res. Canton, m. William PAYNE, farmer, ae 25,
b. Barkhamsted, res. same, Jan. [ ], 1850, by William Goodwin — 233

Mehetable, d. Ezra & Mehetable, b. July 31, 1781 — 18

Mehetabel, d. Feb. 4, 1800 — 18

Melisa, d. Zabad & Sarah, b. Mar. 10, 1812 — 100

Melissa R., of Hitchcockvill, m. Charles W. ENSIGN, of Tarriffvill, Sept.
16, 1845, by Luther H. Barber — 215

Merriam, d. Eliphelet & Rachel, b. Mar. 29, 1794 — 132

Page

CASE, (cont.)

Page

CASE, (cont.)
Zabad Dillon, s. Zabad & Sarah, b. Feb. 26, 1798   100
Zophar, s. Amos & Elizabeth, b. Oct. 2, 1773   25
CASTER, William P., m. Hariott WILDER, Dec. 10, 1839, by J. W. Alvord   209
CASTLE, Elisabeth, m. Phineas STANNARD, b. of Barkhamsted, Apr. 29,
1843, by Rev. Reuben S. Hazen   212
Polly M., of Winchester, m. Anson E. BARNS, of Barkhamsted, Mar. 30,
1851, by Rev. Luther H. Barber, of Hitchcockville   223
CHADWICK, Elizabeth, m. Nelson MOORE, b. of Barkhamsted, June 21,
1847, by George B. Atwell   219
CHAMBERLIN, William H., of Hartland, m. Sarah HART, of Barkhamsted,
Mar. 23, 1842, by Rev. S. W. Smith, of M. E. Ch.   211
CHANDER, Daniel, d. Jan. 22, 1805   66
Esther, w. Daniel, d. Jan. 18, 1793, in her 72nd y.   66
CHASE, Henry W., b. Granville, Mass., married, d. Oct. 11, 1855, ae 28   212
CHUBB, Alexander, m. Mindwell WHEELER, Mar. 9, 1786   49
Alexander, m. Mindwell WHEELER, Mar. 9, 1786   94
Alexander, s. Alexander & Mindwell, b. June 20, 1790   94
Claret, d. Alexander & Mindwell, b. Sept. 1, 1788   94
Rebecca, m. Ambrose HUMPHRY, Sept. 24, 1772   50
Stephen Nash, s. Alexander & Mindwell, [b.] Dec. 9, 1786   94
CHURCH, Orvill, farmer, ae 25, b. Barkhamsted, res. same, m. Ellen CASE,
ae 16, b. Granby, Mar. 22, 1849   230
Orvill, farmer, ae 26 & Ellen, ae 17, had d. [ ], b. Sept. 18, 1850   235
CLARK, CLARKE, George H. m. Lucy Ann MOORE, b. of Barkhamsted,
Dec. 9, 1824, by Rev. James Beach, of Winsted   167
George H., m. Huldah WOODRUFF, Sept. 24, 1829, by Rev. Erastus
Doty, of Colebrook   191
Lydia, b. Hamden, res. Barkhamsted, d. Dec. 11, 1849, ae 72   234
Orlando, farmer, ae 33, had s. [ ], b. July 30, 1851   235
CLEVELAND, CLEAVELAND, Alex P., married, d. July 31, 1861, ae 51   215
Clarissa, m. Daniel WHITE, July 4, 1799   118
Ellen, single, d. Aug. 20, 1861, ae 19   215
Polly, of Barkhamsted, m. Almon ALCOX, of Wolcott, Dec., 7, 1828, by
Rev. James Beach, of Winsted   123
Sally, married, d. Apr. 17, 1854, ae 51   211
CLINTON, Eleanor, d. Henry, Jr. & Eleanor, b. May 26, 1788   57
Hannah, d. Samuel & Lydia, b. Oct. 24, 1787   64
Henry, Jr., b. Nov. 27, 1763; m. Eleanor DARROW, Oct. 19, 1786   57
Henry, s. Henry, Jr. & Eleanor, b. Jan. 4, 1790   57
Henry, Jr., & Eleanor, had twin sons, b. Apr. 23, 1792; one d. Apr. 24,
1792. the other d. Apr. 25, 1792   57
Lydia, d. Samuel & Lydia, b. Oct. 10, 1789   64
Rachel, d. Samuel & Lydia, b. Apr. 1, 1786   64
Samuel, m. Lydia ALLING, Nov. 3, 1785   64
Sheldon, m. Pelia HARRINGTON, Sept. 30, 1792   66
Stephen Person, s. Samuel & Lydia, b. Oct. 11, 1791   64
COE, Amanda M., of Colebrook, m. Henry H. HEWITT, of Winchester, Oct.

EELLS, (cont.

Hannah, d. Rev. Ozias & Phebe, b. Apr. 29, 1793   61

Hannah, m. Hezekiah **WADSWORTH**, Oct. 1, 1812   152

Ozias, Rev., m. Phebe **ELY**, Sept. 19, 1787   61

Ozias Sheldon, s. Ozias & Phebe, b. Dec. 20, 1794   61

Phebe, d. Rev. Ozias & Phebe, b. Feb. 3, 1802   61

Phebe, of Barkhamsted, m. Erastus **LATIMER**, of Simsbury, Feb. 6,
1828, by Saul Clark   190

Richard, s. Rev. Ozias & Phebe, b. Feb. 23, 1800   61

Richard, of Barkhamsted, m. Jane **BESTER**, of Simsbury, Oct. 4, 1826,
by Allen McLean   177

William Edward, s. Rev. Ozias & Phebe, b. Oct. 5, 1805   61

EGGLESTON, EDGLESTON, David, d. Aug. 30, 1850, ae 15   237

Elisabeth L., m. Eben C. **WOODRUFF,** b. of Barkhamsted, Apr. 21,
1842, by Daniel Coe   211

Ellen, ae 17, b. Barkhamsted, m. John **HOWEL,** mechanic, ae 22, b.
Salisbury, res. Barkhamsted, Nov. [ ], 1850 , by Rev. H. Chase   236

Hector, of Middletown, m. Isabella **LEE,** of Barkhamsted, Sept. 7, 1823,
by Saul Clark   188

Henriette H., ae 20, b. Barkhamsted, m. Roswell **ANDRUSS,** mechanic,
res. Barkhamsted, Nov. 12, 1848, by [ ]   230

ELLIS,Catharine, tayloress, b. Granby, res. Barkhamsted, d. Jan. 3, 1848, ae 24   228

ELWELL, Caroline, of Mass., m. William S. **SMITH,** of Westfield, Mass.,
Sept. 9, 1838, in Hitchcockvill, by Rev. Isaac Jones   206

Charles J., d. Oct. 21, 1860, ae 6   214

Jenett, d. Isaac, ae 25 & Thankful, ae 22, b. Jan. 17, 1849   229

Jerome, s. Joseph, Jr. farmer, ae 33, b. Sept. 7, 1849   232

John, basketmaker, mohegan & Mary, mohegan, had child, b. July 20,
1849   229

Joseph, Jr., of Barkhamsted, m. Catharine **EDGHCOME,** of S. Canaan,
Sept. 12, 1842, by Rev. Erastus Doty, of Colebrook   211

Phebe, d. Isaac, day laborer, ae 27, & Thankfull, ae 27, b. Dec. 24, 1850   235

Stephen, b. Southington, d. Jan. 24, 1859, ae 85   213

ELY, Phebe, m. Rev. Ozias **EELLS,** Sept. 19, 1787   61

EMMONS, Harris, m. Sebre **MERRITT,** Oct. 2, 1794   110

Harris Hiram, s. Harris & Sebre, b. July 31, 1795   110

Lester, s. Harriss & Sebre, b. May 18, 1802   110

Loisa, d. Harris & Sebre, b. Nov. 17, 1799   110

Sebre Lovina, d. Harris & Sebre, b. July 19, 1797   110

ENSIGN, Charles W., of Tarriffvill, m. Melissa R. **CASE,** of Hitchcockvill,
Sept. 16, 1845, by Luther H. Barber   215

Freedom, m. Hiram **ROCKWELL,** Mar. 25, 1823, by Rev. Saul Clarks   183

Harriet, Mrs. of Barkhamsted, m. Elisha **ROCKWELL,** of Westfield,
Mass., Mar. 25, 1823, by Saul Clark   188

Jerusha, m. Hezekiah **RICHARDS,** Apr. 10, 1800   158

FANCES, [see also **FRANCES**], Mary Jane*, m. John **JOHNSON,** Feb. 26,
1854, by P. T. Holley   *("Mary Jane **FRANCES**"?)   239

FANCHER, Robert, m. Julia **BURWELL,** May 29, 1828, by Saul Clark   190

Page

FARGOT, Mary, d. John, farmer, b. Apr. [ ], 1850   232
FARNAM, Lutia, m. Levi CASE, May 11, 1824, by Gershom Pierce   166
Matilda, of Barkhamsted, m. Gurdon TILLOTSON, of Granville, Mass.,
    Aug. 12, 1828, by Saul Clark   190
FELON, [see under PHELAN]
[FERGUSON], FEUGERSON, Albert G., of New Hartford, m. Amerza
    ROBERTS of Barkhamsted, Sept. 26, 1824, by Rev. James Beach,
    of Winsted   167
FISH, Sara, m. William AUSTIN, Jr., Aug. 23, 1771   11
FIST, Eliza Ann, b. Boston, res. Barkhamsted, d. Dec. 18, 1848, ae 42   231
FLOWER, Clarisa, m. Abner SLADE, Sept. 26, 1825, by Samuel Munson, J.P.   175
FORD, Alven E., d. Apr. 13, 1850, ae 22   234
Sylvia Ophelia, of Barkhamsted, m. Frederick T. WALLACE, of Otis,
    Mass., May 10, 1846, by Rev. Luther H. Barber, of Hitchockville 216
FORDUM, Eliza, m. Gordon TURNER, Mar. 31, 1844, by Edward Camp, J.P.   213
FORSTER, Chester, s. Phinahas [& Hannah], b. Apr. 29, 1802   48
Chole, d. Eli & Caty, b. Jan. 29, 1799   82
Electa, d. Phinahas & Hannah, b. Oct. 28, 1797   48
Eli, m. Caty BARKER, Dec. 19, 1793   82
Hannah, d. Phinahas & Hannah, b. Oct. 30, 1808   48
Harvey, s. Eli & Caty, b. July 28, 1796   82
Laura, d. Eli & Caty, b. July 27, 1801   82
Lemuel, s. Phinahas & Hannah, b. Nov. 24, 1799   48
Lewis, s. Phinahas & Hannah, b. Feb. 5, 1807   48
Lucy, d. Phinahas & Hannah, b. July 24, 1804   48
Marvin, s. Eli & Caty, b. Oct. 6, 1794   82
Milton, s. Eli & Caty, b. July 8, 1804   82
Phinahas, m. Hannah KILBORN, Sept. 22, 1796   48
FOX, Joseph, of Granby, m. Charity TUTTLE, of Barkhamsted, June 9, 1823,
    by Asa Bushnel, L. M.   (Entry crossed out)   164
FRANCES, [see also FANCES], Oliver S., of Avon, m. Achsah C. HARGER,
    of Barkhamsted, Dec. 23, 1833, by Rev. William R. Gould   202
FRAZIER, FRAZER, FRAZUR, Abigael, d. Thomas & Deborah, b. Aug. 22,
    1790   143
Allanson, s. John & Hannah, b. June 8, 1782   14
Ameret, d. Thomas & Deborah, b. May 12, 1801   143
Deborah, d. Thomas & Deborah, b. July 20, 1794   143
Eliphelet, s. Thomas & Deborah, b. June 14, 1806   143
Filander, s. John & Hannah, b. May 26, 1784   14
Jarvis, of Granby, m. Matilda PHELPS, of Barkhamsted, Nov. 26, 1822,
    by Saul Clark   187
John, m. Hannah HUDSON, Oct. 4, 1781   14
John, s. Thomas & Deborah, b. Jan. 1, 1804   143
Joseph, s. Thomas & Deborah, b. Oct. 14, 1796   143
Maria, d. Thomas & Deborah, b. Jan. 24, 1799   143
Mary, m. Ashbel CASE, July 19, 1801   145
Mary Matilda, d. Philander & Polly Matilda (MILLER), b. July 31, 1806   136
Permelia, d. Philander & Polly Matilda (MILLER), b. Aug. 26, 1803   136

Page

GILBERT, (cont.)

Nelson, s. Asa & Mary, b. Feb. 20, 1807   125
GILLETT, GILLET, Anna, m. Joseph WILDER, 2nd, Aug. 27, 1812   158
Joel, d. July 22, 1863, ae 1 y. 5 m.   217
Junius, of Colebrook, m. Pearly (?) ROSE, of Barkhamsted, Sept. 23,
    1838, by Rev. Isaac Jones, of Hitchockvill   206
Mary, m. Pelatiah ALLYN, Dec. 13, 1781   41
Miles, of Colebrook, m. Sarah TUTTLE, of Barkhamsted, Dec. 9, 1823,
    by Saul Clark   188
Pantha, m. Lovel ROSE, June 10, 1812   137
Theron B., m. Mary Ann BIDWELL, b. of Colebrook, May 29, 1853, by
    Rev. Luther H. Barber, of Hitchcockville   238
Tryphena, m. Aaron PHELPS, Sept. 30, 1784   106
GODARD, GODDARD, Elizabeth, m. Ezekiel BARBER, Jan. 15, 1779   3
Jerome, of Granby, m. Harriet A. WHITE, of Barkhamsted, July 22,
    1838, by Rev. William R. Gould   208
GOLDSMITH, GOOLDSMITH, Edward, of Plymouth, m. Harriet SEGAR,
    of Barkhamsted, Dec. 23, 1847, by George Merrill, J. P.   218
Edward L., stonecutter, ae 23, b. Plymouth, res. same, m. Harriet SEGAR,
    ae 19, b. Barkhamsted, Dec. 23, 1847, by G. Merrell   227
GOODWILL, Stephen, s. Samuel P., mechanic, b. July [ ], 1850   232
GOODWIN, GOODNON, Beecher, farmer, ae 24, b. New Hartford, res. same,
    m. Hyla AUSTIN, ae 20, b. Colebrook, Feb. 9, 1849   230
Beecher A., of Farmington, m. Hyler AUSTIN, Feb. 21, 1850, by Rev.
    George B. Atwell   221
George H., m. Melissa JOHNSON, Dec. 25, 1853, by P. T. Holley   240
Hiram, single, d. Apr. 2, 1855, ae 17   212
GOSS, Eunice, d. Thomas & Eunice, b. Aug. 25, 1767   1
Jemima, m. George SHEPARD, June 9, 1775   42
Jemima, d. Thomas & Sarah, b. Feb. 13, 1778   1
Jesse, s. Thomas & Sarah, b. Feb. 17, 1780   1
Judith, d. Thomas & Eunice, b. Oct. 22, 1769   1
Sarah, d. Philip, b. July 1, 1782   9
Simeon, s. Thomas & Sarah, b. May 27, 1784   1
Thomas, m. Sarah DERBY, May 29, 1777   1
Thomas, s. Thomas & Sarah, b. Mar. 24, 1782   1
GRAHAM, Flavel B., Dr., m. Caroline PHELPS, of Barkhamsted, Oct. 13,
    1833, by Rev. Asahel Morse   199
GRANGER, Giles A., m. Jenette TUCKER, b. of Barkhamsted, Jan. 12, 1840,
    by Daniel Coe   209
GRANT, Harriot, of Courtland Village, N. Y., m. William Kenyon PARKER,
    Oct. 22, 1838, by Rev. Isaac Jones   206
GREEN, Calice, of North Adams, Mass., m. Henry HODGE, of Londonderry,
    Ireland, Mar. 10, 1839 , by Rev. Isaac Jones   207
Eugene, d. [ ], ae 6 m.   234
Rachel, d. [ ], ae 17   231
GREENWOODS, Francis, m. Lucy F. MESSENGER, Nov. 4, 1850, by
    George Merrill, J. P.   220

Page

HART, (cont)

Page

HART, (cont.)

Rebecca, of Barkhamsted, m. Lorenzo C. **STEPHENS**, of Hartland, Oct.
2, 1831, by Rev. John A. Hempsted — 196

Sally, d. Levy & Elizabeth, b. Sept. 10, 1796 — 115

Sally, d. Aaron & Annice, b. Feb. 10, 1801 — 99

Sally, d. Levi & Elizabeth, d. Sept. 20, 1807, ae 11 y. 10 d. — 115

Salmon, s. Aaron & Anna, b. Sept. 19, 1807 — 99

Sarah, d. Hawkins & Lois, b. Jan. 24, 1818 — 171

Sarah, of Barkhamsted, m. William H. **CHAMBERLIN**, of Hartland, Mar.
23, 1842, by Rev. S. W. Smith, of M. E. Ch. — 211

Sidney L., m. Electa **HUMPHREY**, Oct. 20, 1840, by J. W. Alvord — 210

Susan Jane, d. Lyman, farmer, ae 51 & Julia L., ae 41, b. Feb. 7, 1848 — 226

William H., s. Hawkins & Lois, b. Aug. 28, 1812 — 171

HASKINS, Emily, of Barkhamsted, m. Everitt **CASE**, of Granby, Nov. 22,
1836, by Asa Bushnell — 201

HAYDEN, HADEN, HAYDON, Amelia Mariette, m. Salmon **HOWD**, b. of
Barkhamsted, Nov. 18, 1830, by Rev. James Beach, of Winsted — 195

Amelia Marietta, m. Salmon **HOWD**, Jr., b. of Barkhamsted, Nov. 18,
1830, by Rev. James Beech, of Winsted — 196

Catherine, of Barkhamsted, m. Gaylord **BARBER**, of Canton, May 8,
1850, by Luther H. Barber — 223

Catherine, ae 25, b. Barkhamsted, res. same, m. Gaylord **BARBER**,
farmer, ae 26, b. Canton, res. same, May 8, 1850, by Luther Barber — 233

Julia A., of Barkhamsted, m. Asa **HOWES**, of Oak Creek, Wis., Apr. 9,
1844, by Rev. Reuben S. Hazen — 213

Luke, b. Torringford, married, d. Mar. 5, 1854, ae 77 — 211

Martha, wid., d. Jan. 11, 1864, ae 74 — 218

Mary Lucretia, d. Rachel Lucretia **MILLER**, b. Aug. 16, 1818 — 13

Minerva, of Barkhamsted, m. Jared **THOMPSON**, of Mansfield, Jan. 21,
1827, by Saul Clark — 190

HAYES, HAYS, HAYSE, Albert, of Barkhamsted, m. Austria S. **BEMAN**, of
Granby, Mar. 15, 1840, by Leister Loomis, J. P. — 209

Eliza L., of Barkhamsted, m. Christopher **GATES**, of Harwinton, Feb. 27,
1845, by Rev. James C. Houghton, of Hartland — 215

Elizabeth, m. William Clark **JONES**, Dec. 28, 1784 — 52

Jerome, m. Lorinda **BLISS**, b. of Barkhamsted, Mar. 19, 1850, by Rev. A.
B. Pulling — 220

Jerome, farmer, ae 27, b. Barkhamsted, res. Granby, m. Lorinda **BLISS**, ae
22, Mar. 19, 1850, by Rev. Mr. Pulling — 233

Melissa, single, d. Dec. 6, 1862, ae 57 — 216

Olive, m. Martin **COSSET**, Feb. 9, 1779 — 43

Silas, of Colebrook, m. Ruby **SLADE**, of Barkhamsted, [   ], 1824, by
Saul Clark — 188

HAYWARD, William, b. England, res. Barkhamsted, d. Feb. 10, 1850, ae 56 — 234

HAZARD, HAZZERD, Franklin, negro, b. Winchester, married, d. Dec. 24,
1854, ae 33 — 211

James S., of Winchester, m. Lovesa **SALES**, of Barkhamsted, Jan. 1,
1839, by Rev. William R. Gould — 203

Page

HODGE, HODGES, (cont.)

Thomas N., m. Maria W. PARSONS, b. of Barkhamsted, Aug. 2, 1842,
by Rev. Lewis Gunn — 211

HOLCOMB, Alpheus, s. Eli & Hannah, b. Jan. 10, 1779 — 38

Alury, d. Eli & Hannah, b. Feb. 17, 1773 — 38

Alury, d. Eli & Hannah, d. Aug. 4, 1774, ae 1 y. 5 m. 18 d. — 38

Cynthy, d. Eli & Hannah, b. Mar. 17, 1783 — 38

Eli, m. Hannah CROFUT, Dec. 20, 1764 — 38

Eli, s. Eli & Hannah, b. Sept. 20, 1765 — 38

Eli, s. Eli & Hannah, d. Feb. 24, 1782, ae 16 y. 5 m. 4 d. — 38

Ella E., b. Southwick, d. Sept. 11, 1855, ae 2 — 212

Hannah, d. Eli & Hannah, b. Apr. 3, 1771 — 38

Herman, of New Hartford, m. Sophronia AVERY, of Barkhamsted, Nov.
27, 1828, by Cyrus Yale — 126

Hugh, s. Eli & Hannah, b. Oct. 14, 1774 — 38

Jared, s. Eli & Hannah, b. Nov. 4, 1780 — 38

Jonathan, of Granby, m. Lois HART, of Barkhamsted, Jan. 1, 1845, by
Rev. Reuben S. Hazen — 215

Rachel, d. Eli & Hannah, b. Dec. 17, 1785 — 38

Selah, s. Eli & Hannah, b. Sept. 4, 1767 — 38

Sterlin, s. Eli & Hannah. b. Oct. 10, 1776 — 38

Trueman, s. Eli & Hannah, b. Aug. 10, 1769 — 38

HOLABIRD, [see under HURLBURT]

HOLIDAY, Mary, m. Samuell MERIOTT, Nov. 17, 1774 — 4

HOOD, Orville, d. Mar. [ ], 1849, ae 52 — 231

HOPKINS, Anson, m. Sally WALTER, b. of Winchester, Aug. 6, 1837, by
Anson Wheeler, J. P. — 204

HORROX, Patience, married, d. May 11, 1864, ae 45 — 218

HOSKINS, Lyman, b. Granby, married, d. Jan. 2, 1865, ae 74 — 218

HOTCHKISS, Charles, farmer, res. Colebrook m. Martha C. BROWN ae 34,
b. Colebrook, Dec. 24, 1848 — 230

HOUGH, Caleb, m. Rebecca ANDREWS, Nov. 27, 1777 — 62

Caleb, s. Caleb & Rebbecca, b. June 23, 1782 — 62

Erastus, s. Caleb & Rebecca, b. Sept. 25, 1790 — 62

Josiah, of Canton, m. Laura RICE, of Barkhamsted, Dec. 8, 1830, by
Amos Beecher, J. P. — 195

Lydia, d. Caleb & Rebecca, b. Oct. 3, 1778 — 62

Orrin, s. Caleb & Rebbecca, b. May 20, 1785 — 62

Patta, d. Caleb & Rebecca, b. June 27, 1780 — 62

Rebecca, d. Caleb & Rebecca, b. Sept. 30, 1787 — 62

HOWD, Darcos, m. Seth BARBER, Dec. 20, 1796 — 96

Georgina, of Barkhamsted, m. Jonathan A. MILLER, of West Hartland,
Mar. 16, 1853, by Rev. Augustus B. Collins — 225

Hannah, m. George MERRELLS, Sept. 21, 1809 — 152

Julia, d. Orville & Anna, b. June 8, 1825 — 170

Julia T., of Barkhamsted, m. Salmon GIDDINGS, of Hartland, Sept. 20,
1843, by Reuben S. Hazen — 212

Julius, single, d. May 13, 1866, ae 32 — 220

HOWD, (cont)

Mary, m. Samuel **MUNSON,** Nov. 13, 1800	122
Mary L., d. Jan 28, 1857, ae 1	212
Orville, m. Anna **WILDER,** June 20, 1822	170
Orvill, m. Anna **WILDER,** June 20, 1822, by Saul Clark	187
Rhoda, w. Salmon, d. Feb. 4, 1804	101
Rhoda, d. Orville & Anna, b. May 3, 1823	170
Rhoda, d. Orville & Anna, d. Apr. 1, 1824	170
Ruth, b. Burlington, wid., d. Apr. 28, 1858, ae 60	213
Salmon, m. Amelia Mariette **HAYDEN,** b. of Barkhamsted, Nov. 18, 1830, by Rev. James Beach of Winsted	195
Salmon, Jr., m. Amelia Mariette **HAYDEN,** b. of Barkhamsted, Nov. 18, 1830, by Rev. James Beech, of Winsted	196

HOWE, HOWES, Asa, of Oak Creek, Wis., m. Julia A. **HADEN,** of

Barkhamsted, Apr. 9, 1844, by Rev. Reuben S. Hazen	213
Elizabeth, d. Apr. 25, 1859	214

HOWEL, John, mechanic, ae 22, b. Salsbury, res. Barkhamsted, m. Ellen

EGGLESTON, ae 17, b. Barkhamsted, Nov. [ ], 1850, by Rev. H. Case	236

HUBBARD, Julia, of Granby, m. Oliver **HULL,** of Springfield, Mass., Apr. 1,

1833, by Leister Loomis, J. P.	198

HUBBELL, Catherine, m. Abraham **BENNETT,** Nov. 11, 1790 | 107

Frances, m. Liverius, **MUNSON,** Mar. [ ], 1802	126

HUDSON, Ebenezer, m. Lydia **BUMPUS,** Jan. 1, 1783 | 22

Ebenezer, d. July 2, 1784, in the 23rd y. of his age	22
Hannah, m. John **FRAZER,** Oct. 4, 1781	14
John, Jr., d. Feb. 29, 1780, ae 31 y.	1
Lovise, d. Ebenezer & Lydia, b. Sept. 4, 1783	22
Lucy, m. Bennoni **JONES,** July 16, 1777	44

HULL, [see also **HALL & HALE**], Adaline A., m. Leander T. **SMITH,** July

26, 1843, at the house of Apollas Moore, by Rev. William H. Frisbie, of Hitchcocksvill	212
John H., m. Lucinda **MOORE,** Apr. 14, 1824, by Erastus Doty, Elder	1
Oliver, of Springfield, Mass., m. Julia **HUBBARD,** of Granby, Apr. 1, 1833, by Leister Loomis, J. P.	198

HUMPHREY, HUMPHREYS, HUMPHRY, Ambrose, m. Rebecca **CHUBB,**

Sept. 24, 1772	50
Ambrose & Rebecca, had s. [ ], b. July 28, 1775 ; d. same day	50
Ambrose & Rebeca, had s. [ ], b. July [ ], 1782 ; d. same day	50
Ambrose & Rebeca, had sons, one [ ], b. Sept. 3, 1783 ; d. same day & the other [ ], , b. July [ ], 1784 ; d. same day	50
Augustus, b. Canton, married, d. July 9, 1859, ae 90	214
Electa, m. Sidney L. **HART,** Oct. 20, 1840, by J. W. Alvord	210
Eveline S., d. [ ], 1864, ae 6	218
Mindwell, d. Ambrose & Rebeca, b. Oct. 4, 1779	50
Rebeca, d. Ambrose & Rebeca, b. Aug. 22, 1773 ; d. Nov. 15, 1773	50
Rebeca, d. Ambrose & Rebeca, b. July 2, 1776	50
Ruth, d. Ambrose & Rebeca, b. Oct. 16, 1785	50
Sarah, wid., d. July 2, 1864, ae 88	218

Page

JOHNSON, (cont.)

21, 1844, by Rev. Luther H. Barber, of Hitchcocksville	214
Emily S., married, d. Feb. 15, 1860, ae 24	214
Erastus, twin with Ralp[h], s. Jonathan & Lydia, b. July 11, 1797	134
Felus, s. Jonathan & Lydia, b. July 25, 1788	134
Frank, d. Mar. 22, 1862, ae 4	216
Harriet E., d. Orrin, farmer, ae [ ] Charlotte, b. Dec. 31, 1849	232
Hiram, s. Reubin & Bethiah, b. May 31, 1793	46
Hiram, s. Reubin & Bethiah, d. Dec. 30, 1795	46
John, m. Mary Jane FANCES, Feb. 26, 1854, by P. T. Holley	239
Laura, d. Jonathan & Lydia, b. June 16, 1803	134
Laura, of Barkhamsted, m. Titus S. CASE, of Canton, June 7, 1848, by Rev. Ira Pettibone	218
Luther, s. Jonathan & Lydia, b. Oct. 12, 1790	134
Lydia, b. Wallingford, res. Barkhamsted, d. Sept. 15, 1849, ae 85	234
Melissa, m. George H. GOODNON, Dec. 25, 1853, by P. T. Holley	240
Nancy, d. Jonathan & Lydia, b. Aug. 24, 1792	134
Olive, d. Jonathan & Lydia, b. Nov. 5, 1799	134
Olive, of Barkhamsted, m. [ ] SMITH, of Torringford, Jan. 31, 1828, by Saul Clark	190
Orrin, m. Charlotte SQUIRE, b. of Barkhamsted, Sept. 9, 1834, by Rev. Asahel Morse	200
Polly, d. Jonathan & Lydia, b. Jan. 25, 1795	134
Ralp[h], twin with Erastus, s. Jonathan & Lydia, b. July 11, 1797	134
Ralph, m. Beulah CASE, Jan. 24, 1827, by Saul Clark	189
Reuben, m. Bethiah KING, June 1, 1786	46
Reubin, d. Nov. 19, 1795	46
Reubin Merriman, s. Reubin & Bethiah, b. Aug. 12, 1795	46
Roxanna, d. Reubin & Bethiah, b. Jan. 12, 1787	46
Sabrina, d. Reubin & Bethiah, b. Feb. 7, 1789	46

JONES, Amos, s. Benjamin & Esther, b. Dec. 16, 1785 | 21

Anson, s. Israel & Rhoda, b. Dec. 24, 1780	4
Armenta, d. Israel & Rhoda, b. June 29, 1788	4
Bennoni, m. Lucy HUDSON, July 16, 1777	44
Bennoni, s. Bennoni & Lucy, b. Nov. 1, 1780	44
Betsy, d. Samuel & Ruth, b. Apr. 22, 1789	10
Chauncey, s. Thomas & Susannah, b. May 11, 1780	35
Clarasey, d. Thomas & Susannah, b. Feb. 7, 1874	35
Dency, d. Israel & Rhoda, b. Oct. 25, 1782	4
Dorcas, d. Bennoni & Lucy, b. June 29, 1779	44
Drayton, s. Israel, Jr. & Rhoda, b. Sept. 15, 1786	4
Edward. s. Israel & Lois, b. Apr. 29, 1806	97
Elam, s. Samuell & Ruth, b. Sept. 29, 1774	10
Electa, d. Samuel [& Ruth], b. June 17, 1787	10
Elijah, s. Samuel & Ruth, b. May 1, 1783	10
Elijah, m. Thankful COLES, Sept. 12, 1804	135
Elijah, d. July 7, 1850, ae 67	234
Elisha Cole, s. Elijah & Thankful, b. July 14, 1807	13

KING, (cont.)

Charles H., b. New London, married, d. Dec. 19, 1863, ae 40   217

KNAPP, Desire, b. Norfolk, m. Edward **CAMP**,farmer, b. Winchester, res.

Barkhamsted, [·]   236

KNIGHT, , Mary, of Colebrook, m.henry B. **BELDEN**, of Sandisfield, Mass.,

Aug. 30, 1853, by Rev. Luther H. Barber, of Hitchcockville   238

LaFOGG, Marilla, b. Colebrook married, d. Oct. 26, 1863, ae 52   217

LANDON, Betsey, m. Humphrey **QUAMOIN**, Nov. 25, 1778, by John Lay, J.

P.   26

LANE, Aaron, farmer, ae 36, had d. [   ], b. Oct. 20, 1850   235

-----, d. Nov. 3, 1859, ae 1   214

LATHAM, Ruba, Mrs., m. Henry **CASE**, Apr. 26, 1841, by Hira Case, J. P.   210

LATIMER, Erastus, of Simsbury, m. Phebe **EELLS**, of Barkhamsted, Feb. 6,

1828, by Saul Clark   190

LAWRENCE, Patience, m. Jacob **BARBER**, Jan. 24, 1765   114

LEE, Dennis, of Sheffield, Mass., m. Caroline **SQUIRE**, of Barkhamsted, Oct.

8, 1833, by Rev. William R. Gould   199

Henry, his w. [   ], b. New Hartford, d. Dec. 4, 1863, ae 57   217

Henry, b. Granby, married, d. Sept. 16, 1865, ae 65   219

Isabella, of Barkhamsted, m. Hector **EGLESTON**, of Middletown, Sept.

7, 1823, by Saul Clark   188

Laura, of Barkhamsted, m. Thaddeus **TULLER**, of Simsbury, Oct. 10,

1821, by Saul Clark   186

-----, wid., d. Mar. 12, 1861, ae 72   215

LEWIS, Elizabeth, m. Dan **WEED**, May 4, 1780   37

Manna, s. Thomas & Abigail, b. Mar. 3, 1793   91

Morgan, of West Stockbridge, m. Roby **WAIT**, of Barkhamsted, Mar. 4,

1830, by Rev. James Beach, of Winsted   191

Rachel, m. Jared **RAXFORD**, Aug. 17, 1794   88

Thomas, m. Abigail **HOLIBURD**, Aug. 10, 1790   91

Thomas, s. Thomas & Abigail, b. Mar. 15, 1795   91

LINSLEY*, Edmund B., m. Susan Janette **SQUIRE**, b. of Granby, Oct. 14,

1835, by W[illia]m R. Gould   * (Perhaaps "LINSEY")   162

LOOMIS, Clarisa Ann, m. Hart **DOOLITTLE**, b. of Barkhamsted, May 18,

1834, by Rev. William R. Gould   202

Laura, of Barkhamsted, m. Orson **GATES**, of Hartland, May 11, 1843, by

Rev. Reuben S. Hazen   212

Leister, b. Vernon, married, d. July 2, 1859, ae 67   213

Lucinda, m. Harvey **CASE**, b. of Barkhamsted, Sept. 18, 1849, by Rev. A.

B. Pulling   220

Luther, m. Catherine Maria **ROCKWELL**, b. of Barkhamsted, Aug. 2,

1829, by Amasa Jerome   185

Maria Ann, b. Granville, married, d. Sept. 6, 1865, ae 63   219

Miles, married, d. Sept. 13, 1854, ae 55   211

Norman, of Otis, Mass., m. Dincy **WILDER**, of Barkhamsted, May 5,

1831, by Amos Beecher, J. P.   195

Sarah, m. Aaron **ALLYN**, Jan. 18, 1782   11

W[illia]m, b. Winsted, married, d. Mar. 25, 1866, ae 61   210

Page

MERRILL, MERRELLS, MERRELL, (cont.)

Caroline, d. Merlin & Clarrissa, b. Nov. 19, 1825	95
Caroline, d. Merlin & Clarissa, d. June 19, 1827	95
Charles, s. George & Marcy, b. Dec. 9, 1831	152
Clarra, d. John & Elizabeth, b. May 6, 1793	154
Clarissa, married, d. Apr. 4, 1857, ae 56	213
Clarry, 2nd, d. John & Elizabeth, b. Oct. 12, 1794	154
Clarry, [d. John & Elizabeth], d. Oct. 17, 1794, in the 18th m. of her age	154
Elisabeth, d. John & Elisabeth, b. Sept. 13, 1783, at New Hartford	154
Elizabeth, w. John, d. May 23, 1823, ae 61	154
Elisabeth, m. Sharlock **MUNSON**, b. of Barkhamsted, by Saul Clark (No date given)	63
Francis E., of Barkhamsted, m. Heman H. **BARBOUR**, of Columbus, Ind., Oct. 23, 1845, by Reubin S. Hough	216
Frances Elizabeth, d. Merlin & Clarrissa, b. May 25, 1824	95
George, s. John & Elizabeth, b. May 10, 1788	154
George, m. Hannah **HOWD**, Sept. 21, 1809	152
George, d. Mar. 12, 1865	152
George, wid., d. Mar. 12, 1865, ae 77	219
Hannah, d. George & Hannah, b. [ ]	152
Helen, d. Merlin & Clarissa, b. Jan. 9, 1828	95
Hepzibah L., b. Strubridge, Mass., married, d. Apr. 11, 1862, ae 51	216
John, m. Elisabeth **SHEPARD**, July 4, 1782, at New Hartford	154
John, s. John & Elizabeth, b. Feb. 23, 1805	154
John, m. Murilla **RICHARDSON**, [ ], 1824, by Saul Clark	188
John, d. Mar. 30, 1848, ae 85	154
John, blacksmith, b. Hew Hartford, res. Barkhamsted, d. Mar. 30, 1848, ae 85	228
Julia, d. Erastus & Lucenda, b. Jan. 26, 1815	156
Marilla, ae 48, b. Barkhamsted, res. same, m. 2nd h. Virgil **TAYLOR**, farmer, ae 58, b. Canton, res. Barkhamsted, Mar. [ ], 1851, by Rev. Hugh Gibson	236
Mercy, w. George, d. Feb. 5, 1860	152
Merlin, s. John & Elizabeth, b. Jan. 23, 1797	154
Merlin, m. Clarrissa **NEWTON**, May 28, 1823, at New Hartford	95
Merlin, s. Merlin & Clarissa, b. Oct. 17, 1830	95
Merlin, s. Merlin & Clarissa, d. Sept. 4, 1833	95
Merlin Clark, s. Merlin & Clarissa, b. Sept. 23, 1834	95
Nelson, s. Erastus & Lucenda, b. Oct. 6, 1810	156
Rhoda, d. George & Hannah, b. Aug. 17, 1810	152
Rhoda, of Barkhamsted, m. Hiram D. **PARSONS**, of Granville, Mass., Nov. 27, 1833, by Rev. William R. Gould	200
Sally, d. John & Elizabeth, b. Sept. 12, 1785, at New Hartford	154
Samuel, s. John & Elizabeth, b. Aug. 30, 1799	154
Sarah, d. George & Hannah, b. Sept. 4, 1822	152
Sarah C., teacher, d. Apr. 11, 1848, ae 20	228
Sheldon, s. George & Marcy, b. Feb. 25, 1833	152
Sheldon, of Barkhamsted, m. Lucie M. **MOSES**, of Shanealites, N. Y.,	

Page

MERRILL, MERRELLS, MERRELL, (cont)
May 27, 1858, by Rev. W[illia]m B. Dada   240
Sylvia, d. John & Elisabeth, b. Aug. 6, 1791   154
Sylvia, m. Peter MERRITT, Dec. 13, 1809   147
Vashti, of Barkhamsted, m. Dwight M. WHEELER, of Granville, Mass.,
      Feb. 15, 1837, by S. W. Edson   203
Vashti, d. George & Hannah, b. [ ]   152
Webster, [s. George & Hannah], d. July 24, 1868   152
Webster, s. George & Hannah, b. [ ]   152
William, s. Erastus & Lucenda, b. Sept. 8, 1812   156
MERRITT, MERRETT, MERIOTT, MIRROTT, MERRIOTT, Celisha, d.
      Samuel & Lucy, b. July 10 , 1809   148
Emeline, d. Peter & Sylvia, b. Nov. 3, 1811   147
Esther, d. James & Hannah, b. Mar. 8, 1771   2
Freedom, d. John & Sarah, b. Oct. 18, 1792   10
Freeman, m. Patty CARRINGTON, Oct. 26, 1805   142
Hannah, d. James & Hannah, b. Mar. 31, 1769   2
James, m. Hannah PHELPS, June 16, 1768   2
James, s. James & Hannah, b. July 3, 1773   2
James, s. James & Hannah, d, June 15, 1777   2
James, s. James & Hannah, b. Feb. 1, 1785   2
Jerusha, d. John & Sarah, b. June 13, 1779   10
Jerusha, d. John & Lucy, b. May 22, 1798   111
John, m. Sarah MILLER, Aug. 24, 1769   10
John, s. John & Sarah, b. May 9, 1770   10
John, Jr., m. Lucy MILLS, Sept. 20, 1793   111
Julia, d. Samuel & Lucy, b. Mar. 11, 1808   148
Julia, m. Frederick ANDREWS, Jan. 28, 1830, by Asa Bushnel, L. M. P.   192
Lois, d. James & Hannah, b. Oct. 13, 1777   2
Lucenda, d. Samuel & Lucy, b. June 2, 1810   148
Lucy, d. Samuel & Mary, b. July 10, 1791   4
Lucy Cristeen, d. John & Lucy, b. Nov. 15, 1796   111
Lydia, d. James & Hannah, b. Apr. 25, 1780   2
Mary, d. Samuell & Mary, b. Jan. 27, 1781   4
Nama *, d. John & Sarah, b. July 27, 1781   *(Perhaps "Narna")   10
Oliver, s. John & Sara, b. Aug. 4, 1784   10
Peter, s. James & Hannah, b. Oct. 31, 1788   2
Peter, m. Sylvia MERRELLS, Dec. 13, 1809   147
Phelena, d. Freeman & Patty, b. Oct. 23, 1806   142
Ruth, d. James & Hannah, b. Sept. 29, 1782   2
Ruth, d. James & Hannah, d. Jan. 29, 1786, ae 3 y. 4 m.   2
Ruth, d. James & Hannah, b. Feb. 11, 1793   2
Sebre *, d. John & Sarah, b. June 1, 1776   *("Sabra")   10
Sebre, m. Harris EMMONS, Oct. 2, 1794   110
Samuell, m. Mary HOLIDAY, Nov. 17, 1774   4
Samuel, s. Samuell & Mary, b. Apr. 6, 1777   4
Samuel, Jr., m. Lucy BUSHNELL, Dec. 24, 1804   148
Samuel m. Mrs. Lucy MESSINGER, Mar. 18, 1842, by Hira Case, J. P.   211

Page

MILLS, (cont.)

"Ursula Chlois") 46

MOODY, Sara, m. Jonas WEED, Jr., May 6, 1773 3

MOORE, Adelaide, m. William KEENEY, b. of Winchester, Sept. 17, 1848,
by Rev. Luther H. Barber, of Hitchockville 219

Almira, of Barkhamsted, m. DeWit FREEMAN, of Hartford, Oct. 21,
1846, by George B. Atwell 219

Alpheus, his w. [   ], d. Aug. 20, 1865, ae 61 219

Avis, Mrs., m. Miles DAVIS, Jan. 31, 1827, by Erastus Doty 177

Azubah, m. Jehiel WILLCOCKS, Apr. [   ], 1779 55

Belinda, m. Gilbert DEMING, Nov. 16, 1825, by Rev. Erastus Doty, of
Colebrook 168

Betsy, d. William, Jr. & Sarah, b. Aug. 30, 1794 90

Charlotte, d. William, Jr. & Sarah, b. July 1, 1785 90

D. Cary Y. Kujo, m. Thankfull ROBERTS, Dec. 19, 1823, by Erastus
Doty, Elder 8

Harriet, married, d. Aug. 1, 1865, ae 34 219

Harriet C., of Barkhamsted, m. John D. SCOTT, of Seymour, Sept. 18,
1851, by Rev. Charles R. Adams, of Colebrook River 221

Henretta M., of Barkhamsted, m. James R. SMITH, of Winchester, Oct.
12, 1852, by Rev. Luther H. Barber, of Hitchcockville 224

King Cyrus, s. David, b. July 20, 1786 60

Laury, of Barkhamsted, m. Richard A. DOOLITTLE, of Hartland, June
29, 1826, by Adolphus Terry, V. D. M. 176

Lucinda, m. John H. HULL, Apr. 14, 1824, by Erastus Doty, Elder 1

Lucy Ann, m. George H. CLARK, b. of Barkhamsted, Dec. 9, 1824, by
Rev. James Beach, of Winsted 167

Mary, d. David, b. Oct. 5, 1788 60

Nelson, m. Elisabeth CHADWICK, b. of Barkhamsted, June 21, 1847,
by George B. Atwell 219

Osbert, b. Colebrook, married, d. Mar. 27, 1858, ae 28 213

Rosel, s. William, Jr. & Sarah, b. Apr. 3, 1790 90

Sally, d. William, Jr. & Sarah, b. Mar. 27, 1792 90

Sarah, w. William, Jr., b. Dec. 17, 1767 90

William, Jr., b. Aug. 13, 1765 ; m. Sarah [   ], [   ] 90

William, s. William, Jr. & Sarah, b. Dec. 13, 1787 90

MOSES, Almira, d. Roger [& Patience Talitha], b. Jan. 14, 1795 117

Clifford S., d. Feb. 23, 1862, ae 4 216

Hannah, d. Roger & Patience (?) Talitha, b. Mar. 4, 1805 117

Hannah, of Barkhamsted, m. Tracy ANDREWS, of Canton, Aug. 27,
1823, by Saul Clark 188

Hannah, m. Noah HART, Oct. 12, 1826, by Saul Clark 189

Hannah, m. Noah [   ], Oct. 26, 1826* *(Entry added in a later hand) 115

Homer, d. Sept. 7, 1864, ae 11 218

Lois, d. Roger [& Patience Talitha], b. June 12, 1806 117

Lucie M., of Shanealities, N. Y., m. Sheldon MERRELL, of
Barkhamsted, May 27, 1858, by Rev. W[illia]m B. Dada 240

Maritta, m. Wayne CASE, May 19, 1853, by Asa Bushnell, Sr. 225

Page

MUNSON, MONSON , (cont)
    1828, by Saul Clark   191
    Nancy Amoret, d. Horice & Harit, b. Jan. 6, 1808   151
    Rachel, d. Ephraim & Hannah, b. Jan. 21, 1779   68
    Reubin J., m. Anna MILLER, Feb. 28, 1803   121
    Reubin Johnson, s. Ephraim & Hannah, b. Feb. 27, 1780   68
    Samuel, s. Ephraim & Hannah, b. Aug. 17, 1777   68
    Samuel, m. Mary HOWD, Nov. 13, 1800   122
    Sherlock, s. Medad & Sibbel, b. Aug. 14, 1798   105
    Sharlock, m. Elisabeth MERRELLS, b. of Barkhamsted, by Saul Clark
      (No date given)   63
    Sibel Mariah, [d. Horice & Harit], b. May 23, 1810   151
    William Beers, s. Liverius & Francis, b. Jan. 30, 1803   126
MURPHY, George W., b. E. Granby, d. Jan. 14, 1862, ae 5   215
    ----, d. Mar. 17, 1860, ae 28 1/2 d.   214
NEALE, Amarella M., m. Erastus CASE, Nov. 2, 1820, by Amos Beecher, J. P   194
    Lavinia M., m. Josiah CASE, Nov. 5, 1821, by Amos Beecher, J. P.   193
NEWELL, Anna, d. Riverius & Sarah, b. Mar. 23, 1784   32
    Gordon, s. Riverus & Sarah, b. Oct. 24, 1779   32
    Riverious, m. Sarah PECK, Nov. 9, 1778   32
    Rollin, married, d. Mar. 27, 1858, ae 76   213
    Salla, d. Riverius & Sarah, b. June 8, 1782   32
    Sally, wid., d. Dec. 8, 1860, ae 72   214
NEWTON, Caroline, m. Pelatiah RANSOM, Dec. [ ], 1809, at New Hartford   160
    Clarrissa, m. Merlin MERRILL, May 28, 1823, at New Hartford   95
NORTHROP, Hiram J., of Pompey, N. Y., m. Louisa JONES, of
      Barkhamsted, June 15, 1836, by Rev. Aaron Gates, of E. Hartland   201
NORTON, Ann, m. Hermon MESSENGER, Apr. 16, 1837, by George Merrill,
      J. P.   207
    Leveritt J., of Owego, N. Y., m. Sarah A. DOOLITTLE, of
      Barkhamsted, July 23, 1851, by Rev. Luther H. Barber, of
      Hitchcockville   224
NOTT, Deborah, b. Mar. 30, 1770 ; m. Thomas FRAZIER, June 17, 1787   143
OATMAN, Loyal, of Sandisfield, Mass., m. Emily JOHNSON, of
      Barkhamsted, Oct. 21, 1844, by Rev. Luther H. Barber, of
      Hitchcocksville   214
OLMSTED, OLMSTEAD, Mercy, wid., d. Jan. 10, 1857, ae 77   212
    Olive, of Barkhamsted, m. Philetus WOODWARD, of East Hartford,
      Sept. 27, 1830, by Daniel Coe   195
ORK, John, mason, had d. [ ], b. May [ ], 1850   232
PALMER, Mary, m. Reuben SWEET, Sept. 21, 1774   31
PARKER, Atwater, s. Joel & Abigail, b. Dec. 12, 1800 ; d. Oct. 6, 1801   123
    Benjamin, s. Lovel & Hannah, b. Jan. 9, 1796   98
    David, s. Lovel & Hannah, b. Aug. 2, 1802   98
    Joel, b. May 2, 1768 ; m. Abigail HART, Dec. 17, 1795   123
    Loly, d. Joel & Abigail, b. May 20, 1799   123
    Lovel, m. Hannah HART, May 22, 1792   98
    Lovel Elon, s. Lovel & Hannah, b. June 4, 1800   98

Page

PARKER (cont.),

Lynus, s. Lovel & Hannah, b. Feb. 20, 1798   98

Moses Atwater, s. Joel & Abigail, b. Sept. 1, 1802   123

Noyse, s. Lovel & Hannah, b. Jan. 24, 1794   98

Orpha, d. Lovel & Hannah, b. Dec. 20, 1803   98

Rufus, s. Lovel & Hannah, b. Mar. 17, 1807   98

William Kenyon, m. Harriot **GRANT**, of Courtland Village, N. Y., Oct. 22, 1838, by Rev. Isaac Jones   206

PARMALEE, PARMELY, PARMERLY, Desire, m. Partridge **PARSONS**, Jan. 18, 1792   81

Pain, m. Sarah A. **TAYLOR**, b. of Barkhamsted, Nov. 8 , 1841, by Rev. S. W. Smith   210

Perren, b. Windsor, married, d. Apr. 30, 1863, ae 43   217

Eliza L., tailoress, b. Tringham, Mass., m. Emery C. **HART**, tailor, b. Durham, res. Barkhamsted, [   ], by George B. Atwell   233

Elisabeth, m. Emery **HART**, b. of Sandersfield, Mass., May 1, 1850, by Rev. George B. Atwell   221

Hiram D., of Granville, Mass., m. Rhoda **MERRILL**, of Barkhamsted, Nov. 27, 1833, by Rev. William R. Gould   220

Laura L., m. Timothy C. **RANSOM**, b. of Barkhamsted, July 9, 1848, by Rev. Luther H. Barber, of Hitchcockville   218

Maria W., m. Thomas N. **HODGES**, b. of Barkhamsted, Aug. 2, 1842, by Rev. Lewis Gunn   211

Mary Merrillia, d. Sarah, b. Sept. 18, 1786   133

Nabby, d. Partridge & Desire, b. Apr. 22, 1793   81

Partridge, m. Desire **PARMELY**, Jan. 18, 1792   81

Rhoda, m. Israel **JONES**, Jan. 19, 1779   4

Sarah, b. Aug. 18, 1761 ; m. James **PIKE**, May 20, 1788 ; had d. Mary Merrillia, b. Sept. 18, 1786   133

Sarah, had d. Mary Merrillia, b. Sept. 18, 1786   133

PAYNE, Mary, b. Canton, married, d. Oct. 25, 1863, ae 38   217

Mary A., d. Henry H., farmer, ae 30, & Mary A., ae 26, b. July 25, 1848   226

Tirza, b. "Chish", married, d. Oct. 17, 1861, ae 75   215

William, farmer, ae 25, b. Barkhamsted, res. Barkhamsted, m. Mary **CASE**, ae 21, b. Canton, res. Canton, Jan. [   ], 1850, by William Goodwin   233

W[illia]m H., farmer, ae 29, & Mary, ae 22, had d. [   ], b. Mar. 10, 1851   235

PEASE, Annah, m. Gad **TERRY**, Oct. 27, 1794   95

Luman, m. Marcia **CASE**, July 4, 1854, by P. T. Holley   240

PECK, Sarah, m. Riverious **NEWELL**, Nov. 9, 1778   32

PELTON, James B., of Saybrook, m. Sarah Ann **TAYLOR**, of Barkhamsted, Nov. 6, 1842, by George Merrill, J. P.   213

Sarah Ann, ae 23, b. Barkhamsted, m. George B. **KIBBE**, farmer, ae 24, b. Tolland, Mass., res. Tolland, June 10, 1849   230

PERCEVAL, Priscilla, of Winchester, m. Ransley **SHATTUCK**, of Colebrook, May 12, 1844, by Luther H. Barber   214

PERKINS, PERKENS, Gideon, m. wid. Thankful **COWLES**, Dec. 26, 1804   16

Sarah, w. Gideon, d. Feb. 1, 1804   16

Page

PERKINS, PERKENS, (cont.)

Susanna, m. Clark **GIDDINGS,** Feb. 26, 1807   15

PETERS, James, of Granby, m. Caroline **DOLPHIN,** of Barkhamsted, May 30,
   1850, by Rev. Luther H. Barber   223

Joseph, of Hartland, m. Sally **TIFFANY,** of Barkhamsted, Nov. 10, 1824,
   by Saul Clark   189

PETTIBONE, Elisha, b. Simsbury, married, d. Sept. 29, 1859, ae 78   214

Mary, m. Cook **JEWETT,** Oct. 6, 1833, by Timothy M. Cooley   199

[PHELAN], PHELON, FELAN, Joseph, m. Margaret **CARPENTER,** June 20,
   1849   230

Lorenzo, m. Mary **STILES,** Dec. 14, 1850, at Pleasant Valley, by Rev.
   George B. Atwell   221

Lorenzo, farmer, b. Granville, Mass., res. same, m. Mary **STILES,** b.
   Barkhamsted, [   ], by George B. Atwell   233

PHELPS, Aaron, m. Tryphena **GILLET,** Sept. 30, 1784   106

Aaron, s. Aaron & Tryphena, b. Jan. 13, 1786   106

Aaron, d. July 19, 1816   106

Aaron, s. Chauncy & Sally, b. Oct. 15, 1818   106

Abigail, m. Manna **CASE,** Nov. 25, 1807   138

Abigail, w. Elkanah, d. June 11, 1813   51

Abigail, w. Elkanah, d. June 11, 1813 *   *(Entry erased)   103

Abigail, m. West G. **WINSLOW,** Dec. 16, 1836, by Asa Bushnell   203

Abijah, m. Elisabeth **BONNY,** Mar. 14, 1815   156

Caroline, m. Dr. Flavel B. **GRAHAM,** Oct. 13, 1833, by Rev. Asahel
   Morse   199

Chauncey, s. Aaron & Tryphena, b. Mar. 2, 1794   106

Chauncy, m. Sally **SHEPARD,** June 1, 1813   106

Cynthia, m. Asel J. **MUNSON,** Nov. 3, 1803   128

Daniel, s. Chauncy & Sally, b. July 9, 1822   106

Elihu, s. Aaron & Tryphena, b. Feb. 22, 1807   106

Elkanah, Capt., d. Dec. 5, 1803   51

Elkanah, s. Oliver & Olive, b. June 17, 1804   103

Elkanah, s. Oliver & Olive, d. Nov. 3, 1819   103

Frederick s. Elkanah & Abigail, b. Oct. 6, 1784   51

Hannah, m. James **MERIOTT,** June 16, 1768   2

Israel Whiting, s. Chauncy & Sally, b. May 17, 1824   106

John, of Granby, m. Dorcas **CASE,** of Barkhamsted, Nov. 19, 1840, by J.
   W. Alvord   210

Julia, m. Christopher **BASSET,** Mar. 15, 1805   137

Martha, b. Hebron, single, d. Jan. 5, 1862, ae 75   215

Mary, d. Oliver & Olive, b. June 19, 1806   103

Mary Ann, d. Chauncy & Sally, b. June 28, 1820   106

Matilda, of Barkhamsted, m. Jarvis **FRAZIER,** of Granby, Nov. 26, 1822,
   by Saul Clark   187

Nathan, s. Chauncy & Sally, b. Apr. 2, 1814   106

Olive, twin with Orrela, d. Oliver & Olive, b. June 30, 1808   103

Olive, [d. Oliver & Olive], d. July 4, 1808   103

Olive, d. Oliver & Olive, b. Oct. 20, 1811   103

Page

PHELPS, (cont.)

Page

PRESTON, (cont.)

Page

RANSOM, (cont.)
Rev. Isaac Jones, of Hitchocksville 204
Polly, d. Pelatiah & Sarah, b. Nov. 23, 1796 53
Salla, d. Pelatiah & Sarah, b. Nov. 23, 1780 53
Sarah E., single, d. Sept. 14, 1862, ae 18 216
Timothy C., m. Laura L. **PARSONS,** b. of Barkhamsted, July 9, 1848, by
Rev. Luther H. Barber, of Hitchcockville 218
Willie, d. Jan. 16, 1863, ae 10 m. 216
William, s. Pelatiah & Sarah, b. Nov. 6, 1778 53
RAU, James M., farmer, ae 26, res. Colebrook, m. Sylvia **AUSTIN,** ae 24, b.
Granvill, Mar. 4, 1849 230
RAXFORD, [see under **REXFORD**]
REED, Amos, of Orleans, N. Y., m. wid. Thankful **CASE,** of Barkhamsted,
Sept. 14, 1824, by Amos Beecher, J. P. 194
Amy, m. Titus **CASE,** Mar. 12, 1792 106
Daniel, of Granby, m. Serena **CASE,** of Barkhamsted, Mar. 1, 1827, by
Saul Clark 190
Sylvia, m. John **KIBBEY,** June 21, 1820, by Amos Beecher, J. P. 194
REXFORD, RAXFORD, Alling, s. Daniel & Sarah, b. Sept. 9, 1791 12
Benjamin, s. Daniel & Sarah, b. Jan. 1, 1776 12
Betsey, d. William & Denis, b. Aug. 15, 1781 19
Daniel, Jr., m. Sarah **ALLYN,** Feb. 23, 1775 12
Daniel, Jr., d. July 28, 1793 12
Daniel, m. Clarinda **ALLYN,** b. of Barkhamsted, Sept. 10, 1834, by Rev.
John A. Hempstead 200
Jared, m. Rachel **LEWIS,** Aug. 17, 1794 88
Jared & Rachel, had s. [ ], b. Sept. 9, 1795 ; d. Nov. 12, 1795 88
Jason, s. William & Denis, b. May 7, 1776 19
Jason, s. William & Denis, d. Sept. 11, 1778, ae 2 y. 4 m. 19
Joel, m. Rhoda **SPENCER,** Jan. 23, 1774 20
Joel, m. Susannah **WEED,** July 2, 1792 109
John, s. Daniel & Sarrah, b. Apr. 10, 1786 12
John, married, d. June 12, 1862, ae 76 216
Leverett, s. William & Dennis, b. Feb. 21, 1787 19
Lyman, s. Joel & Rhoda, b. Apr. 24, 1784 20
Martha, d. Joel & Rhoda, b. Dec. 9,. 1779 20
Martha, d. Joel & Rhoda, d. Aug. 9, 1780, ae 8 m. 20
Martha, d. Daniel & Sarah, b. Apr. 22, 1789 12
Micha, s. Daniel & Sarah, b. Feb. 1, 1780 12
Polly, d. Joel & Susannah, b. July 20, 1794 109
Rachel, w. Jared, d. Apr. 19, 1796 88
Rachel, d. Joel & Susannah, b. July 27, 1802 109
Sarah, d. Daniel & Sarah, b. Jan. 16, 1784 12
Simeon, s. Joel & Rhoda, b. Mar. 7, 1776 20
William, m. Denis **SPERRY,** Dec. 30, 1772 19
William, s. William & Denis, b. Dec. 22, 1773 19
William, s. William & Denis, d. Sept. 14, 1778, ae 4 y. 9 m. 19
William, twin with [ ], s. William & Denis, b. Dec. 23, 1779 19

Page

REXFORD, RAXFORD, (cont.)

William & Denis, had twin s. [   ], d. Dec. 25, 1779, ae 2 d.   19

Zinah, s. Daniel & Sarah, b. Sept. 17, 1777   12

----, twin with William s. William & Denis, b. Dec. 23, 1779   19

REYNOLDS, W[illia]m, b. Exeter, R. I., married, d. July 9, 1865, ae 57 y. 8 m   219

RICE, Aaron, m. Hannah **TULLER,** Nov. 11, 1824, by Samuel Munson, J. P.   175

Almon, d. Jan. [   ], 1850, ae 10   234

Edward, m. Avis **ROBERTS,** b. of Barkhamsted, Feb. 28, 1847, by
Luther H. Barber   217

Frederick W., d. Jan. 2, 1858, ae 2 y. 16 m.   213

Laura, of Barkhamsted, m. Josiah **HOUGH,** of Canton, Dec. 8, 1830, by
Amos Beecher, J. P.   195

Lucius, m. Mrs. Ann **WEBSTER,** b. of Barkhamsted, Jan. 9, 1847, by
George Merrell, J. P.   217

Luther, m. Cloe **BLISS,** Dec. 8, 1803   24

Nahum, s. Luther & Cloe, b. May 2, 1804   24

Reuben, m. Emily **BARNES,** Aug. 17, 1824, by Eli Barnet, Elder   30

Wait, of Canton, m. Laura **CASE,** of Barkhamsted, Oct. 11, 1835, by
Leister Loomis, J. P.   201

Wait, of Canton, m. Lura **CASE,** of Barkhamsted, Sept. 18, 1836, by
Leister Loomis, J. P.   201

RICHARDS, Caroline, d. Hezekiah & Jerusha, b. Jan. 8, 1801   158

Hezekiah, m. Jerusha **ENSIGN,** Apr. 10, 1800   158

Hezekiah, s. Hezekiah & Jerusha, b. Feb. 2, 1809   158

Lemuel, farmer, ae 21, b. Barkhamsted, res. same, m. Martha **TIFFANY,**
ae 18, b. Barkhamsted, res. same, Oct. 22, 1849, by Aron Gates   233

Sarah, d. Hezekiah & Jerusha, b. Sept. 18, 1806   158

RICHARDSON, Ann, ae 44, b. Barkhamsted, res. same, m. Salmon **BARBER,**
farmer, ae 47, b. Canton, res. Barkhamsted, Apr. 7, 1850, by Rev.
Mr. Leadbetter   233

Daniel **WOODRUFF,** s. Daniel & Sukey, b. May 1, 1822   81

Edwin Treat, s. Daniel & Suky, b. June 20, 1809   81

Elizabeth Ellen, d. Daniel & Suky, b. June 21, 1817   81

Emily M., of Barkhamsted, m. James F. **ROWLEY,** of Winsted, Dec. 25,
1851, by Rev. A. B. Pulling   222

Gideon Humphrys, s. Daniel [& Suky], b. May 28, 1815   81

Julia Maria, d. Daniel & Sukey, b. Dec. 21, 1823   81

Lemuel, Jr., m. Martha M. **TIFFANY,** b. of Barkhamsted, Oct. 22, 1849,
by Rev. Aaron Gates   220

Lucia Annet, d. Daniel & Sukey, b. July 3, 1826   81

Murilla, m. John **MERRELL,** [   ], 1824, by Saul Clark   188

Sarah, b. Stockbridge, wid., d. Apr. 8, 1866, ae 72   220

Sarah Ann, d. Daniel & Suky, b. Dec. 9, 1813   81

Sukey Cornelia, d. Daniel [& Suky], b. Sept. 4, 1819   81

William Mills, s. Daniel & Suky, b. Feb. 22, 1811   81

RIGBY, Cora Elizabeth, d. Apr. 4, 1860, ae 4 m.   214

RISLEY, Jane C., d. Andrew, farmer, ae 25, & Dealia, ae 25, b. Oct. 7, 1849   232

ROBERTS, Amerza, of Barkhamsted, m. Albert G. **FEUGERSON,** of New

Page

ROBERTS, (cont.)

Hartford, Sept. 26, 1824, by Rev. James Beach of Winsted 167

Avis, m. Edward **RICE,** b. of Barkhamsted, Feb. 28, 1847, by Luther H.
Barber 217

Clerk, s. Paul * & Mindwell, b. Apr. 14, 1787 *("Robert" written first
and erased) 7

John, b. Middletown, res. Barkhamsted, d. Aug. 30, 1848, ae 77 231

Levi, s. Paul & Mindwell, b. Mar. 20, 1785 7

Lucy, d. Paul & Mindwell, b. Mar. 5, 1781 7

Lucy, m. Fisher **CASE,** Sept. 12, 1803 124

Mindwell, d. Paul & Mindwell, b. July 21, 1778 7

Paul, m. Mindwell **HALL,** Apr. 20, 1775 7

Paul, s. Paul & Mindwell, b. Jan. 13, 1776 7

Paul & Mindwell, had d. [ ], b. Mar. 7, 1777 7

Paul & Mindwell, had d. [ ], d. May 7, 1777 7

Paul & Mindwell, had s. [ ], b. Apr. 3, 1783 7

Paul & Mindwell, had s. [ ], d. May 3, 1783 7

Paul, b. Windsor, married, d. Mar. 24, 1854, ae 78 211

Paul, married, d. Jan. 7, 1862, ae 61 215

Thankfull, m. D. Cary Y. Kujo **MOORE,** Dec. 19, 1823, by Erastus Doty,
Elder 8

ROBINSON, Martha G., of Hitchcockville, m. Elliott D. **BODWELL,** of
Collinsville, May 1, 1853, by Rev. L. S. Weed. Witnesses Emory
M. Davis & Charlott A. Davis 240

ROCKWELL, Abel, s. John & Dorithy, b. June 12, 1787 28

Abel, m. Lucretia **SPENCER,** July 4, 1822, by Saul Clark 187

Catherine Maria, m. Luther **LOOMIS,** b. of Barkhamsted, Aug. 2, 1829,
by Amasa Jerome 185

Charles, m. Martha **COOMB,** Feb. 24, 1808 140

Elisha, of Westfield, Mass., m. Mrs. Harriet **ENSIGN,** of Barkhamsted,
Mar. 25, 1823, by Saul Clark 188

Henry E., of Winchester, m. Emeritt **MUNSON,** of Barkhamsted, Nov. 2,
1837, by Rev. James Beach, of Winsted 205

Hiram, m. Freedon **ENSIGN,** Mar. 25, 1823, by Rev. Saul Clarke 183

Hiram Stilwell, s. Hiram & Freedon, b. Jan. 13, 1824 183

John, Jr., of Barkhamsted, m. Malissa **TAYLOR,** of Hartland, Mar. 18,
1823, by Saul Clark 187

Lyman, m. Lucy **BURROWS,** Oct. 3, 1837, in Hitchcockville, by Rev.
Isaac Jones 204

Mariah, d. Charles & Martha, b. Feb. 14, 1809 140

Nancy Hellena, d. Hiram & Freedom, b. Dec. 29, 1827 183

Phebe, d. John & Dorithy, b. June 10, 1790 28

Phebe, d. John & Dorithy, d. Sept. 3, 1793, ae 3 y. 2 m. 23 d. 28

Seth, s. John & Dorithy, b. Jan. 17, 1785 28

Seth, s. John & Dorithy, d. Sept. 2, 1793, ae 8 y. 7 m. 16 d. 28

ROGERS, Emily, of Colebrook, m. Horatio N. **KEEP,** of Winsted, Feb. 9,
1845, by Rev. Luther H. Barber, of Hitchcocksville 215

ROOT, Charles W., s. Orrin, farmer, ae 39, & Emily, ae 33, b. Oct. 28, 1847 226

Page

ROOT, (cont)
Frederick H., of West Meridan, m. Almira A. STEWART, of
    Barkhamsted, Sept. 19, 1852, by Rev. David Miller   222
George A., single, d. June 5, 1866, ae 38, (soldier, 4 y. in Army)   220
Nancy, m. Norman N. BIDWELL, Sept. 28, 1845, by Reuben S. Hazen   215
Orrin, b. New Hartford, married, d. Aug. 19, 1865, ae 65   219
Samuel F. J., b. Marlboro, married, d. Feb. 28, 1863, ae 45   217
ROSE, Arther, s. Lovel & Pantha, b. May 16, 1814   137
Carrell, s. Lovel & Panthy, b. Oct. 11, 1818   137
Jane Caroline, d. Lovel & Panthy, b. Apr. 2, 1817   137
John, s. Lovel & Panthy, b. July 20, 1822   137
Julia, b. Barkhamsted, m. Abner HART, farmer, b. Barkhamsted, Mar. 20,
    1848, by R. S. Hazen   227
Julia Pantha, d. Lovel & Pantha, b. July 12, 1825   137
Lovel, m. Pantha GILLET, June 10, 1812   137
Lovel & Pantha, had d. [   ], b. Nov. 20, 1820 ; d. Nov. 21, 1820   137
Lucius Lovel, s. Lovel & Pantha, b. Sept. 25, 1815   137
Marquiss, m. Sally CASE, Feb. 1, 1809   139
Pearly (?), of Barkhamsted, m. Junius GILLETT, of Colebrook, Sept. 23,
    1838, by Rev. Isaac Jones, of Hitchcockvill   206
Philo Zelotes, s. Marquiss & Sally, b. July 8, 1809   139
Richard, s. Lovel & Pantha, b. May 2, 1813   137
Sally, of Barkhamsted, m. John SCHAMMERHORN, of New Hartford,
    Oct. 23, 1831, by Jesse Ives, J. P.   197
ROWLEY, Emely, married, d. Feb. 8, 1855, ae 23   212
James F., of Winsted, m. Emily M. RICHARDSON, of Barkhamsted,
    Dec. 25, 1851, by Rev. A. B. Pulling   222
RUST, Charles H., s. Norman, farmer, ae 40, & Mary S., ae 39, b. July 10,
    1849   229
Cherosoa, m. Austin MESSENGER, Feb. 4, 1838, by George Merrells, J.
    P.   207
Deney, of Barkhamsted, m. Benjamin TUCKER, of New Hartford, Sept.
    16, 1839, by George Merrell, J. P.   213
Mariah, m. Nelson TUCKER, Nov. 22, 1835, by George Merrills, J. P.   207
Martin, m. Sarah L. ATWATER, b. of Barkhamsted, Sept. 4, 1838, by
    Rev. William R. Gould   208
Martin, married, d. Dec. 24, 1854, ae 41   211
Olive, m. Homan SEGAR, Apr. [   ], 1826, by Saul Clark   189
Perlin F., single, d. Oct. 29, 1863, ae 21 (soldier)   217
Sarah J., d. Martin, farmer, ae 37, & Sarah L., ae 30, b. Oct. 12, 1850   235
SAGE, Byron, b. Sandisfield, single, d. Mar. 27, 1854, ae 26   211
Henry W., of Norfold, m. Mary BRIGHT, of Colebrook, Apr. 9, 1848,
    by Luther H. Barber   218
SALES, SALLES, Lovesa, of Barkhamsted, m. James S. HAZARD, of
    Winchester, Jan. 1, 1839, by Rev. William R. Gould   208
Nancy, m. Charles SELEY, Nov. 26, 1835, by George Merrells, J. P.   207
SANDERSON, Charlotte A., of Hitchcockville, m. Emory M. DAVIS, of West
    Granville, Mass., Nov. 17, 1852, by Rev. L. S. Weed   225

Page

SQUIRES, SQUIRE, (cont.)

Page

STRONG, (cont.)

1852, by Rev. Augustus B. Collins — 224

STUART, Jane E., of Barkhamsted, m. Alexander **PINNEY,** of Tarrifvill, Feb. 27, 1845, by Rev. Erastus Doty — 215

Susan, b. Hampton, res. Barkhamsted, [d.   ], ae 28 — 234

W[illia]m A., b. Blanford, Mass., res. Barkhamsted, d. Apr. 14, 1850, ae 41 — 234

STURGES, Edwin, m. Charlotte **HEWITT,** b. of Barkhamsted, May 20, 1828, by Rev. James Beach, of Winsted — 181

SWEET, Fanny, b. Hartland, married, d. Dec. 21, 1854, ae 23 — 211

James, s. Reuben & Mary, b. Dec. 11, 1777 — 31

Mary, d. Reuben & Mary, b. Nov. 17, 1782 — 31

Rachel, d. Reuben & Mary, b. May 9, 1780 — 31

Reuben, m. Mary **PALMER,** Sept. 21, 1774 — 31

TAINTOR, TAINTER, Jane, d. Harvey & Mary, b. Feb. 20, 1817 — 164

Jane, of Barkhamsted, m. Charles B. **HINE,** of Middlebury, Oct. 25, 1835, by Rev. James Beach, of Winsted — 200

Ruth A., d. Harvey & Mary, b. Apr. 7, 1822 — 164

TALMADGE, TALMAGE, Rebecca, b. Torrington, wid., d. Aug. 27, 1862, ae 82 — 216

Rhoda A., m. Edwin E. **CASE,** Oct. 25, 1852, by Rev. Augustus B. Collins — 22

TAYLOR, Covil, d. Jan. 2, 1866, ae 2 d. — 219

Edor, married, d. Feb. [   ], 1857, ae 79 — 213

Electa, d. Apr. 6, 1850, ae 56 — 234

Eliza, m. Hiram **CARTER,** b. of Barkhamsted, Feb. 3, 1833, by Rev. William R. Gould — 198

Hannah, b. Jan. 24, 1768; m. Joseph **GREGORY,** Nov. 8, 1787 — 89

Jefferson, of Colebrook River, m. Mary **HART,** of Winsted, Sept. 1, 1850, by George B. Atwell — 220

Malissa, of Hartland, m. John **ROCKWELL,** Jr., of Barkhamsted, Mar. 18, 1823, by Saul Clark — 187

Nancy, m. Joseph **CARTER,** b. of Barkhamsted, Nov. 1, 1833, by Rev. William R. Gould — 199

Otis, of Hartland, m. Abigail **CASE,** of Barkhamsted, Nov. 27, 1822, by Saul Clark — 187

Sarah A., m. Pain **PARMALEE,** b. of Barkhamsted, Nov. 8, 1841, by Rev. S. W. Smith — 210

Sarah Ann, of Barkhamsted, m. James B. **PELTON,** of Saybrook, Nov. 6, 1842, by George Merrill, J. P. — 213

Sherdian, single, d. Feb. 27, 1863, ae 31 — 217

Sophia, m. Henry **ALLEN,** Oct. 14, 1813 — 173

Virgil, farmer, ae 58, b. Canton, res. Barkhamsted, m. 2nd w. Marilla **MERRELL,** ae 48, b. Barkhamsted, res. same, Mar. [   ], 1851, by Rev. Hugh Gibson — 236

Virgil, married, d. Dec. 16, 1861, ae 70 — 215

TERRY, Alven, s. Ebenezer & Susanna, b. Mar. 4, 1799 — 105

Gad, m. Annah **PEASE,** Oct. 27, 1794 — 95

Page

TERRY, (cont.)
Gad, s. Gad & Annah, b. Oct. 25, 1795; d. [ ]   95
Gad, d. [ ]   95
Naomi, d. Ebenezer & Susanna, b. Mar. 5, 1790   105
Roseanne, m. Richard ADAMS, May 12, 1768   27
Sally, d. Ebenezer & Susanna, b. Oct. 9, 1787   105
Susanna, d. Ebenezer & Susanna, b. Oct. 21, 1792   105
TEW, Eliza, of Coventry, R. I., m. Romanta TUTTLE, of Barkhamsted, June
    22, 1834, by Rev. William G. Gould   202
THOMPSON, Belinda P., of Tyringham, Mass., m. David H. BUTLER, of
    New Haven, July 16, 1843, by Rev. David Bennet   212
Jared, of Mansfield, m. Minerva HAYDEN, of Barkhamsted, Jan. 21,
    1827, by Saul Clark   190
THORP, Joseph L, s. Henry, day laborer, colored, ae 25, & Ann, res. Canaan,
    b. Feb. 23, 1851   235
Ruby Ann, m. Elisha SMITH, Sept. 29, 1833, in Hitchcocksville, by Rev.
    John D. Smith, of Simsbury, Granby & Bark.   198
TIFFANY, Amelia, b. Hartland, single, d. Aug. 7, 1864, ae 72   218
Ann, of Barkhamsted, m. Orsman CASE, of Canton, Nov. 24, 1842, by
    Rev. Jairus Burt   211
Daniel, of Hartland, m. Sylvia PHELPS, of Barkhamsted, [ ], 1824, by
    Saul Clark   188
Elija, m. Martha M. BURWELL, b. of Barkhamsted, Sept. 20, 1829, by
    Amasa Jerome   140
Ella J., d. James, joiner, ae 37 & Sophrona, ae 34, b. June [ ], 1851   235
Ephraim, farmer, ae 24, b. Barkhamsted, res. Hartland, m. Mary J.
    VOSBURG, ae 21, b. Barkhamsted, Sept. 12, 1850, by Rev. Hugh
    Gibson   236
Frances Elisabeth, d. William, farmer, ae 30, & Eliesabeth M., ae 25, b.
    Nov. 22, 1847   226
James, m. Sophronia CASE, b. of Barkhamsted, May 2, 1839, by George
    Merrell, J. P.   213
James Bryon, s. James, joiner & Sophronia, b. Dec. 9, 1849   232
Jemima, m. Ebenezer CRANE, May 21, 1778   11
Levi, m. Mrs. Fanny IVES, June 8, 1830, by Rev. Luther Meed   192
Martha, ae 18, b. Barkhamsted, res. same, m. Lemuel RICHARDS,
    farmer, ae 21, b. Barkhamsted, res. same, Oct. 22, 1849, by Aron
    Gates   233
Martha M., m. Lemuel RICHARDSON, Jr., b. of Barkhamsted, Oct. 22,
    1849, by Rev. Aaron Gates   220
Minerva, d. May 29, 1850, ae 36   234
Philemon, married, d. Jan. 2, 1862, ae 61   215
Sally, of Barkhamsted, m. Joseph PETERS, of Hartland, Nov. 10, 1824,
    by Saul Clark   189
Salmon C., of Barkhamsted, m. Fanny BEECH, of Hartland, Jan. 1, 1854,
    by Luther H. Barber   239
Salmon C., married, d. Jan. 4, 1857, ae 43   212
Sarah, married, d. Sept. 27, 1863, ae 55   217

Page

TUTTLE, (cont.)
Phebe, d. Isaiah & Hannah, b. Jan. 2, 1783   9
Phebe, of Barkhamsted, m. Titus CASE, of Canton, July 3, 1822, by Saul
    Clark   187
Penul Case, s. Charles & Rosette, b. Sept. 29, 1792   59
Romanta, of Barkhamsted, m. Eliza TEW, of Conventry, R. I., June 22,
    1834, by Rev. William R. Gould   202
Romanta, s. Isaiah & Hannah, b. [   ]   9
Samuel, s. Isaiah & Hannah, b. June 4, 1781   9
Samuel, m. Else JONES, Jan. 5. 1803   120
Sarah, m. Joseph SHEPARD, Jr., [   ], 1785   84
Sarah, d. Isaiah & Hannah, b. June 14, 1798   9
Sarah, of Barkhamsted, m. Miles GILLET, of Colebrook, Dec. 9, 1823,
    by Saul Clark   188
Sylva, d. Isaiah & Hannah, b. Jan. 12, 1791   9
Theophilus, s. Samuel & Else, b. Feb. 26, 1804   120
UPSON, Amanda, m. Albert STEPHENS, b. of Barkhamsted, Dec. 10, 1854,
    by Luther H. Barber   239
Garry, m. Mariah WILNER, Jan, 8, 1829, by Rev. Erastus DOTY, of
    Colebrook   185
Jane M., of Barkhamsted, m. Charles H. COMMINGS, of Waterbury,
    Nov. 9, 1853, by Luther H. Barber   238
VIETS, A. P., Rev. of Canton, m. Hannah WEBSTER, of Barkhamsted, Sept.
    4, 1848, by George B. Atwell   219
A. P., clergyman, ae 28, b. Granby, res. Canton, m. Henriette WEBSTER,
    ae 18, b. Bethlem, Oct. 25, 1848   230
VINING, John W., of Granby, m. Susan BEERS, of Barkhamsted, Dec. 31,
    1826, by John Merrell, J. P.   178
Sarah, m. Herschel P. CASE, b. of Barkhamsted, July 18, 1847, by Asa
    Bushnell, Sr.   217
VOSBURG, Mary, b. Hartford, married, d. Apr. 4, 1866, ae 60   220
Mary J., ae 21, b. Barkhamsted, m. Ephraim TIFFANY, farmer, ae 24, b.
    Barkhamsted, res. Hartland, Sept. 12, 1850, by Rev. Hugh Gibson   236
WADSWORTH, Hannah, Mrs. of Barkhamsted, m. Horatio WRIGHT, of
    Norwich, June 19, 1822, by Saul Clark   186
Hezekiah, m. Hannah EELLS, Oct. 1, 1812   152
Hezekiah, s. Hezekiah & Hannah, b. Feb. 15, 1814   152
Louis, m. Israel JONES, Jr., Dec. 27, 1796   97
WAIT, Aline, of Barkhamsted, m. Bezaleel ADAMS, of Sandisfield, Mass.,
    Feb. 13, 1823, by James Beach   165
Roby, of Barkhamsted, m. Morgan LEWIS?, of West Stockbridge, Mar. 4,
    1830, by Rev. James Beach, of Winsted   191
WALKER, Philon A., d. June 29, 1855, ae 9   212
WALLACE, Frederick T., of Otis, Mass., m. Sylvia Ophelia FORD, of
    Barkhamsted, May 10, 1846, by Rev. Luther H. Barber, of
    Hitchcockville   216
WALLING, Rachel, m. Nathaniel COLLINS, Sept. 6, 1781   9
WALTER, Sally, m. Anson HOPKINS, b. of Winchester, Aug. 6, 1837, by

Page

WALTER, (cont.)
Anson Wheeler, J. P. 204
WARD, Aldrack, s. James & Huldah, b. Dec. 31, 1785 65
Bethiah, d. James & Huldah, b. Oct. 28, 1781 65
Dolla, d. James & Huldah, b. Apr. 16, 1792 65
Eliphalet, s. James & Huldah, b. Apr. 1, 1789 65
Elizabeth, m. Amos **CASE,** Dec. 17, 1767 25
Elizabeth A., wid., d. Apr. 12, 1866, ae 82 220
Huldah, d. James & Huldah, b. Oct. 19, 1783 65
James, m. Huldah **GIBBS,** ,Jan. 25, 1781 65
Roxeny, m. Jared **TUTTLE,** July 28, 1785 48
Sarah, d. James & Huldah, b. Oct. 2, 1794 65
W[illia]m H., m. Martha A. **PINNEY,** of Barkhamsted, Apr. 28, 1852, by
Rev. J. H. Betts, of New Hartford 222
WARRINER, Martha, married, d. Oct. 16, 1858, ae 30 213
WATSON, William S., of Norfolk, m. Eliza J. **BEECHER,** of Barkhamsted,
Oct. 11, 1853, by Rev. George B. Atwell 241
WAUGH, George F., m. Corneila A. **MESSENGER,** Jan. 10, 1854, by P. T.
Holley 240
WEBB, Sarah, of Otis, Mass., m. Timothy **TIFFANY,** of Barkhamsted, July 1,
1832, by Rev. William R. Gould 197
WEBSTER, Abner S., of Sandisfield, Mass., m. Mary Matilda **ALFORD,** of
Barkhamsted, Oct. 28, 1829, by Amasa Jerome 150
Ann, Mrs., m. Lucius **RICE,** b. of Barkhamsted, Jan. 9, 1847, by George
Merrell, J. P. 217
Hannah, of Barkhamsted, m. Rev. A. P. **VIETS,** of Canton, Sept. 4, 1848,
by George B. Atwell 219
Henriette, ae 18, b. Bethlem, m. A. P. **VIETS,** clergyman, ae 28, b.
Granby, res. Canton, Oct. 25, 1848 230
Henry, d. May [ ], 1848, ae 3 w. 228
Hinry, s. Gum, basket maker (colored), res. Southington, b. May [ ], 1848 226
Sara, d. July 21, 1850, ae 46 234
Solomon, of Southington, m. Mary **WILSON,** of Barkhamsted, Oct. 6,
1850, by Rev. Luther H. Barber 223
Solomon, day laborer, ae 22, & Mary, ae 20, had d. [ ], b. July 30, 1851 235
Stephen, s. Montgomery, basketmaker, mohegan & Sibel, creole, b. June
15, 1849 229
----, female, d. Jan. 18, 1861, ae 4 m. 215
WEED, Amelia, d. Jonas & Sara, b. Apr. 7, 1778 3
Anna, d. Jonas & Sara, b. Sept. 22, 1787 3
Claray, d. Jonas & Sara, b. May 13, 1782 3
Cyrus Woodworth, s. Eber & Nancy, b. Jan. 23, 1796 104
Dan, m. Elizabeth **LEWIS,** May 4, 1780 37
Dan & Elizabeth, had s. [ ], b. June 27, 1781 37
Dan & Elizabeth, had s. [ ], d. Aug. 5, 1781, ae 1 m. 8 d. 37
Dan, s. Dan & Elizabeth, b. Sept. 10, 1784 37
Eber, m. Eunice **BACON,** Mar. 22, 1793 104
Eber, m. Nancy **WOODWORTH,** Apr. 16, 1795 104

Page

WILDER, (cont.)

Electa, d. Joseph & Anna, b. July 9, 1813   158

Elijah & Hannah, had s. [   ], b. Apr. 9, 1780 ; d. June 6, 1780   7

Hannah, m. James **AUSTIN**, Dec. 9, 1779   5

Hannah, d. Thomas & Tahpenes, b. Jan. 18, 1783   5

Hannah, w. Elijah, d. Mar. 31, 1789   7

Hariott, m. William P. **CASTER**, Dec. 10, 1839, by J. W. Alvord   209

Henry, s. Thomas & Tahpenes, b. Oct. 17, 1779   5

Henry, s. Joseph & Anna, b. July 3, 1824   158

Ira, s. Jonathan & Sara, b. Aug. 22, 1780   6

James, s. Thomas & Tahpenes, b. Mar. 16, 1781   5

Jonathan, m. Sara **AUSTIN**, Apr. 1, 1779   6

Joseph, s. Thomas & Tahpenes, b. Feb. 5, 1787   5

Joseph, 2nd, m. Anna **GILLET**, Aug. 27, 1812   158

Joseph, s. Joseph & Anna, b. Feb. 1, 1817   158

Mathew Gillet, s. Joseph & Anna, b. Jan. 2, 1819   158

Phebe, d. Thomas, b. Sept. 9, 1799   5

Phebe, of Barkhamsted, m. Calvin **WILDER**, of Hartland, Dec. 26, 1821,

  by Saul Clark   186

Polly, d. Thomas, b. Mar. 22, 1793   5

Sally, d. Thomas & Tahpenes, b. Mar. 12, 1791   5

Susa, d. Thomas, b. Nov. 4, 1803   5

Susan, m. Ichabad **HURLBERT**, b. of Barkhamsted, Sept. 18 1827, by

  John Merrell, J. P.   180

Thomas, s. Thomas & Tahpenes, b. Jan. 15, 1785   5

Thomas, m. Tahpenes **AUSTIN** [   ]   5

William, s. Thomas & Tahpenes, b. Jan. 12, 1789   5

William, s. Joseph & Anna, b. June 27, 1815   158

WILCOX WILLCOCKS, Azubah, d. Jehiel & Azubah, b. July 9, 1787   55

Cloe, d. Joseph & Hannah, b. Aug. 17, 1785   56

George, d. Mar. 24, 1866, ae 21, d.   219

Hira, s. Jehiel & Azubah, b. Apr. 29, 1785   55

Ira, s. Jehiel & Azubah, b. June 21, 1783   55

Jehiel, m. Azubah **MOOR**, Apr. [   ], 1779   55

Jehiel, s. Jehiel & Azubah, b. July 16, 1781   55

Joseph, Jr., m. Hannah **BANNING**, Dec. [   ], 1784   56

Julia A., ae 25, b. Canton, m. Eli S. **CASE**, farmer, ae 30, b.

  Barkhamsted, res. same, July 4, 1849   230

Luman, s. Joseph & Hannah, b. Feb. 1, 1789   56

Malista, m. Mathew **MOSES**, June 10, 1821, by Saul Clark   186

Samuel, s. Joseph & Hannah, b. May 2, 1787   56

Samuel, s. Joseph, Jr. & Hannah, d. Aug. 16, 1788   56

Thanks, m. Zimri **BARBER**, [   ]   131

WILLEY, Hannah, m. David **BRISTOL**, Jan. 20, 1795   129

WILLIAMS, Albert, of Barkhamsted, m. Julia M. **LOVELAND**, of Colebrook

  River, July 8, 1851, at the house of Mr. Loveland, by Rev. Luther

  H. Barber   223

Phillips, b. New Hartford, d. Apr. 6, 1864, ae 12 y. 11 m.   218

BERLIN VITAL RECORDS
1785 - 1850

Vol.   Page

ANDREWS, ANDRUS, (cont.)

Robert, of New Haven, m. Elizabeth A. **TUTTLE,** of Berlin,
May 1, 1843, by Rev. John Moore, of Hartford   1   91

Rosena, of Berlin, m. Adna **HAMLIN,** of Farmington, May 10,
1829, by Rev. Samuel Goodrich   1   35

Roxana, m. Enos M. **SMITH,·**b. of Berlin, May 20, 1835, by
Rev. Noah Porter, of Farmington   1   57

Sarilla M., of Southington, m. Hiram H. **HURLBERT,** of New
Britain, May 19, 1845, by Rev. L. F. Barney, of New
Britain   1   104

Seth, of Meriden, m. Charlotte **CLARK,** Oct. 14, 1832, by
Rev. Samuel Goodrich   1   48

Sophia, m. Maj. Samuel **STANLEY,** Oct. 13, 1844, by Rev.
Samuel W. Law   1   98

Thesta, m. Buyon **PORTER,** Nov. 27, 1823, by Newton
Skinner   1   11

Walter, m. Emily **BUCKLEY*,** b. of Berlin, Oct. 10, 1831, by
Rev. John Nixon   *("**BECKLEY**"?)   1   44

ARNOLD, Charlotte, of Berlin, m. Alvin **ROBERTS,** of
Middletown, Jan. 14, 1844, by William W. Woodworth   1   95

Nancy M., m. Linus B. **COOLEY,** b. of Middletown, Dec. 29,
1844, by W. W. Woodworth   1   101

ASHTON,John, of Newburyport,Mass., m. Sophia M. **GOODRICH,**
of Berlin, Dec. 3, 1844, by Charles A. Goodrich   1   101

ATKINS, Kesiah, of Southington, m. Samuel B. **MURRY,** of
Woodbury, Nov. 28, 1849, by Rev. Stephen Rushmore   1   134

Lewis M., of South Hampton, Mass., m. Harriet N. **ALLEN,** of
New Britain, Dec. 4, 1839, by Walter W. Brewer   1   76

ATWATER, Bryan, m. Mary J. **SAGE,** b. of Berlin, Oct. 31, 1849,
W. W. Woodworth   1   135

Mary M., m. W[illia]m **MARKLAND,** Oct. 4, 1835, at New
Britain, by Rev. Amos D. Watrous   1   59

Walter D., m. Catharine S. **CASE,** b. of Berlin, Oct. 31, 1849,
by W. W. Woodworth   1   135

ATWOOD, Caroline, of Berlin, m. Heman **WHITE,** of Mereden,
July 7, 1835, by Rev. Abraham S. Francis   1   58

Emily, m. George J. **HOOKER,** b. of Berlin, Oct. 28, 1829,
by Royal Robbins   1   38

Jameson, m. Sophia **HOOKER,** b. of Berlin, July 21, 1822, by
Rev. Royal Robbins   1   7

Laura, of Berlin, m. Theron J. **FINCH,** of Southington, Oct. 8,
1832, by Royal Robbins   1   48

Lucetta, m. Leonard **NORTON** , Dec. 10, 1832, by Rev. John
Boyden   1   49

Mary E., m. Samuel S. **TAYLOR,** b. of Berlin, Nov. 25, 1844,
by W. W. Woodworth   1   100

Nelson, m. Deliaett **NEFF,** Sept. 16, 1827, by Rev. Samuel
Goodrich   1   28

	Vol.	Page

ATWOOD, (cont.)

Sabrah, d. Hosea, decd., m. Samuel B. **COWLES**, b. of Berlin,
Jan. 18, 1847, by Rev. Royal Robbins ... 1 ... 115

AUSTIN, Caleb H., m. Lois **WINCHEL**, b. of Berlin, Feb. 26,
1830, by Rev. Theron Osborn ... 1 ... 38

Calvin H., of Litchfield, m. Sally F. **EDWARDS**, of Benton,
Nov. 13, 1820, by Samuel Goodrich ... 1 ... 2

Lindsley, m. Mary **ROOT**, b. of Berlin, Mar. 20, 1842, by Rev.
Royal Robbins ... 1 ... 88

Stephen, of Mereden, m. Mary T. **JUDD**, of Berlin, May 27,
1830, by Royal Robbins ... 1 ... 39

AVERY, Emily, m. Leonard D. **BELDEN**, Aug. 11, 1844, by
William Whittlesey ... 1 ... 97

Levi A. m. Emily Ann **STOW**, b. of Berlin, Sept. 14, 1847,
by Rev. W. A. Stickney ... 1 ... 119

Martha, of Berlin, m. Henry **DEMING**, of Wethersfield, Dec.
19, 1836, by Rev. J. Brace, of Newington ... 1 ... 66

Russell, m. Tamour **HUNT**, Sept. 6, 1838, by Dwight M.
SEWARD ... 1 ... 72

BAILEY, Aurelia A., m. Eli B. **KELSEY**, May 13, 1832, by Rev.
Samuel Goodrich ... 1 ... 45

Clarissa, m. Evelin **TRYON**, b. of Berlin, Sept. 5, 1831, by
Rev. John Nixon ... 1 ... 43

Horace, Jr., m. Martha **DEMING**, Oct. 3, 1844, by Rev. Joseph
L. Morse ... 1 ... 98

Jason, m. Henrietta **WILCON** *, b. of Berlin, Jan. 23, 1831,
by Royal Robbins *(Probably "WILCOX") ... 1 ... 41

Norris, m. Cornelia **PARMELEE**, b. of Berlin, Sept. 26, 1843,
by William W. Woodworth ... 1 ... 95

Norris, m. Roxy D. **BULKLEY**, d. William, Apr. 1, 1850, by
W. W. Woodworth ... 1 ... 137

Rozilla C., of Berlin, m. Henry W. **TIBBALS**, of Chatham,
June 16, 1841, by Rev. Stephen Alonzo Loper, of Middle
Haddam ... 1 ... 84

Thomas L., of Middletown, m. Phebe **BLINN**, of Berlin, Feb.
14, 1840, by Walter W. Brewer ... 1 ... 76

BAIRD, Aaron, m. Emily **TAYLOR**, Apr.30, 1835, by Amos D.
Watrous ... 1 ... 57

BAKER, John S., of New Hartford, m. Martha A. **MOORE**, of
Berlin, Jan. 4, 1846, by Rev. Samuel Rockwell, of New
Britain ... 1 ... 108

BALDWIN, Antoinette R., m. Samuel L. **NORTON**, b. of Berlin,
Nov. 25, 1847, by W. W. Woodworth ... 1 ... 120

Charles L., of Berlin, m. Jennette A. **SHARP**, of New Haven,
Dec. 24, 1848, by Rev. Philo Hawkes ... 1 ... 128

Delia A., d. Ira M., of Berlin, m. Charles N. **ALLING**, of
Hamden, Apr. 29, 1849, by Rev. Royal Robbins ... 1 ... 131

Lucius, of Mereden, m. Maria **WILLARD**, of Berlin, May 29,

	Vol.	Page
BASSETT, (cont.)		
June 3, 1838, by Dwight M. Seward	1	70
BEACH, Philander J., m. Lydia **GOFF**, b. of Berlin, Aug. 1, 1841,		
by W. W. Brewer	1	84
BEAVINS, Alvan, m. Vashti **TAYLOR**, b. of Southington, Oct. 19,		
1826, by Royal Robbins	1	24
BECKLEY, Almira, of Rocky Hill, m. Horace **BOOTH**, of New		
Britain, May 5, 1847, by Charles S. Sherman	1	116
Amelia O., m. Horace **SHELDON**, b. of Berlin, May 13, 1835,		
by Rev. James M. McDonald	1	57
Betsey, m. Herman **CULLENDER**, b. of Berlin, Jan. 4, 1821,		
by Samuel Goodrich	1	3
Clarissa P., m. Laton **PORTER**, b. of Berlin, Oct. 27, 1822,		
by Rev. Samuel Goodrich	1	8
E. M., m. Sarah Jane **STEEL**, b. of Berlin, Apr. 8, 1845, by		
Rev. John Moore, of Hartford	1	101
Edgar, m. Jane E. **WARNER**, d. Edmund, b. of Berlin, July 11,		
1849, by Rev. Royal Robbins	1	132
Elias, m. Abigail **STANLEY**, Apr. 14, 1828, by Rev. Samuel		
Goodrich	1	31
Eliza, Mrs., m. Elijah **STANLEY**, b. of Berlin, Dec. 23, 1834,		
by Rev. W. A. Stickney	1	57
Elvia, m. Alden **SAVAGE**, b. of Berlin, Dec. 15, 1833, by E.		
E. Griswold	1	54
Emily*?, m. Walter **ANDREWS**, b. of Berlin, Oct. 10, 1831,		
by Rev. John Nixon *(Arnold Copy has "Emily		
BUCKLEY")	1	44
Emily, m. Rev. H. G. **SMITH**, b. of Berlin, Nov. 29, 1840,		
by Rev. John Moore, of Hartford	1	80
Emma, of Berlin, m. Horace **PORTER**, of Hamden, May 7,		
1821, by Samuel Goodrich	1	4
Franklin W., of Rocky Hill, m. Eliza M. **BELDEN**, of		
Berlin, Jan. 1, 1849, by W. W. Woodworth	1	128
Harriet M., of Berlin, m. James F. **LEWIS**, of New Britain,		
July 15, 1850, by Rev. Samuel Rockwell	1	139
Harriet* P., of Berlin, m. James F. **MOSES**, of Boston, Apr.		
22, 1846, by W. W. Woodworth *(Note says "d. of		
Benjamin, decd.")	1	109
Harriet* P., of Berlin, m. Augustus P. **COLLINS**, of Windham,		
Apr. 15, 1846, by Rev. Augustus B. Collins *(Note		
says, "d. of Orin, decd.")	1	109
Horace, m. Mary **ROBERTS**, Apr. 16, 1826, by Rev. Samuel		
Goodrich	1	20
Julia M., of Berlin, m. Sidney S. **ALCOTT**, of Marshall,		
Mich., Sept. 8, 1836, by Rev. W[illia]m A. Stickney	1	64
Lois, d. Daniel & Martha, b. Nov. 17, 1730; m. Peet **GALPIN**,		
s. of Caleb & Elizabeth, Nov. 15, 1753	Lr1	513
Louisa L., m. Linus **PORTER**, b. of Berlin, Nov. 9, 1823, by		

	Vol.	Page
BECKLEY, (cont.)		
Rev. Samuel Goodrich	1	11
Lyman, m. Comelia H. **ANDRUS,** d. of Dr. A. **HALL,** decd.,		
b. of Berlin, Mar. 13, 1850, by Rev. Samuel Rockwell	1	136
Milley, of Berlin, m. Nathaniel **PERMELE,** of Middletown,		
May 8, 1821, by Samuel Goodrich	1	4
Miranda, m. Leonard **PATTISON,** Sept. 17, 1826, by Rev.		
Henry Jones	1	22
Nancy, of Berlin, m. Chester **KELSEY,** of Middletown, Nov.		
24, 1825, by Rev. Samuel Goodrich	1	18
Polly, of Dover, O., m. Henry **SANFORD,** of Berlin, Apr. 29,		
1842, by W. W. Brewer	1	88
Ralph, m. Lucinda **MILES,** June 24, 1832, by Rev. John Boyd	1	47
Walter, m. Maria **BUTLER,** b. of Berlin, Jan. 12, 1832, by		
Rev. John Boyde, Jr.	1	45
William, m. Roxey **DEMING,** Apr. 18, 1822, by Samuel		
Goodrich	1	6
W[illia]m S., of Berlin, m. Caroline B. **DICKENSON,** of		
Wethersfield, May 9, 1839, by Rev. W. A. Stickney	1	75
BEEMAN, [see also **BEMENT**], Cecelia, of Middletown, m.		
Robbins **HART,,** of Berlin, Dec. 18, 1836, by Rev. W. A.		
Stickney	1	65
BELDEN, Adaline, of Berlin, m. Martin **WILSON,** of West		
Springfield, Mass., Apr. 3, 1837, by Rev. W. A. Stickney	1	67
Alvin, m. Mrs. Emeline **CORNWELL,** b. of Berlin, Nov. 9,		
1831, by Rev. J. Cogswell	1	44
Aurelia, of Middletown, m. Orrin C. **CLARK,** of Berlin, Jan.		
18, 1849, by W. W. Woodworth	1	130
Edwin, m. Mary Ann **ELLIS,** b. of Berlin, Sept. 7, 1835, by		
Charles A. Goodrich	1	58
Eliza M., of Berlin, m. Franklin W. **BECKLEY,** of Rocky Hill,		
Jan. 1, 1849, by W. W. Woodworth	1	128
Esther M., m. Sheldon J. **ROBERTS,** b. of Berlin, Oct. 24,		
1848, by Rev. William P. Pattison	1	128
Henry m. Nancy **LEE,** Sept. 27, 1826, by Rev. Henry Jones	1	23
Ira C., of New Britain, m. Comelia A. **BUCK,** of Kensington,		
Dec. 7, 1845, by Rev. Asahel Chapin	1	107
Jerusha, m. Amon **JUDD,** Aug. 4, 1824, by Rev. Newton		
Skinner	1	13
Joshua, of Wethersfield, m. Lorena **KELSEY,** of Berlin, Sept.		
17, 1825, by Rev. Samuel Goodrich	1	18
Laura A., of Rocky Hill, m. J. D. **BARBER,** of Palmer Depart,		
Mass., Apr. 25, 1847, by W. W. Woodworth	1	117
Leonard D., m. Emily **AVERY,** Aug. 11, 1844, by William		
Whittlesey	1	97
Lucina, m. George **STEEL,** Jan. 11, 1824, by Rev. Newton		
Skinner	1	12
Lucinia, m. William J. **BULKLEY,** Feb. 9, 1841, by Rev. D.		

	Vol.	Page

BELDEN, (cont.)

M. Seward — 1 — 84

Maria, of Wethersfield, m. Jabez **PECK**, of Berlin, June 8, 1823, by Rev. Roger Robbins — 1 — 10

Mary, m. Chauncey **HILLS**, Apr. 6, 1828, by Rev. Samuel Goodrich — 1 — 30

Matilda, of Wethersfield, m. Elizur **STEELE**, of Berlin, May 5, 1840, by Joseph Whittlesey — 1 — 77

Nancy, of Berlin, m. Henry **NEWBURY**, of Wethersfield, Dec. 9, 1824, by Rev. Samuel Goodrich — 1 — 15

Polly, of Berlin, m. Eli **WARNER**, of Bristol, Mar. 8, 1827, by Samuel Hart, J. P. — 1 — 26

Robert S., of New Britain, m. Evelina S. **SHELDON**, of Farmington, Dec. 20, 1845, at New Britain, by Rev. Samuel Rockwell — 1 — 114

Sophia, of Berlin, m. Warren J. **HUBBARD**, of Middletown, Aug. 16, 1847, by Rev. W. P. Pattison, of New Britain — 1 — 119

BEMENT, [see also **BEEMAN**], Mary, of Middletown, m. David P. **HOUSE**, of Windsor, [ ], by Rev. H. Gardner Smith. Recorded Oct. 5, 1841 — 1 — 85

BENHAM, Roswell G., of New Hartford, m. Mary Jane **NORTHROP**, of Berlin, Jan. 14, 1846, by William W. Woodworth — 1 — 108

BENTON, Henry, m. Sarah E. **BUTLER**, Dec. 23, 1840, by Rev. D. M. Seward — 1 — 81

BIDWELL, Henry L., of Farmington, m. Julia Anne **STANLEY**, of Berlin, Dec. 21, 1830, by Rev. J. Cogswell — 1 — 41

BILL, Asa G., m. [ ] **CROWELL**, Jan. 19, 1834, by E. E. Griswold — 1 — 54

BINGHAM, Jane, m. George **DEWEY**, b. of Berlin, June 23, 1842, by Rev. John M. Guion, of New Britain — 1 — 88

William, m. Jane E. **TODD**, d. Josiah, b. of Berlin, Nov. 5, 1843, by Rev. John M. Guion, of Berlin — 1 — 93

BIRD, Isaac, of Hartford, m. Lucy A. **EDDY**, Nov. 1, 1837, by Jared R. Avery — 1 — 69

BISHOP, Easther, m. Peet **GALPIN**, Feb. 19, 1795 — Lr1 — 513

BLAKE, Lucius D., of Winchester, m. Susan M. **GRISWOLD**, of New Britain, Mar. 29, 1843, by Rev. C. S. Lyman — 1 — 91

BLAKESLEY, Mima, b. Aug. 2, 1774 ; m. James **GALPIN**, Dec. 12, 1790 — Lr1 — 511

BLINN, BLIN, Bitsey, m. William B. **BOOTH**, b. of Berlin, Mar. 31, 1838, by Rev. J. Brace — 1 — 70

Daniel, m. Thesiah **KELSEY**,b. of Berlin, May 6, 1829, by Rev. Samuel Goodrich — 1 — 35

Eliza Ann, of Berlin, m. Charles S. **ELLIS**,of Southbridge, Nov. 1, 1840, by Rev. Herman S. Haven — 1 — 83

Elizabeth N., of Berlin, m. Alfred **DAVIS**, of Wethersfield, Oct. 26, 1826, by Rev. Samuel Goodrich — 1 — 23

BLINN, BLIN, (cont.)

Harriet M., m. Olcott **CHEYNEY**, b. of Berlin, Oct. 2, 1822,
by Rev. Samuel Goodrich   1   8

Luanah E., m. Frederick J. **BOOTH**, of New Britain, May 1,
1842, in New Britain, by Rev. Aaron S. Hill   1   91

Lucy, m. David **STEEL**, Jr., b. of Berlin, July 23, 1826, by
Rev. Samuel Goodrich   1   22

Lucy D., m. John M. **THATCHER**, b. of Berlin, July 8, 1832,
by Rev. William Bentley   1   47

Nancy, of Berlin, m. Purmont B. **BRADFORD**, of Haddam,
May 12, 1838, by Rev. J. Brace, of Newington   1   71

Phebe, of Berlin, m. Thomas L. **BAILEY**, of Middletown, Feb.
14, 1840, by Walter W. Brewer   1   76

William, m. Nancy Jane **PARSONS**, b. of Berlin, Feb. 14,
1840, by W. W. Brewer   1   76

Zerah, m. Lovina **STEEL**, Feb. 6, 1826, by Rev. Samuel
Goodrich   1   19

BLOOD, W[illia]m, of Berlin, m. Louisa **JEROME**, of Bristol, Nov.
18, 1841, by Rev. John M. Guion, of New Britain   1   86

BLUE, Jesse S., m. Emeline **CHURCHILL**, b. of Berlin, Mar. 8,
1850, by Rev. Stephen Rushmore   1   136

BOARDMAN, Albert, of Middletown, m. Mary **WIER***,, of
Mereden, Oct. 4, 1827, by Rev. Samuel Goodrich   *(In
pencil **RICE**"?)   1   28

Asa, of Middletown, m. Loisa **COLE**, of Berlin, Sept. 25,
1828, by Royal Robbins   1   33

Emeline, of Westfield, Conn., m. Amasa **SAVAGE**, of Berlin,
Apr. 17, 1836, by Rev. James McDonald   1   61

Emily C., of New Britain, m. James A. **SMITH**, of
Middletown, Dec. 12, 1847, by Rev. W. P. Pattison, of
New Britain   1   121

Eunice, m. Lorenzo **STOW**, b. of Berlin, Oct. 8, 1826, by
Charles A. Goodrich   1   29

BODWELL, Woodbridge, m. Sarah **HULL**, Sept. 26, 1843, by C. S.
Lyman   1   93

BOOTH, BOOTHE, Almira, m. Russell **TREADWAY**, Nov. 5,
1826, by Samuel Goodrich   1   23

Amny*, [d. Joseph, 2nd & Hannah], b. Mar. 8, 1798
*("Anny"?)   Lr1   507

Anna, m. Hiram **MYGATT**, July 13, 1823, by Rev. Samuel
Goodrich   1   10

Cyrus, m. Menta **LOPEN**, July 1, 1825, by Rev. Royal
Robbins   1   16

David, Jr., of Berlin, m. Lydia **RUSSEL**, of Bristol, July 7,
1828, by Samuel Goodrich   1   31

Edmond F., m. Mary B. **BOOTH**, June 1, 1826, by Royal
Robbins   1   21

Edwin, [s. Joseph, 2nd & Hannah], b. May 6, 1796   Lr1   507

	Vol.	Page

BOOTH, BOOTHE, (cont.)

Edwin, m. Sally M. **PORTER,** b. of Berlin, Oct. 29, 1821, by
　　Samuel Goodrich — 1 — 5

Elizabeth, m. George **HART,** b. of Berlin, Sept. 11, 1832,
　　by Royal Robbins — 1 — 47

Frederick J., m. Luanah E. **BLINN,** b. of New Britain, May 1,
　　1842, at New Britain, by Rev. Aaron S. Hill — 1 — 91

George W., m. Abigail S. **CORNWELL,** b. of Berlin, Oct. 2,
　　1828, by Royal Robbins — 1 — 33

Henry, m. Sophia **BULLARD,** b. of Berlin, Mar. 23, 1828, by
　　Royal Robbins — 1 — 31

Horace, of New Britain, m. Almira **BECKLEY,** of Rocky Hill,
　　May 5, 1847, by Charles S. Sherman — 1 — 116

Joseph, 2nd, m. Hannah **HENRY,** May 14, 1795 — Lr1 — 507

Joseph, Jr., m. Caroline M. **STEEL,** Nov. 22, 1827, by Rev.
　　Samuel Goodrich — 1 — 29

Laura S., of New Britain, m. William A. **LEE,** of West
　　Bloomfield, N. Y., Nov. 25, 1847, at New Britain, by
　　Rev. Samuel Rockwell — 1 — 120

Lucetta, of Berlin, m. Henry B. **PHELPS,** of New Harmony,
　　Ind., Sept. 28, 1836, by Charles A. Goodrich — 1 — 64

Lyman W., m. Keziah L. **ANDREWS,** b. of Berlin, May 5,
　　1825, by Rev. Joab Brace, of Wethersfield — 1 — 15

Martha A., of Southington, m. Elam **SLATER,** of Berlin, Jan.
　　31, 1849, at New Britain, by Rev. Samuel Rockwell — 1 — 130

Mary B., m. Edmond F. **BOOTH,** June 1, 1826, by Royal
　　Robbins — 1 — 21

Nancy N., of New Britain, m. David P. **HUGHES,**. of Canton,
　　Sept. 19, 1837, by Jared R. Avery — 1 — 69

Polly, d. Thomas & Eunice, b. May 22, 1818 — Lr12 — 544

Robert, s. Robert & Abigail, b. Dec. 8, 1794 — Lr1 — 506

Robert, s. Robert & Abigail, b. Aug. 1, 1796 — Lr1 — 506

William B., m. Bitsey **BLINN,** b. of Berlin, Mar. 31, 1838,
　　by Rev. J. Brace — 1 — 70

William S., m. Julia A. **CORNWELL,** d. Chauncey, b. of New
　　Britain, Sept. 4, 1849, at New Britain, by Rev. Samuel
　　Rockwell — 1 — 133

BOTSFORD, Lewis, m. Caroline **BARNS,** b. of Berlin, Oct. 20,
　　1828, by Rev. Irenus Atkins, of Southington — 1 — 34

Lewis, m. Mary L. **COWLES,** b. of Berlin, May 29, 1832, by
　　Royal Robbins — 1 — 46

Lydia, m. Russel U. **PECK,** b. of Berlin, Oct. 7, 1827, by
　　Royal Robbins — 1 — 29

Mary, of Berlin, m. Anson **MERIAM,** of Mereden, Oct. 22,
　　1826, by Royal Robbins — 1 — 24

BRACE, Samuel, of Newington, m. Sarah R. **NORTH,** d. of Alvin,
　　Aug. 19, 1847, by Rev. J. Brace — 1 — 119

BRADFORD, Purmont B., of Haddam, m. Nancy **BLINN,** of Berlin,

Vol.   Page

BRADFORD, (cont.)

May 12, 1838, by Rev. J. Brace, of Newington   1   71

BRADLEY, James H., m. Catharine E. **SMITH,** b. of Hartford, Feb.

3, 1849, by Rev. Royal Robbins   1   130

Jason, m. Phebe **BARNS,** Feb. 16, 1825, by Rev. Smith Dayton   1   15

John, of Stafford, m. Laura S. **WOODRUFF,** of Farmington,

Oct. 26, 1828, by Rev. Samuel Griswold   1   33

Wyllys, of Southington, m. Fanny **STEADMAN,** of Berlin,

[Nov.], 27, 1820, by Royal Robbins   1   3

BRAINARD, Delia, of Haddam, m. John D. **ACKLEY,** of East

Haddam, Oct. 18, 1826, by Rev. Samuel Goodrich   1   23

BRANDEGEE, BRANDEGA, Elisha, [s. Elishama & Lucy], b.

Nov. 5, 1783   Lr1   514

Elishama, m. Lucy **WESTON,** Mar. 10, 1778   Lr1   514

Elishama, m. Mrs. Anna **MYGATT,** b. of Berlin, Nov. 29,

1835, by Rev. James M. McDonald   1   60

Elishama, Jr., of Berlin, m. Florence **STICTT** (?), of

Petersburg, Va., Apr. 28, 1841, by Rev. Aaron J.

Leavenworth   1   85

Jacob T., m. Sarah M. **HINSDALE,** b. of Berlin, May 15,

1839, by Joseph Whittlesey   1   73

Job*, [s. Elishama & Lucy], b. Nov. 11, 1778 *[Probably

"Jacob"]   Lr1   514

John, [s. Elishama & Lucy], b. Nov. 19, 1786   Lr1   514

John, m. Mary A. N. **BULKLEY,** Nov. 11, 1845, by W. W.

Woodworth   1   108

Lucy, [d. Elishama & Lucy], b. July 18, 1781   Lr1   514

Lucy, m. Giles **CURTISS,** b. of Berlin, Sept. 1, 1824, by Rev.

Samuel Goodrich   1   14

Sally, [d. Elishama & Lucy], b. Aug. 2, 1793   Lr1   514

BRASH, Elizabeth, of Burlington, m. David **SQUIRE,** of Berlin,

Nov. 10, 1829, by Charles A. Goodrich   1   38

BRIDGHAM, Hezekiah C., m. Clarissa **NORTH,** b. of Berlin, Oct.

21, 1833, by Rev. Ambrose Edson   1   52

Hezekiah C., of Middletown, m. Clarissa **NORTH** [d. Jedediah

& Betsey], Oct. 21, 1833   1   126

BRONSON, BROWNSON, Abel, [s. Luke], b. Jan. 23, 1780   Lr1   509

Amey, [d. Luke], b. Sept, 8, 1776 ; d. Sept. 20, 1777   Lr1   509

Amey, [d. Luke], b. Mar. 31, 1786   Lr1   509

Asahel, m. Ruth **WOODRUFF,** Oct. 24, 1785   Lr1   505

Charles, s. [Asahel & Ruth], b. July 10, 1788   Lr1   505

Charlotte, d. [Asahel & Ruth], b. Aug. 24, 1786   Lr1   505

Chester, of Salisbury, N. Y., m. Patty **NORTH,** of Berlin,

[July] 14, 1833, by Rev. Ambrose Edson   1   51

Ira, [s. Luke], b. Aug. 14, 1784   Lr1   509

Jane F., d. Theodore & Maria C., of New Britain, m. Mortimer

F. **LEE,** of Bristol, s. Nelson & Abba, May 16, 1848, by

Rev. C. S. Sherman   1   124

	Vol.	Page
BRONSON, BROWNSON, (cont.)		
Luke, m. [ ], Nov. 11, 1737* *(Arnold says probably		
"1773")	Lr1	509
Lydia, [d. Luke], b. Apr. 10, 1787	Lr1	509
Marcia M., m. Levi R. **JUDD**, b. of Berlin, Sept. 1, 1841,		
by W. W. Brewer	1	85
Martha, m. James H. **GLADDING**,, b. of Berlin, Feb. 28,		
1836, by Rev. Royal Robbins	1	61
Sarah, [d. Luke], b. Sept. 1, 1774	Lr1	509
Sophrona C., m. James D. **HUNTER**, b. of Berlin, Nov. 4,		
1833, by Rev. Theron Osborn	1	53
BROWN, Anstra, m. Miley M. **WEBSTER**, July 15, 1827, by Rev.		
Henry Jones	1	27
Charles H., of East Boston, Mass., m. Emeline J. **HUBBARD**,		
of Berlin, May 24, 1847, by W. W. Woodworth	1	117
Charles M., m. Cornelia S. **THRASHER**, d. Nathan, b. of		
Kensington, May 24, 1848, by Rev. Royal Robbins	1	123
Edwin, of Chatham, m. Lucy M. **SKINNER**, Oct. 29, 1840, by		
Joseph Whittlesey	1	81
Horace H., m. Harriet S. **SMITH**, b. of Berlin, May 14, 1845,		
by Rev. Samuel Rockwell, of New Britain	1	104
Hubert M., m. Jane M. **DALOON**, b. of Berlin, Oct. 21, 1840,		
by Rev. W. W. Brewer	1	79
Joseph, m. Lovina **TRYON**, b. of Berlin, Sept. 27, 1830, by		
Rev. Timothy Benedict	1	40
Lucy Ann, m. Nelson **ALLEN**, b. of Berlin, July 10, 1836, by		
Rev. J. Brace, of Newington	1	65
Lydia, of Berlin, m. William **LEWIS**, of Southington, Mar. 20,		
1821, by Samuel Goodrich	1	4
Roxy, m. John **KENT**, b. of Berlin, June 29, 1829, by Royal		
Robbins	1	36
BUCK, Anson A., m. Rebecka **CRAPON**, Sept. 30, 1832, by Rev.		
John Boyden	1	49
Apollos W., of Middletown, m. Mary **OSGOOD**, of Berlin,		
Apr. 12, 1832, by Rev. Irenus Atkins, of Southington	1	46
Cornelia A., of Kensington, m. Ira C. **BELDEN**, of New		
Britain, Dec. 7, 1845, by Rev. Asahel Chapin	1	107
Sophia A., m. William **LOVELAND**, b. of Berlin, Oct. 7,		
1845, by Rev. Royal Robbins	1	106
BUCKLEY, [see also **BULKLEY & BECKLEY**], Emily*, m.		
Walter **ANDREWS**, b. of Berlin, Oct. 10, 1831, by Rev.		
John Nixon *("Emily **BECKLEY**"?)	1	44
BUCKNALL, Stephen Gittins, of Springfield, Mass., m. Maria Eliza		
RICE, of Berlin, Aug. 19, 1847, by Rev. John M. Guion,		
of Saybrook	1	118
BULKLEY, [see also **BUCKLEY**], Betsey, d. Justus, b. Aug. 3,		
1793, at Rocky Hill ; m. Jedediah **NORTH**, s. Levi, Mar.		
10, 1813	1	126

	Vol.	Page

BULKLEY, (cont.)

Maria L., m. Lyman **WILCOX**, b. of Berlin, Sept. 26, 1843,
by William W. Woodworth — 1 — 94

Mary A. N., m. John **BRANDEGEE**, Nov. 11, 1845, by W. W.
Woodworth — 1 — 108

Roxy D., d. William, m. Norris **BAILEY**, Apr. 1, 1850, by W.
W. Woodworth — 1 — 137

William, m. Carolina **HART**, b. of Berlin, Sept. 11, 1827,
by Rev. Samuel Goodrich — 1 — 27

William J., m. Lucinia **BELDEN**, Feb. 9, 1841, by Rev. D. M.
Seward — 1 — 84

BULL, Susan, of Guilford, m. Denison A. **SPENCER**, of [ ], June
30, 1828, by Royal Robbins — 1 — 32

BULLARD, Sophia, m. Henry **BOOTH**, b. of Berlin, Mar. 23,
1828, by Royal Robbins — 1 — 31

BUNCE, Margarette, m. Lyman M. **TUTTLE**, b. of New Britain,
July 7, 1844, by Rev. Samuel Rockwell — 1 — 97

Rhoda M., m. Amon **STEEL**, b. of Berlin, Nov. 16, 1840, by
Rev. W. W. Brewer — 1 — 79

BUNNELL, BUNNEL, Catharine, of Southington, m. Luther
GRAHAM, of Chatham, May 15, 1831, by Rev. Ambrose
Edson — 1 — 42

Julius, m. Sarah A. **TRACY**, b. of New Britain, May 2, 1848,
by W. P. Pattison — 1 — 123

Lucy, of Berlin, m. Nelson **SPERRY**, of New Haven, July 31,
1822, by Rev. Royal Robbins — 1 — 7

BURGSTRAM, Elizabeth H., Mrs. of New Haven, m. Selah S.
PORTER,, of West Haven, Sept. 17, 1848, by W. W.
Woodworth — 1 — 125

BURNHAM, Edwin H., m. A. Eliza **DOWD**, b. of Berlin, Nov. 28,
1849, by W. W. Woodworth — 1 — 135

BURRITT, BURRET, BURRETT, Almira B., m. Stephen L.
STRICTLAND, Nov. 24, 1836, by Dwight M. Seward — 1 — 65

Elizabeth, of Berlin, m. Hezekiah **SEYMOUR**, of Hartford,
Aug. 24, 1829, by J. Cogswell — 1 — 37

Eunice W., m. Jabez **CORNWELL**, Apr. 24, 1833, by J.
Cogswell — 1 — 51

Mary, m. Warner **WILLIAMS**, b. of Berlin, May 26, 1825, by
Rev. Royal Robbins — 1 — 16

William, m. Clarissa **COLE**, b. of Berlin, May 4, 1826, by
Royal Robbins — 1 — 20

BURT, Alfred L., m. Adaline L. **ALLEN**, June 7, 1846, by Rev.
John H. Kent — 1 — 111

Charles M., m. Nancy E. **ALLEN**, b. of New Britain, June 28,
1840, by Rev. W. W. Brewer — 1 — 78

BUSH, Eliza Ann, of Southington, m. Hubert R. **FRANCIS**, of
Berlin, Aug. 3, 1830, by Rev. Irenus Atkins, of
Southington — 1 — 40

	Vol.	Page
BUTLER, George, m. Harriet RUSSELL, of Middletown, Sept. 21, 1835, by Rev. Abraham S. Francis	1	59
Harriet Elizabeth, m. Sylvester STONE, b. of Berlin, Nov. 2, 1828, by Royal Robbins	1	34
Maria, m. Walter BECKLEY, b. of Berlin, Jan. 12, 1832, by Rev. John Boyde, Jr.	1	45
Oscar M., m. Julia A. HART, b. of Berlin, Apr. 10, 1850, at New Britain, by Rev. Samuel Rockwell	1	137
Reuel, m. Luciet FINCH, May 1, 1839, by Rev. Dwight M. Seward	1	74
Sarah, of Berlin, m. John A. COLE, of New Haven, Jan. 3, 1831, by Rev. Timothy Benedict	1	41
Sarah E., m. Henry BENTON, Dec. 23, 1840, by Rev. D. M. Seward	1	81
Walter C., m. Cynthia S. GRISWOLD, d. Riley & Naomi, b. of New Britain, Nov. 15, 1848, by Rev. Charles S. Sherman	1	129
BUTTERFIELD, Daniel, of Pepperill, Mass., m. Sarah HUBERT, of Berlin, Sept. 23, 1827, by Rev. Samuel Goodrich	1	28
BYINGTON, Ensign, m. Harriet MORGAN, Dec. 25, 1838, by Dwight M. Seward	1	73
Miranda, of Berlin, m. Andrew J. NORTON, of Southington, Dec. 8, 1843, by Rev. David H. Plumb	1	94
Olive, of Southington, m. Don Carlos LITTLEFIELD, of Wolcott, Oct. 30, 1839, by Joseph Whittlesey	1	77
CADWELL, Henry S., of Portland, m. Patience GRAHAM, of Berlin, Dec. 25, 1845, at the house of John Graham, by Rev. Samuel M. Emery, of Portland	1	107
Lucius F., of Torringford, m. Electa J. MILEY, May 23, 1828* by Dwight M. Seward, in New Britain *(Probably "1838")	1	70
CAMERON, George A., of Southington, m. Amanda M. DAYTON, of Southington, Dec. 20, 1841, by Rev. J. Marshall Guion, of New Britain	1	87
CAMP, Curtis C., m. Sabina A. HART, Jan. 18, 1844, by Rev. David Miller	1	95
John T., of Durham, m. Eliza A. PERRY, of Berlin, June 21, 1840, by Rev. Herman S. Haven	1	83
Lyman C., of Middletown, m. Ulysea E. SAVAGE, of Berlin, May 21, 1844, by William W. Woodworth	1	96
CANDAY, Asa, of Hartland, m. Phebe ANDREWS, of Berlin, Aug. 17, 1823, by Rev. Benoni Upson	1	10
CAREY, Henry L., s. Elijah & Tabitha, of Windham, m. Martha R. GRISWOLD, d. Riley & Naomi, of New Britain, Jan. 13, 1848, by Rev. C. S. Sherman	1	122
CARPENTER, George, m. Abi GLADDIN, b. of Berlin, Sept. 2, 1835, by Rev. Royal Robbins	1	58
Horaace H., m. Emily WILLIAMS, Sept. 17, 1826, by Rev.		

	Vol.	Page

CARPENTER, (cont.)

Henry Jones — 1 — 23

James B., m. Huldah T. **LAMB**, b. of Berlin, Dec. 25, 1835,
by Rev. William A. Stickney — 1 — 60

James B., m. Louisa M. **LAMB**, b. of Berlin, July 22, 1844,
by Rev. David H. Plumb — 1 — 97

Joshua, m. Betsey **HULL**, b. of Berlin, Sept. 2, 1829, by Royal
Robbins — 1 — 37

CARRINGTON, C[h]loe, of Farmington, m. John **STEELE**, of
Berlin, Dec. 2, 1822, by Rev. Samuel Goodrich — 1 — 8

Sarah, m. Amasa **COBLEIGH**, Dec. 26, 1836, by Rev. C. W.
Turner — 1 — 66

CARTER, Almira, m. Benjamin **HART**, b. of Berlin, July 15, 1832,
by Royal Robbins — 1 — 47

Asahel, m. Jeanette **CURTISS**, b. of Southington, Apr. 12,
1837, by Charles A. Goodrich — 1 — 67

Catharine, Mrs. of Mereden, m. William W. **KELSEY**, of
Berlin, Sept. 13, 1835, by Rev. Abraham S. Francis — 1 — 58

Francis H., m. Hannah A. **MORSE**, d. Orson & Amand[a], of
Burlington, Conn., Oct. 19, 1848, in New Britain, by [ ] — 1 — 127

Francis H., of New Britain, m. Hannah A. **MORSE**, d. Orson
& Amanda, of Burlington, Conn., Oct. 19, 1848, by Rev.
Charles S. Sherman — 1 — 129

CARY, Lorenzo, of Norwich, m. Mrs. Sarah **PECK**, of Berlin, Aug.
11, 1839, by Joseph Whittlesey — 1 — 73

CASE, Aaron R., m. Maria Jane **RICHARDSON**, b. of Berlin, May
22, 1839, by Joseph Whittlesey — 1 — 73

Catharine S., m. Walter D. **ATWATER**, b. of Berlin, Oct. 31,
1849, by W. W. Woodworth — 1 — 135

Esther M., m. James C. **NORTH**, b. of Berlin, Nov. 3, 1844,
by Rev. D. H. Plumb — 1 — 99

CASTLON, James, of New York, m. Polly **DUNHAM**, of Berlin,
Sept. 23, 1830, by Royal Robbins — 1 — 40

CHAKER, Eunice, of Hartford, m. William R. **LEACH**, of Berlin,
July 14, 1844, by Rev. Royal Robbins — 1 — 97

CHAPMAN, David, m. Amey **COLE**, Apr. 8, 1834, by Theron
Osborn — 1 — 56

CHAPPELL, Fanny, m. John W. **TIBBITTS**, b. of New London,
May 22, 1843, by Joseph Whittlesey — 1 — 93

CHENEY, CHEYNEY, Clarissa, b. Feb. 5, 1794; m. Joseph
SAVAGE, Feb. 19, 1818 — Lr12 — 544

Olcott, m. Harriet M. **BLIN**, b. of Berlin, Oct. 2, 1822, by
Rev. Samuel Goodrich — 1 — 8

Orry, of Berlin, m. Walter **WARNER**, of Wethersfield, Apr.
13, 1825, by Rev. William S. Pease — 1 — 16

Polly, of Berlin, m. Richard **COWLES**, of Southington, Oct.
8, 1826, by Rev. Eli Denniston — 1 — 25

CHILDS, Frances M., of Haddam, m. William A. **WENTWORTH**,

	Vol.	Page
CHILDS, (cont.)		
of Middletown, July 29, 1831, by Rev. John Nixon	1	43
CHURCHILL, Clarissa A., of Newington, m. Almon B.		
GOODWIN, of New Britain, Dec. 24, 1841, by W. W.		
Brewer	1	87
Emeline, m. Jesse S. **BLUE,** b. of Berlin, Mar. 8, 1850, by		
Rev. Stephen Rushmore	1	136
Laura, m. Giles **COLVIN,** b. of Berlin, Nov. 20, 1837, by		
Charles A. Goodrich	1	69
Lucy, m. Jeremiah H. **OSGOOD,** Oct. 2, 1754	Lr1	508
Olive, b. Sept. 19, 1784	Lr1	517
Olive, m. Amos **EDWARDS,** s. Josiah & Mary, Mar. 13, 1806	Lr1	517
Samuel C., m. Emily **NORTH,** [d. Jedediah & Betsey], Aug.		
[ ], 1840	1	126
Sarah A., m. Sylvester **ELTON,** Jr., July 31, 1836, by Rev.		
Amos D. Watrous	1	63
William, m. Eliza J. **FRANCIS,** b. of Berlin, Sept. 14, 1835,		
by Rev. Noah Porter, of Farmington	1	59
CLAPP, Horace, m. Sarah **WOODRUFF,** Oct. 8, 1838, by Dwight		
M. Seward	1	72
CLARK, CLERK, Alvin, [s. Ezekiel], b. Aug. 18, 1793	Lr4	492
Charlotte, m. Seth **ANDREWS,** of Meriden, Oct. 14, 1832, by		
Rev. Samuel Goodrich	1	48
Dan, m. Mary **WHITTLESEY,** Sept. 4, 1827, by Rev. Henry		
Jones	1	27
Eliza, d. Chauncey & Mary, m. James P. **MOORE,** s. Perry &		
Lovira, b. of New Britain, June 22, 1848, by Rev. Charles		
S. Sherman	1	124
Elizabeth, m. Oliver **LOOMIS,** b. of East Windsor, Aug. 3,		
1829, by Rev. J. Cogswell	1	36
Emily, of Berlin, m. Ambrose Ives **DOWNS,** of Wolcott, Oct.		
14, 1841, by Rev. Royal Robbins	1	86
George, of Hartford, m. Lucetta **ROBERTS,** of Berlin, Feb. 24,		
1845, by Rev. Joseph L. Morse	1	101
Henry, m. Emily **STANLEY,** Oct. 21, 1832, by Rev. J.		
Cogswell	1	49
Huldah, [d. Ezekiel], b. Mar. 5, 1791	Lr4	492
James, [s. Ezekiel], b. Mar. 26, 1799	Lr4	492
Jane L., of New Britain, m. Deming W. **SAXTON,** of		
Chatham, Apr. 9, 1845, by Rev. Philo Hawkes	1	102
Jerusha, m. George **HART,** of Glastonbury, Feb. 1, 1821, by []	1	3
Jesse, [s. Ezekiel], b. Feb. 1, 1788	Lr4	492
Julia A., m. Miles **BALDWIN,** Apr. 12, 1846, by William S.		
Stilwell	1	109
Laura, of Newington, m. Nelson **HURLBERT,** of Hartford,		
Jan. 6, 1848, by Rev. Joseph Holdick	1	122
Linus, m. Maria L. **BASSETT,** b. of Berlin, Nov. 26, 1837,		
by Luther Beckley, J. P.		

Vol. Page

CLARK, CLERK,, (cont.)

Louisa L., m. Elizur N. **SMITH** b. of New Britain, Dec. 22,
1846, by C. S. Sherman   1   114

Maria, m. Willis A. **PIERCE**, b. of Hartford, Oct. 7, 1849,
at the house of Mr. Pierce, Berlin, by Rev. Alexander
Capron   1   133

Mary, m. Timothy **WETMORE**, May 18, 1836, by Rev.
Dwight Seward, of New Britain   1   62

Mary, m. Henry **EDWARDS**, b. of Berlin, Aug. 6, 1837, by,
Rev. Royal Robbins   1   68

Mary Eliza Ann, m. Andrew N. **RICHARDSON**, b. of Berlin,
Jan. 11, 1843, by William W. Woodworth   1   90

Orrin C., of Berlin, m. Aurelia **BELDEN**, of Middletown, Jan.
18, 1849, by W. W. Woodworth   1   130

Sarah, m. James **FRANCIS**, Oct. 22, 1827, by Rev. Henry
Jones   1   28

Sarah, m. Orrin S. **NORTH**, Feb. 5, 1831, by J. Cogswell   1   42

Teresa, of Berlin, m. Sherman **LAWRENCE**, of Mereden,
Aug. 16, 1832, by Rev. Samuel Goodrich   1   47

William E., of Windsor, m. Mary **EDDY**, of Berlin, Apr. 27,
1841, by Rev. Herman S. Haven   1   83

COBLEIGH, Amasa, m. Sarah **CARRINGTON**, Dec. 26, 1836, by
Rev. C. W. Turner   1   66

COE, George S., m. Almira **STANLEY**, June 15, 1843, by C. S.
Lyman   1   92

John, m. Ursula **WOODRUFF**, of Granville, Mass., Oct. 10,
1830, by Rev. Samuel Goodrich   1   40

COGSWELL, Abigail M., m. W[illia]m **JUDD**, Jr. May 6, 1829, by
Rev. J. Cogswell, of New Britain   1   36

Mary, of Berlin, m. Franklin S. **KINNEY**, of New York, Oct.
16, 1833, by Rev. J. Cogswell   1   53

COLE, [see also **COWLES**], Albert, [s. Capt. Stephen], b. May 13,
1790   Lr1   507

Alva, m. Eliza **GOODRICH**, b. of Berlin, Sept. 14, 1823, by
Royal Robbins   1   10

Amey, m. David **CHAPMAN**, Apr. 8, 1834, by Theron Osbom   1   56

Anner, [d. Selah & Rebecca], b. May 9, 1781   Lr1   506

Betsey, of Berlin, m. Richard **COWLES**, of Lima, N. Y., Oct.
21, 1839, by T. Clark   1   74

Charlotte, [d. Selah & Rebecca], b. Sept. 20, 1782   Lr1   506

Chloe, [d. Selah & Rebecca], b. Dec. 14, 1778   Lr1   506

Clarissa, m. William **BURRET**, b. of Berlin, May 4, 1826, by
Royal Robbins   1   20

Eunice, [d. Selah & Rebecca], b. Nov. 6, 1785   Lr1   506

Ira, [s. Capt. Stephen], b. Aug. 11, 1779   Lr1   507

Ira, of Cahawba, Ala., m. Melissa **ALLYN**, of Berlin, Oct.
15, 1838, by Rev. Royal Robbins   1   71

Jared, m. Mary Ann **DUNHAM**, b. of Berlin, Aug. 21, 1839,

	Vol.	Page
COLE, (cont.)		
by Joseph Whittlesey	1	74
John A., of New Haven, m. Sarah **BUTLER**, of Berlin, Jan. 3, 1831, by Rev. Timothy Benedict	1	41
Loisa, of Berlin, m. Asa **BOARDMAN**, of Middletown, Sept. 25, 1828, by Royal Robbins	1	33
Lucy, [d. Capt. Stephen], b. May 24, 1782	Lr1	507
Lydia, [d. Capt. Stephen], b. Oct. 9, 1774	Lr1	507
Mary Hall, [d. Selah & Rebecca], b. Feb. 14, 1780	Lr1	506
Orpha, of Berlin, m. Philemon **WOODRUFF**, of Southington, Aug. 19, 1832, by Royal Robbins	1	47
Orrein, [s. Selah & Rebecca], b. Nov. 13, 1804	Lr1	506
Rebecca, [d. Selah & Rebecca], b. Feb. 19, 1784	Lr1	506
Russel, [s. Capt. Stephen], b. Oct. 18, 1772	Lr1	507
Selah, m. Rebecca **RICE**, May 14, 1778	Lr1	506
Selah, [s. Selah & Rebecca], b. Dec. 26, 1787	Lr1	506
Selah, m. Martha **STRICTLAND**, Mar. 5, 1810	Lr1	506
Stephen, [s. Capt. Stephen], b. Jan. 22, 1777	Lr1	507
Truman, m. Maria B. **HART**, b. of Berlin, Oct. 2, 1836, by Rev. David Plumb. Witnesses Thomas Hart & James Elton	1	65
COLLINS, Augustus P., of Windham, m. Harriet *P. **BECKLEY**, of Berlin, Apr. 15, 1846, by Rev. Augustus B. Collins *(Note says "d. of Orin, decd.")	1	109
Gilbert E., m. Jerusha E. **DICKINSON**, d. Ralph, decd., b. of Berlin, May 1, 1850, by Rev. John M. Guion	1	138
COLVIN, Elihu H., of Manchester, m. Charlotte R. **STOCKER**, of Berlin, Aug. 14, 1831, by Levi Knight	1	43
Giles, m. Laura **CHURCHILL**, b. of Berlin, Nov. 20, 1837, by Charles A. Goodrich	1	69
Lois, of Berlin, m. Sylvester **MICHAEL**, of Mereden, Apr. 16, 1837, by Rev. D. Plumb. Witnesses Newell Moses & Nancy Moses	1	67
CONE, Emily H., of Lee, Mass., m. Henry E. **PATTISON**, of Berlin, Dec. 31, 1843, by William W. Woodworth	1	95
COOK, Cornelia E., d. Augustus & Mary, of Litchfield, m. Henry W. **FLAGG**, of New Britain, Nov. 15, 1848, by Rev. Charles S. Sherman	1	129
Nathan R., of Mereden, m. Lucy B. **JUDD**, of Berlin, Sept. 13, 1836, by Charles A. Goodrich	1	64
Ozias A., m. Martha M. **JUDD**, Oct. 17, 1836, by Dwight M. Seward	1	65
COOLEY, Linus B., m. Nancy M. **ARNOLD**, b. of Middletown, Dec. 29, 1844, by W. W. Woodworth	1	101
CORBIN, Philip, Jr., of New Britain, s. Philip & Lois, of West Hartford, m. Francina T. **WHITING**, d. Henry W. & Sarah, of New Britain, [June 22, 1848], by Rev. Charles S. Sherman	1	124

	Vol.	Page
CORNWELL, Abigail S., m. George W. **BOOTH**, b. of Berlin, Oct. 2, 1828, by Royal Robbins	1	33
Adaline, m. Timothy W. **STANLEY**, Oct. 18, 1841, by Rev. Dwight M. Seward	1	87
Betsey S., m. Richard T. **PORTER**, Oct. 20, 1824, by Rev. Newton Skinner	1	14
Emeline, Mrs., m. Alvin **BELDEN**, b. of Berlin, Nov. 9, 1831, by Rev. J. Cogswell	1	44
Jabez, m. Eunice W. **BURRETT**, Apr. 24, 1833,by J. Cogswell	1	51
Julia A., d. Chauncey, m. William S. **BOOTH**, of New Britain, Sept. 4, 1849, at New Britain, by Rev. Samuel Rockwell	1	133
Julia Ann, m. Harvey **DUNHAM**, Oct. 3, 1822, by Newton Skinner	1	8
Mary R., m. W[illia]m G. **DAVIDSON**, July 26, 1829, by Samuel Goodrich	1	36
Ralph, m. Emeline **EDDY**, b. of Berlin, Oct. 12, 1823, by Rev. Samuel Goodrich	1	11
Richard T., m. Mary **ROOT**, Oct. 12, 1825, by Rev. Samuel Goodrich	1	18
Stephen W., s. Capt. Timothy, of Middletown, m. Abigail **STANLEY**, July 25, 1796	Lr1	488
William, of Middletown, m. Mary A. **STEEL**, of Berlin, July 11, 1836, by James M. McDonald	1	63
COSSLETTE, Lydia S., m. Josiah **DEWEY**, Jr., May 8, 1823, by Newton Skinner	1	9
COSTELLOW, Polly, Mrs. of Berlin, m. Ephraim **ROBBERTS**, of Mereden, Apr. 27, 1845, by Rev. Joseph L. Morse	1	102
COWLES, [see also COLE], Edward, of Avon, m. Mary **KENT**, of Berlin, June 11, 1837, by Rev. Royal Robbins	1	68
Elisha A., of Ala., m. Rebecca **DICKENSON**, d. Azel, of Berlin, Aug. 10, 1846, by Rev. Royal Robbins	1	111
Emily L., of Berlin, m. Alfred W. **MORRIS**, of Wisconsin Territory, [Oct.] 25, 1840, by Rev. Royal Robbins, of Kensington	1	79
George, m. Betsey Ann **NORTON**, b. of Berlin, Jan. 7, 1838, by Rev. Royal Robbins	1	70
James A., m. Catharine **DUNHAM**, b. of Berlin, May 2, 1842, by Joseph Whittlesey	1	93
John E.,of Farmington, m. Margaret **STANLEY**,of New Britain Dec. 30, 1844, by Rev. C. S. Lyman, of New Britain	1	100
Kirtland, m. Mary **DEMING**, b. of Wethersfield, Feb. 5, 1837, by Rev. D. Plumb. Witness Frederick A. Beliw	1	66
Lois, of Berlin, m. Denison A. **SPENCER**, of Middletown, July 4, 1827, by Royal Robbins	1	27
Lucy A., m. Isaac W. **JUDD**, b. of Berlin, June 17, 1838, by Rev. Royal Robbins	1	71
Mary Ann, of Berlin, m. Howell **MERRIMAN**, of Mereden, July 24, 1843, by Rev. Royal Robbins	1	92

	Vol.	Page

COWLES, (cont.)

Mary L., m. Lewis **BOTSFORD**, b. of Berlin, May 29, 1832,
by Royal Robbins — 1 — 46

Richard, of Southington, m. Abigail **HAILE**, of Mereden, Nov.
12, 1823, by Eli Barnett, Elder — 1 — 11

Richard, of Southington, m. Polly **CHENEY**, of Berlin, Oct. 8,
1826, by Rev. Eli Denniston — 1 — 25

Richard, of Lima, N. Y., m. Betsey **COLE**, of Berlin, Oct.
21, 1839, by T. Clark — 1 — 74

Samuel B., m. Sabrah **ATWOOD**, d. Hosea, decd., b. of Berlin,
Jan. 18, 1847, by Rev. Royal Robbins — 1 — 115

Seldon, of Southington, m. Mary Ann **DICKINSON**, of Berlin,
May 30, 1833, by Royal Robbins — 1 — 51

Seth, m. Lucy **PECK**, Nov. 27, 1825, by Royal Robbins — 1 — 18

COX, Ambrose, of Scottsville, N. Y., m. Sarah G. **GALPIN**, of
Berlin, Feb. 26, 1844, by W. W. Woodworth — 1 — 96

CRAPON, Ama Ann, of Berlin, m. James **HURLBURT**, of
Augusta, Ga., Oct. 16, 1838, by Joseph Whittlesey — 1 — 71

Rebecka, m. Anson A. **BUCK**, Sept. 30, 1832, by Rev. John
Boyden — 1 — 49

CROCKER, Abraham, of Berlin, m. Harriet P. **RICHMAN**, of
Southington, Sept. 22, 1836, by Charles A. Goodrich — 1 — 64

CROSBY, Elisha, m. Mary **JUDD**, Dec. 17, 1844, by Rev. L. F.
Barney, of New Britain — 1 — 103

CROSS, Nancy, of Berlin, m. Rev. W[illia]m **DICKENS**, of
Middletown, Oct. 21, 1839, by Rev. Herman S. Havens — 1 — 76

CROWELL, Levana, of Middletown, m. William **WILSON**, of
Berlin, Jan. 5, 1847, by Rev. Royal Robbins — 1 — 115

----, m. Asa G. **BILL**, Jan. 19, 1834, by E. E. Griswold — 1 — 54

CULLENDAR, Herman, m. Betsey **BECKLEY**, b. of Berlin, Jan. 4,
1821, by Samuel Goodrich — 1 — 3

CURTIS, CURTISS, Edward, of Pepperil, Mass., m. Clarissa
HULBERT, of Berlin, July 4, 1824, by Rev. Samuell
Goodrich — 1 — 13

Emeline L., m. Benjamin F. **EDDY**, Nov. 4, 1849, by Rev.
Stephen Rushmore — 1 — 134

Giles, m. Lucy **BRANDEGEE**, b. of Berlin, Sept. 1, 1824, by
Rev. Samuel Goodrich — 1 — 14

Homer, of Mereden, m. Julia Ann **UPSON**, of Berlin, Nov. 26,
1835, by Rev. J. Brace, of Newington — 1 — 60

Jeanette, m. Asahel **CARTER**, b. of Southington, Apr. 12,
1837, by Charles A. Goodrich — 1 — 67

Marshall, of Stockbridge, m. Lydia E. **PARKER**, of Lenox,
Mass., June 14, 1842, by Rev. John M. Guion, of New
Britain — 1 — 88

Nancy, of Berlin, m. Leonard **SMITH**, of Wayne, N. Y., Aug.
4, 1833, by Rev. Royal Robbins — 1 — 52

Samuel E., of Southington, m. Mary B. **ANDREWS**, of Berlin,

	Vol.	Page
CURTIS, CURTISS, (cont.		
Apr. 21, 1830, by J. Cogswell	1	39
W[illia]m, m. Lucy A. **PENFIELD,** b. of Berlin, Sept. 1, 1840,		
by Rev. John Marshall Guien	1	78
CUSHMAN, George, m. Azaria **HOWD,** b. of New Britain, Sept.		
10, 1835, by Rev. Abraham S. Francis	1	59
DALOON, Jane M., m. Hubert M. **BROWN,** b. of Berlin, Oct. 21,		
1840, by Rev. W. W. Brewer	1	79
DANIELS, Chester, m. Matilda **GLADWIN,** May 29, 1836, by Rev.		
Amos D. Watrous	1	63
George, m. Susan **THOMSON,** b. of Berlin, Oct. 16, 1828,		
by Royal Robbins	1	33
Maria Ann, of Windsor, m. Ira **GILBERT,** of Berlin, May 17,		
1826, by Royal Robbins	1	21
William, m. Jane P. **DUNHAM,** decd., b. of Kensington, Feb.		
6, 1848, by Rev. Royal Robbins	1	122
DAVIDSON, W[illia]m G., m. Mary R. **CORNWELL,** July 26,		
1829, by Samuel Goodrich	1	36
DAVIS, Alfred, of Wethersfield, m. Elizabeth N. **BLIN,** of Berlin,		
Oct. 26, 1826, by Rev. Samuel Goodrich	1	23
DAYTON, Amanda M., of Southington, m. George A. **CAMERON,**		
of Southington, Dec. 20, 1841, by Rev. J. Marshall Guion,		
of New Britain	1	87
Jeremiah, of North Haven, m. Laura Ann, **STEWERT,** Berlin,		
June 22, 1832, by Luther Beckley, J. P.	1	46
DEAN, DEANE, Eliza A., m. Alfred **ROOT,** b. of Berlin, Jan. 6,		
1850, by Rev. Royal Robbins	1	135
Henry W., m. Loisa U. **KENT,** b. of Berlin, Mar. 15, 1838,		
by Rev. Royal Robbins	1	70
Margrett, of Berlin, m. John **DEKIN,** of Hartford, Feb. 17,		
1850, at New Britain, by Rev. Samuel Rockwell	1	135
Stephen M., of Chatham, m. Ira **HART,** of Berlin, Dec. 19,		
1827, by Royal Robbins	1	29
William M., m. Elizabeth A. **WAY,** b. of Berlin, Oct. 15,		
1840, by Rev. Royal Robbins, of Kensington	1	79
DECATUR, Ellen, m. Peter **NORTON,** b. of Berlin (colored),		
Oct. 10, 1839. by Joseph Whittlesey	1	75
DEKIN, John, of Hartford, m. Margrett **DEAN,** of Berlin, Feb.		
17, 1850, at New Britain, by Rev. Samuel Rockwell	1	135
DEMING, Alfred, [s. Moses], b. Mar. 8, 1792	Lr1	542
Anson, [s. Moses], b. Feb. 9, 1790	Lr1	542
Barzillai, of Middletown, m. Ann Jane **RECOR,** of Berlin,		
Oct. 18, 1839, by Rev. Herman S. Havens	1	76
Catharine, m. Gordon S. **ANDREWS,** b. of Berlin, Nov. 17,		
1844, by Rev. L. F. Barney, of New Britain	1	99
Cornelia M., of Berlin, m. Lyman **DUNBAR,** of Buffalo, N. Y.,		
Oct. 28, 1833, by Rev. Ambrose Edson	1	53
Demas, [child of Seth & Hannah], b. Mar. 22, 1787	Lr1	514

	Vol.	Page
DEMING, (cont.)		
Emily, [d. Moses], b. July 7, 1801	Lr1	542
Fenn Wadsworth, [s. Seth & Hannah], b. Jan. 13, 1783	Lr1	514
Francis, m. Julia A. **TUTTLE**, b. of Berlin, July 5, 1847, by		
H. G. Smith	1	118
Hannah, 1st child [Seth & Hannah], b. Mar. 31, 1778	Lr1	514
Henry, of Wethersfield, m. Martha **AVERY**, of Berlin, Dec. 19,		
1836, by Rev. J. Brace, of Newington	1	66
Hepzibah, m. Abijah **NORTH**, Jan. 14, 1824, by Rev. Royal		
Robbins	1	12
Herbert, [s. Moses], b. July 17, 1796	Lr1	542
Julia A., of Berlin, m. True P. **TUCKER**, of Buffalo, N. Y.,		
May 20, 1835, by Rev. James M. McDonald	1	57
Lane A., of Berlin, m. William **KETCHAM**, of Washington,		
N. C., Mar. 6, 1837, by James M. MacDonald	1	66
Lucy, m. Silas **NORTH**, of Berlin, Apr. 14, 1825, by Rev.		
William S. Pease	1	16
Lucy, m. Omri **ANDRUS**, Jan. 9, 1845, by Rev. Joseph L.		
Morse	1	100
Martha, m. Horace **BAILEY**, Jr., Oct. 3, 1844, by Rev. Joseph		
L. Morse	1	98
Mary, m. Kirtland **COWLES**, b. of Wethersfield, Feb. 5, 1837,		
by Rev. D. Plumb. Witness Frederick A. Beliw	1	66
Moses*, [s. Moses], b. Mar. 17, 1803 *(Note says "perhaps		
Moses C.")	Lr1	542
Nancy, [d. Moses], b. Sept. 10, 1787	Lr1	542
Olive E., m. Giles **WRIGHT**, b. of Berlin, Nov. 23, 1841,		
by Rev. Royal Robbins	1	86
Ralph*, [s. Moses], b. July 8, 1798 *(Note says "perhaps		
Ralph P.")	Lr1	542
Rhoda, m. Allen **JUDD**, Mar. 10, 1844, by Rev. David Miller	1	96
Roxey, m. William **BECKLEY**, Apr. 18, 1822, by Samuel		
Goodrich	1	6
Sally, [d. Moses], b. Feb. 17, 1794	Lr1	542
Sarah, b. May 25, 1753; m. Roger **RILEY**, Oct. 19, 1775	Lr1	509
Seth, b. May 21, 1748; m. Hannah **GILBERT**, d. Ebenezer,		
of Middletown, June 11, 1777	Lr1	514
Seth, 2nd Child [Seth & Hannah], b. Mar. 28, 1781	Lr1	514
Seth, Jr., m. Sophia **GALPIN**, Jan. 29, 1804	Lr1	515
Sophia, [d. Seth & Hannah], b. Feb. 10, 1793	Lr1	514
Treat, m. Chloe **LEE**, Oct. 8, 1820, by N. Skinner	1	2
W[illia]m H., m. Laura C. **STEEL**, May 4, 1826, by Rev.		
Samuel Goodrich	1	20
DEWEY, Arabella, of Berlin, m. William **GAYLORD**, of		
Middletown, Dec. 23, 1845, by Rev. Samuel Rockwell, of		
New Britain	1	107
Asahel, s. Josiah, b. Nov. 14, 1794	Lr1	506
George, m. Jane **BINGHAM**, b. of Berlin, June 23, 1842, by		

Vol. Page

DEMING, (cont.)

Rev. John M. Guion, of New Britain	1	88
Josiah, Jr., m. Lydia S. COSSLETTE, May 8, 1823, by Newton Skinner	1	9
Mary, m. Elnathan PECK, June 18, 1827, by Rev. Henry Jones	1	26
Mehitable, m. Edmond HART, June 2, 1824, by Rev. Newton Skinner	1	13
Oliver, s. David, m. Mary STANLEY, Nov. 2, 1792	Lr1	488

DICKENS, W[illia]m, Rev., of Middletown, m. Nancy CROSS, of

Berlin, Oct. 21, 1839, by Rev. Herman S. Havens	1	76

DICKINSON, DICKENSON, Abby, Mrs., m. Asaph SMITH, b. of

Berlin, Feb. 6, 1840, by Joseph Whittlesey	1	77
Ashbel, m. Lydia PORTER, Sept. 21, 1823, by Rev. Samuel Goodrich	1	10
Caroline B., of Wethersfield, m. W[illia]m S. BECKLEY, of Berlin, May 9, 1839, by Rev. W. A. Stickney	1	75
Emeline, of Berlin, m. Osman D. GOODRICH, of New Hartford, N. Y., May 15, 1832, by Royal Robbins	1	46
Esther, m. Jonathan WEBSTER, Jan. 7, 1827, by Rev. Samuel Goodrich	1	25
Jerusha E., d. Ralph, decd., m. Gilbert E. COLLINS, b. of Berlin, May 1, 1850, by Rev. John M. Guion	1	138
Jiry, m. Abby KELSEY, b. of Berlin, Dec. 7, 1825, by Rev. Samuel Goodrich	1	18
Julia Maria, m. Allen M. GALPIN, b. of Berlin, [ ], by Joseph Whittlesey	1	98
Louisa M., m. Horatio S. HOUGH, b. of Berlin, May 9, 1841, by Rev. Herman S. Haven	1	83
Lucy, m. Samuel HART, Jr., Nov. 28, 1825, by Royal Robbins	1	18
Lucy B., d. Henry, of Kensington, m. Lewis MERRIMAN, of Southington, Apr. 2, 1850, by Rev. Royal Robbins	1	137
Margaretta, of Southington, m. Samuel UPSON, Sept. 12, 1841, by Rev. Royal Robbins	1	86
Mary Ann, of Berlin, m. Seldon COWLES, of Southington, May 30, 1833, by Royal Robbins	1	51
Nathaniel, of Springfield, m. Harriet HEART, of Berlin, June 11, 1844, by William W. Woodworth	1	97
Rebecca, d. Azel, of Berlin, m. Elisha A. COWLES, of Ala., Aug. 10, 1846, by Rev. Royal Robbins	1	111
Rollin, m. Marilla JUDD, Dec. 18, 1820, by Newton Skinner	1	3
Seth, m. Patty HOTCHKISS, b. of Berlin, Nov. 23, 1820, by Royal Robbins	1	2
Sophia, m. Horace STANLEY, b. of Berlin, Aug. 24, 1820, by Royal Robbins	1	2
Susan L., m. Sheldon MOORE, b. of Berlin, Nov. 1, 1831, by Royal Robbins	1	45

DICKMAN, Caroline A., m. Ariel PARISH, b. of Berlin, Apr. 3,

1836, by Charles A. Goodrich	1	61

	Vol.	Page
DIX, DICKS, Charlotte, m. Martin **PENFIELD,** b. of Berlin, Dec. 6, 1840, by Rev. Herman S. Haven	1	83
Maria, m. Horatio N. **TUCKER,** Nov. 8, 1835, by Rev. Amos D. Watrous	1	60
DIXON, Elizabeth, of New Haven, m. Elisha A. **PECK,** of Berlin, Aug. 22, 1841, by Rev. Royal Robbins	1	85
DOBSON, Mary, m. William H. **EDDY,** Sept. 23, 1827, by Rev. Samuel Goodrich	1	28
DOOLITTLE, Curtis M., m. Ann C. **HART,** Dec. 14, 1823, by Rev. Newton Skinner	1	12
Reuben, m. Eliza **STANLEY,** b. of Berlin, Nov. 4, 1832, by Royal Robbins	1	49
DORAN, Jarvis, of New York City, m. Selina **SOUTHWORTH,** of Berlin, Jan. 17, 1836, by Rev. J. Brace, of Wethersfield. Recorded Jan. 16, 1836	1	61
DOWD, DOUD, A. Eliza, m. Edwin H. **BURNHAM,** b. of Berlin, Nov. 28, 1849, by W. W. Woodworth	1	135
Amey, of Berlington, m. Andrew B. **HOPKINS,** of Harwinton, July 27, 1834, by Amos D. Watrous	1	56
Julius N., of Madison, m. Eliza D. **WILCOX,** of Berlin, Dec. 18, 1831, by Rev. Samuel Goodrich	1	44
DOWNS, Ambros Ives, of Wolcott, m. Emily **CLARK,** of Berlin, Oct. 14, 1841, by Rev. Royal Robbins	1	86
DUDLEY, Amos E., of Guilford, m. Minerva L. **GLADDING,** of New Britain, Oct. 7, 1846, by C. S. Sherman	1	113
DUNBAR, Liman, of Plymouth, m. Julia **PATTISON,** of Berlin, Aug. 21, 1822, by Rev. Samuel Goodrich	1	7
Lyman, of Buffalo, N. Y. m. Cornelia M. **DEMING,** of Berlin, Oct. 28, 1833, by Rev. Ambrose Edson	1	53
DUNHAM, Adaline, [d. Reuben & Betsey], b. Sept. 6, 1808	Lr9	563
Albert, m. Mehitable **PICKET,** b. of Berlin, Sept. 19, 1822, by Rev. Royal Robbins	1	8
Ann E., of Kensington, m. Hiram **RICHMOND,** of Mereden, Oct. 20, 1844, by Rev. Royal Robbins	1	98
Brainard, m. Julia Ann **SQUIRE,** Mar. 11, 1832, by Rev. Samuel Goodrich	1	45
Catharine, m. James **RICHARDSON,** [Dec.] 1, 1839, by Rev. Royal Robbins	1	76
Catharine, m. James A. **COWLES,** b. of Berlin, May 2, 1842, by Joseph Whittlesey	1	93
Cornelius, m. Jerusha **KELSEY,** b. of Berlin, [Sept.] 16, 1833, by Rev. Ambrose Edson	1	52
Dennis, m. Mary **HOLLESTER,** b. of Berlin, Jan. 19, 1826, by Royal Robbins	1	19
Eliza, [d. Reuben & Betsey], b. Aug. 27, 1800	Lr9	563
Eliza, m. Lewis **EDWARDS,** Aug. 31, 1823, by Rev. Samuel Goodrich	1	10
Elizabeth Ann, of Berlin, m. Samuel N. **SPERRY,** of		

	Vol.	Page

DUNHAM, (cont.)

Woodbridge, Nov. 28, 1843, by Rev. Samuel Rockwell, of New Britain — 1 — 94

Frederick, [s. Reuben & Betsey], b. Apr. 13, 1804 — Lr9 — 563

George, [s. Reuben & Betsey], b. Oct. 7, 1798 — Lr9 — 563

Gideon, m. Mary LEWIS, b. of Berlin, Dec. 2, 1832, by Royal Robbins — 1 — 50

Harvey, m. Julia Ann CORNWELL, Oct. 3, 1822, by Newton Skinner — 1 — 8

Irene, m. Stephen WINCHET, b. of Berlin, Jan. 22, 1823, by Rev. Royal Robbins — 1 — 9

Jane P., d. William, decd., m. William DANIELS, b. of Kensington, Feb. 6, 1848, by Rev. Royal Robbins — 1 — 122

Julia E., of Berlin, m. Franklin K. WILCOX, of Cuqahoga Falls, O., Apr. 21, 1845, by W. W. Woodworth — 1 — 102

Laura Ann, m. George B. GRANNIS, Aug. 22, 1832, by Rev. John Boyd — 1 — 47

Lucina, m. Mortin JUDD, b. of Berlin, Jan. 28, 1828, by Royal Robbins — 1 — 30

Lucy, [d. Reuben & Betsey], b. Feb. 20., 1802 — Lr9 — 563

Lucy, m. Abijah HART, Oct. 26, 1828, by Rev. Henry Jones — 1 — 25

Mariah, [d. Reuben & Betsey], b. Aug. 6, 1806 — Lr9 — 563

Maria, of Berlin, m. Lucius F. NEWTON, of Munson, Mass., Apr. 12, 1830, by Royal Robbins — 1 — 39

Maria Smith, m. Charles Joseph GILBERT, of Hartford, Sept. 2, 1834, by N. G. Wheaton — 1 — 56

Mary Ann, m. Jared COLE, b. of Berlin, Aug. 21, 1839, by Joseph Whittlesey — 1 — 74

Orson, m. Hannah WEBSTER, b. of Southington, Mar. 23, 1836, by Rev. Royal Robbins — 1 — 61

Polly, of Berlin, m. James CASTLON, of New York, Sept. 23, 1830, by Royal Robbins — 1 — 40

Ralph, m. Sophia HART, July 3, 1826, by Rev. Henry Jones — 1 — 21

Reuben, m. Betsey NORTON, Dec. 14, 1797 — Lr9 — 563

Sarah, of Berlin, m. Unni ROBBINS, of Wethersfield, Apr. 19, 1826, by Royal Robbins — 1 — 20

DURAND, Samuel, m. Rebecca ROOT, b. of Berlin, May 1, 1834, by Rev. Ambrose Edson — 1 — 54

EDDY, Abi L., of Berlin, m. Charles PARKER, of Mereden, Oct. 6, 1831, by Rev. Russel Jennings — 1 — 44

Benjamin F., m. Emeline L. CURTIS, Nov. 4, 1849, by Rev. Stephen Rushmore — 1 — 134

Charlotte, m. Henry HILL, May 9, 1836, by Rev. Dwight M. Steward, of New Britain — 1 — 62

Emeline, m. Ralph CORNWELL, b. of Berlin, Oct. 12, 1823, by Rev. Samuel Goodrich — 1 — 11

Frederick, m. Julia Ann BASSETT, b. of Berlin, Sept. 21, 1841, by Joseph Whittlesey — 1 — 85

	Vol.	Page
EDDY, (cont.)		
Horace, m. Mary Ann **WRIGHT**, b. of Berlin, [Sept.] 22,		
1829, by Rev. J. Cogswell	1	37
Lorenzo, m. Nancy **JUDD**, Nov. 25, 1832, by J. Cogswell	1	49
Lucy A., m. Isaac **BIRD**, of Hartford, Nov. 1, 1837, by Jared		
R. Avery	1	69
Martha, m. Daniel b. **FOWLER**, Oct. 16, 1839, by Rev. D.		
M. Seward	1	75
Mary, m. Theodore **RILEY**, Oct. 4, 1835, at New Britain,		
by Rev. Amos D. Watrous	1	59
Mary, of Berlin, m. William E. **CLARK**, of Windsor, Apr.		
27, 1841, by Rev. Herman S. Haven	1	83
Mary J., m. Nathaniel E. **JAMES**, of New York City, Jan.		
6, 1841, by Joseph Whittlesey	1	82
Rebeckah, m. Albert **NORTON**, b. of Berlin, June 28, 1825,		
by Rev. Royal Robbins	1	16
Rebecca B., d. William H. & Mary, m. Elbridge J. **STEELE**,		
s. Russell & Abigail, Feb. 22, 1848, by Rev. C. S.		
Sherman	1	122
William H., m. Mary **DOBSON,** Sept. 23, 1827, by Rev.		
Samuel Goodrich	1	28
EDWARDS, Alfred, m. Sophia W. **NORTH**, Feb. 28, 1830, by Rev.		
Samuel Goodrich	1	38
Amos, [s. Josiah & Mary], b. Oct. 1, 1778; m. Olive		
CHURCHILL, Mar. 13, 1806	Lr1	517
Elisha, [s. Josiah & Mary], b. Feb. 21, 1773	Lr1	517
Elisha, m. Sarah **FENN**, of Milford, Nov. 26, 1795	Lr1	498
Elisha, m. 2nd w. Bethiah **MARCY**, of Ashford, Jan. 29, 1798	Lr1	498
Eliza, d. [Elisha & Bethiah], b. Feb. 6, 1799	Lr1	498
Eliza, of Berlin, m. Elisha M. **HALL**, of Wallingford,		
Feb. 12, 1829, by Rev. Samuel Goodrich	1	34
Henry, [s. Amos & Olive], b. Dec. 4, 1813	Lr1	517
Henry, m. Mary **CLARK**, b. of Berlin, Aug. 6, 1837, by		
Rev. Royal Robbins	1	68
Josiah, b. Dec. 21, 1739; m. Mary **FOSTER**, Mar. 16, 1768	Lr1	517
Josiah, [s. Josiah & Mary], b. Nov. 15, 1774	Lr1	517
Lewis, m. Eliza **DUNHAM**, Aug. 31, 1823, by Rev. Samuel		
Goodrich	1	10
Mary, [d. Josiah & Mary], b. Jan. 25, 1777	Lr1	517
Mary, w. Josiah, d. Oct. 10, 1799	Lr1	517
Phebe, b. Feb. 19, 1770; m. Samuel **NORTON**, Jan. 22, 1789	Lr1	514
Sally F., of Benton*, m. Calvin H. **AUSTIN**, of Litchfield,		
Nov. 13, 1820, by Samuel Goodrich *("Berlin"?)	1	2
Sarah, d. [Elisha & Sarah], b. Oct. 24, 1796	Lr1	498
Sarah, [w. Elisha], d. Oct. 26, 1796	Lr1	498
Walter, [s. Amos & Olive], b. Jan. 8, 1807	Lr1	517
ELDERKIN, Vine, Dr., m. Nancy **NORTON**, Mar. 29, 1826, by		
Rev. Samuel Goodrich	1	20

	Vol.	Page
ELDRIDGE, Elisha, s. Mulford, b. Jan. 28, 1789	Lr1	516
ELLIOTT, John, m. Margaret FRY, Sept. 3, 1843, by W. W.		
Woodworth	1	92
William, m. Agnes FRY, of Ireland, Sept. 27, 1843, by		
Joseph Whittlesey	1	92
ELLIS, Charles S., of Southbridge, m. Eliza Ann BLINN, of Berlin,		
Nov. 1, 1840, by Rev. Herman S. Haven	1	83
Charlotte W., of New Britain, m. Thomas J. HUDDLESTON,		
of Columbus, Miss., Sept. 1, 1846, by C. S. Sherman,		
Int. Pub.	1	112
Mary Ann, m. Edwin BELDEN, b. of Berlin, Sept. 7, 1835,		
by Charles A. Goodrich	1	58
ELLSWORTH, Lydia T., of Berlin, m. Joseph SPALDING, of		
Janesville, Wis., Feb. 7, 1839, by Joseph Whittlesey	1	75
Martha, of Berlin, m. George E. KNAPP, of Westfield,		
Mass., May 15, 1838, by Rev. Joseph Whittlesey	1	70
Sarah, of Berlin, m. Mathew PECK, of Washington, Ala.,		
Aug. 13, 1824, by Rev. Royal Robbins	1	13
ELTON, Sylvester, Jr., m. Sarah A. CHURCHILL, July 31, 1836,		
by Rev. Amos D. Watrous	1	63
ERICKSON, Abraham, m. Maria HOWEL, Oct. 5, 1843, by Rev.		
David Miller	1	93
ERWIN, Cornelius B., m. Maria NORTH, May 18, 1836, by Rev.		
Dwight M. Seward, of New Britain	1	62
ESPY, Robert, m. Elizabeth McKAY, May 20, 1849, by Joseph		
Whittlesey	1	131
EVANS, Jesse, m. Alvira C. GOODRICH, Jan. 8, 1837, by Rev. C.		
W. Turner	1	66
EVAR, Lois, of Southington, m. William BASSETT, of New		
Britain, June 3, 1838, by Dwight M. Seward	1	70
FAIRCHILD, Daniel, of Stockbridge, m. Rebecca WHITTLESEY,		
of New Britain, Jan. 1, 1845, by C. S. Lyman	1	100
FANNING, Benjamin R., m. Charlotte KIMBERLEY, b. of Berlin,		
Oct. 6, 1844, by Joseph Whittlesey	1	99
FARNHAM, Lucy C., m. William SAGE, b. of Berlin, Oct. 19,		
1840, by Joseph Whittlesey	1	81
FELIX, Frances Augustine, d. Henry, of Cuba, m. Rev. Francis		
PECK, of Baltimore, Md., Aug. 31, 1847, by Rev. John		
M. Guion, of Saybrook	1	118
FENN, Richard, of Watertown, m. Prudena N. RICHARDSON, of		
Berlin, June 24, 1832, by Rev. Samuel Goodrich	1	46
Sarah, of Milford, m. Elisha EDWARDS, Nov. 26, 1795	Lr1	498
FENTON, Oliver W., of Vernon, m. Harriet MORSE, of New		
Britain, May 12, 1845, by Rev. L. F. Barney	1	104
FILEY, Levina, m. John HICKSON, Mar. 2, 1795	Lr1	507
FINCH, Luciet, m. Reuel BUTLER, May 1, 1839, by Rev. Dwight		
M. Seward	1	74
Theron J., of Southington, m. Laura ATWOOD, of Berlin,		

	Vol.	Page
FINCH, (cont.)		
Oct. 8, 1832, by Royal Robbins	1	48
FISHER, Hester Ann, m. Henry **NELSON**, Sept. 8, 1833, by Edwin		
E. Griswold	1	52
FITCH, Lucy, m. James **KILBORN**, Nov. 8, 1789	Lr1	511
FLAGG, George, m. Susan **MÒRGAN**, Apr. 30, 1826, by Rev.		
Samuel Goodrich	1	20
Henry W., of New Britain, m. Cornelia E. **COOK**, d. Augustus		
& Mary, of Litchfield, Nov. 15, 1848, by Rev. Charles S.		
Sherman	1	129
Martha, m. Asahel **PECK**, b. of Berlin, Sept. 23, 1829, by		
Royal Robbins	1	37
FLETCHER, Thomas G., of New York City, m. Almira **BARNS**, of		
Berlin, May 5, 1830, by Rev. Samuel Goodrich	1	39
FORBES, Lucy, m. Alfred **HULBURT**, Nov. 16, 1826, by Rev.		
Samuel Goodrich	1	24
FOSTER, Chester M., of Utica, N. Y., m. Harriet M. **LEE**, of		
New Britain, Dec. 3, 1849, at New Britain, by Rev.		
Samuel Rockwell	1	134
Ira, of Mereden, m. Harriet F. **KELSEY**, of Berlin, May 28,		
1837, by Rev. David Plumb	1	68
Mary, b. Jan. 22, 1741; m. Josiah **EDWARDS**, Mar. 16, 1768;		
d. Oct. 10, 1799	Lr1	517
FOWLER, Adaline, m. Daniel **SALISBURY**, Sept. 3, 1835, at New		
Britain, by Rev. Amos D. Watrous	1	59
Daniel B., m. Martha **EDDY**, Oct. 16, 1839, by Rev. D. M.		
Seward	1	75
Ozias, of Durham, m. Ester P. **SAVAGE**, of Berlin, Sept.		
21, 1820, by Samuel Goodrich	1	1
Reuel, m. Densey **NORTON**, (colored), Sept. 10, 1848, by		
W. W. Woodworth	1	126
FOX, Dudley, of Hartford, m. Clarinda **GRANT**, of Berlin, Nov.		
20, 1844, by Rev. John M. Guion, of New Britain	1	100
FRANCIS, Abi, m. James **NORTH**, Feb. 26, 1828, by Rev. J.		
Brace, of Wethersfield	1	30
Charlotte W., m. Horatio A. **PRATT**, b. of Berlin, Sept.		
24, 1832, by Royal Robbins	1	48
Cyrus, m. Nancy D. **PRATT**, July 8, 1827, by Rev. Samuel		
Spring, of Hartford	1	27
Darwin, m. Henrietta W. **HART**, d. Elijah, b. of Berlin,		
Sept. 14, 1846, by Rev. Royal Robbins	1	112
Edwin, m. Dorothy **PERCIVAL**, b. of Berlin, Sept. 15, 1825,		
by Rev. Charles A. Goodrich	1	17
Eliza J., m. William **CHURCHILL**, b. of Berlin, Sept. 14,		
1835, by Rev. Noah Porter, of Farmington	1	59
Emma Mariah, m. Lewis **MITCHEL**, Oct. 23, 1832, by Theron		
Osborn	1	49
Harriet, d. Robert J. & Mary T., of Newington, m. Levi S.		

	Vol.	Page
FRANCIS, (cont.)		
WELLS, of New Britain, s. Horace & Pamela, Apr. 27, 1848, by Rev. C. S. Sherman	1	124
Hubert R., of Berlin, m. Eliza Ann **BUSH**, of Southington, Aug. 3, 1830, by Rev. Irenus Atkins, of Southington	1	40
James, m. Sarah **CLARK**, Oct. 22, 1827, by Rev. Henry Jones	1	28
Mary L., m. John **STANLEY**, May 28, 1843, in New Britain, by George J. Wood. Certified by C. S. Lyman	1	92
Mason B., m. Elizabeth L. **STANLEY**, Dec. 13, 1843, by C. S. Lyman	1	95
FREEMAN, John R., m. Catharine A. **RILEY**, d. Moses, May 1, 1850, by W. W. Woodworth	1	137
FRY, Agnes, of Ireland, m. William **ELLIOTT**, Sept. 27, 1843, by Joseph Whittlesey	1	93
Margaret, m. John **ELLIOTT**, Sept. 3, 1843, by W. W. Woodworth	1	92
Mary, m. Daniel **GOULD**, b. of Berlin, Sept. 22, 1845, by William W. Woodworth	1	105
GAINES, Eliza A., m. W[illia]m C. **MARSHALL**, Oct. 12, 1836, by Dwight M. Seward	1	65
GALLEGHER, John, of New Britain, m. Mary **KEECH**, of Wethersfield, Mar. 17, 1850, by W. W. Woodworth	1	136
GALPIN, Abby, of Berlin, m. Norman **PORTER**, of Lexington, Kty., Mar. 2, 1823, by Rev. Samuel Goodrich	1	9
Albert, [s. Joseph & Catharine], b. Apr. 23, 1789; d. June 11, 1790	Lr1	512
Allen M., m. Julia Maria **DICKINSON**, b. of Berlin, [ ], by Joseph Whittlesey	1	98
Betsey, [d. James & Mima], b. Mar. 3, 1800	Lr1	511
Caleb, [s. Peet & Lois], b. July 23, 1761; d. Mar. 20, 1764	Lr1	513
Caleb, [s. Peet & Lois], b. Nov. 29, 1771	Lr1	513
Caroline, [d. Peet & Lois], b. Apr. 2, 1765	Lr1	513
Catharine, w. Joseph, d. July 15, 1791	Lr1	512
Catharine Parsons, [d. Joseph & Catharine], b. June 19, 1791; d. July 23, 1791	Lr1	512
Caty, [d. Joseph & Rhoda], b. Nov. 7, 1793	Lr1	512
Clarrissa, [d. James & Mima], b. Feb. 20, 1804	Lr1	511
David, [s. Peet & Lois], b. Sept. 19, 1754	Lr1	513
Emeline, [d. James & Mima], b. Aug. 5, 1797	Lr1	511
George, [s. Joseph & Catharine], b. Nov. 13, 1781	Lr1	512
Hetty D., of Berlin, m. Rev. Seth **SACKETT**, of Warren, [Oct.] 19, 1831, by Rev. Ambrose Edson	1	44
Huldah, m. Harvey **HUBBARD**, Apr. 10, 1825, by Rev. Samuel Goodrich	1	15
James, b. Aug. 3, 1771; m. Mima **BLAKESLEY**, Dec. 12, 1790	Lr1	511
Jehiel, [s. Peet & Lois], b. Dec. 22, 1756	Lr1	513
Jehiel, [s. Peet & Lois], d. Nov. [ ], 1793	Lr1	513

	Vol.	Page
GALPIN, (cont.)		
Joseph, b. Sept. 6, 1754; m. Catharine **PARSONS**, Apr. 16,		
1778	Lr1	512
Joseph, [s. Joseph & Catharine], b. Aug. 14, 1779	Lr1	512
Joseph, m. Rhoda **GUIRNSEY**, Nov. 7, 1792	Lr1	512
Lois, [d. Peet & Lois], b. Dec. 10, 1758	Lr1	513
Lois, 1st w. [Peet], d. Sept. 19, 1793	Lr1	513
Lucy, [d. James & Mima], b. Mar. 17, 1795	Lr1	511
Marietta M., of Berlin, m. Seldon **BARNES**, of East Hartford,		
Apr. 30, 1833, by Rev. Robert A. Hallam, of Mereden	1	50
Mary S., of Berlin, m. Hiram W. **HUBBARD**, of Middletown,		
June 13, 1837, by Rev. James M. McDonald	1	68
Milly, 1st child [James & Mima], b. June 26, 1792	Lr1	511
Mima, w. [James], d. Feb. 9, 1813	Lr1	511
Nabby, [d. Joseph & Rhoda], b. July 6, 1796	Lr1	512
Orrel, [s. Peet & Lois], b. July 5, 1767	Lr1	513
Peet, s. Caleb & Elizabeth, b. Oct. 5, 1731; m. Lois		
BECKLEY, d. Daniel & Martha, Nov. 15, 1753	Lr1	513
Pete & Lois, had s. [ ], b. June 1, 1769; d. [ ], ae 3 da.	Lr1	513
Peet, m. 2nd w. Easther **BISHOP**, Feb. 19, 1795	Lr1	513
Samuel W., m. Amanda E. **SKINNER**, b. of Berlin, May 2,		
1844, by William W. Woodworth	1	96
Sarah G., of Berlin, m. Ambrose **COX**, of Scottsville, N. Y.,		
Feb. 26, 1844, by W. W. Woodworth	1	96
Seth, [s. Joseph & Catharine], b. Aug. 12, 1786	Lr1	512
Silena, m. John **RICHARDSON**, b. of Berlin, Sept. 6, 1835,		
by Rev. Royal Robbins	1	58
Sophia, [d. Joseph & Catharine], b. Sept. 4, 1783	Lr1	512
Sophia, m. Seth **DEMING**,Jr., Jan. 29, 1804	Lr1	515
GAYLORD, William, of Middletown, m. Arabella **DEWEY**, of		
Berlin, Dec. 23, 1845, by Rev. Samuel Rockwell, of New		
Britain	1	107
GILBERT, Aaron B., of New York, m. Caroline **GILBERT**, of		
Berlin, Aug. 31, 1841, by Rev. Herman S. Haven	1	83
Caroline, of Berlin, m. Aaron B. **GILBERT**, of New York,		
Aug. 31, 1841, by Rev. Herman S. Haven	1	83
Charles Joseph, of Hartford, m. Maria Smith **DUNHAM**,		
Sept. 2, 1834, by N. G. Wheaton	1	56
David S., m. Almira **WADSWORTH**, Jan. 1, 1827, by Ira E.		
Smith, J. P.	1	25
Hannah, d. Ebenezer, of Middletown, b. Apr. 7, 1758; m.		
Seth **DEMING**, June 11, 1777	Lr1	514
Ira, of Berlin, m. Maria Ann **DANIELS**, of Windsor, May		
17, 1826, by Royal Robbins	1	21
Moses, of Berlin, m. Lucelia J. **STEELE**, of Farmington, Mar.		
11, 1850, by Rev. S. Rushmore	1	136
GLADDING, GLADDIN, GLADIN, GLADDEN, Abi, m. George		
CARPENTER, b. of Berlin, Sept. 2, 1835, by Rev.		

	Vol.	Page
GLADDING, GLADDIN, GLADIN, GLADDEN, (cont.)		
Royal Robbins	1	58
Elmina, m. Jason **PECK**, b. of Berlin, Nov. 4, 1838, by		
Rev. Albert Case	1	71
Hannah A., m. Sherman **THOMSON**, Mar. 7, 1830, by Elijah		
Willard, Elder	1	38
Henry, m. Betsey **JUDD**, Oct. 3, 1832, by J. Cogswell	1	48
Henry, m. Eliza **HILLS**, Mar. 9, 1836, by Rev. Dwight M.		
Seward, of New Britain	1	62
James H., m. Martha **BRONSON**, b. of Berlin, Feb. 28, 1836,		
by Rev. Royal Robbins	1	61
Jesse, m. Almira **STOWEL**, b. of Berlin, Aug. 7, 1831, by		
Royal Robbins	1	42
Jesse, m,. Almira **STOWE**, b. of Berlin, Aug. 7, 1831, by		
Royal Robbins	1	43
Maria, of Berlin, m. Enos **HUNN**, of Wethersfield, June 17,		
1829, by Royal Robbins	1	36
Minerva L., of New Britain, m. Amos E. **DUDLEY**, of		
Guilford, Oct. 7, 1846, by C. S. Sherman	1	113
Nancy, m. Henry **PECK**, b. of Berlin, Nov. 26, 1826, by		
Royal Robbins	1	24
Orson, m. Lucy Ann **STEELE**, Oct. 20, 1847, by W. P.		
Pattison	1	120
Patience, m. Reuben **PECK**, b. of Berlin, Sept. 6, 1829,		
by Royal Robbins	1	37
Phebe, m. Roger **HART**, Oct. 24, 1824, by Rev. Newton		
Skinner	1	14
GLADWIN, Alfred H., of Berlin, m. Mrs. Lucy **SPERRY**, of		
Hamden, Mar. [ ], 1836, by Rev. Abraham S. Francis	1	62
Matilda, m. Chester **DANIELS**, May 29, 1836, by Rev. Amos		
D. Watrous	1	63
GOFF, Betsey, 2nd, m. Jefferson **STEELE**, b. of Berlin, Feb. 16,		
1823, by Rev. Royal Robbins	1	9
Lydia, m. Philander J. **BEACH**, b. of Berlin, Aug. 1, 1841,		
by W. W. Brewer	1	84
Polly, of Berlin, m. [ ] **TUCKER**, of R. I., Sept. 14,		
1831, by Charles A. Goodrich	1	44
Roxy Ann, m. Solomon B. **YALE**, b. of Berlin, Mar. 5, 1837,		
by Rev. Royal Robbins	1	67
GOODRICH, Alvira C., m. Jesse **EVANS**, Jan. 8, 1837, by Rev. C.		
W. Turner	1	66
Cyprian, m. Nancy **ROOT**, May 5, 1839, by [ ]	1	73
Eliza, m. Alva **COLE**, b. of Berlin, Sept. 14, 1823, by		
Royal Robbins	1	10
Emily C., of Berlin, m. Darius **MEAD**, of Greenwich, May 8,		
1833, by Rev. Samuel Goodrich	1	51
Hannah, of Wethersfield, m. Jonathan **SQUIRES**, of Berlin,		
May 20, 1827, by Samuel Goodrich	1	26

	Vol.	Page
GOODRICH, (cont.)		
Henry, [s. Jeremiah D. & Aurelia], on July 27, 1833, ae 10 y.	Lr12	544
John, of Berlin, m. Henriette **SQUIRES**, of Berlin, Jan.		
15, 1840, by Herman S. Haven	1	76
Laura Smith, m. John Jansen **TAPPIN**, Nov. 30, 1826, by		
Rev. Henry Jones	1	24
Lucy Ann, [d. Jeremiah D. & Aurelia], on Dec. 17, 1832,		
ae 11 y.	Lr12	544
Mary W., m. Homer **HASKELL**, b. of Berlin, May 2, 1831, by		
Royal Robbins	1	42
Milley, m. Isaac **NORTON**, Dec. 28, 1823, by Rev. Samuel		
Goodrich	1	12
Norman K., m. Ruth A. **BARBER**, June 22, 1835, by Rev.		
Amos D. Watrous, at New Britain	1	58
Osman D., of New Hartford, N. Y., m. Emeline **DICKINSON**,		
of Berlin, May 15, 1832, by Royal Robbins	1	46
Sarah N., m. William W. **WOODWORTH**, Oct. 9, 1845, by		
Charles A. Goodrich	1	106
Sophia M., of Berlin, m. John **ASHTON**, of Newburyport,		
Mass., Dec. 3, 1844, by Charles A. Goodrich	1	101
GOODWIN, Almon B., of New Britain, m. Clarissa A.		
CHURCHILL, of Newington, Dec. 24, 1841, by W. W.		
Brewer	1	87
John H., m. Nancy D. **STANLEY**, Nov. 15, 1838, by Dwight		
M. Seward	1	72
Sarah, of Berlin, m. William **PECKHAM**. of New Haven, Nov.		
7, 1841, by Rev. John M. Guion, of New Britain	1	86
GOULD, Daniel, m. Mary **FRY**, b. of Berlin, Sept. 22,. 1845,		
by William W. Woodworth	1	105
Rachel, Mrs. of Middletown, m. Waight **SMITH**, of Berlin,		
May 5, 1823, by Rev. Frederick Wightman, of		
Middletown	1	9
GRAHAM, John, of Chatham, m. Mary **HUBBARD**, of Berlin, Feb.		
3, 1833, by Rev. Samuel Goodrich	1	50
Luther, of Chatham, m. Catharine **BUNNEL**, of Southington,		
May 15, 1831, by Rev. Ambrose Edson	1	42
Mary Ann, m. George W. **WELTON**, of Waterbury, Dec. 15,		
1840, by Joseph Whittlesey	1	82
Patience, of Berlin, m. Henry S. **CADWELL**, of Portland,		
Dec. 25, 1845, at the house of John Graham, by Rev.		
Samuel M. Emery, of Portland	1	107
Sarah C., of Chatham, m. Calvin **WILKIE**, of Alexandra, N.		
Y., Oct. 9, 1836, by Rev. David Plumb, Witnesses		
Hervey Lounsbury, John H. Hubbard	1	64
GRANNIS, George B., m. Laura Ann **DUNHAM**, Aug. 22, 1832,		
by Rev. John Boyd	1	47
Julia, m. Simeon **STEADMAN**, Jan. 1, 1822, by Newton		
Skinner	1	5

	Vol.	Page
GRANT, Clarinda, of Berlin, m. Dudley **FOX**, of Hartford, Nov. 20, 1844, by Rev. John M. Guion, of New Britain	1	100
GREEN, Eliza, of Berlin, m. William R. **SLADE**, of Plymouth, [Dec.] 17, 1836, by Rev. Royal Robbins	1	65
GRIDLEY, Abel, [s. Abel], b. Oct. 9, 1782	Lr1	508
Clement, [s. Abel], b. June 23, 1800	Lr1	508
Cyprian, [s. Abel], b. Jan. 24, 1786	Lr1	508
Elizabeth, m. Benjamin **ALLYN**, b. of Berlin, Feb. 17, 1830, by Royal Robbins	1	38
Eunice, [d. Abel], b. Nov. 13, 1801	Lr1	508
Harriet, [twin with Henry, d. Abel], b. June 19, 1792	Lr1	508
Henry, [twin with Harriet, s. Abel], b. June 19, 1792	Lr1	508
John, [s. Abel], b. Oct. 13, 1798	Lr1	508
Julia, m. David **KEYES**, Jan. 20, 1836, by Rev. Dwight M. Seward, of New Britain	1	62
Leonard, [s. Abel], b. Jan. 28, 1789	Lr1	508
Lois, [d. Abel], b. Feb. 15, 1794	Lr1	508
Lucy, [d. Abel], b. Apr. 14, 1780	Lr1	508
Lucyna, [d. Abel], b. Sept. 7, 1790	Lr1	508
Polly, [d. Abel], b. Dec. 31, 1795	Lr1	508
Rhoda, [d. Abel], b. Jan. 24, 1788	Lr1	508
Sally, [d. Abel], b. June 15, 1781	Lr1	508
Sally, of Berlin, m. Jonathan **TAYLOR**, of Owego, N. Y., June 21, 1829, by Royal Robbins	1	36
Walter, m. Mary **HUNTER**, b. of Berlin, Feb. 14, 1840, by Rev. Herman S. Haven	1	83
GRISWOLD, Cynthia S., d. Riley & Naomi, m. Walter C. **BUTLER**, b. of New Britain, Nov. 15, 1848, by Rev. Charles S. Sherman	1	129
George, of Wethersfield, m. Ester **STODDARD**, of Berlin, June 10, 1821, by Samuel Goodrich	1	5
George, of Wethersfield, m. Sarah M. **SIMONS**, of Berlin, Apr. 25, 1847, by W. W. Woodworth	1	117
Laura B., of New Britain, m. Ransom **HILL**, of East Hartford, June 10, 1846, by C. S. Sherman. Int. Pub.	1	112
Lucy J., m. Albert **MASON**, May 14, 1840, by Rev. D. M. Seward	1	80
Luther D., m. Sarah **SMITH**, b. of Elyria Lorain Co. O., Mar. 25, 1835, by Edwin E. Griswold	1	57
Martha R., d. Riley & Naomi, of New Britain, m. Henry L. **CAREY**, s. Elijah & Tabitha, of Windham, Jan. 13, 1848, by Rev. C. S. Sherman	1	122
Susan M., of New Britain, m. Lucius D. **BLAKE**, of Winchester, Mar. 29, 1843, by Rev. C. S. Lyman	1	91
GUERNSEY, GUERNSLEY, GOURNSEY, GUIRNSEY, Caroline E., m. Henry S. **HOADLEY**, of Augusta, Ga., Oct. 29, 1840, by Joseph Whittlesey	1	81
Catharine Helen, of Berlin, m. Harvey Seward **HOADLEY**, of		

	Vol.	Page

GUERNSEY, GUERNSLEY, GOURNSEY, GUIRNSEY, (cont.)

New Haven, Nov. 14, 1830, by Rev. Samuel Goodrich   1   41

Elizabeth Louisa, of Berlin, m. John James JONES, of

Louisburgh, N. C., Nov. 4, 1832, by Rev. Ambrose Edson   1   49

Rhoda, m. Joseph GALPIN, Nov. 7, 1792   Lr1   512

GUION, Franklin G., of Kinderhook, N. Y., m. Cordelia L.

WARNER, d. Norman, of Berlin, Oct. 1, 1849, in St.

Marks Ch., New Britain, by Rev. John M. Guion   1   133

GUSET, Sheldon, m. Amanda JOHNSON, b. of Southington, Mar.

18, 1824, by Rev. Benoni Upson   1   12

HALE, HALLE, Abigail, of Mereden, m. Richard COWLES, of

Southington, Nov. 12, 1823, by Eli Barnett, Elder   1   11

Harriet M., of Glastonbury, m. George S. TAYLOR, of Berlin,

July 23, 1845, by Rev. Royal Robbins   1   105

Lucy, of Glastonbury, m. Cornelius W. PECK, of Berlin,

Mar. 22, 1848, by Rev. Henry Miller, of Meriden   1   123

HALL, Cornelia H., m. George ANDRUS, Feb. 11, 1842, by

Rev. Dwight M. Seward   1   87

Cornelia H., see Cornelia H. ANDRUS   1   136

Elisha M., of Wallingford, m. Eliza EDWARDS, of Berlin,

Feb. 12, 1829, by Rev. Samuel Goodrich   1   34

John, m. Lydia M. JUDD, b. of Berlin [ ], by Rev. Royal

Robbins. Recorded Jan. 31, 1841   1   82

Sarah A., m. Henry E. NORTON, b. of Berlin, June 15, 1846,

by Rev. Royal Robbins   1   110

HAMILTON, William, m. Mary Ann VINCENT, b. of Berlin, May

25, 1847, by W. W. Woodworth   1   117

HAMLIN, HAMBLIN, Adna, of Farmington, m. Rosena

ANDREWS, of Berlin, May 10, 1829, by Rev. Samuel

Goodrich   1   35

John, m. Esther M. SWEET, Nov. 10, 1828, by Rev. Samuel

Goodrich   1   33

Linus, of Farmington, m. Abigail HUNT, of Berlin, Dec.

18, 1828, by Royal Robbins   1   34

Lurana, of Farmington, m. Robert POTTER, of Waterbury,

Apr. 30, 1843, in New Britain, by Rev. William Bentley   1   91

Maria, of Farmington, m. Norris SLATER, of Berlin, Oct.

25, 1836, by Rev. J. Brace, of Newington   1   64

Noah, m. Eliza WRIGHT, Jan. 24, 1825, by Rev. Newton

Skinner   1   15

Samuel A., m. Lavinia HART, Dec. 9, 1824, by Rev. Newton

Skinner   1   15

Solomon, m. Mary STEEL, Nov. 1, 1825, by Rev. Henry

Jones   1   18

HART HEART, Aaron C., m. Abigail ANDRUS, Nov. 29, 1827, by

Rev. Henry Jones   1   29

Abigail, m. Isaiah NORTON, Mar. 27, 1789   Lr1   505

Abigail, wid. Jonathan, m. Rev. Cyprain STRONG, Aug. 3,

	Vol.	Page
HART, HEART, (cont.)		
1797	Lr1	507
Abigail, m. Oliver **MOORE,** b. of Berlin, Nov. 3, 1830, by		
Royal Robbins	1	41
Abigail B., wid., d. John & Caroline Andrews, of New		
Britain, m. Comfort **HEWLET,** of Chester, Mass., s.		
Comfort & Patty, of Groton, May 11, 1848, by Rev. C. S.		
Sherman	1	124
Abijah, m. Lucy **DUNHAM,** Oct. 26, 1826, by Rev. Henry		
Jones	1	25
Adaline, of Berlin, m. Levi **WELLS,** of Wethersfield, Nov.		
26, 1845, by Rev. Samuel Rockwell, of New Britain	1	106
Alces Evelon, s. Jonathan & Abigail, b. Oct. 10, 1782	Lr1	505
Angeline C., m. Imley B. **VIETS,** June 28, 1843, by William		
Whittlesey	1	92
Ann C., m. Curtis M. **DOOLITTLE,** Dec. 14, 1823, by Rev.		
Newton Skinner	1	12
Antoinette, of New Britain, m. Andrew **RAPELYE,** of		
Cabotville, Mass., May 24, 1846, by Rev. E. Cushman	1	111
Benjamin, m. Almira **CARTER,** b. of Berlin, July 15, 1832,		
by Royal Robbins	1	47
Betsey, m. John **JUDD,** Jr., Apr. 10, 1822, by Newton Skinner	1	6
Carolina, m. William **BULKLEY,** b. of Berlin, Sept. 11,		
1827, by Rev. Samuel Goodrich	1	27
Caroline, of Berlin, m. Dennis **SWEET,** of Farmington, July		
3, 1828, by Rev. J. Brace, of Wethersfield	1	32
Caroline M., of Avon, m. Merrils **ROBERTS,** of Berlin, Dec.		
1, 1845, by Rev. Samuel Rockwell, of New Britain	1	106
Chauncy m. Polly **MARKHAM,** May 3, 1821, by Royal		
Robbins	1	5
Chauncey m. Jane **HOOPER,** Sept. 16, 1832, by Rev. Luman		
Andrus	1	48
Chester, m. Hannah **WELLS,** Sept. 19, 1821, by Newton		
Skinner	1	5
Chester, m. Elva **WELLS,** May 12, 1824, by Rev. Newton		
Skinner	1	13
Cryus Wadsworth, s. Samuel & Polly, b. Mar. 8, 1794	Lr9	564
Edmond, m. Mehitable **DEWEY,** June 2, 1824, by Rev.		
Newton Skinner	1	13
Eliphaz, s. Judah & Sarah, b. June 28, 1789	Lr1	506
Eliza, m. Ralph **PEARL,** Apr. 18, 1824, by Rev. Newton		
Skinner	1	13
Eliza A., d. Elijah, of New Britain, m. Hector F.		
HUMPHREY, of Bloomfield, May 31, 1849, at New		
Britain, by Rev. Samuel Rockwell	1	132
Fidelia, m. Mansfield **STACEY,** b. of Berlin, Oct. 22,		
1846, by Rev. E. Cushman	1	113
Freedom, m. Harriet **NORTON,** Nov. 8, 1824, by Rev. Samuel		

	Vol.	Page
HART, HEART, (cont.)		
Goodrich	1	14
George, of Glastonbury, m. Jerusha **CLERK**, Feb. 1, 1821, by [ ]	1	3
George, m. Mary **ANDREWS**, Mar. 2, 1826, by Henry Jones	1	20
George, m. Elizabeth **BOOTH**, b. of Berlin, Sept. 11, 1832, by Royal Robbins	1	47
Harriet, late of Berlin, m. N·rris **WILCOX**, Mar. 3, 1822, by Royal Robbins	1	6
Harriet, of Berlin, m. Nathaniel **DICKINSON**, of Springfield, June 11, 1844, by William W. Woodworth	1	97
Henrietta W., d. Elijah, m. Darwin **FRANCIS**, b. of Berlin, Sept. 14, 1846, by Rev. Royal Robbins	1	112
Henry A., m. Eliza **SHIPMAN**, Apr. 24, 1827, by Rev. Henry Jones	1	26
Ira, of Berlin, m. Stephen M. **DEAN**, of Chatham, Dec. 19, 1827, by Royal Robbins	1	29
Jesse, m. Mindwell **PENTON**, b. of Berlin, Mar. 14, 1822, by Samuel Goodrich	1	6
Julia A., m. Oscar M. **BUTLER**, b. of Berlin, Apr. 10, 1850, at New Britain, by Rev. Samuel Rockwell	1	137
Juliaetta A., of New Britain, m. Imley B. **VIETS**, of Granby, June 5, 1826, by Dwight M. Seward	1	70
Laura, m. Horace **STEEL**, b. of Berlin, Aug. 26, 1839, by Rev. John Boyden, Jr.	1	74
Laurana C., of Farmington, m. Charles P. **JAMES**, of Hartford, June 18, 1837, by Jared R. Avery	1	68
Lavinia, m. Samuel A. **HAMBLIN**, Dec. 9, 1824, by Rev. Newton Skinner	1	15
Leander S., m. Emeline **THOMPSON**, Aug. 23, 1824, by Rev. Newton Skinner	1	13
Linus O., m. Mary Ann **PENFIELD**, Oct. 30, 1839, by Rev. D. M. Seward	1	75
Lucinda, m. William H. **SMITH**, Apr. 27, 1842, by Rev. D. M. Seward	1	88
Lucy H., m. Selden **PECK**, b. of Berlin, Nov. 1, 1826, by Royal Robbins	1	24
Lydia, d. Judah & Sarah, b. Dec. 14, 1786	Lr1	506
Lydia, m. Theron **HART**, b. of Berlin, Apr. 27, 1834, by Edwin E. Griswold	1	55
Maria B., m. Truman **COLE**, b. of Berlin, Oct. 2, 1836, by Rev. David Plumb. Witnesses Thomas Hart & James Elton	1	65
Nancy, m. Dr. William **ALLEN**, Jr., b. of Berlin, July 31, 1839, by William W. Brewer	1	73
Nancy A., of New Britain, m. George **HITCHCOCK**, of Southington, Dec. 14, 1845, by Rev. C. S. Sherman, of New Britain	1	108

	Vol.	Page
HART, HEART, (cont.)		
Philip, m. Mary **JUDD,** b. of Berlin, Nov. 16, 1831, by		
Rev. J. Cogswell	1	44
Rhoda, of Berlin, m. Asaph **TULLER,** of Simsbury, Mar. 28,		
1839, by Joseph W. Whittlesey	1	72
Robbins, of Berlin, m. Cecelia **BEEMAN,** of Middletown,		
Dec. 18, 1836, by Rev. W. A. Stickney	1	65
Roger, m. Phebe **GLADDING,** Oct. 24, 1824, by Rev. Newton		
Skinner	1	14
Roswell, m. Eliza **STEEL,** Feb. 13, 1826, by Rev. Noah		
Porter, of Farmington	1	21
Roxana, d. Judah & Sarah, b. Oct. 23, 1783	Lr1	505
Ruth, m. Albert **NORTON,** b. of Berlin, [Mar.] 25, 1829,		
by Royal Robbins	1	35
Sabina A., m. Curtis C. **CAMP,** Jan. 18, 1844, by Rev.		
David Miller	1	95
Salviner, m. Henry **JUDD,** Jan. 30, 1822, by Newton Skinner	1	5
Samuel, Jr., m. Lucy **DICKINSON,** Nov. 28, 1825, by Royal		
Robbins	1	18
Sarah A., of Berlin, m. Orrin B. **SAVAGE,** of Camden, Ala.,		
Sept. 24, 1845, by William W. Woodworth	1	105
Selah, Jr., m. Mrs. Sarah **NORTH,** Nov. 11, 1829, by Rev.		
J. Cogswell	1	38
Sophia, m. Ralph **DUNHAM,** July 3, 1826, by Rev. Henry		
Jones	1	21
Theron, m. Lydia **HART,** b. of Berlin, Apr. 27, 1834, by		
Edwin E. Griswold	1	55
William, m. Rhoda **JUDD,** b. of Berlin, July 21, 1830, by		
Rev. J. Coggswell, of New Britain	1	39
HASKELL, Homer, of Berlin, m. Mary W. **GOODRICH,** of Berlin,		
May 2, 1831, by Royal Robbins	1	42
HAZARD, John, m. Mary M. **STEEL,** Jan. 13, 1833, by George W.		
Appleton	1	50
HEATH, Buckley P., of Warehouse Point, m. Eunice D. **SMITH,**		
of Berlin, Feb. 12, 1838, by Charles A. Goodrich	1	69
HENRY, Hannah, m. Joseph **BOOTH,** 2nd, May 14, 1795	Lr1	507
HEROD, Eliza, m. Richard **JUDD,** Dec. 22, 1833, by J. Cogswell	1	54
HEWIT, Elias, of Albany, N. Y., m. Lois **LOVELAND,** of Berlin,		
Oct. 2, 1833, by Nathaniel Hervey	1	53
HEWLET, Comfort, of Chester, Mass., s. Comfort & Patty, of		
Groton, m. wid. Abigail B. **HART,** d. John & Caroline		
ANDREWS, of New Britain, May 11, 1848, by Rev. C.		
S. Sherman	1	124
Harriet, of Berlin, m. Barzillai **LEE,** of Southington,		
Feb. 24, 1833, by Charles J. Hinsdale	1	50
HICKSON, John, m. Levina **FILEY,** Mar. 2, 1795	Lr1	507
Rebecah, [d. John & Levina], b. Nov. 29, 1796, in Hartford	Lr1	507
Sally, [d. John & Levina], b. June 27, 1798	Lr1	507

	Vol.	Page
HIGBY, Candice B., of Middletown, m. John McMANNAMAN, of		
New Hartford, Nov. 22, 1835, by A. S. Francis	1	60
HIGGINS, William, m. Mary J. SANFORD, b. of Berlin, Oct. 25,		
1839, by T. Clark	1	75
HILLS, HILL, Chauncey, m. Mary BELDEN, Apr. 6, 1828, by		
Rev. Samuel Goodrich	1	30
Edwin C., of East Hartford, m. Margaret STANLEY, d. Ira		
J. & Eliza, of New Britain, Apr. 5, 1848, in New Britain,		
by Rev. C. S. Sherman	1	124
Eliza, m. Henry GLADDEN, Mar. 9, 1836, by Rev. Dwight M.		
Seward, of New Britain	1	62
Henry, m. Charlotte EDDY, May 9, 1836, by Rev. Dwight M.		
Seward, of New Britain	1	62
Ransom, of East Hartford, m. Laura B. GRISWOLD, of New		
Britain, June 10, 1846, by C. S. Sherman. Int. Pub.	1	112
Sheldon, m. Almedia N. RECOY, b. of Berlin, May 6, 1845,		
by Rev. L. F. Barney	1	103
HINSDALE, George, m. Dolly WILLIAMS, b. of Berlin, May 26,		
1822, by Rev. Royal Robbins	1	7
Lorrain, of Torrington, m. Aurora J. SLATER, Feb. 28,		
1847, by Charles S. Sherman	1	116
Mary Louisa, d. Gilman & Ann, m. Israel T. WELLS, b. of		
New Britain, Apr. 11, 1849, by Rev. Charles S. Sherman	1	130
Ruth, m. Allen STEEL, b. of Berlin, Feb. 5, 1821, by Samuel		
Goodrich	1	3
Sarah M., m. Jacob T. BRANDEGEE, b. of Berlin, May 15,		
1839, by Joseph Whittlesey	1	73
HITCHCOCK, Benajah, of Berlin, m. Nancy A. MIX, of Bristol,		
Sept. 4, 1849, by Rev. Albert Nash	1	132
George, of Southington, m. Nancy A. HART, of New Britain,		
Dec. 14, 1845, by Rev. C. S. Sherman, of New Britain	1	108
HOADLEY, Harvey Seward, of New Haven, m. Catharine Helen		
GOURNSEY, of Berlin, Nov. 14, 1830, by Rev. Samuel		
Goodrich	1	41
Henry S., of Augusta, Ga., m. Caroline E. GUERNSLEY,		
Oct. 29, 1840, by Joseph Whittlesey	1	81
HOLBROOK HOLLBROOK, Caroline, Mrs. of Berlin, m. William		
HUBBARD, of Mereden, Jan. 27, 1841, by Walter W.		
Brewer	1	82
William R., m. Caroline MORGAN, Dec. 26, 1836, by Rev.		
C. W. Turner	1	66
HOLLISTER, HOLLESTER, Mary, m. Dennis DUNHAM, b. of		
Berlin, Jan. 19, 1826, by Royal Robbins	1	19
Melisent, m. Henry C. SMITH, b. of Berlin, Sept. 24,		
1826, by Royal Robbins	1	23
Nelson E., of Glastonbury, m. Olive A. ALLEN, of Plymouth,		
Nov. 28, 1849, at New Britain, by Rev. Samuel Rockwell	1	134
HOLMES, Everett C., of Winsted, m. Laura P. PEASE, d. Asaph &		

	Vol.	Page
HOLMES,(cont.)		
Clotila, of New Britain, Nov. 1, 1848, in New Britain, by		
Rev. Charles S. Sherman	1	129
Mary, of Rocky Hill, m. David **WEBSTER**, of Berlin, Jan.		
10, 1847, at New Britain, by Rev. Samuel Rockwell	1	114
HOOKER, Elizabeth N., m. William **WARNER**, b. of Berlin, May		
3, 1832, by Royal Robbins	1	46
George, of Berlin, m. Sally **WOODRUFF**, of Southington,		
Aug. 27, 1826, by Royal Robbins	1	22
George J., m. Emily **ATWOOD**, b. of Berlin, Oct. 28, 1829,		
by Royal Robbins	1	38
James, m. Mrs. Jennette **SWEET**, b. of Farmington, June 14,		
1840, in New Britain, by W. W. Brewer	1	78
Jane A., d. George, of New Britain, m. Isaac **NORTON**, of		
Berlin, [ ], by Rev. Samuel Rockwell. Recorded July 4,		
1850	1	138
Seth, m. Electa **LEONARD**, Feb. 23, 1826, by Royal Robbins	1	19
Sophia, m. Jameson **ATWOOD**, b. of Berlin, July 21, 1822,		
by Rev. Royal Robbins	1	7
HOOPER, Jane, m. Chauncey **HART**, Sept. 16, 1832, by Rev.		
Luman Andrus	1	48
HOPKINS, Andrew B., of Harwinton, m. Amey **DOUD**, of		
Berlington, July 27, 1834, by Amos D. Watrous	1	56
Benjamin, b. Sept. 28, 1752; m. Ruth [ ], Mar. 13, 1777	Lr1	515
Benjamin, [s. Benjamin & Ruth], b. Apr. 22, 1793; bp.	Lr1	
Aug. 4, 1793		
Betsey, [d. Benjamin & Ruth], b. Mar. 23, 1785; bp.	Lr1	515
May 22, 1785		
Clarissa, [d. Benjamin & Ruth], b. Jan. 29, 1778; bp.	Lr1	515
June 9, 1778		
Edmond, [s. Benjamin & Ruth], b. Sept. 8, 1804; bp.	Lr1	515
Feb. 10, 1805		
George, [s. Benjamin & Ruth], b. Nov. 19, 1800; bp.	Lr1	515
Mar. 8, 1801		
Horace, [s. Benjamin & Ruth], b. Nov. 13, 1790; bp.	Lr1	515
Jan. 16, 1791		
Mary, [d. Benjamin & Ruth], b. Apr. 21, 1781; bp.	Lr1	515
June 3, 1781		
Parsis, [child Benjamin & Ruth], b. Sept. 20, 1787; bp.	Lr1	515
Dec. 1, 1787	Lr1	
Ruth, w. Benjamin, b. Nov. 28, 1757		515
Ruth, [d. Benjamin & Ruth], b. Sept. 24, 1796; bp.	Lr1	515
Nov. 27, 1796		
Samuel J., of Michigan, m. Mary A. **KEENEY**, of Lenox,	1	515
Mass., July 4, 1831, by Rev. J. Cogswell		
Willys, of Newington, m. Harriet N. **LANDON**, of Plainville,	1	43
Apr. 24, 1849, at New Britain, by Rev. Samuel Rockwell		
HORTON, Mathias, m. Evelina **SMITH**, b. of Berlin, Apr. 2, 1836,		131

	Vol.	Page
HORTON, (cont.)		
by Rev. Royal Robbins	1	61
HOTCHKISS, Alvin, m. Mary P. **ROBERTS**, b. of Berlin, Aug.		
24, 1825, by Rev. Royal Robbins	1	17
Patty, m. Seth **DICKINSON**, b. of Berlin, Nov. 23, 1820,		
by Royal Robbins	1	2
HOUGH, Horatio S., m. Louisa M. **DICKINSON**, b. of Berlin, May		
9, 1841, by Rev. Herman S. Haven	1	83
Manny, m. Keron **JONES**, Apr. 26, 1840, by Rev. Dwight M.		
Seward	1	80
Nancy, m. Andrew **NORTON**, Apr. 18, 1829, by Samuel		
Goodrich	1	35
HOUSE, David P., of Windsor, m. Mary **BEMENT**, of		
Middletown,[ ], by Rev. H. Gardner Smith. Recorded		
Oct. 5, 1841	1	85
Nelson S., of Glastonbury, m. Sarah S. **HUBBARD**, of		
Middletown, Jan. 6, 1839, by Joseph Whittlesey	1	72
HOVEY, Clarissa, of Berlin, m. Jedediah **WILCOX**, 2nd, of		
Middletown, Sept. 6, 1848, by Rev. Aaron Snow, of		
Glastonbury	1	125
HOWD, Azaria, m. George **CUSHMAN**, b. of New Britain, Sept.		
10, 1835, by Rev. Abraham S. Francis	1	59
HOWEL, Maria, m. Abraham **ERICKSON**, Oct. 5, 1843, by Rev.		
David Miller	1	93
HUBBARD, Abiathea, m. Mary D. **STEEL**, b. of Berlin, Apr. 14,		
1845, by Rev. Royal Robbins	1	103
Ann M., m. Henry **MAYNARD**, b. of New Britain, Sept. 30,		
1844, by Rev. L. F. Barney, of New Britain	1	99
Benjamin, [s. Jonathan & Catharine], b. Sept. 21, 1772;		
d. Jan. 29, 1776	Lr1	516
Benjamin, [s. Jonathan & Catharine], b. Feb. 4, 1776	Lr1	516
Calvin L., of Perry, N. Y., m. Maria M. **KELLOGG**, of Berlin,		
Mar. 11, 1841, by Rev. Royal Robbins	1	83
Catharine, [d. Jonathan & Catharine], b. Sept. 28, 1765	Lr1	516
Delia C., of Berlin, m. Sidney S. **OLCOTT**, of Rochester,		
Dec. 20, 1825, by Rev. Samuel Goodrich	1	19
Edwin, m. Hannah **NORTH**, b. of Berlin, [Oct.] 21, 1832, by		
Rev. Ambrose Edson	1	48
Emeline J., of Berlin, m. Charles H. **BROWN**, of East Boston,		
Mass., May 24, 1847, by W. W. Woodworth	1	117
Harvey, m. Huldah **GALPIN**, Apr. 10, 1825, by Rev. Samuel		
Goodrich	1	15
Hiram W., of Middletown, m. Mary S. **GALPIN**, of Berlin,		
June 13, 1837, by Rev. James M. McDonald	1	68
Jonathan, m. Catharine **ROBBERTS**, Feb. 3, 1763	Lr1	516
Jonathan, [s. Jonathan & Catharine], b. Aug. 28, 1767	Lr1	516
Jonathan, [s. Jonathan & Catharine], b. July 1, 1784	Lr1	516
Jonathan, [s. Jonathan & Catharine], d. July 13, 1784	Lr1	516

	Vol.	Page
HUBBARD, (cont.)		
Jonathan, 2nd, [s. Jonathan & Catharine], d. Feb. 9, 1788	Lr1	516
Lemuel, [s. Jonathan & Catharine], b. Mar. 19, 1778	Lr1	516
Linus P., of Buffalo, N. Y., m. Mary **HULBURT,** of		
Berlin, Oct. 23, 1833, by Rev. Ambrose Edson	1	53
Mary, m. Jarvis **TUTTLE,** May 21, 1832, by Rev. John		
Boyd, Jr.	1	46
Mary, of Berlin, m. John **GRAHAM,** of Chatham, Feb. 3,		
1833, by Rev. Samuel Goodrich	1	50
Richard, [s. Jonathan & Catharine], b. Jan. 15, 1770	Lr1	516
Russell, m. Mahala **WRIGHT,** Oct. 23, 1834, by Rev. John		
Boyden, Jr.	1	56
Samuel, m. Rhoda **STEEL,** Aug. 11, 1836, by Rev. Amos D.		
Watrous	1	63
Sarah, [d. Jonathan & Catharine], b. Nov. 7, 1763	Lr1	516
Sarah, [d. Jonathan & Catharine], d. Jan. 29, 1779	Lr1	516
Sarah, b. Feb. 22, 1780; m. Hart **HULBERT,** Oct. 21, 1798	Lr1	512
Sarah S., of Middletown, m. Nelson S. **HOUSE,** of		
Glastonbury, Jan. 6, 1839, by Joseph Whittlesey	1	72
Sidney, m. Mary **SMITH,** b. of Berlin, May 4, 1845, by Rev.		
L. F. Barney	1	103
Warren J., of Middletown, m. Sophia **BELDEN,** of Berlin,		
Aug. 16, 1847, by Rev. W. P. Pattison, of New Britain	1	119
Wells, m. Electa **LEE,** Aug. 20, 1826, by Rev. Henry Jones	1	22
William, of Mereden, m. Mrs. Caroline **HOLBROOK,** of		
Berlin, Jan. 27, 1841, by Walter W. Brewer	1	82
HUBERT, [see also **HURLBURT**], Sarah, of Berlin, m. Daniel		
BUTTERFIELD, of Pepperill, Mass., Sept. 23, 1827, by		
Rev. Samuel Goodrich	1	28
HUDDLESTON, Thomas J., of Columbus, Miss., m. Charlotte W.		
ELLIS, of New Britain, Sept. 1, 1846, by C. S. Sherman.		
Int. Pub.	1	112
HUGHES, Alpheus, of Newark, N. J., m. Cynthia **ROSE,** of Berlin,		
Sept. 1, 1841, by Rev. Royal Robbins	1	85
David P., of Canton, m. Nancy N. **BOOTH,** of New Britain,		
Sept. 19, 1837, by Jared R. Avery	1	69
HULL, Betsey, m. Joshua **CARPENTER,** b. of Berlin, Sept. 2,		
1829, by Royal Robbins	1	37
George, of Berlin, m. Sally **SPENCER,** of Killingworth,		
Jan. 10, 1828, by Charles A. Goodrich	1	30
Sarah, m. Woodbridge **BODWELL,** Sept. 26, 1843, by C. S.		
Lyman	1	93
William S., m. Betsey L. **STEEL,** b. of Berlin, Oct. 23,		
1842, by Irenus Atkins	1	90
HUMPHREY, Harlow, m. Mrs. Julia M. **OSGOOD,** July 6, 1830,		
by J. Cogswell	1	39
Hector F., of Bloomfield, m. Eliza A. **HART,** d. Elijah,		
of New Britain, May 31, 1849, at New Britain, by		

	Vol.	Page
HUMPHREY,(cont.)		
Rev. Samuel Rockwell	1	132
HUNN, Enos, of Wethersfield, m. Maria **GLADDIN,** of Berlin,		
June 17, 1829, by Royal Robbins	1	36
HUNT, Abigail, of Berlin, m. Linus **HAMLIN,** of Farmington, Dec.		
18, 1828, by Royal Robbins	1	34
Andrew K., of Charlestown, Mass., m. Almira Stanley **LEE,**		
of New Britain, Oct. 17, 1837, by Jared R. Avery	1	69
Tamour, m. Russell **AVERY,** Sept. 6, 1838, by Dwight M.		
Seward	1	72
HUNTER, James D., m. Sophrona C. **BRONSON,** b. of Berlin,		
Nov. 4, 1833, by Rev. Theron Osborn	1	53
Mary, m. Walter **GRIDLEY,** b. of Berlin, Feb. 14, 1840, by		
Rev. Herman S. Haven	1	83
Roswell, m. Esther **VAN NORDEN,** b. of Berlin, Oct. 12,		
1826, by Royal Robbins	1	24
HURLBURT, HULBERT, HULBURT, HURLBERT, [see also		
HUBERT], Abijah, m. Maria **WILCOX,** b. of Berlin,		
May 1, 1837, by Rev. James M. MacDonald	1	67
Alfred, m. Lucy **FORBES,** Nov. 16, 1826, by Rev. Samuel		
Goodrich	1	24
Clarinda, [d. Hart & Sarah], b. Nov. 22, 1800	Lr1	512
Clarissa, of Berlin, m. Edward **CURTISS,** of Pepperil,		
Mass., July 4, 1824, by Rev. Samuel Goodrich	1	13
Hart, b. June 28, 1776; m. Sarah **HUBBARD,** Oct. 21, 1798	Lr1	512
Hart, Jr., [s. Hart & Sarah], b. June 11, 1812	Lr1	512
Hiram H., of New Britain, m. Sarilla M. **ANDREWS,** of		
Southington, May 19, 1845, by Rev. L. F. Barney, of		
New Britain	1	104
James, of Augusta, Ga., m. Ama Ann **CRAPON,** of Berlin,		
Oct. 16, 1838, by Joseph Whittlesey	1	71
James Hart, [s. Hart & Sarah], b. May 8, 1805	Lr1	512
Mary, [twin with William, d. Hart & Sarah], b. Oct. 23, 1809	Lr1	512
Mary of Berlin, m. Linus P. **HUBBARD,** of Buffalo, N. Y.,		
Oct. 23, 1833, by Rev. Ambrose Edson	1	53
Nelson, of Hartford, m. Laura **CLARK,** of Newington, Jan.		
6, 1848, by Rev. Joseph Holdick	1	122
Sarah, Mrs., m. Abijah **PORTER,** b. of Berlin, [Aug.] 28,		
1833, by Rev. Ambrose Edson	1	52
Sarah Hubbard, [d. Hart & Sarah], b. Apr. 25, 1803	Lr1	512
William, [twin with Mary, s. Hart & Sarah], b. Oct. 23, 1809	Lr1	512
JACKSON, William, of Wethersfield, m. Harriet O. **LEWIS,** of		
Berlin, Aug. 6, 1843, by Rev. Royal Robbins	1	92
JACOBS, Naomi, d. Mar. 17, 1803, in the 56th y. of her age	Lr1	511
JAMES, Charles P., of Hartford, m. Laurana C. **HART,** of		
Farmington, June 18, 1837, by Jared R. Avery	1	68
Nathaniel E., of New York City, m. Mary J. **EDDY,** Jan. 6,		
1841, by Joseph Whittlesey	1	82

	Vol.	Page

JENNINGS, Abraham, of New Milford, m. Abigail SPENCER, of
Berlin, Apr. 3, 1836, by Rev. Abraham S. Francis   1   62
JEROME, Andrew, of New Haven, m. Julia E. THRESHER, of
Kensington, May 8, 1849, at New Britain, by Rev.
Samuel Rockwell   1   131
Hiram, of Bristol, m. Rachel SPENCER, of Berlin, Apr. 8,
1829, by Royal Robbins   1   35
Louisa, of Bristol, m. W[illia]m BLOOD, of Berlin, Nov.
18, 1841, by Rev. John M. Guion, of New Britain   1   86
JEWETT, Stafford D., Rev. of Griswold, m. Abigail G. SHIPMAN,
of Berlin, Dec. 22, 1830, by Rev. J. Cogswell   1   41
JOHNSON, Amanda, m. Sheldon GUSET, b. of Southington, Mar.
18, 1824, by Rev. Benoni Upson   1   12
Ann, of Mereden, m. Lemuel WHITE, of Middletown, [ ],
by Benoni Upson   1   10
Jerome, m. Mary ALLEN, Nov. 26, 1835, by Rev. Amos D.
Watrous   1   62
JONES, John James, of Louisburgh, N. C., m. Elizabeth Louisa
GUERNSEY, of Berlin, Nov. 4, 1832, by Rev. Ambrose
Edson   1   49
Keron, m. Manny HOUGH, Apr. 26, 1840, by Rev. Dwight M.
Seward   1   80
JUDA,* Annette, m. Burnham H. PENFIELD, May 10, 1846, by
Rev. Gurdon Robbins, of Hartford *("JUDD"?)   1   110
JUDD, Allen, m. Sarah THIRLEY *, b. of Berlin, Dec. 19, 1830,
by Rev. Timothy Benedict *(Perhaps (SHIRLEY")   1   41
Allen, m. Rhoda DEMING, Mar. 10, 1844, by Rev. David
Miller   1   96
Amon, m. Jerusha BELDEN, Aug. 4, 1824, by Rev. Newton
Skinner   1   13
Ann, m. Lawrence RICHARDS, b. of Berlin, Mar. 26, 1826,
by Rev. Joel S. Linsley, of Hartford   1   20
Annette*, m. Burnham H. PENFIELD, May 10, 1846, by Rev.
Gurdon Robbins, of Hartford *(Written "Annette JUDA")   1   110
Betsey, m. Henry GLADDIN, Oct. 3, 1832, by J. Cogswell   1   48
Cyrus, m. Lina POND, b. of Berlin, Oct. 16, 1849, by Rev.
Stephen Rushmore   1   133
Henrietta, m. Justus R. MORGAN, Nov. 30, 1843, by Rev.
David Miller   1   94
Henry, m. Salviner HART, Jan. 30, 1822, by Newton Skinner   1   5
Isaac W., m. Lucy A. COWLES, b. of Berlin, June 17, 1838,
by Rev. Royal Robbins   1   71
John, Jr., m. Betsey HART, Apr. 10, 1822, by Newton Skinner   1   6
Levi R., m. Marcia M. BROWNSON, b. of Berlin, Sept. 1,
1841, by W. W. Brewer   1   85
Lucy B., of Berlin, m. Nathan R. COOK, of Mereden, Sept.
13, 1836, by Charles A. Goodrich   1   64
Lydia M., m. John HALL, b. of Berlin, [ ], by Rev. Royal

	Vol.	Page
JUDD, (cont.)		
Robbins. Recorded Jan. 31, 1841	1	82
Marilla, m. Rollin **DICKERSON**, Dec. 18, 1820, by Newton		
Skinner	1	3
Martha M., m. Ozias A. **COOK**, Oct. 17, 1836, by Dwight		
M. Seward	1	65
Mary, d. John, m. Gad **STANLEY**, s. Thomas, 2nd, Oct. 29,		
1767	Lr1	488
Mary, m. Philip **HART**, b. of Berlin, Nov. 16, 1831, by		
Rev. J. Cogswell	1	44
Mary, m. Elisha **CROSBY**, Dec. 17, 1844, by Rev. L. F.		
Barney, of New Britain	1	103
Mary T., of Berlin, m. Stephen **AUSTIN**, of Mereden, May		
27, 1830, by Royal Robbins	1	39
Mortin, m. Lucina **DUNHAM**, b. of Berlin, Jan. 28, 1828,		
by Royal Robbins	1	30
Nancy, m. Lorenzo **EDDY**, Nov. 25, 1832, by J. Cogswell	1	49
Polly, m. William **BASSETT**, Apr. 23, 1823, by Newton		
Skinner	1	9
Rhoda, m. William **HART**, b. of Berlin, July 21, 1830, by		
Rev. J. Coggswell, of New Britain	1	39
Richard, m. Eliza **HEROD**, Dec. 22, 1833, by J. Cogswell	1	54
William, m. Lydia **KELLOGG**, b. of Berlin, Feb. 1, 1829,		
by Royal Robbins	1	35
W[illia]m, Jr., m. Abigail M. **COGSWELL**, May 6, 1829, by		
Rev. J. Cogswell, of New Britain	1	36
Willaim Samuell, s. Maj. William, of Farmington, m.		
Esther **STANLEY**, Mar. 26, 1789	Lr1	488
JUDSON, Birdsey, m. Emeline **ROBERTS**, Mar. 30, 1831, by Rev.		
Samuel Goodrich	1	42
KEACH, KEECH, Mary, of Wethersfield, m. John **GALLEGHER**,		
of New Britain, Mar. 17, 1850, by W. W. Woodworth	1	136
Sarah W., of Wethersfield, m. Samuel H. **WELDON**, of New		
Britain, Mar. 15, 1840, by Herman S. Haven	1	77
KEENEY, Mary A., of Lenox, Mass., m. Samuel J. **HOPKINS**, of		
Michigan, July 4, 1831, by Rev. J. Cogswell	1	43
KELLIN, Mary, m. Francis **NORTON**, May 6, 1846, by William		
W. Woodworth	1	111
KELLOGG, Jane A., of Berlin, m. Curtis R. **PARSONS**, of Macon,		
Ga., [Sept.] 20, 1842, by Rev. Royal Robbins	1	89
Lydia, m. William **JUDD**, b. of Berlin, Feb. 1, 1829, by		
Royal Robbins	1	35
Maria M., of Berlin, m. Calvin L **HUBBARD**, of Perry, N. Y.,		
Mar. 11, 1841, by Rev. Royal Robbins	1	83
KELSEY, Abby, m. Jiry **DICKINSON**, b. of Berlin, Dec. 7, 1825,		
by Rev. Samuel Goodrich	1	18
Almira, m. Willis **WILCOX**, Jan. 29, 1826, by Rev. Samuel		
Goodrich	1	19

	Vol.	Page

KELSEY, (cont)

Amelia, m. Philo **ANDREWS**, b. of Berlin, Nov. 27, 1828,
by Royal Robbins | 1 | 34

Asahel, b. Nov. 10, 1743; m. Content **PARSONS**, May 21,
1767 | Lr1 | 510

Asahel Allis, [s. Asahel & Content], b. July 17, 1768 | Lr1 | 510

Chester, of Middletown, m. Nancy **BECKLEY**, of Berlin,
Nov. 24, 1825, by Rev. Samuel Goodrich | 1 | 18

Eli B., m. Aurelia A. **BAILEY**, May 13, 1832, by Rev.
Samuel Goodrich | 1 | 45

Erastus, of Kensington, m. Fanny **WAY**, of Mereden, Apr.
6, 1847, by Rev. Royal Robbins | 1 | 116

Francis, [s. Asahel & Content], b. Jan. 4, 1773 | Lr1 | 510

Francis, [s. Asahel & Content], d. July 21, 1775 | Lr1 | 510

Francis, 2nd, [s. Asahel & Content], b. Sept. 3, 1776 | Lr1 | 510

Harriet F., of Berlin, m. Ira **FOSTER**, of Mereden, May 28,
1837, by Rev. David Plumb | 1 | 68

Jerusha, m. Cornelius **DUNHAM**, b. of Berlin [Sept.] 16,
1833, by Rev. Ambrose Edson | 1 | 52

Levi L., of Hartford, m. Emma **STEVENS**, of Berlin, Mar.
27, 1828, by Rev. Samuel Goodrich | 1 | 30

Lorena, of Berlin, m. Joshus **BELDEN**, of Wethersfield,
Sept. 17, 1825, by Rev. Samuel Goodrich | 1 | 18

Lucinda, [d. Asahel & Content], b. Nov. 5, 1781 | Lr1 | 510

Miranda, m. Alfred **WILCOX**, May 16, 1822 | 1 | 6

Sarah, [d. Asahel & Content], b. May 10, 1771 | Lr1 | 510

Sarah Ann, m. Henry W. **WHITING**, Sept. 6, 1826, by Rev.
Henry Jones | 1 | 22

Thesiah, m. Daniel **BLIN**, b. of Berlin, May 6, 1829, by
Rev. Samuel Goodrich | 1 | 35

Urbana, [d. Asahel & Content], b. June 16, 1787 | Lr1 | 510

William W., of Berlin, m. Mrs. Catharine **CARTER**, of
Mereden, Sept. 13, 1835, by Rev. Abraham S. Francis | 1 | 58

Zenus, [s. Asahel & Content], b. Dec. 12, 1774; d. Aug.
4, 1775 | Lr1 | 510

Zenus, 2nd, [s. Asahel & Content], b. June 17, 1778 | Lr1 | 510

KENT, John, m. Roxy **BROWN**, b. of Berlin, June 29, 1829, by
Royal Robbins | 1 | 36

Loisa U., m. Henry W. **DEAN**, b. of Berlin, Mar. 15, 1838,
by Rev. Royal Robbins | 1 | 70

Mary, of Berlin, m. Edward **COWLES**, of Avon, June 11,
1837, by Rev. Royal Robbins | 1 | 68

Susan, m. Jeremiah **MUNSON**, b. of Berlin, June 24, 1833,
by Rev. John Boyden, Jr. | 1 | 56

KETCHAM, William, of Washington, N. C., m. Lane A. **DEMING**,
of Berlin, Mar. 6, 1837, by James M. MacDonald | 1 | 66

KEYES, David, m. Julia **GRIDLEY**, Jan. 20, 1836, by Rev. Dwight
M. Seward, of New Britain | 1 | 62

	V ol.	Page
KILBOURN, KILBORN, Bryon, [s. James & Lucy], b. Sept. 8,		
1801	Lr1	511
Erastus, m. Elmira **RUGG,** Apr. 21, 1826, by Rev. Henry Jones	1	21
Harriet, [d. James & Lucy], b. Apr. 26, 1795	Lr1	511
Hector, [s. James & Lucy], b. Apr. 25, 1791	Lr1	511
James, m. Lucy **FITCH,** Nov. 8, 1789	Lr1	511
Larra, [child of James & Lucy], b. May 26, 1797	Lr1	511
Lucy, [d. James & Lucy], b. Feb. 1, 1793	Lr1	511
Orrel, [s. James & Lucy], b. Nov. 28, 1799; d. Oct. 26, 1800	Lr1	511
KILBY, KILBEY, Daniel, of Wethersfield, m. Hannah		
WILLIAMS, of Berlin, May 31, 1821, by Elijah Willard,		
Elder	1	4
Hannah, of Berlin, m. Benjamin **ROLAND,** of Hartford,		
Sept. 26, 1840, by Rev. J. Marshall Guien	1	78
Marie, m. Henry **MINOR,** b. of Berlin May 1, 1832, by Rev.		
J. Cogswell	1	45
KIMBERLY, KIMBERLEY, , Charlotte, m. Benjamin R.		
FANNING, b. of Berlin, Oct. 6, 1844, by Joseph		
Whittlesey	1	99
Edward A., m. Charlotte **LEE,** b. of Berlin, [Oct.] 10,		
1832, by Rev. Ambros Edson	1	48
KING, Lois, m. Seth **SAVAGE,** b. of Berlin, Jan. 24, 1824, by		
Rev. Samuel Goodrich	1	12
KINNEY, Franklin s., of New York, m. Mary **COGSWELL,** of		
Berlin, Oct. 16, 1833, by Rev. J. Cogswell	1	53
KNAPP, George E., of Westfield, Mass., m. Martha		
ELLSWORTH, of Berlin, May 15, 1838, by Rev. Joseph		
Whittlesey	1	70
KNOWLES, Samuel M., of Farmington, m. Julia Ann **PENFIELD,**		
of New Britain, Nov. 25, 1841, by Rev. Aaron S. Hills, in		
New Britain	1	87
LAMB, Huldah T., m. James B. **CARPENTER,** b. of Berlin, Dec.		
25, 1835, by Rev. William A. Stickney	1	60
Louisa M., m. James B. **CARPENTER,** b. of Berlin, July 22,		
1844, by Rev. David H. Plumb	1	97
LAMPSON, Emeline P., of New Britain, m. Levi F. **PARISH,** of		
Hartford, Dec. 7, 1845, by Rev. Asahel Chapin	1	107
LANGDON, LANDON, Eliza, m. Norris **PECK,** b. of Berlin, Oct.		
6, 1823, by Royal Robbins	1	11
Emma Ann, of Berlin, m. Walter **WOODWORTH,** of East		
Hartford, Oct. 28, 1840, by Rev. Royal Robbins	1	79
Frederic, of Warehouse Point, m. Eliza N. **SEYMOUR,** of		
New Britain, Sept. 14, 1847, at New Britain, by Rev.		
Samuel Rockwell	1	120
Harriet N., of Plainville, m. Willys **HOPKINS,** of		
Newington, Apr. 24, 1849, at New Britain, by Rev.		
Samuel Rockwell	1	131
Rodney, m. Caroline **SANFORD,** Nov. 24, 1830, by Theron		

	Vol.	Page
LANGDON, LANDON,(cont.)		
Osbom	1	41
Samuel P., m. Minerva **ALLYN**, b. of Berlin, Dec. 18, 1832,		
by Royal Robbins	1	50
LAWRENCE, Shurman, of Mereden, m. Teresa **CLARK**, of Berlin,		
Aug. 16, 1832, by Rev. Samuel Goodrich	1	47
LEACH, William R., of Berlin, m. Eunice **CHAKER**, of Hartford,		
July 14, 1844, by Rev. Royal Robbins	1	97
LEE, Abigail, m. Cyrus **STANLEY**, Sept. 7, 1806	Lr1	516
Almira, 5th d.[Thomas, 2nd & Electa], b. Aug. 9, 1812	Lr12	524
Almira Stanley, of New Britain, m. Andrew K. **HUNT**, of		
Charlestown, Mass., Oct. 17, 1837, by Jared R. Avery	1	69
Barzillai, of Southington, m. Harriet **HEWLET**, of Berlin,		
Feb. 24, 1833, by Charls J. Hinsdale	1	50
Caroline, 4th d. [Thomas, 2nd & Electa], b. Nov. 8, 1810	Lr12	524
Caroline, m. Joshua **PHELPS**, Oct. 14, 1840, by Rev. D. M.		
Seward	1	80
Charlotte, m. Edward A. **KIMBERLY**, b. of Berlin, [Oct.]		
10, 1832, by Rev. Ambrose Edson	1	48
Chloe, m. Treat **DEMING**, Oct. 8, 1820, by N. Skinner	1	2
Electa, 3rd d.[Thomas, 2nd & Electa], b. Mar. 22, 1806	Lr12	524
Electa, m. Wells **HUBBARD**, Aug. 20, 1826, by Rev. Henry		
Jones	1	22
Elizabeth, m. Curtis **WHAPLES**, June 11, 1827, by Rev.		
Henry Jones	1	26
Harriet M., of New Britain, m. Chester M. **FOSTER**, of		
Utica, N. Y., Dec. 3, 1849, at New Britain, by Rev.		
Samuel Rockwell	1	134
Harvey W., of Montgomery, Mass., m. Minerva **WILLIAMS**,		
of Berlin, Aug. 8, 1841, by W. W. Brewer	1	84
Isaac N., m. Orpah **SHIPMAN**, b. of Berlin, Oct. 20, 1833,		
by Rev. J. Cogswell	1	53
John, 2nd, of Berlin, m. Emeline B. **MORTON**, of Hartford,		
June 13, 1841, by Rev. Royal Robbins	1	84
John Riley, 2nd s. [Thomas, 2nd & Electa], b. Apr. 22, 1804	Lr12	524
Lorenzo Porter, 1st s. Thomas, 2nd & Electa], b. Apr. 12, 1800	Lr12	524
Minerva, 1st d. [Thomas, 2nd & Electa], b. Apr. 22, 1798	Lr12	524
Mortimer F., of Bristol, s. Nelson & Abba, m. Jane F.		
BRONSON, d. Theodore & Maria C., of New Britain,		
May 16, 1848, by Rev. C. S. Sherman	1	124
Nancy, m. Henry **BELDEN**, Sept. 27, 1826, by Rev. Henry		
Jones	1	23
Olyeline, 6th d. [Thomas, 2nd & Electa], b. Jan. 4, 1824	Lr12	524
Phillip, m. Nancy **NORTH**, Dec. 28, 1823, by Rev. Newton		
Skinner	1	12
Polly, d. Isaac, Jr., b. Dec. 22, 1783	Lr1	505
Polly, m. Rodney **PICKET**, b. of Berlin, Oct. 22, 1823,		
by Royal Robbins	1	11

	Vol.	Page

LEE, (cont.)

Thomas, 2nd s. Isaac, Jr., b. Nov. 28, 1770; m. Electa
 RILEY, d. John [ ], 1797 — Lr12 — 524

Thomas Goodrich, 3rd s. [Thomas, 2nd & Electa], b. Sept.
 1, 1808 — Lr12 — 524

Tireza, 2nd d. [Thomas, 2nd & Electa], b. Nov. 19, 1801 — Lr12 — 524

William A., of West Bloomfield, N. Y., m. Laura S. **BOOTH**,
 of New Britain, Nov. 25, 1847, at New Britain, by Rev.
 Samuel Rockwell — 1 — 120

William Henry, 4th s. [Thomas, 2nd & Electa], b. Feb. 10,
 1816; d. Dec. 27, 1816 — Lr12 — 524

William Henry, 5th s. [Thomas 2nd & Electa], b. May 19, 1818 — Lr12 — 524

LEONARD, Electa, m. Seth **HOOKER**, Feb. 23, 1826, by Royal
 Robbins — 1 — 19

LESTON, Eliza Ann, of Berlin, m. Aurora **MORIL** (?)*, of
 Wolcottville, July 3, 1831, by Royal Robbins *(Perhaps
 Aurora Marie [ ]") — 1 — 42

LEWIS, Almira, m. Calvin **SWEARES**(?), Nov. 26, 1835, by Rev.
 Amos D. Watrous — 1 — 62

Edward, m. Eliza **PARSONS**, Apr. 22, 1839, by Dwight M.
 Seward — 1 — 73

Harriet O., of Berlin, m. William **JACKSON**, of Wethersfield,
 Aug. 6, 1843, by Rev. Royal Robbins — 1 — 92

James F., m. Emily R. **ROBERTS**, b. of Berlin, Aug. 25,
 1845, by W. W. Woodworth — 1 — 104

James F., of New Britain, m. Harriet M. **BECKLEY**, of Berlin,
 July 15, 1850, by Rev. Samuel Rockwell — 1 — 139

Mary, m. Gideon **DUNHAM**, b. of Berlin, Dec. 2, 1832, by
 Royal Robbins — 1 — 50

Merrick L., of Westfield, Mass., m. Julia E. **STEELE**, of
 Berlin, Apr. 21, 1846, by Rev. John M. Guion, of New
 Britain — 1 — 110

Sally, d. Adonijah, b. Nov. 15, 1776; m. William **SMITH**,
 3rd s. Samuel, [ ], 1797 — Lr12 — 526

Sarah A., of Kensington, m. Charles W. **RISLEY**, of East
 Hartford, Apr. 8, 1845, by Rev. Royal Robbins — 1 — 102

William, of Southington, m. Lydia **BROWN**, of Berlin, Mar.
 20, 1821, by Samuel Goodrich — 1 — 4

W[illia]m G., m. Eliza L. **SOUTHWORTH**, Dec. 5, 1830, by
 Rev. J. Cogswell — 1 — 41

LIMSON, Asahel, m. Maria **SWEARS**, Nov. 24, 1836, by Dwight
 M. Seward — 1 — 65

LITTLEFIELD, Don Carlos, of Wolcott, m. Olive **BYINGTON**, of
 Southington, Oct. 30, 1839, by Joseph Whittlesey — 1 — 77

LOOMIS, Grove W., m. Sarah M. **SMITH**, May 1, 1839, by Rev.
 D. M. Seward — 1 — 74

Oliver, m. Elizabeth **CLARK**, b. of East Windsor, Aug. 3,
 1829, by Rev. J. Cogswell — 1 — 36

	Vol.	Page
LOOMIS, (cont.)		
Timothy W., m. Chloe **RILEY**, Nov. 23, 1840, by Rev. D. M. Seward	1	80
LOPEN, Harriet, m. Rowe B. **NEWELL**, b. of Berlin, Aug. 14, 1825, by Rev. Charles A. Goodrich	1	17
Menta, m. Cyrus **BOOTH**, July 1, 1825, by Rev. Royal Robbins	1	16
LOVELAND, Adaline, of Berlin, m. Brian **NEWELL**, of Southington, [Feb.] 2, 1840, by Rev. Royal Robbins	1	77
Azuba Ann, of Berlin, m. Briar **NEWELL**, of Granville, Ga., Aug. 22, 1831, by Royal Robbins	1	43
Comfort, b. Nov. [ ], 1737; m. Roger **RILEY**, Feb. 12, 1761	Lr1	509
Lois, of Berlin, m. Elias **HEWIT**, of Albany, N. Y., Oct. 2, 1833, by Nathaniel Hervey	1	53
Maria, m. Horace **ROBERTS**, Oct. 8, 1838, by Rev. Charles Chittenden	1	71
William, m. Sophia A. **BUCK**, b. of Berlin, Oct. 7, 1845, by Rev. Royal Robbins	1	106
McKAY, Elizabeth, m. Robert **ESPY**, May 20, 1849, by Joseph Whittlesey	1	131
John, m. Emily **NORTH**, b. of Berlin, Apr. 5, 1848, by W. W. Woodworth	1	125
McKINLEY, William, of Lexington, Ga., m. L. Anne **SIMS**, d. Prof. A. E. **ANDREW**, of Berlin, Oct. 26, 1848, at New Britain, by Rev. Samuel Rockwell	1	128
McMANNAMAN, John, of New Hartford, m. Candice B. **HIGBY**, of Middletown, Nov. 22, 1835, by A. S. Francis	1	60
MAGUIRE, Patrick, of Berlin, m. Avatha **METCALF**, of East Hartford, Apr. 6, 1823, by Rev. Samuel Goodrich	1	9
MARCY, Bethiah, of Ashford, m. Elisha **EDWARDS**, Jan. 29, 1798	Lr1	498
MARKHAM, Polly, m. Chauncy **HART**, May 3, 1821, by Royal Robbins	1	5
Sarah M., m. Edwin **SMITH**, b. of Berlin, Apr. 19, 1841, by Rev. W. W. Brewer	1	83
MARKLAND, W[illia]m, m. Mary M. **ATWATER**, Oct. 4, 1835, at New Britain, by Rev. Amos D. Watrous	1	59
MARSHALL, Alexander, of Berlin, m. Mary **BARRET**, of Mereden, Dec. 12, 1847, by Rev. Royal Robbins	1	121
W[illia]m C., m. Eliza A. **GAINES**, Oct. 12, 1836, by Dwight M. Seward	1	65
MASON, Albert, m. Lucy J. **GRISWOLD**, May 14, 1840, by Rev. D. M. Seward	1	80
Herve Green, of Dublin, m. Mary **WHITAKE**, of Great Britain, Aug. 10, 1836, by Rev. Amos D. Watrous	1	63
MASTERS, Sally, m. William **SQUIRES**, b. of Berlin, Nov. 8, 1840, by Joseph Whittlesey	1	81
MATHER, Persea, m. Thomas **SUGDEN**, Dec. 7, 1780	Lr1	505
MATTHEW, Rebecca, m. Norman C. **SMITH**, May 13, 1822, by		

	Vol.	Page
MATTHEW, (cont.)		
Newton Skinner	1	7
MAYNARD, Henry, m. Ann M. **HUBBARD**, b. of New Britain, Sept. 30, 1844, by Rev. L. F. Barney, of New Britain	1	99
MEAD, Darius, of Greenwich, m. Emily C. **GOODRICH**, of Berlin, May 8, 1833, by Rev. Samuel Goodrich	1	51
MECLENTIC (?), James, of Berlin, m. Martha L. **WARNER**, of Wethersfield, Nov. 24, 1833, by Rev. Theron Osborn	1	54
MERIAM, [see also **MERRIMAN**], Anson, of Mereden, m. Mary **BOTSFORD**, of Berlin, Oct. 22, 1826, by Royal Robbins	1	24
MERRELLS, Judeth, m. Austin **MOSIEUR**, Sept. 21, 1826, by Rev. Henry Jones	1	23
MERRIMAN, [see also **MERIAM**], Emily, of Kensington, m. Franklin A. **NEWBERRY**, of Hartford, July 24, 1848, by Rev. Royal Robbins	1	125
Howell, of Mereden, m. Mary Ann **COWLES**, of Berlin, July 24, 1843, by Rev. Royal Robbins	1	92
John, of N. Carolina, m. Mrs. Polly **MERRIMAN**, of Berlin, Sept. 10, 1826, by Samuel Hart, J. P.	1	22
Lewis, of Southington, m. Lucy B. **DICKINSON**, of Kensington, d. Henry, Apr. 2, 1850, by Rev. Royal Robbins	1	137
Mary, of Kensington, m. Samuel **TERRY**, of Bristol, May 8, 1844, by Rev. Royal Robbins	1	96
Polly, Mrs. of Berlin, m. John **MERRIMAN**, of N. Carolina, Sept. 10, 1826, by Samuel Hart, J. P.	1	22
METCALF, Avatha, of East Hartford, m. Patrick **MAGUIRE**, of Berlin, Apr. 6, 1823, by Rev. Samuel Goodrich	1	9
MICHAEL, Sylvester, of Mereden, m. Lois **COLVIN**, of Berlin, Apr. 16, 1837, by Rev. D. Plumb. Witnesses Newell Moses & Nancy Moses	1	67
MILDRUM, William A., of Middletown, m. Adelia M. **WILCOX**, of Berlin, Oct. 15, 1845, by Joseph Whittlesey	1	105
MILES, Lucinda, m. Ralph **BECKLEY**, June 24, 1832, by Rev. John Boyd	1	47
W[illia]m, of Goshen, m. Jane **ANDREWS**, of Berlin, Sept. 7, 1837, by Charles A. Goodrich	1	69
MILEY, Electa J., m. Lucius F. **CADWELL**, of Torringford, May 23, 1828*, in New Britain, by Dwight M. Seward *(Probably "1838")	1	70
MILL, Roger H., m. Harriet B. **NORTH**, July 17, 1839, by Rev. Dwight M. Seward	1	74
MILLARD, John D., m. Laura **BARNS**, Nov. 16, 1829, by Rev. Samuel Goodrich	1	37
MILLER, Laura A., m. Amazi H. **STEEL**, b. of Berlin, Oct. 30, 1843, by Rev. David Miller	1	94
Lois Ann, m. Chauncey **MORGAN**, b. of Berlin, Oct. 5, 1835, by Rev. Abraham S. Francis	1	59

	Vol.	Page
MINOR, Henry, m. Marie **KILBY**, b. of Berlin, May 1, 1832, by Rev. J. Cogswell	1	45
MITCHEL, Lewis, m. Emma Mariah **FRANCIS**, Oct. 23, 1832, by Theron Osborn	1	49
MIX, Nancy A., of Bristol, m. Benajah **HITCHCOCK**, of Berlin, Sept. 4, 1849, by Rev. Albert Nash	1	132
MOORE, Eliza S., m. Charles N. **STANLEY**, b. of Berlin, Feb. 15, 1842, by Rev. J. Marshall Guion, of New Britain	1	87
Fanny L., m. Gad **STANLEY**, b. of New Britain, May 11, 1846, by Rev. Samuel Rockwell, of New Britain	1	109
James P., s. Perry & Lovira, of New Britain, m. Eliza **CLARK**, d. Chauncey & Mary, of New Britain, June 22, 1848, by Rev. Charles S. Sherman	1	124
Lucretia, d. Abijah, b. May 20, 1789; m. William **SMITH**, [ ], 1812	Lr12	526
Martha A., of Berlin, m. John S. **BAKER**, of New Hartford, Jan. 4, 1846, by Rev. Samuel Rockwell, of New Britain	1	108
Oliver, m. Abigail **HART**, b. of Berlin, Nov. 3, 1830, by Royal Robbins	1	41
Sheldon, m. Susan L. **DICKINSON**, b. of Berlin, Nov. 1, 1831, by Royal Robbins	1	45
MORAN, Almira, m. Philo **RICOR**, b. of New Britain, Dec. 7, 1845, by Rev. C. S. Sherman, of New Britain	1	108
MORGAN, Caroline, m. William R. **HOLLBROOK**, Dec. 26, 1836, by Rev. C. W. Turner	1	66
Chauncey, m. Lois Ann **MILLER**, b. of Berlin, Oct. 5, 1835, by Rev. Abraham S. Francis	1	59
Eliza, m. Salmon **STEEL**, Nov. 29, 1832, by Rev. Luman Andrus	1	49
George, Jr., of Berlin, m. Louisa O. **THOMPSON**, of South Windsor, Feb. 21, 1847, by Rev. E. Cushman	1	115
Harriet, m. Ensign **BYINGTON**, Dec. 25, 1838, by Dwight M. Seward	1	73
Justus R., m. Henrietta **JUDD**, Nov. 30, 1843, by Rev. David Miller	1	94
Prudence, of Berlin, m. Lyman **WETHERELL**, of Chatham, Sept. 21, 1840, by Rev. W. W. Brewer	1	78
Susan, m. George **FLAGG**, Apr. 30, 1826, by Rev. Samuel Goodrich	1	20
MORIL, Aurora*, of Wolcottville, m. Eliza Ann **LESTON**, of Berlin, July 3, 1831, by Royal Robbins *(Perhaps "Aurora Marie [ ]")	1	42
MORLEY, Jonathan, of Glastonbury, m. Eliza **SAVAGE**, of Berlin, May 22, 1845, by W. W. Woodworth	1	104
MORRIS, Alfred W., of Wisconsin Territory, m. Emily L. **COWLES**, of Berlin, [Oct.] 25, 1840, by Rev. Royal Robbins, of Kensington	1	79
MORSE, Hannah A., d. Orson & Amand, of Burlington, Conn., m.		

	Vol.	Page
MORSE, (cont.)		
Francis H. **CARTER**, Oct. 19, 1848, at New Britain, by [ ]	1	127
Hannah A., d. Orson & Amanda, of Burlington, Conn., m. Francis H. **CARTER**, of New Britain, Oct. 19, 1848, in New Britain, by Rev. Charles S. Sherman	1	129
Harriet, of New Britain, m. Oliver W. **FENTON**, of Vernon, May 12, 1845, by Rev. L. F. Barney	1	104
MORTON, Emeline B., of Hartford, m. John **LEE**, 2nd, of Berlin, June 13, 1841, by Rev. Royal Robbins	1	84
MOSES, James F., of Boston, m. Harriet * P. **BECKLEY**, of Berlin, Apr. 22, 1846, by W. W. Woodworth *(Note says "d. of Benjamin, decd.")	1	109
MOSIEUR (?), Austin, m. Judeth **MERRELLS**, Sept. 21, 1826, by Rev. Henry Jones	1	23
MUNSON, Isaac, m. Lucey **STANLEY**, Mar. 8, 1832, by Rev. John Boyde, Jr.	1	45
Jeremiah, m. Susan **KENT**, b. of Berlin, June 24, 1833, by Rev. John Boyden, Jr.	1	56
Roxana, m. George J. **NORTON**, b. of Berlin, May 9, 1841, by Rev. Royal Robbins	1	83
MURPHY, John W., of Coventry, m. Eliza **WINCHEL**, of Berlin, Nov. 26, 1828, by Royal Robbins	1	34
MURRY, Samuel, m. Elizabeth A. **ROBBINS**, May 8, 1843, by William Whittlesey	1	92
Samuel B., of Woodbury, m. Kesiah **ATKINS**, of Southington, Nov. 28, 1849, by Rev. Stephen Rushmore	1	134
MYGATT, Anna, Mrs., m. Elishama **BRANDEGEE**, b. of Berlin, Nov. 29, 1835, by Rev. James M. McDonald	1	60
Hiram, m. Anna **BOOTH**, July 13, 1823, by Samuel Goodrich	1	10
NAMANN, Sherman B., m. Clestia **NORTON**, d. David (colored), May 3, 1850, by W. W. Woodworth	1	138
NASH, Harriet C., of Berlin, m. Rundell **SCOFIELD**, of Greenwich, Apr. 8, 1845, by Rev. Joseph L. Morse	1	101
NEALE, **NEAL**, Abram, m. Diadama **STEEL**, Feb. 8, 1821, by Newton Skinner	1	4
Joseph, of Southington, m. Matilda **BARNES**, of Berlin, Aug. 26, 1828, by Rev. Irenus Atkins, of Southington	1	33
NEFF, Deliaett, m. Nelson **ATWOOD**, Sept. 16, 1827, by Rev. Samuel Goodrich	1	28
NELSON, Henry, m. Hester Ann **FISHER**, Sept. 8, 1833, by Edwin E. Griswold	1	52
NEWBERRY, **NEWBURY**, Franklin A., of Hartford, m. Emily **MERRIMAN**, of Kensington, July 24, 1848, by Rev. Royal Robbins	1	125
Henry, of Wethersfield, m. Nancy **BELDEN**, of Berlin, Dec. 9, 1824, by Rev. Samuel Goodrich	1	15
Lovisa, of Hartford, m. Nathaniel **TILLOTSON**, of Suffield,		

	Vol.	Page

NEWBERRY, NEWBURY, (cont.)

Conn., Apr. 16, 1838, by Rev. W. A. Stickney — 1 — 70

NEWELL, Brian, of Southington, m. Adaline **LOVELAND,** of
Berlin, [Feb.] 2, 1840, by Rev. Royal Robbins — 1 — 77

Briar, of Granville, Ga., m. Azuba Ann **LOVELAND,** of
Berlin, Aug. 22, 1831, by Royal Robbins — 1 — 43

Rowe B., m. Harriet **LOPEN,** b. of Berlin, Aug. 14, 1825,
by Rev. Charles A. Goodrich — 1 — 17

NEWTON, Lucius F., of Munson, Mass., m. Maria **DUNHAM,** of
Berlin, Apr. 12, 1830, by Royal Robbins — 1 — 39

NICHOLS, W[illia]m S., of Middletown, m. Harriet **PARKMAN,** of
Berlin, May 22, 1827, by Samuel Goodrich — 1 — 26

NORTH, Abijah, m. Hepzibah **DEMING,** Jan. 14, 1824, by Rev.
Royal Robbins — 1 — 12

Adaline, [d. Jedediah & Betsey], b. Oct. 8, 1824; d.
Feb. 15, 1844, at Norwich — 1 — 126

Albert, s. Stephen & Susanna, b. July 18, 1789 — Lr1 — 505

Alfred, m. Mary O. **WILCOX,** b. of Berlin, May 8, 1834,
by Rev. Ambrose Edson — 1 — 55

Alvin, s. James, m. Anne **STANLEY,** July 15, 1804 — Lr1 — 488

Augusta Ann, [d. Jedediah & Betsey], b. Sept. 16, 1830 — 1 — 126

Caroline Sophia, [d. Jedediah & Betsey], b. Mar. 6, 1836 — 1 — 126

Charlotte, m. John **STANLEY,** Jan. 4, 1824, by Newton
Skinner — 1 — 12

Clarissa, [d. Jedediah & Betsey], b. May 19, 1814; d.
Sept. 5, 1843, at Norwich — 1 — 126

Clarissa, m. Hezekiah C. **BRIDGHAM,** b. of Berlin, Oct. 21,
1833, by Rev. Ambrose Edson — 1 — 52

Clarissa, [d. Jedediah & Betsey], m. Hezekiah C.
BRIDGHAM, of Middletown, Oct. 21, 1833 — 1 — 126

Edmund, m. Almira **WILCOX,** May 7, 1850, by W. W.
Woodworth — 1 — 138

Eliza S., m. Henry **STANLEY,** June 10, 1829, by J. Cogswell — 1 — 36

Emily, [d. Jedediah & Betsey], b. Oct. 23, 1816; d. Aug.
14, 1841, at Akron, O. — 1 — 126

Emily, [d. Jedediah & Betsey], m. Samuel C. **CHURCHILL,**
Aug. [ ], 1840 — 1 — 126

Emily, m. John **McKAY,** b. of Berlin, Apr. 5, 1848, by W.
W. Woodworth — 1 — 125

Ethel, s. Reuben & Amanda, of Goshen, m. Mabel C.
STRICKLAND, d. Stephen & Nancy, of Glastonbury,
now residents of Berlin, Nov. 23, 1847, by C. S. Sherman — 1 — 121

Fidelia Maria, [twin with Frederic Marie], d. [Jedediah
& Betsey], b. June 5, 1833 — 1 — 126

Frederick A., m. Mary **NORTH,** d. Henry, b. of New
Britain, Aug. 28, 1850, by Rev. Samuel Rockwell — 1 — 139

Frederic Marie, [twin with Fidelia Maria, child of
Jedediah & Betsey], b. June 5, 1833 — 1 — 126

	Vol.	Page

NORTH, (cont.)

Hannah, m. Edwin **HUBBARD,** b. of Berlin, [Oct.] 21, 1832,
by Rev. Ambrose Edson   1   48
Harriet B., m. Roger H. **MILL,** July 17, 1839, by Rev.
Dwight M. Seward   1   74
Henry, m. Laucretta **SMITH,** Jan. 24, 1821, by Newton
Skinner   1   4
James, m. Abi **FRANCIS,** Feb. 26, 1828, by Rev. J. Brace,
of Wetherfield   1   30
James C., m. Esther M. **CASE,** b. of Berlin, Nov. 3, 1844,
by Rev. D. H. Plumb   1   99
Jane Elizabeth, [d. Jedediah & Betsey], b. June 9, 1821;
d. Dec. 15, 1844, at Berlin   1   126
Jedediah, s. Levi, b. June 22, 1789; m. Betsey **BULKLEY,**
d. Justus, Mar. 10, 1813   1   126
Julia, m. Titus **PENFIELD,** b. of Berlin, Nov. 25, 1830,
by Charles A. Goodrich   1   41
Levi, Jr., m. Ann **TAYLOR,** May 19, 1833, by Rev. J.
Brace, of Newington   1   51
Maria, m. William H. **SMITH,** b. of Berlin, Aug. 7, 1825,
by Rev. Joab Brace, of Wethersfield   1   17
Maria, m. Cornelius B. **ERWIN,** May 18, 1836, by Rev.
Dwight M. Seward, of New Britain   1   62
Mary, of Berlin, m. Samuel **RAYMOND,** of Bethlem, [May]
23, 1834, by Rev. J. Cogswell   1   55
Mary, d. Henry, m. Frederick A. **NORTH,** b. of New Britain,
Aug. 28, 1850, by Rev. Samuel Rockwell   1   139
Nancy, m. Phillip **LEE,** Dec. 28, 1823, by Rev. Newton
Skinner   1   12
Orrin S., m. Sarah **CLARK,** Feb. 5, 1831, by J. Cogswell   1   42
Patty, of Berlin, m. Chester **BRONSON,** of Salisbury, N.
Y., [July] 14, 1833, by Rev. Ambrose Edson   1   51
Sarah, Mrs., m. Selah **HART,** Jr., Nov. 11, 1829, by Rev.
J. Cogswell   1   38
Sarah R., d. Alvin, m. Samuel **BRACE,** of Newington, Aug.
19, 1847, by Rev. J. Brace   1   119
Seth J., s, James, m. Elizbeth **STANLEY,** Sept. 27, 1801   Lr1   488
Silas, m. Lucy **DEMING,** b. of Berlin, Apr. 14, 1825, by
Rev. William S. Pease   1   16
Sophia W., m. Alfred **EDWARDS,** Feb. 28, 1830, by Rev.
Samuel Goodrich   1   38
Stephen, b. Jan. 26, 1767; m. Susanna **SAVAGE,** Jan. 1, 1788   Lr1   505
NORTHROP, Mary Jane, of Berlin, m. Roswell G. **BENHAM,** of
New Hartford, Jan. 14, 1846, by William W. Woodworth   1   108
NORTON, Albert, m. Rebeckah **EDDY,** b. of Berlin, June 28, 1825,
by Rev. Royal Robbins   1   16
Albert, m. Ruth **HART,** b. of Berlin, [Mar.] 25, 1829, by
Royal Robbins   1   35

	Vol.	Page
NORTON, (cont.)		
Albert R., m. Elizabeth E. **STOCKING**, d. Luther, decd., b. of Berlin, Oct. 4, 1846, by Rev. Royal Robbins	1	112
Andrew, m. Nancy **HOUGH**, Apr. 18, 1829, by Rev. Samuel Goodrich	1	35
Andrew J., of Southington, m. Miranda **BYINGTON**, of Berlin, Dec. 8, 1843, by Rev. David H. Plumb	1	94
Betsey, [d. Samuel & Phebe], b. Aug. 13, 1791	Lr1	514
Betsey, m. Reuben **DUNHAM**, Dec. 14, 1797	Lr9	563
Betsey, m. Norton **WRIGHT**, b. of Berlin, Jan. 27, 1820, by Samuel Goodrich	1	1
Betsey Ann, m. George **COWLES**, b. of Berlin, Jan. 7, 1838, by Rev. Royal Robbins	1	70
Charles, of Bristol, m. Martha **STOCKING**, d. Luther, decd., of Berlin, Oct. 6, 1846, by Rev. Royal Robbins	1	112
Clestia, d. David, m. Sherman B. **NAMANN** (colored), May 3, 1850, by W. W. Woodworth	1	138
Dency, of Berlin, m. Ralsey **TOWNSEND**, of Windsor (b. colored), July 3, 1839, by Joseph Whittlesey	1	73
Densey, m. Reuel **FOWLER** (colored), Sept. 10, 1848, by W. W. Woodworth	1	126
Edward, [s. Samuel & Phebe], b. Feb. 15, 1790	Lr1	514
Francis, m. Mary **KELLIN**, May 6, 1846, by William W. Woodworth	1	111
George, [s. Samuel & Phebe], b. Feb. 11, 1810	Lr1	514
George J., m. Roxana **MUNSON**, b. of Berlin, May 9, 1841, by Rev. Royal Robbins	1	83
Harriet, [d. Samuel & Phebe], b. Apr. 27, 1796	Lr1	514
Harriet, of Berlin, m. John **SHAD**, of Savannah, Ga., June 5, 1820, by Royal Robbins	1	1
Harriet, m. Freedom **HART**, Nov. 8, 1824, by Rev. Samuel Goodrich	1	14
Henry, [s. Samuel & Phebe], b. Apr. 10, 1803	Lr1	514
Henry E., m. Sarah A. **HALL**, b. of Berlin, June 15, 1846, by Rev. Royal Robbins	1	110
Hiram, [s. Samuel & Phebe], b. Oct. 17, 1798	Lr1	514
Isaac, m. Milley **GOODRICH**, Dec. 28, 1823, by Rev. Samuel Goodrich	1	12
Isaac, of Berlin, m. Jane A. **HOOKER**, d. George, of New Britain, [ ], by Rev. Samuel Rockwell. Recorded July 4, 1850	1	138
Isaiah, m. Abigail **HART**, Mar. 27, 1789	Lr1	505
Leonard, m. Lucetta **ATWOOD**, Dec. 10, 1832, by Rev. John Boyden	1	49
Nancy, [d. Samuel & Phebe], b. Sept. 17, 1793	Lr1	514
Nancy, m. Dr. Vine **ELDERKIN**, Mar. 29, 1826, by Rev. Samuel Goodrich	1	20
Peter, m. Ellen **DECATUR**, b. of Berlin (colored), Oct. 10, 1839, by Joseph Whittlesey	1	75

	Vol.	Page
NORTON, (cont.)		
Phillip, [s. Samuel & Phebe], b. Mar. 2, 1801	Lr1	514
Rebeckah, m. Abraham **WRIGHT**, Mar. 6, 1777, by Rev.		
Thomas Miner	Lr1	495
Samuel, b. Sept. 30, 1759; m. Phebe **EDWARDS**, Jan. 22,		
1789	Lr1	514
Samuel, Jr., [s. Samuel & Phebe], b. Sept. 7, 1806	Lr1	514
Samuel L., m. Antionette R. **BALDWIN**, b. of Berlin, Nov.		
25, 1847, by W. W. Woodworth	1	120
Sarah A., m. William E. **SMITH**, b. of Berlin, May [ ],		
1845, by W. W. Woodworth	1	102
William, [s. Samuel & Phebe], b. June 21, 1812	Lr1	514
Zachariah, s. [Isaiah & Abigail], b. Apr. 30, 1790	Lr1	505
OLCOTT, Sidney S., of Rochester, m. Delia C. **HUBBARD**, of		
Berlin, Dec. 20, 1825, by Rev. Samuel Goodrich	1	19
ORVIS, Edmund S., of Farmington, m. Maria **PIER**, of New		
Britain, Oct. 22, 1846, by Rev. E. Cushman	1	113
OSBORN, Elihu, of Derby, m. Esther **STRONG**, of Torrington,		
Nov. 12, 1828, by Rev. Epaphras Goodman	1	34
OSGOOD, Charlotte, m. Milton **ANDREWS**, May 3, 1827, by Rev.		
Henry Jones	1	26
Chloe, m. Hiram **SMITH**, Apr. 11, 1831, by Rev. Nathan E.		
Shailer	1	42
Janna, [child of Jeremiah H. & Lucy], b. June 26, 1766	Lr1	508
Jeremiah, [s. Jeremiah H. & Lucy], b. July 3, 1755	Lr1	508
Jeremiah H., m. Lucy **CHURCHILL**, Oct. 2, 1754	Lr1	508
John, [s. Jeremiah H. & Lucy], b. June 1, 1764	Lr1	508
Josiah, [s. Jeremiah H. & Lucy], b. Sept. 23, 1759	Lr1	508
Julia M., Mrs., m. Harlow **HUMPHREY**, July 6, 1830, by		
J. Cogswell	1	39
Lucy, [d. Jeremiah H. & Lucy], b. May 3, 1757	Lr1	508
Mary, [d. Jeremiah H. & Lucy], b. June 5, 1776	Lr1	508
Mary, of Berlin, m. Apollos W. **BUCK**, of Middletown,		
Apr. 12, 1832, by Rev. Irenus Atkins, of Southington	1	46
Rebecah, [d. Jeremiah H. & Lucy], b. July 9, 1773	Lr1	508
William, [s. Jeremiah H. & Lucy], b. Oct. 14, 1770	Lr1	508
PARISH, Ariel, m. Caroline A. **DICKMAN**, b. of Berlin, Apr. 3,		
1836, by Charles A. Goodrich	1	61
Levi F., of Hartford, m. Emeline P. **LAMPSON**, of New		
Britain, Dec. 7, 1845, by Rev. Asahel Chapin	1	107
PARKER, Charles, of Mereden, m. Abi L. **EDDY**, of Berlin, Oct.		
6, 1831, by Rev. Russel Jennings	1	44
Lydia E., of Lenox, Mass., m. Marshall **CURTIS**, of		
Stockbridge, June 14, 1842, by Rev. John M. Guion, of		
New Britain	1	88
Sarah E., m. Ezekiel **ANDREWS**, Jr., Aug. 7, 1833, by Rev.		
J. Cogswell	1	51
PARKHAM, Harriet, of Berlin, m. W[illia]m S. **NICHOLS**, of		

	Vol.	Page
PARKHAM, (cont.)		
Middletown, May 22, 1827, by Samuel Goodrich	1	26
PARMELEE, PARMELE, Cornelia, m. Noris **BAILEY**, b. of		
Berlin, Sept. 26, 1843, by William W. Woodworth	1	95
Nathaniel, of Middletown, m. Milley **BECKLEY**, of Berlin,		
May 8, 1821, by Samuel Goodrich	1	4
PARSONS, Catharine, b. Aug. 2, 1757; m. Joseph **GALPIN**, Apr.		
16, 1778	Lr1	512
Content, b. Feb. 5, 1743; m. Asahel **KELSEY**, May 21, 1767	Lr1	510
Curtis R., of Macon, Ga., m. Jane A. **KELLOGG**, of Berlin,		
[Sept] 20, 1842, by Rev. Royal Robbins	1	89
Eliza, m. Edward **LEWIS**, Apr. 22, 1839, by Dwight M.		
Seward	1	73
Jane E., d. Henry L., m. Eli H. **PORTER**, b. of New Britain,		
June 28, 1849,in New Britain,by Rev. Charles S. Sherman	1	132
Nancy Jane, m. William **BLINN**, b. of Berlin, Feb. 14,		
1840, by W. W. Brewer	1	76
Orville W., m. Ruah **TULLER**, Feb. 5, 1834, by J. Cogswell	1	54
PATTISON, Edward, m. Sally **SQUIRES**, July 7, 1827, by Ira E.		
Smith, J. P.	1	28
Henry E., of Berlin, m. Emily H. **CONE**, of Lee, Mass.,		
Dec. 31, 1843, by William W. Woodworth	1	95
Hipsibah Maria, m. Charles F. **BARTLETT**, Feb. 1, 1827,		
by Rev. Samuel Goodrich	1	25
Julia, of Berlin, m. Liman **DUNBAR**, of Plymouth, Aug.		
21, 1822, by Rev. Samuel Goodrich	1	7
Leonard, m. Miranda **BECKLEY**, Sept. 17, 1826, by Rev.		
Henry Jones	1	22
Lois, m. Calvin **WINCHEL**, b. of Berlin, May 5, 1824, by		
Rev. Royal Robbins	1	13
Sarah, of Berlin, m. Michael **STOCKING**, of Middletown,		
Nov. 4, 1822, by Rev. Joshua L. Williams, of Middletown	1	9
PAYNE, William, of Mereden, m. Julia A. **THORP**, of		
Southampton, Mass., June 15, 1834, by Amos L.		
Watrous	1	55
PEARL, Catharine, m. George M. **SANDERS**, of Mass., Apr. 17,		
1839, by Charles A. Goodrich	1	72
Ralph, m. Eliza **HART**, Apr. 18, 1824, by Rev. Newton		
Skinner	1	13
PEASE, Laura P., d. Asaph & Clotila, of New Britain, m.		
Everett C. **HOLMES**, of Winsted, Nov. 1, 1848, in New		
Britain, by Rev. Charles S. Sherman	1	129
PECK, Anna S., m. Samuel C. **WILCOX**, June 9, 1846, by William		
W. Woodworth	1	111
Asahel, m. Martha **FLAGG**, b. of Berlin, Sept. 23, 1829,		
by Royal Robbins	1	37
Cordelia N., m. Oliver **STANLEY**, b. of New Britain, Aug. 29,		
1850, at New Britain, by Rev. Samuel Rockwell	1	139

	Vol.	Page

PECK, (cont.)

Cornelius W., of Berlin, m. Lucy **HALE**, of Glastonbury,
Mar. 22, 1848, by Rev. Henry Miller, of Meriden   1   123

Elisha A., of Berlin, m. Elizabeth **DIXON**, of New Haven,
Aug. 22, 1841, by Rev. Royal Robbins   1   85

Elizabeth C., m. Henry E. **RUSSELL**, b. of Berlin, Aug.
3, 1843, by Rev. John M. Guion, of New Britain   1   91

Elnathan, m. Mary **DEWEY**, June 18, 1827, by Rev. Henry
Jones   1   26

Everard, of Raetanten (?), N. Y., m. Chloe **PORTER**, of
Berlin, Oct. 12, 1820, by Samuel Goodrich   1   2

Francis, Rev. of Baltimore, Md., m. Frances Augustine
FELIX, d. Henry, of Cuba, Aug. 31, 1847, by Rev. John
M. Guion, of Saybrook   1   118

Hannah S., m. Norman **PORTER**, Jr., Nov. 30, 1846, by W.
W. Woodworth   1   115

Henry, m. Nancy **GLADIN**, b. of Berlin, Nov. 26, 1826, by
Royal Robbins   1   24

Jabez, of Berlin, m. Maria **BELDEN**, of Wethersfield,
June 8, 1823, by Rev. Roger Robbins   1   10

Jason, m. Elmina **GLADDING**, b. of Berlin, Nov. 4, 1838,
by Rev. Albert Case   1   71

Lucy, m. Seth **COWLES**, Nov. 27, 1825, by Royal Robbins   1   18

Lucy, m. Willis **WILLIAMS**, b. of Berlin, Aug. 9, 1835,
by Rev. William A. Stickney   1   58

Mathew, of Washington, Ala., m. Sarah **ELLSWORTH**, of
Berlin, Aug. 13, 1824, by Rev. Royal Robbins   1   13

Norris, m. Eliza **LANGDON**, b. of Berlin, Oct. 6, 1823,
by Royal Robbins   1   11

Reuben, m. Patience **GLADDEN**, b. of Berlin, Sept. 6,
1829, by Royal Robbins   1   37

Russel U., m. Lydia **BOTSFORD**, b. of Berlin, Oct. 7,
1827, by Royal Robbins   1   29

Sarah, Mrs. of Berlin, m. Lorenzo **CARY**, of Norwich, Aug.
11, 1839, by Joseph Whittlesey   1   73

Sarah M., of Berlin, m. Timothy H. **PLANT**, of Augusta,
Ga., Aug. 28, 1834, by Charles A. Goodrich   1   56

Selden, m. Lucy H. **HART**, b. of Berlin, Nov. 1, 1826, by
Royal Robbins   1   24

PECKHAM, William, of New Haven, m. Sarah **GOODWIN**, of
Berlin, Nov. 7, 1841, by Rev. John M. Guion, of New
Britain   1   86

PENFIELD, Alvina, m. Benjamin **SMITH**, Dec. 9, 1824, by Rev.
Newton Skinner   1   14

Amelia, m. Henry **STEEL**, b. of Berlin, Nov. 26, 1827, by
Rev. Noah Porter, of Farmington   1   29

Burnham H., m. Annette **JUDA***, May 10, 1846, by Rev.
Gurdon Robbins, of Hartford   ***("JUDD"?)**   1   110

	Vol.	Page

PLANT, (cont.)

Berlin, Aug. 28, 1834, by Charles A. Goodrich   1   56

POND, Dewitt C., of New Britain, m. Mary E. **TUCKER**, d. Erastus
& Emma A., of New Britain, Nov. 15, 1848, by Rev.
Charles S. Sherman   1   129

Lina, m. Cyrus **JUDD**, b. of Berlin, Oct. 16, 1849, by
Rev. Stephen Rushmore   1   133

PORTER, Abijah, m. Mrs. Sarah **HULBERT**, b. of Berlin, [Aug.]
28, 1833, by Rev. Ambrose Edson   1   52

Buyon*, m. Thesta **ANDREWS**, Nov. 27, 1823, by Newton
Skinner   *("Bryon"?)   1   11

Chloe, of Berlin, m. Everard **PECK**, of Raetanten(?), N.
Y., Oct. 12, 1820, by Samuel Goodrich   1   2

Eli H., m. Jane E. **PARSONS**, d. Henry L., b. of New Britain,
June 28, 1849, in New Britain, by Rev. Charles S.
Sherman   1   132

Emily, of New Britain, m. Andrew **PIERPOINT**, of New
Hartford, Dec. 5, 1847, by Rev. W. P. Pattison, of New
Britain   1   121

Horace, of Hamden, m. Emma **BECKLEY**, of Berlin, May 7,
1821, by Samuel Goodrich   1   4

Isaac, m. Caroline **BARNES**, b. of Berlin, Aug. 9, 1820,
by Samuel Goodrich   1   1

Job, of East Hartford, m. Harriet **WILCOX**, of Berlin,
Sept. 24, 1828, by Rev. Samuel Goodrich   1   32

Laton, m. Clarissa P. **BECKLEY**, b. of Berlin, Oct. 27,
1822, by Rev. Samuel Goodrich   1   8

Laura Ann, m. Sherman **SLATER**, b. of Berlin, Nov. 14,
1832, by Irenus Atkins   1   50

Linus, m. Louisa L. **BECKLEY**, b. of Berlin, Nov. 9, 1823,
by Rev. Samuel Goodrich   1   11

Lucetta W., m. Hiram B. **SMITH**, [Sept.] 16, 1833, by Rev.
Ambrose Edson   1   52

Lydia, m. Ashbel **DICKENSON**, Sept. 21, 1823, by Rev.
Samuel Goodrich   1   10

Mercy H., of Berlin, m. Jarvis **TUTTLE**, of Waterbury,
Sept. 13, 1823, by Rev. Samuel Goodrich   1   10

Norman, of Lexington, Kty., m. Abby **GALPIN**, of Berlin,
Mar. 2, 1823, by Rev. Samuel Goodrich   1   9

Norman, Jr., m. Hannah S. **PECK**, Nov. 30, 1846, by W. W.
Woodworth   1   115

Richard T., m. Betsey S. **CORNWELL**, Oct. 20, 1824, by
Rev. Newton Skinner   1   14

Rosanna, of Berlin, m. William **TALCOTT**, of Ohio, Apr. 28,
1830, by Royal Robbins   1   39

Sally M., m. Edwin **BOOTH**, b. of Berlin, Oct. 29, 1821,
by Samuel Goodrich   1   5

Selah S., of West Haven, m. Mrs. Elizabeth H. **BURGSTRAM**,

	Vol.	Page

PORTER, (cont.)

of New Haven, Sept. 17, 1848, by W. W. Woodworth — 1 — 125

POST, Anna, Mrs., m. Seth **SAVAGE,** b. of Berlin, Nov. 29,
1828, by Rev. Samuel Goodrich — 1 — 34

POTTER, Roberts, of Waterbury, m. Lurana **HAMLIN,** of
Farmington, Apr. 30, 1843, in New Britain, by Rev.
William Bentley — 1 — 91

PRATT, Betsey W., m. Amon W. **RICHARDS,** May 31, 1826, by
Rev. Henry Jones — 1 — 21

Horatio A., m. Charlotte W. **FRANCIS,** b. of Berlin, Sept.
24, 1832, by Royal Robbins — 1 — 48

Nancy D., m. Cryus **FRANCIS,** July 8, 1827, by Rev.
Samuel Spring, of Hartford — 1 — 27

William T., m. Eliza H. **STEELE,** May 6, 1825, by Rev.
Samuel Goodrich — 1 — 17

RAPELYE, Andrew, of Cabotville, Mass., m. Antionette **HART,** of
New Britain, May 24, 1846, by Rev. E. Cushman — 1 — 111

RAYMOND, Samuel, of Bethlem, m. Mary **NORTH,** of Berlin,
[May] 23, 1834, by Rev. J. Cogswell — 1 — 55

RECOR, RICOR, Ann Jane, of Berlin, m. Barzillai **DEMING,** of
Middletown, Oct. 18, 1839, by Rev. Herman S. Havens — 1 — 76

Horatio, m. Elizabeth **SHELLEY,** b. of Berlin, Mar. 24,
1829, by Rev. J. Brace, of Wethersfield — 1 — 35

Maria, m. Dennis **ROOT,** Nov. 26, 1829, by Rev. J. Cogswell — 1 — 38

Philip, m. Mary D. **STEEL,** Sept. 1, 1836, by Rev. Amos D.
Watrous — 1 — 63

Philo, of New Britain, m. Almira **MORAN,** of New Britain,
Dec. 7, 1845, by Rev. C. S. Sherman, of New Britain — 1 — 108

Samuel, m. Almira **STEEL,** Nov. 25, 1829, by Rev. J.
Cogswell — 1 — 38

RECOY, Almedia N., m. Sheldon **HILLS,** b. of Berlin, May 6,
1845, by Rev. L. F. Barney — 1 — 103

REDFIELD, Manning, of Manchester, N. Y., m. Millisent G.
SMITH, of Berlin, Sept. 26, 1828, by Rev. Samuel
Goodrich — 1 — 33

REED, William, of New Haven, m. Cynthia G. **WILLARD,** of
Berlin, May 15, 1828, by Rev. Lucius Baldwin — 1 — 31

REYNOLDS, Rufus K., m. Lovetta **STANNARD,** b. of Berlin, Feb.
19, 1843, by Rev. Samuel W. Smith — 1 — 90

RICE, [see also **ROYCE**], Maria Eliza, of Berlin, m. Stephen
Gittins **BUCKNALL,** of Springfield, Mass., Aug. 19,
1847, by Rev. John M. Guion, of Saybrook — 1 — 118

Mary*, of Mereden, m. Albert **BOARDMAN,** of Middletown,
Oct. 4, 1827, by Rev. Samuel Goodrich *(Arnold Copy
has "Mary Wier" — 1 — 28

Rebecca, m. Selah **COLE,** May 14, 1778 — Lr1 — 506

RICH, Laura, m. Henry **ANDREWS,** b. of Berlin, Nov. 30, 1843,
by William W. Woodworth — 1 — 94

	Vol.	Page
RICH, (cont.)		
Martha H., of Berlin, m. Rollin C. **SMITH**, of Southington, May 9, 1844, by William W. Woodworth	1	96
Sarah C., of Berlin, m. William W. **SMITH**, of Haddam, Aug. 13, 1843, by William W. Woodworth	1	91
RICHARDS, Amon, m. Betsey W. **PRATT**, May 31, 1826, by Rev. Henry Jones	1	21
Lawrence, m. Ann **JUDD**, b. of Berlin, Mar. 26, 1826, by Rev. Joel S. Linsley, of Hartford	1	20
Maritty, m. Eben **STEEL**, Dec. 22, 1825, by Rev. J. T. Nichols	1	19
RICHARDSON, Andrew N., m. Mary Eliza Ann **CLARK**, b. of Berlin, Jan. 11, 1843, by William W. Woodworth	1	90
James, m. Catharine **DUNHAM**, [Dec.] 1, 1839, by Rev. Royal Robbins	1	76
John, m. Silena **GALPIN**, b. of Berlin, Sept. 6, 1835, by Rev. Royal Robbins	1	58
Maria Jane, m. Aaron R. **CASE**, b. of Berlin, May 22, 1839, by Joseph Whittlesey	1	73
Prudena N., of Berlin, m. Richard **FENN**, of Watertown, June 24, 1832, by Rev. Samuel Goodrich	1	46
RICHMOND, RICHMAN, Harriet P., of Southington, m. Abraham **CROCKER**, of Berlin, Sept. 22, 1836, by Charles A. Goodrich	1	64
Hiram, of Mereden, m. Ann E. **DUNHAM**, of Kensington, Oct. 20, 1844, by Rev. Royal Robbins	1	98
RILEY, Aaron, twin with Moses, [s. Roger & Sarah], b. June 10, 1786	Lr1	509
Aaron, [s. Roger & Sarah], d. Oct. 18, 1811	Lr1	509
Abigail, [d. Roger & Sarah], b. Aug. 1, 1776	Lr1	509
Abigail, [d, Roger & Sarah], d. Dec. 21, 1795	Lr1	509
Asahel, [s. Roger & Sarah], b. Dec. 28, 1777	Lr1	509
Catharine A., d. Moses, m. John R. **FREEMAN**, May 1, 1850, by W. W. Woodworth	1	137
Chloe, m. Timothy W. **LOOMIS**, Nov. 23, 1840, by Rev. D. M. Seward	1	80
Comfort, [d. Roger & Comfort, Apr. 30, 1765	Lr1	509
Comfort, w. Roger, d. Nov. 22, 1773	Lr1	509
Comfort, [d. Roger & Comfort], d. Oct. 3, 1798	Lr1	509
Cynthia, [d. Roger & Comfort], b. Sept. 13, 1772; d. Sept. 28, 1775	Lr1	509
Electa, d. John, b. Dec. 13, 1776; m. Thomas **LEE**, 2nd, s. Isaac, Jr., [ ], 1797	Lr12	524
Isaac, [s. Roger & Comfort], b. Nov 29, 1770	Lr1	509
Lucy, 1st child [Roger & Comfort], b. Dec. 2, 1761	Lr1	509
Milecent, [d. Roger & Sarah], b. Apr. 25, 1784	Lr1	509
Milecent, [d. Roger & Sarah], d. Oct. 1, 1811	Lr1	509
Moses, twin with Aaron, [s. Roger & Sarah], b. June 10, 1786	Lr1	509
Roger, b. Feb. 6, 1737; m. Comfort **LOVELAND**,Feb. 12,1761	Lr1	509

	Vol.	Page
RILEY, (cont.)		
Roger, [s. Roger & Comfort], b. Mar. 9, 1764	Lr1	509
Roger, m. Sarah **DEMING**, Oct. 19, 1775	Lr1	509
Roger, d. May 18, 1803	Lr1	509
Theodore, m. Mary **EDDY**, Oct. 4, 1835, at New Britain,		
by Rev. Amos D. Watrous	1	59
William,[s. Roger & Sarah], b. Sept. 14, 1779	Lr1	509
William, [s. Roger & Sarah], d. Nov. 14, 1811	Lr1	509
RISLEY, Charles W., of East Hartford, m. Sarah A. **LEWIS**, of		
Kensington, Apr. 8, 1845, by Rev. Royal Robbins	1	102
ROBBINS, Augustus, m. Mary **BARNS**, Apr. 16, 1827, by Rev.		
Henry Jones	1	26
Elizabeth A., m. Samuel **MURRY**, May 8, 1843, by William		
Whittlesey	1	92
Unni, of Wethersfield, m. Sarah **DUNHAM**, of Berlin, Apr.		
19, 1826, by Royal Robbins	1	20
ROBERTS, ROBBERTS, Alvin, of Middletown, m. Charlotte		
ARNOLD, of Berlin, Jan. 14, 1844, by William W.		
Woodworth	1	95
Catharine, m. Jonathan **HUBBARD**, Feb. 3, 1763	Lr1	516
Electa, of Berlin, m. Harvey **WARD**, of Middletown, May 5,		
1824, by Rev. Samuel Goodrich	1	13
Emeline, m. Birdsey **JUDSON**, Mar. 30, 1831, by Rev.		
Samuel Goodrich	1	42
Emily R., m. James F. **LEWIS**, b. of Berlin, Aug. 25,		
1845, by W. W. Woodworth	1	104
Ephraim, of Mereden, m. Mrs. Polly **COSTELLOW**, of Berlin,		
Apr. 27, 1845, by Rev. Joseph L. Morse	1	102
Horace, m. Maria **LOVELAND**, Oct. 8, 1838, by Rev. Charles		
Chittenden	1	71
Julia, of Berlin, m. Russell **STANNARD**, of Killingworth,		
Feb. 26, 1838, by Charles A. Goodrich	1	69
Lucetta, of Berlin, m. George **CLARK**, of Hartford, Feb.		
24, 1845, by Rev. Joseph L. Morse	1	101
Luke G., m. Wealthy **ALLEON**, b. of Bristol, Mar. 22, 1826,		
by Rev. Samuel Goodrich	1	19
Mary, m. Horace **BECKLEY**, Apr. 16, 1826, by Rev. Samuel		
Goodrich	1	20
Mary P., m. Alvin **HOTCHKISS**, b. of Berlin, Aug. 24,		
1825, by Rev. Royal Robbins	1	17
Merrils, of Berlin, m. Caroline M. **HART**, of Avon, Dec. 1,		
1845, by Rev. Samuel Rockwell, of New Britain	1	106
Sheldon J., m. Esther M. **BELDEN**, b. of Berlin, Oct. 24,		
1848, by Rev. William P. Pattison	1	128
ROBINSON, George, m. Nancy **WOOD**, b. of Pawtucket, R. I., Jan.		
21, 1827, by Rev. E. Washburn	1	25
ROCKWELL, Samuel, m. Charlotte N. **STANLEY**, b. of Berlin,		
July 29, 1844, by Rev. William Wright, of Farmington	1	97

	Vol.	Page
ROGERS, Asa, m. Lucy WELDIN, b. of Berlin, July 11, 1830, by Rev. Timothy Benedict	1	39
ROLAND, Benjamin, of Hartford, m. Hannah KILBY, of Berlin, Sept. 26, 1840, by Rev. J. Marshall Guien	1	78
ROOTS, Alfred, m. Eliza A. DEANE, b. of Berlin, Jan. 6, 1850, by Rev. Royal Robbins	1	135
Amanda, of Berlin, m. Mannice O. BARNES, of Clinton, N. Y., Dec. 14, 1834, by Charles A. Goodrich	1	58
Asahel, m. Nancy WILLIAMS, b. of Berlin, June 7, 1821, by Samuel Goodrich	1	4
Charlotte M., m. Silas SPENCER, Mar. 30, 1836, by Rev. Amos D. Watrous	1	63
Cyrus, of Southington, m. Delia Ann STOCKING, of Berlin, Nov. 26, 1828, by David L. Ogden	1	118
Dennis, m. Maria RECOR, Nov. 26, 1829, by Rev. J. Cogswell	1	38
Mary, m. Richard T. CORNWELL, Oct. 12, 1825, by Rev. Samuel Goodrich	1	18
Mary, m. Lindsley AUSTIN, b. of Berlin, Mar. 20, 1842, by Rev. Royal Robbins	1	88
Nancy, m. Cyprian GOODRICH, May 5, 1839, by [ ]	1	73
Rebecca, m. Samuel DURAND, b. of Berlin, May 1, 1834, by Rev. Ambrose Edson	1	54
Timothy, of Berlin, m. Eliza WILCOX, of Canton, Feb. 18, 1844, by W. W. Woodworth	1	95
ROSE, Cynthia, of Berlin, m. Alphens HUGHES, of Newark, N. J., Sept. 1, 1841, by Rev. Royal Robbins	1	85
[ROYCE], ROYS, Franklin, m. Emily SAVAGE, Oct. 10, 1830, by Rev. Samuel Goodrich	1	40
RUGG, Elmira, m. Erastus KILBOURN, Apr. 21, 1826, by Rev. Henry Jones	1	21
Polly, m. Nathaniel PENFIELD, Oct. 3, 1822, by Newton Skinner	1	8
RUSSELL RUSSEL, Harriet, of Middletown, m. George BUTLER, Sept. 21, 1835, by Rev. Abraham S. Francis	1	59
Henry E., m. Elizabeth C. PECK, b. of Berlin, Aug. 3, 1843, by Rev. John M. Guion, of New Britain	1	91
Lydia, of Bristol, m. David BOOTH, Jr., of Berlin, July 7, 1828, by Samuel Goodrich	1	31
SACKETT, Seth, Rev. of Warren, m. Hetty D. GALPIN, of Berlin, [Oct.] 19, 1831, by Rev. Ambrose Edson	1	44
SAGE, Edwin, m. Hannah WOOD, b. of Berlin, Jan. 15, 1843, by William W. Woodworth	1	90
Enos Fairchild, [s. Solomon, Jr.], b. Feb. 27, 1787	Lr1	510
Hannah, [d. Solomon, Jr.], b. Sept. 1, 1789	Lr1	510
Harriet, [d. Solomon, Jr.], b. Oct. 23, 1784	Lr1	510
Hiram, [s. Solomon, Jr.], b. Feb. 16, 1796	Lr1	510
Hosia, [s. Solomon, Jr.], b. Dec. 5, 1782	Lr1	510

	Vol.	Page
SAGE, (cont.)		
Julia, [d. Solomon, Jr.], b. July 25, 1791	Lr1	510
Lois, [d. Solomon, Jr.], b. June 11, 1781	Lr1	510
Mary J., m. Bryan **ATWATER**, b. of Berlin, Oct. 31, 1849, by W. W. Woodworth	1	135
Solomon, Jr., b. Aug. 25, 1759; m. [ ], June 29, 1780	Lr1	510
Solomon, Jr., his w. [ ]. b. Apr. 13, 1761	Lr1	510
William, m. Lucy C. **FARNHAM**, b. of Berlin, Oct. 19, 1840, by Joseph Whittlesey	1	81
SALISBURY, Daniel, m. Adaline **FOWLER**, Sept. 3, 1835, at New Britain, by Rev. Amos D. Watrous	1	59
SANDERS, George M., of Mass., m. Catharine **PEARL**, Apr. 17, 1839, by Charles A. Goodrich	1	72
SANFORD, Caroline, m. Rodney **LANGDON**, Nov. 24, 1830, by Theron Osborn	1	41
Henry, of Berlin, m. Polly **BECKLEY**, of Dover, O., Apr. 29, 1842, by W. W Brewer	1	88
Lucy E., m. Harvey **PENFIELD**, Oct. 21, 1839, by Rev. D. M. Seward	1	75
Mary J., m. William **HIGGINS**, b. of Berlin, Oct. 25, 1839, by T. Clark	1	75
SANGER, Ithiel, of Ludlow, Mass., m. Ann Jane **WHIPPLE**, Mar. 14, 1831, by J. Cogswell	1	42
SAVAGE, Alden, m. Elvia **BECKLEY**, b. of Berlin, Dec. 15, 1833, by E. E. Griswold	1	54
Amasa, of Berlin, m. Emeline **BOARDMAN**, of Westfield, Conn., Apr. 17, 1836, by Rev. James McDonald	1	61
Eliza, of Berlin, m. Jonathan **MORLEY**, of Glastonbury, May 22, 1845, by W. W. Woodworth	1	104
Elliot, [s. Joseph & Clarissa], b. Jan. 6, 1822	Lr12	544
Emily, m. Franklin **ROYS**, Oct. 10, 1830, by Rev. Samuel Goodrich	1	40
Ester P., of Berlin, m. Ozias **FOWLER**, of Durham, Sept. 21, 1820, by Samuel Goodrich	1	1
Harriet, [d. Joseph & Clarissa], b. Aug. 11, 1819	Lr12	544
Jamin(?), m. Emily **STRICTLAND**, Sept. 11, 1826, by Rev. Samuel Goodrich	1	22
Joseph, b. Mar. 8, 1795; m. Clarissa **CHENEY**, Feb. 19, 1818	Lr12	544
Joseph A., [s. Joseph & Clarissa], b. Feb. 3, 1827	Lr12	544
Orrin B., of Camden, Ala., m. Sarah A. **HART**, of Berlin, Sept. 24, 1845, by William W. Woodworth	1	105
Seth, m. Lois **KING**, b. of Berlin, Jan. 24, 1824, by Rev. Samuel Goodrich	1	12
Seth, m. Mrs. Anna **POST**, b. of Berlin, Nov. 29, 1828, by Rev. Samuel Goodrich	1	34
Susanna, b. Apr. 14, 1765; m. Stephen **NORTH**, Jan. 1, 1788	Lr1	505
Ulysea E., of Berlin, m. Lyman C. **CAMP**, of Middletown, May 21, 1844, by William W. Woodworth	1	96

	Vol.	Page
SAXTON, Alva, of Berlin, m. Rachel Minerva **SAXTEN**, of Guilford, Dec. 5, 1823, by Rev. Royal Robbins	1	12
Deming W., of Chatham, m. Jane L. **CLARK**, of New Britain, Apr. 9, 1845, by Rev. Philo Hawkes	1	102
Rachel Minerva, of Guilford, m. Alva **SAXTEN**, of Berlin, Dec. 5, 1823, by Rev. Royal Robbins	1	12
SCOFIELD, Rundell, of Greenwich, m. Harriet C. **NASH**, of Berlin, Apr. 8, 1845, by Rev. Joseph L. Morse	1	101
SCRANTON, Jared M., of Durham, m. Jane C. **STEPHENS**, of Berlin, Sept. 6, 1840, by Rev. W. W. Brewer	1	78
SELLECK, Elizabeth, of Greenwich, m. Henry **TIBBALS**, of Durham, Nov. 20, 1842, by William W. Woodworth	1	90
SEYMOUR, Eliza N., of New Britain, m. Frederick **LANGDON**, of Warehouse Point, Sept. 14, 1847, at New Britain, by Rev. Samuel Rockwell	1	120
Hezekiah, of Hartford, m. Elizabeth **BURRETT**, of Berlin, Aug. 24, 1829, by J. Congswell	1	37
Orson H. m. Maria **STANLEY**, b. of Berlin, Sept. 16, 1827, by Joshua Williams. V. D. M.	1	27
SHAD, John, of Savannah, Ga., m. Harriet **NORTON**, of Berlin, June 5, 1820, by Royal Robbins	1	1
SHARP, Jennette A., of New Haven, m. Charles L. **BALDWIN**, of Berlin, Dec. 24, 1848, by Rev. Philo Hawkes	1	128
SHELDON, Evelina S., of Farmington, m. Robert S. **BELDEN**, of New Britain, Dec. 20, 1845, at New Britain, by Rev. Samuel Rockwell	1	114
Horace, m. Amelia O. **BECKLEY**, b. of Berlin, May 13, 1835, by Rev. James M. McDonald	1	57
SHELLEY, Elizabeth, m. Horatio **RECOR**, b. of Berlin, Mar. 24, 1829, by Rev. J. Brace, of Wethersfield	1	35
SHEPARD, Isaiah, of Litchfield, m. Mrs. Huldah **WOODRUFF**, of Southington, Feb. 4, 1821, by Samuel Hart, J. P.	1	4
SHIPMAN, Abigail G., of Berlin, m. Rev. Stafford D. **JEWETT**, of Griswold, Dec. 22, 1830, by Rev. J. Cogswell	1	41
Eliza, m. Henry A. **HART**, Apr. 24, 1827, by Rev. Henry Jones	1	26
Mary L., m. Alfred **ANDREWS**, Sept. 15, 1824, by Rev. Newton Skinner	1	14
Orpah, m. Isaac N. **LEE**, b. of Berlin, Oct. 20, 1833, by Rev. J. Cogswell	1	53
Ralph, m. Marilla **WELLS**, Nov. 2, 1825, by Rev. Henry Jones	1	18
SIMONS, Sarah M., of Berlin, m. George **GRISWOLD**, of Wethersfield, Apr. 25, 1847, by W. W. Woodworth	1	117
SIMPSON, Margaret, m. William **VANCE**, b. of Berlin, Mar. 26, 1848, by Joseph Whittlesey, V. D. M.	1	123
SIMS, Edward D., Prof. of Tuscaloosa, Ala., m. L. Anne **ANDREWS**, d. Prof. E. A., of Berlin, Aug. 24, 1842, by Charles A. Goodrich	1	89

	Vol.	Page

SIMS, (cont.)

L. Anne, d. Prof. A. E. **ANDREWS,** of Berlin, m. William
McKINLEY, of Lexington, Ga., Oct. 26, 1848, at New
Britain, by Rev. Samuel Rockwell — 1 — 128

SKINNER, Amanda E., m. Samuel W. **GALPIN,** b. of Berlin, May
2, 1844, by William W. Woodworth — 1 — 96

Lucy M., m. Edwin **BROWN,** of Chatham, Oct. 29, 1840, by
Joseph Whittlesey — 1 — 81

SLADE, William R., of Plymouth, m. Eliza **GREEN,** of Berlin,
[Dec.] 17, 1836, by Rev. Royal Robbins — 1 — 65

SLATER, Aurora J., m. Lorrain **HINSDALE,** of Torrington, Feb.
28, 1847, by Charles S. Sherman — 1 — 116

Elam, m. Matilda **WRIGHT,** Nov. 4, 1832, by Rev. J.
Cogswell — 1 — 49

Elam, of Berlin, m. Martha A. **BOOTH,** of Southington,
Jan. 31, 1849, at New Britain, by Rev. Samuel Rockwell — 1 — 130

Lucy M., m. William **WRIGHT,** b. of Berlin, May 15, 1836,
by Rev. Edwin R. Gilbert, of Wallingford — 1 — 61

Norris, of Berlin, m. Maria **HAMLIN,** of Farmington, Oct.
25, 1836, by Rev. J. Brace, of Newington — 1 — 64

Sherman, m. Laura Ann **PORTER,** b. of Berlin, Nov. 14, 1832,
by Irenus Atkins — 1 — 50

SLOPER, Lambert E., of Southington, m. Emma **BARNS,** of
Berlin, Sept. 30, 1830, by Rev. Irenus Atkins, of
Southington — 1 — 40

SMITH, Abigail, m. Seth **STANSBURY,** Sept. 30, 1822, by Rev.
Samuel Goodrich — 1 — 8

Amey, of Southington, m. Sheldon **STANLEY,** of Berlin,
Sept. 22, 1824, by Samuel Hart, J. P. — 1 — 14

Ann Jane, m. Thomas **TRACY,** b. of Berlin, Nov. 26, 1835,
by Rev. Royal Robbins — 1 — 60

Asaph, m. Mrs. Abby **DICKINSON,** b. of Berlin, Feb. 6,
1840, by Joseph Whittlesey — 1 — 77

Benjamin, m. Alvina **PENFIELD,** Dec. 9, 1824, by Rev.
Newton Skinner — 1 — 14

Betsey, Mrs., m. Col. Richard **WILSON,** Nov. 11, 1827, by
Rev. Samuel Goodrich — 1 — 28

Betsey L., 1st d. [William & Sally], b. Nov. 24, 1797 — Lr12 — 526

Caroline, m. Henry **WILLIAMS,** June 29, 1840, by Rev. D.
M. Seward — 1 — 81

Catharine E., m. James H. **BRADLEY,** b. of Hartford, Feb.
3, 1849, by Rev. Royal Robbins — 1 — 130

Edwin, m. Sarah M. **MARKHAM,** b. of Berlin, Apr. 19, 1841,
by Rev. W. W. Brewer — 1 — 83

Elizur N., m. Louisa L. **CLARK,** b. of New Britain, Dec.
22, 1846, by O. S. Sherman — 1 — 114

Enos M., m. Roxana **ANDREWS,** b. of Berlin, May 20, 1835,
by Rev. Noah Porter, of Farmington — 1 — 57

	Vol.	Page

SMITH, (cont.)

Eunice D., of Berlin, m. Buckley P. HEATH, of Warehouse
Point, Feb. 12, 1838, by Charles A. Goodrich — 1 — 69

Evelina, m. Mathias HORTON, b. of Berlin, Apr. 2, 1836,
by Rev. Royal Robbins — 1 — 61

H. G. Rev., m. Emily BECKLEY, b. of Berlin, Nov. 29,
1840, by Rev. John Moore, of Hartford — 1 — 80

Harriet E., of New Britain, m. Eli YALE, of Mereden,
Oct. 15, 1837, by Jared R. Avery — 1 — 69

Harriet S., m. Horace H. BROWN, b. of Berlin, May 14,
1845, by Rev. Samuel Rockwell, of New Britain — 1 — 104

Harriet Strong, [d. William & Lucretia], b. Sept. 29, 1820 — Lr12 — 526

Henry C., m. Melisent HOLLISTER, b. of Berlin, Sept. 24,
1826, by Royal Robbins — 1 — 23

Hiram, m. Chloe OSGOOD, Apr. 11, 1831, by Rev. Nathan E.
Shailer — 1 — 42

Hiram B., m. Lucetta W. PORTER, [Sept.] 16, 1833, by Rev.
Ambrose Edson — 1 — 52

Isaac, of New Burgh, N. Y., m. Ellen WINCHELL, d. Capt.
Jairus, of Berlin, Oct. 2, 1848, by Rev. Royal Robbins — 1 — 127

James A., of Middletown, m. Emily C. BOARDMAN, of New
Britain, Dec. 12, 1847, by Rev. W. P. Pattison, of New
Britain — 1 — 121

Laura, Mrs., m. Col. Richard WILCOX, Nov. 8, 1829, by
Rev. Samuel Goodrich — 1 — 37

Leonard, of Wayne, N. Y., m. Nancy CURTIS, of Berlin,
Aug. 4, 1833, by Rev. Royal Robbins — 1 — 52

Levi O., m. Elizabeth S. WHITING, b. of New Britain,
Oct. 26, 1847, at New Britain, by Rev. Samuel Rockwell — 1 — 119

Levi Omstead, 1st s. [William & Lucretia], b. Mar. 25, 1818 — Lr12 — 526

Lucretta, 2nd d. [William & Sally], b. Sept. 24, 1802 — Lr12 — 526

Laucretta, m. Henry NORTH, Jan. 24, 1821, by Newton
Skinner — 1 — 4

Lucy M., m. Edwin BARNES, b. of Berlin, Apr. 15, 1822,
by Rev. Royal Robbins — 1 — 6

Mary, m. Sidney HUBBARD, b. of Berlin, May 4, 1845, by
Rev. L. F. Barney — 1 — 103

Mary B., of Berlin, m. Samuel BANCRAFT, of East Windsor,
May 15, 1834, by Rev. Ambrose Edson — 1 — 55

Millisent G., of Berlin, m. Manning REDFIELD, of
Manchester, N. Y., Sept. 26, 1828, by Rev. Samuel
Goodrich — 1 — 33

Nancy, of Berlin, m. Horatio WALDO, Jr., of Johnston,
N. Y., May 11, 1832, by Rev. J. Cogswell — 1 — 45

Norman C., m. Rebecca MATTHEW, May 13, 1822, by
Newton Skinner — 1 — 7

Rollin C., of Southington, m. Martha H. RICH, of Berlin,
May 9, 1844, by William W. Woodworth — 1 — 96

	Vol.	Page
SMITH, (cont.)		
Sally, w. William, d. Feb. 4, 1810	Lr12	526
Sally Maria, 1st d. [William & Lucretia], b. Apr. 11, 1816	Lr12	526
Samuel Walter, 2nd s. [William & Sally], b. May 15, 1805	Lr12	526
Sarah, m. Luther D. **GRISWOLD,** b. of Elyria, Lorain Co.,		
O., Mar. 25, 1835, by Edwin E. Griswold	1	57
Sarah M., m. Grove W. **LOOMIS,** May 1, 1839, by Rev. D.		
M. Seward	1	74
Truman*, of Middletown, m. Emeline **WILLIAMS,** of Berlin,		
July 8, 1827, by Royal Robbins *(In pencil "Freeman"?)	1	27
Waight, of Berlin, m. Mrs. Rachel **GOULD,** of Middletown,		
May 5, 1823, by Rev. Frederick Wightman, of		
Middletown	1	9
William, 3rd s. Samuel, b. Sept. 2, 1770; m. Sally **LEWIS,**		
d. Adonijah, [ ], 1797	Lr12	526
William, m. Lucretia **MOORE,** d. Abijah, [ ] , 1812	Lr12	526
William E., m. Sarah A. **NORTON,** b. of Berlin, May [ ],		
1845, by W. W. Woodworth	1	102
William H., Maria **NORTH,** b. of Berlin, Aug. 7, 1825, by		
Rev. Joab Brace, of Wethersfield	1	17
William H., m. Lucinda **HART,** Apr. 27, 1842, by Rev. D.		
M. Seward	1	88
William Henry, 1st s. [William & Sally], b. Oct. 22, 1800	Lr12	526
William W., of Haddam, m. Sarah C. **RICH,** of Berlin, Aug.		
13, 1843, by William W. Woodworth	1	91
SOUTHWORTH, Eliza L., m. W[illia]m G. **LEWIS,** Dec. 5, 1830,		
by Rev. J. Cogswell	1	41
George, m. Sally **WELDON,** of Berlin, [Nov.] 30, [1820],		
by Royal Robbins	1	3
Selina, of Berlin, m. Jarvis **DORAN,** of New York City,		
Jan. 17, 1836, by Rev. J. Brace, of Wethersfield.		
Recorded Jan. 16, 1836	1	61
SPALDING, Joseph, of Janesville, Wis., m. Lydia T.		
ELLSWORTH, of Berlin, Feb. 7, 1839, by Joseph		
Whittlesey	1	75
SPENCER, Abigail, of Berlin, m. Abraham **JENNINGS,** of New		
Milford, Apr. 3, 1836, by Rev. Abraham S. Francis	1	62
Denison A., of Middletown, m. Lois **COWLES,** of Berlin,		
July 4, 1827, by Royal Robbins	1	27
Denison A., m. Susan **BULL,** of Guilford, June 30, 1828,		
by Royal Robbins	1	32
Rachel, of Berlin, m. Hiram **JEROME,** of Bristol, Apr. 8,		
1829, by Royal Robbins	1	35
Sally, of Killingworth, m. George **HULL,** of Berlin, Jan.		
10, 1828, by Charles A. Goodrich	1	30
Silas, m. Charlotte M. **ROOT,** Mar. 30, 1836, by Rev. Amos		
D. Watrous	1	63
SPERRY, Lucy, Mrs. of Hamden, m. Alfred H. **GLADWIN,** of		
Berlin, Mar.[ ], 1836, by Rev. Abraham S. Francis	1	62

	Vol.	Page
SPERRY, (cont.)		
Nelson, of New Haven, m. Lucy **BUNNELL**, of Berlin, July 31, 1822, by Rev. Royal Robbins	1	7
Samuel N. of Woodbridge, m. Elizabeth Ann **DUNHAM**, of Berlin, Nov. 28, 1843, by Rev. Samuel Rockwell, of New Britain	1	94
SQUIRES, SQUIRE, SQUARES, Alvin, b. Mar. 11, 1821	Lr1	510
Amelia, m. Milo **THOMPSON**, b. of Berlin, July 22, 1829, by Royal Robbins	1	37
Daniel, b. Oct. 28, 1816	Lr1	510
David, b. July 4, 1805	Lr1	510
David, of Berlin, m. Elizabeth **BRASH**, of Burlington, Nov. 10, 1829, by Charles A. Goodrich	1	38
Henriette, m. John **GOODRICH**, b. of Berlin, Jan. 15, 1840, by Herman S. Haven	1	76
Horace, b. Oct. 13, 1818	Lr1	510
Jane, m. Franklin **TRYON**, May 11, 1837, by Dwight M. Seward	1	68
Jonathan, b. Sept. 13, 1803	Lr1	510
Jonathan, of Berlin, m. Hannah **GOODRICH**, of Wethersfield, May 20, 1827, by Samuel Goodrich	1	26
Julia Ann, m. Brainard **DUNHAM**, Mar. 11, 1832, by Rev. Samuel Goodrich	1	45
Lois, b. Apr. 16, 1813	Lr1	510
Martin, b. Aug. 13, 1807	Lr1	510
Phinehas, m. Elizabeth **ADKINS**, b. of Berlin, May 12, 1833, by Rev. Samuel Goodrich	1	51
Sally, m. Edward **PATTISON**, July 7, 1827, by Ira E. Smith, J.P.	1	28
William, m. Sally **MASTERS**, b. of Berlin, Nov. 8, 1840, by Joseph Whittlesey	1	81
STACEY, Mansfield, m. Fidelia **HART**, b. of Berlin, Oct. 22, 1846, by Rev. E. Cushman	1	113
STANLEY, Abi, m. Lemuel **WELLS**, Nov. 18, 1827, by Rev. Henry Jones	1	28
Abigail, [d. Gad & Mary], b. Aug. 18, 1774	Lr1	488
Abigail, m. Stephen W. **CORNWELL**, s. Capt. Timothy, of Middletown, July 25, 1796	Lr1	488
Abigail, d. Timothy, Jr. & Abigail, b. July 14, 1798	Lr1	507
Abigail, m. Elias **BECKLEY**, Apr. 14, 1828, by Rev. Samuel Goodrich	1	31
Almira, m. George S. **COE**, June 15, 1843, by C. S. Lyman	1	92
Amelia, d. Amon & Abi S., m. Henry **WALTER**, of England, Feb. 29, 1848, by Rev. C. S. Sherman	1	122
Amzi, [s. Gad & Mary], b. Oct. 23, 1770	Lr1	488
Amzi, m. Lucy **WEBSTER**, d. Joshua, Sept. 27, 1801	Lr1	488
Anne, [d. Gad & Mary], b. Jan. 15, 1783	Lr1	488
Anne, m. Alvin **NORTH**, s. James, July 15, 1804	Lr1	488

Vol.   Page

STANLEY, (cont.)

Margaret, d. Ira J. & Eliza, of New Britain, m. Edwin C.
HILLS, of East Hartford, Apr. 5, 1848, in New Britain,
by Rev. C. S. Sherman 1   124

Maria, m. Orson H. SEYMOUR, b. of Berlin, Sept. 16, 1827,
by Joshua Williams, V. D. M. 1   27

Mary, [d. Gad & Mary], b. Aug. 2, 1772 .... Lr1   488

Mary, m. Oliver DEWEY, s. David, Nov. 2, 1792 ...... Lr1   488

Nancy D., m. John H. GOODWIN, Nov. 15, 1838, by Dwight
M. Seward 1   72

Nancy E., d. Cyprian, decd., of Berlin, m. Noyes BALDWIN,
of Naugatuck, Nov. 8, 1846, by Rev. Royal Robbins 1   113

Noah W., m. Laury F. STANLEY, Oct. 16, 1824, by Rev.
Newton Skinner 1   14

Oliver, m. Cordelia N. PECK, b. of New Britain, Aug. 29,
1850, at New Britain, by Rev. Samuel Rockwell 1   139

Orrin, d. Mar. 2, 1786 .... Lr1   488

Orren, [s. Gad & Mary], b. Nov. 6, 1786 .... Lr1   488

Oswin, m. Jane M. THRESHER, b. of Berlin, Nov. 3, 1844,
by Rev. Royal Robbins 1   98

Phebe, [d. Gad & Mary], b. Aug. 28, 1778 .... Lr1   488

Phebe, m. Thomas STOW, s. Capt. Zebulon, of Middletown,
Sept. 28, 1800 .... Lr1   488

Samuel, Maj., m. Sophia ANDREWS, Oct. 13, 1844, by Rev.
Samuel W. Law 1   98

Sheldon, of Berlin, m. Amey SMITH, of Southington, Sept.
22, 1824, by Samuel Hart, J. P. 1   14

Thomas, m. Nancy S. WHITTLESEY, Feb. 19, 1827, by Rev.
Henry Jones 1   25

Timothy W., m. Adaline CORNWELL, Oct. 18, 1841, by Rev.
Dwight M. Seward 1   87

STANNARD, Lovetta, m. Rufus K. REYNOLDS, b. of Berlin, Feb.
19, 1843, by Rev. Samuel W. Smith 1   90

Russell, of Killingworth, m. Julia ROBERTS, of Berlin,
Feb. 26, 1838, by Charles A. Goodrich 1   69

STANSBURY, Seth, m. Abigail SMITH, Sept. 30, 1822, by Rev.
Samuel Goodrich 1   8

STEADMAN, Fanny, of Berlin, m. Wyllys BRADLEY, of
Southington, [Nov.] 27, 1820, by Royal Robbins 1   3

Simeon, m. Julia GRANNIS, Jan. 1, 1822, by Newton Skinner .. 1   5

STEELE, STEEL, Allen, m. Ruth HINSDALE, b. of Berlin, Feb. 5,
1821, by Samuel Goodrich 1   3

Almira, m. Samuel RECOR, Nov. 25, 1829, by Rev. J.
Cogswell 1   38

Amazi H., m. Laura A. MILLER, b. of Berlin, Oct. 30,
1843, by Rev. David Miller 1   94

Amon, m. Rhoda M. BUNCE, b. of Berlin, Nov. 16, 1840,
by Rev. W. W. Brewer 1   79

Vol.   Page

STEELE, STEEL, (cont.)

Avery, m. Jerusha **WILLIAMS,** Feb. 18, 1826, by Rev. John
  Bentley   1   19

Betsey L., m. William S. **HULL,** b. of Berlin, Oct. 23,
  1842, by Irenus Atkins   1   90

Caroline M., m. Joseph **BOOTH,** Jr., Nov. 22, 1827, by
  Rev. Samuel Goodrich   1   29

Chauncey, Jr., m. Nancy H. **STEEL,** b. of Berlin, Jan. 31,
  1841, by Rev. W. W. Brewer   1   82

David, Jr., m. Lucy **BLIN,** b. of Berlin, July 23, 1826,
  by Rev. Samuel Goodrich   1   22

Diadama, m. Abram **NEAL,** Feb. 8, 1821, by Newton Skinner   1   4

Dyantha S., m. Elijah A. **ANDRUS,** b. of Berlin, Oct. 23,
  1842, by Charles A. Goodrich   1   89

Eben, m. Maritty **RICHARDS,** Dec. 22, 1825, by Rev. J. T.
  Nichols   1   19

Ebenezer, of Berlin, m. Mary W. **PILGRIM,** of Hartford,
  Oct. 24, 1830, by Rev. Timothy Benedict   1   40

Elbridge J., s. Russell & Abigail, m. Rebecca B. **EDDY,**
  d. William H. & Mary, Feb. 22, 1848, by Rev. C. S.
  Sherman   1   122

Eliza, m. Roswell **HART,** Feb. 13, 1826, by Rev. Noah Porter,
  of Farmington   1   21

Eliza H., m. William T. **PRATT,** May 6, 1825, by Rev.
  Samuel Goodrich   1   17

Elizur, of Berlin, m. Matilda **BELDEN,** of Wethersfield,
  May 5, 1840, by Joseph Whittlesey   1   77

Emeline, of Berlin, m. Moses B. **WILSON,** of Providence,
  R. I., July 1, 1832, by Rev. William Bentley   1   47

George, m. Lucina **BELDEN,** Jan. 11, 1824, by Rev. Newton
  Skinner   1   12

Henriette L., of New Britain, m. William A. **TOMPKINS,**
  of Farmington, May 2, 1847, by Charles S. Sherman   1   116

Henry, m. Amelia **PENFIELD,** b. of Berlin, Nov. 26, 1827,
  by Rev. Noah Porter, of Farmington   1   29

Henry A., of Berlin, m. Eliza **WILLIAMS,** of Mass., Aug.
  14, 1831, by Rev. Ambrose Edson   1   42

Hila, of Berlin, m. Isaac W. **TALMAGE,** of Wethersfield,
  Dec. 21, 1831, by Rev. Samuel Goodrich   1   45

Horace, m. Laura **HART,** b. of Berlin, Aug. 26, 1839, by
  Rev. John Boyden, Jr.   1   74

Jefferson, m. Betsey **GOFF,** 2nd, b. of Berlin, Feb. 16,
  1823, by Rev. Royal Robbins   1   9

Jerome L., of Berlin, m. Mary H. **WESTCOAT,** of
  Wethersfield, Jan. 8, 1828, by Ira E. Smith, J. P.   1   30

John, of Berlin, m. Cloe **CARRINGTON,** of Farmington, Dec.
  2, 1822, by Rev. Samuel Goodrich   1   8

Julia, of Berlin, m. Elisha **WHAPLES,** 3rd, of Wethersfield,

	Vol.	Page
STEELE, STEEL, (cont.)		
Sept. 7, 1830, by Rev. Samuel Goodrich	1	40
Julia E., of Berlin, m. Merrick L. **LEWIS**, of Westfield, Mass., Apr. 21, 1846, by Rev. John M. Guion, of New Britain	1	110
Laura C., m. W[illia]m H. **DEMING**, May 4, 1826, by Rev. Samuel Goodrich	1	20
Lovina, m. Zerah **BLIN**, Feb. 6, 1826, by Rev. Samuel Goodrich	1	19
Lucelia J., of Farmington, m. Moses **GILBERT**, of Berlin, Mar. 11, 1850, by Rev. S. Rushmore	1	136
Lucy Ann, m. Orson **GLADDING**, Oct. 20, 1847, by W. P. Pattison	1	120
Martha, of New Britain, m. William **WILSON**, of Pittsfield, Mass., Nov. 20, 1842, by Rev. R. K. Reynolds	1	90
Mary, m. Solomon **HAMLIN**, Nov. 1, 1825, by Rev. Henry Jones	1	18
Mary A., of Berlin, m. William **CORNWELL**, of Middletown, July 11, 1836, by James M. McDonald	1	63
Mary D., m. Philip **RECOR**, Sept. 1, 1836, by Rev. Amos D. Watrous	1	63
Mary D., m. Abiathea **HUBBARD**, b. of Berlin, Apr. 14, 1845, by Rev. Royal Robbins	1	103
Mary M., m. John **HAZARD**, Jan. 13, 1833, by George W. Appleton	1	50
Nancy H., m. Chauncey **STEEL**, Jr., b. of Berlin, Jan. 31, 1841, by Rev. W. W. Brewer	1	82
Nancy S., of New Britain, m. Levi F. **PIERCE**, of Springflield, Dec. 23, 1838, by Rev. John Goodwin	1	72
Rhoda, m. Samuel **HUBBARD**, Aug. 11, 1836, by Rev. Amos D. Watrous	1	63
Salmon, m. Eliza **MORGAN**, Nov. 29, 1832, by Rev. Luman Andrus	1	49
Sarah Jane, m. E. M. **BECKLEY**, b. of Berlin, Apr. 8, 1845, by Rev. John Moore, of Hartford	1	101
Thurza, m. Albert **WILLIAMS**, Apr. 14, 1824, by Rev. Newton Skinner	1	12
STEVENS STEPHENS, Eliza Ann, m. Henry **WATERMAN**, b. Berlin, Nov. 6, 1831, by Royal Robbins	1	45
Emma, of Berlin, m. Levi L. **KELSEY**, of Hartford, Mar. 27, 1828, by Rev. Samuel Goodrich	1	30
Jane C., of Berlin, m. Jared M. **SCRANTON,**, of Durham, Sept. 6, 1840, by Rev. W. W. Brewer	1	78
STEWERT, Laura Ann, of Berlin, m. Jeremiah **DAYTON**, of North Haven, June 22, 1832, by Luther Beckley, J. P.	1	46
STICTT (?),Florence, of Petersburg, Va., m. Elishama **BRANDEGEE**, Jr., of Berlin, Apr. 28, 1841, by Rev. Aaron J. Leavenworth	1	85

	Vol.	Page
STILLMAN, Roger, of Colebrook, m. Mrs. Mary WITHERELL, of		
Berlin, Aug. 2, 1829, by Rev. J. Cogswell	1	36
STOCKER, Charlotte R., of Berlin, m. Elihu H. COLVIN, of		
Manchester, Aug. 14, 1831, by Levi Knight	1	43
STOCKING, Delia Ann, of Berlin, m. Cyrus ROOT, of		
Southington, Nov. 26, 1828, by David L. Ogden	1	118
Elizabeth E., d. Luther, decd., m. Albert R. NORTON, b.		
of Berlin, Oct. 4, 1846, by Rev. Royal Robbins	1	112
John, m. Lucy WHITE, b. of Middletown, July 13, 1828, by		
Elijah Willard, Elder	1	32
Martha, d. Luther, decd., of Berlin, m. Charles NORTON,		
of Bristol, Oct. 6, 1846, by Rev. Royal Robbins	1	112
Michael, of Middletown, m. Sarah PATTISON, of Berlin,		
Nov. 4, 1822, by Rev. Joshua L. Williams, of Middletown	1	9
STODDARD, Ester, of Berlin, m. George GRISWOLD, of		
Wethersfield, June 10, 1821, by Samuel Goodrich	1	5
STONE, Sylvester, m. Harriet Elizabeth BUTLER, b. of Berlin,		
Nov. 2, 1828, by Royal Robbins	1	34
STOWE, STOW, Almira, m. Jesse GLADDIN, b. of Berlin, Aug. 7,		
1831, by Royal Robbins	1	43
Emily Ann, m. Levi A. AVERY, b. of Berlin, Sept. 14,		
1847, by Rev. W. A. Stickney	1	119
Lorenzo, m. Eunice BOARDMAN, b. of Berlin, Oct. 8, 1826,		
by Charles A. Goodrich	1	29
Thomas, s. Capt. Zebulon, of Middletown, m. Phebe		
STANLEY, Sept. 28, 1800	Lr1	488
STOWEL, Almira, m. Jesse GLADDIN, b. of Berlin, Aug. 7, 1831,		
by Royal Robbins	1	42
STRICTLAND, Emily, m. Jamin SAVAGE, Sept. 11, 1826, by		
Rev. Samuel Goodrich	1	22
Mabel C., d. Stephen & Nancy, of Glastonbury, m. Ethel		
NORTH, s. Reuben & Amanda, of Goshen, now residents		
of Berlin, Nov. 23, 1847, by C. S. Sherman	1	121
Martha, m. Selah COLE, Mar. 5, 1810	Lr1	506
Stephen L., m. Almira B. BURRITT, Nov. 24, 1836. by		
Dwight M. Seward	1	65
STRONG, Cyprain, Rev., m. Abigail HART, wid. Jonathan, Aug.		
3, 1797	Lr1	507
Esther, of Torrington, m. Elihu OSBORN, of Derby, Nov.		
12, 1828, by Rev. Epaphras Goodman	1	34
SUGDEN, Elisha, [s. Thomas & Persea], b. Jan. 14, 1786	Lr1	505
Hannah, [d. Thomas & Persea], b. June 13, 1790	Lr1	505
John, [s. Thomas & Persea], b. May 30, 1782	Lr1	505
Sarah, [d. Thomas & Persea], b. July 25, 1788	Lr1	505
Thomas, m. Persea MATHER, Dec. 7, 1780	Lr1	505
Thomas, Jr., [s. Thomas & Persea], b. Feb. 14, 1784	Lr1	505
SWEARS, SWEARES, Calvin, m. Almira LEWIS, Nov. 26, 1835,		
by Rev. Amos D. Watrous	1	62

	Vol.	Page

SWEARS, SWEARES, (cont.)

Maria, m. Asahel **LIMSON,** Nov. 24, 1836, by Dwight M.
Seward ... 1 ... 65

SWEET, Dennis, of Farmington, m. Caroline **HART,** of Berlin,
July 3, 1828, by Rev. J. Brace, of Wethersfield ... 1 ... 32

Esther M., m. John **HAMLIN,** Nov. 10, 1828, by Rev.
Samuel Goodrich ... 1 ... 33

Jennette, Mrs., m. James **HOOKER,** b. of Farmington, June
14, 1840, in New Britain, by W. W. Brewer ... 1 ... 78

TALCOTT, Clark A., m. Mary E. **WHAPLES,** Nov. 11, 1846, by
Charles A. Goodrich ... 1 ... 113

William, of Ohio, m. Rosanna **PORTER,** of Berlin, Apr. 28,
1830, by Royal Robbins ... 1 ... 39

TALMAGE, Isaac W., of Wethersfield, m. Hila **STEEL,** of Berlin,
Dec. 21, 1831, by Rev. Samuel Goodrich ... 1 ... 45

TAPPIN, John Jansen, m. Laura Smith **GOODRICH,** Nov. 30,
1826, by Rev. Henry Jones ... 1 ... 24

TAYLOR, Ann, m. Levi **NORTH,** Jr., May 19, 1833, by Rev. J.
Brace, of Newington ... 1 ... 51

Emily, m. Aaron **BAIRD,** Apr. 30, 1835, by Amos D. Watrous ... 1 ... 57

George S., of Berlin, m. Harriet M. **HALE,** of Glastonbury,
July 23, 1845, by Rev. Royal Robbins ... 1 ... 105

Jonathan, of Owego, N. Y., m. Sally **GRIDLEY,** of Berlin,
June 21, 1829, by Royal Robbins ... 1 ... 36

Samuel S., m. Mary E. **ATWOOD,** b. of Berlin, Nov. 25,
1844, by W. W. Woodworth ... 1 ... 100

Vashti, m. Alvan **BEAVINS,** b. of Southington, Oct. 19,
1826, by Royal Robbins ... 1 ... 24

TERRY, Samuel, of Bristol, m. Mary **MERRIMAN,** of Kensington,
May 8, 1844, by Rev. Royal Robbins ... 1 ... 96

THATCHER, John M., m. Lucy D. **BLINN,** b. of Berlin, July 8,
1832, by Rev. William Bentley ... 1 ... 47

THIRLEY*, Sarah, m. Allen **JUDD,** b. of Berlin, Dec. 19, 1830,
by Rev. Timothy Benedict *(Perhaps "**SHIRLEY**") ... 1 ... 41

THOMPSON, THOMSON, Emeline, m. Leander S. **HART,** Aug.
23, 1824, by Rev. Newton Skinner ... 1 ... 13

Louisa O., of South Windsor, m. George **MORGAN,** Jr., of
Berlin, Feb. 21, 1847, by Rev. E. Cushman ... 1 ... 115

Milo, m. Amelia **SQUIRES,** b. of Berlin, July 22, 1829,
by Royal Robbins ... 1 ... 37

Sherman, m. Hannah A. **GLADDIN,** Mar. 7, 1830, by Elijah
Willard, Elder ... 1 ... 38

Susan, m. George **DANIELS,** b. of Berlin, Oct. 16, 1828,
by Royal Robbins ... 1 ... 33

THORP, Julia A., of Southampton, Mass., m. William **PAYNE,** of
Mereden, June 15, 1834, by Amos L. Watrous ... 1 ... 55

THRASHER, THRESHER, Cornelia S., d. Nathan, m. Charles M.
BROWN, b. of Kensington, May 24, 1848, by Rev.

Vol.   Page

THRASHER, THRESHER, (cont.)

Royal Robbins   1   123

Jane M., m. Oswin **STANLEY,** b. of Berlin, Nov. 3, 1844,
by Rev. Royal Robbins   1   98

Julia E., of Kensington, m. Andrew **JEROME,** of New Haven,
May 8, 1849, at New Britain, by Rev. Samuel Rockwell   1   131

TIBBALS, Henry, of Durham, m. Elizabeth **SELLECK,** of
Greenwich, Nov. 20, 1842, by William W. Woodworth   1   90

Henry W., of Chatham, m. Rozilla C. **BAILEY,** of Berlin,
June 16, 1841, by Rev. Stephen Alonzo Loper, of Middle
Haddam   1   84

TIBBITTS, John W., m. Fanny **CHAPPELL,** b. of New London,
May 22, 1843, by Joseph Whittlesey   1   93

TILLOTSON, Nathaniel, of Suffield, Conn., m. Lovisa
NEWBURY, of Hartford, Apr. 16, 1838, by Rev. W. A.
Stickney   1   70

TODD, Jane E., d. Josiah, m. William **BINGHAM,** b. of Berlin,
Nov. 5, 1843, by Rev. John M. Guion   1   93

TOMPKINS, William A., of Farmington, m. Henriette L. **STEELE,**
of New Britain, May 2, 1847, by Charles S. Sherman   1   116

TOWNSEND, Ralsey, of Windsor, m. Dency **NORTON,** of Berlin
(b. colored), July 3, 1839, by Joseph Whittlesey   1   73

TRACY, Sarah A., m. Julius **BUNNEL,** b. of New Britain, May 2,
1848, by W. P. Pattison   1   123

Thomas, m. Ann Jane **SMITH,** b. of Berlin, Nov. 26, 1835,
by Rev. Royal Robbins   1   60

TREADWAY, Russell, m. Almira **BOOTH,** Nov. 5, 1826, by
Samuel Goodrich   1   23

TRYON, Eliza, of Berlin, m. Enus **TUCKER,** of Worcester, Mass.,
Dec. 3, 1823, by Charles Goodrich   1   11

Evelin, m. Clarissa **BAILEY,** b. of Berlin, Sept. 5, 1831,
by Rev. John Nixon   1   43

Franklin, m. Jane **SQUARES,** May 11, 1837, by Dwight M.
Seward   1   68

Lovina, m. Joseph **BROWN,** b. of Berlin, Sept. 27, 1830,
by Rev. Timothy Benedict   1   40

TUCKER, Enus, of Worcester, Mass., m. Eliza **TRYON,** of Berlin,
Dec. 3, 1823, by Charles Goodrich   1   11

Horatio N., m. Maria **DICKS,** Nov. 8, 1835, by Rev. Amos
D. Watrous   1   60

Mary E., d. Erastus & Emma A., m. Dewitt C. **POND,** b. of
New Britain, Nov. 15, 1848, in New Britain, by Rev.
Charles S. Sherman   1   129

True P., of Buffalo, N. Y., m. Julia A. **DEMING,** of Berlin,
May 20, 1835, by Rev. James M. McDonald   1   57

----, of R. I., m. Polly **GOFF,** of Berlin, Sept. 14, 1831,
by Charles A. Goodrich   1   44

TULLER, Asaph, of Simsbury, m. Rhoda **HART,** of Berlin, Mar.

	Vol.	Page
TULLER, (cont.)		
28, 1839, by Joseph W. Whittlesey	1	72
Ruah, m. Orville W. **PARSONS,** Feb. 5, 1834, by J. Cogswell	1	54
TUTTLE, Elizabeth A., of Berlin, m. Robert **ANDRUS,** of New Haven, May 1, 1843, by Rev. John Moore, of Hartford	1	91
Jarvis, of Waterbury, m. Mercy H. **PORTER,** of Berlin, Sept. 13, 1823, by Rev. Samuel Goodrich	1	10
Jarvis, m. Mary **HUBBARD,** May 21, 1832, by Rev. John Boyd, Jr.	1	46
Julia A., m. Francis **DEMING,** b. of Berlin, July 5, 1847, by H. G. Smith	1	118
Lyman M., m. Margarette **BUNCE,** b. of New Britain, July 7, 1844, by Rev. Samuel Rockwell	1	97
UPSON, Julia Ann, of Berlin, m. Homer **CURTIS,** of Mereden, Nov. 26, 1835, by Rev. J. Brace, of Newington	1	60
Samuel, m. Margaretta **DICKINSON,** of Southington, Sept. 12, 1841, by Rev. Royal Robbins	1	86
VANCE, William, m. Margaret **SIMPSON,** b. of Berlin, Mar. 26, 1848, by Joseph Whittlesey, V. D. M.	1	123
VAN NORDEN, Esther, m. Roswell **HUNTER,** b. of Berlin, Oct. 12, 1826, by Royal Robbins	1	24
Maria, of Berlin, m. Alfred **WARD,** of Middletown, Oct. 21, 1827, by Charles A. Goodrich	1	29
VIETS, Imely B., of Granby, m. Juliaetta A. **HART,** of New Britain, June 5, 1826, by Dwight M. Seward	1	70
Imley B., m. Angeline C. **HART,** June 28, 1843, by William Whittlesey	1	92
VINCENT, Mary Ann, m. William **HAMILTON,** b. of Berlin, May 25, 1847, by W. W. Woodworth	1	117
WADSWORTH, Almira, m. David S. **GILBERT,** Jan. 1, 1827, by Ira E. Smith, J. P.	1	25
WALDO, Horatio, Jr., of Johnston, N. Y., m. Nancy **SMITH,** of Berlin, May 11, 1832, by Rev. J. Cogswell	1	45
WALTER, Henry, of England, m. Amelia **STANLEY,** d. Amon & Abi S., Feb. 29, 1848, by Rev. C. S. Sherman	1	122
WARD, Alfred, of Middletown, m. Maria **VAN NORDEN,** of Berlin, Oct. 21, 1827, by Charles A. Goodrich	1	29
Harvey, of Middletown, m. Electa **ROBERTS,** of Berlin, May 5, 1824, by Rev. Samuel Goodrich	1	13
WARNER, Charlotte, m. Salmon **WARNER,** b. of Berlin, May 14, 1841, by Joseph Whittlesey	1	84
Cordelia L., d. Norman, of Berlin, m. Franklin G. **GUION,** of Kinderhook, N. Y., Oct. 1, 1849, in St. Marks Ch., New Britain, by Rev. John M. Guion	1	133
Edmund, m. Elizabeth **WOODRUFF,** Oct. 8, 1838, by Dwight M. Seward	1	72
Eli, of Bristol, m. Polly **BELDEN,** of Berlin, Mar. 8, 1827, by Samuel Hart, J. P.	1	26

WARNER, (cont.)

Jane E., d. Edmund, m. Edgar **BECKLEY,** b. of Berlin,
July 11, 1849, by Rev. Royal Robbins   1   132

Martha L., of Wethersfield, m. James **MECLENTIC (?),** of
Berlin, Nov. 24, 1833, by Rev. Theron Osborn   1   54

Mary, d. Eli, m. William **WHAPLES,** b. of Berlin, Nov. 29,
1846, by Rev. Royal Robbins   1   114

Mary A., d. Norman, of Berlin, m. Asahel **WELLS,** of
Savannah, Ga., Oct. 1, 1845, by Rev. John M. Guion, of
Berlin   1   105

Salmon, m. Charlotte **WARNER,** b. of Berlin, May 14, 1841,
by Joseph Whittlesey   1   84

Walter, of Wethersfield, m. Orry **CHENEY,** of Berlin, Apr.
13, 1825, by Rev. William S. Pease   1   16

William, m. Elizabeth N. **HOOKER,** b. of Berlin, May 3,
1832, by Royal Robbins   1   46

WARREN, Alanson, m. Almira **WOODRUFF,** Jan. 18, 1837, by
Dwight M. Seward   1   68

WATERMAN, Henry, m. Eliza Ann **STEVENS,** b. of Berlin, Nov.
6, 1831, by Royal Robbins   1   45

WAY, Elizabeth A., m. William M. **DEAN,** b. of Berlin, Oct. 15,
1840, by Rev. Royal Robbins, of Kensington   1   79

Fanny, of Mereden, m. Erastus **KELSEY,** of Kensington, Apr.
6, 1847, by Rev. Royal Robbins   1   116

WEBSTER, Amos, m. Mary Ann **PERKINS,** b. of Berlin, May 13,
1828, by Royal Robbins   1   31

David, of Berlin, m. Mary **HOLMES,** of Rocky Hill, Jan.
10, 1847, at New Britain, by Rev. Samuel Rockwell   1   114

Hannah, m. Orson **DUNHAM,** b. of Southington, Mar. 23,
1836, by Rev. Royal Robbins   1   61

Jonathan, m. Esther **DICKINSON,** Jan. 7, 1827, by Rev.
Samuel Goodrich   1   25

Lucy, d. Joshua, m. Amzi **STANLEY,** Sept. 27, 1801   Lrl   488

Miley M., m. Anstra **BROWN,** July 15, 1827, by Rev. Henry
Jones   1   27

WELDON, WELDEN, WELDIN, Lucy, m. Asa **ROGERS,** b. of
Berlin, July 11, 1830, by Rev. Timothy Benedict   1   39

Sally, of Berlin, m. George **SOUTHWORTH,** of Berlin,
[Nov.] 30, 1820, by Royal Robbins   1   3

Samuel, m. Sally **BARTHOLOMEW,** Oct. 13, 1823, by
Newton Skinner   1   11

Samuel H., of New Britain, m. Sarah W. **KEACH,** of
Wethersfield, Mar. 15, 1840, by Herman S. Haven   1   77

WELLS, Asahel, of Savannah, Ga., m. Mary A. **WARNER,** of
Berlin, d. of Norman, Oct. 1, 1845, by Rev. John M.
Guion, of Berlin   1   105

Elva, m. Chester **HART,** May 12, 1824, by Rev. Newton
Skinner   1   13

	Vol.	Page

WELLS, (cont.)

Hannah, m. Chester **HART**, Sept. 19, 1821, by Newton Skinner	1	5
Israel T., m. Mary Louisa **HINSDALE**, d. of Gilman & Ann, b. of New Britain, Apr. 11, 1849, by Rev. Charles S. Sherman	1	130
Lemuel, m. Abi **STANLEY**, Nov. 18, 1827, by Rev. Henry Jones	1	28
Levi, of Wethersfield, m. Adaline **HART**, of Berlin, Nov. 26, 1845, by Rev. Samuel Rockwell, of New Britain	1	106
Levi S., of New Britain, s. Horace & Pamela, m. Harriet **FRANCIS**, d. Robert J. & Mary T., of Newington, Apr. 27, 1848, by Rev. C. S. Sherman	1	124
Marilla, m. Ralph **SHIPMAN**, Nov. 2, 1825, by Rev. Henry Jones	1	18
Russel, m. Clarissa **WRIGHT**, b. of Berlin, Mar. 29, 1840, by Rev. Royal Robbins	1	77
WELTON, George W., of Waterbury, m. Mary Ann **GRAHAM**, Dec. 15, 1840, by Joseph Whittlesey	1	82
WENTWORTH, Daniel, m. Maria **ALLEN**, Dec. 4, 1834, by Rev. Samuel Goodrich	1	56
William A., of Middletown, m. Frances M. **CHILDS**, of Haddam, July 29, 1831, by Rev. John Nixon	1	43
WESTCOAT, Mary H., of Wethersfield, m. Jerome L. **STEEL**, of Berlin, Jan. 8, 1828, by Ira E. Smith, J. P.	1	30
WESTON, Lucy, m. Elishama **BRANDEGA**, Mar. 10, 1778	Lr1	514
WETHERELL, Lyman, of Chatham, m. Prudence **MORGAN**, of Berlin, Sept. 21, 1840, by Rev. W. W. Brewer	1	78
WETMORE, Timothy, m. Mary **CLARK**, May 18, 1836, by Rev. Dwight Seward	1	62
WHAPLES, Curtis, m. Elizabeth **LEE**, June 11, 1827, by Rev. Henry Jones	1	26
Elisha, 3rd, of Wethersfield, m. Julia **STEEL**, of Berlin Sept. 7, 1830, by Rev. Samuel Goodrich	1	40
Mary E., m. Clark A. **TALCOTT**, Nov. 11, 1846, by Charles A. Goodrich	1	113
William, m. Mary **WARNER**, d. Eli, b. of Berlin, Nov. 29, 1846, by Rev. Royal Robbins	1	114
WHIPPLE, Ann Jane, m. Ithiel **SANGER**, of Ludlow, Mass., m. Mar. 14, 1831, by J. Cogswell	1	42
Charlotte C., m. Cyrus **WILLIAMS**, b. of Berlin, July 31, 1831, by Rev. Laban C. Cheney	1	43
WHITAKE, Mary, of Great Britain, m. Herve Green **MASON**, of Dublin, Aug. 10, 1836, by Rev. Amos D. Watrous	1	63
WHITE, Heman, of Mereden, m. Caroline **ATWOOD**, of Berlin, July 7, 1835, by Rev. Abraham S. Francis	1	58
Lemuel, of Middletown, m. Ann **JOHNSON**, of Mereden, [ ], by Benoni Upson	1	10
Lucy, m. John **STOCKING**, b. of Middletown, July 13, 1828,		

	Vol.	Page
WILCOX, WILCON , (cont.)		
Maria, m. Abijah **HURLBURT**, b. of Berlin, May 1, 1837, by		
Rev. James M. MacDonald	1	67
Mary O., m. Alfred **NORTH**, b. of Berlin, May 8, 1834, by		
Rev. Ambrose Edson	1	55
Norris, m. Harriet **HART**, late of Berlin, Mar. 3, 1822,		
by Royal Robbins	1	6
Richard, [s. Samuel], b. Oct. 24, 1780	Lr1	505
Richard, Col., m. Mrs. Laura **SMITH**, Nov. 8, 1829, by		
Rev. Samuel Goodrich	1	37
Samuel C., m. Anna S. **PECK**, June 9, 1846, by William W.		
Woodworth	1	111
Sylvester, [s. Samuel], b. Apr. 20, 1788	Lr1	505
Thurolin, of Suffield, m. Nancy **WILLIAMS**, of West		
Hartford, Sept. 15, 1831, by Rev. John Nixon	1	44
Willis, m. Almira **KELSEY**, Jan. 29, 1826, by Rev. Samuel		
Goodrich	1	19
WILKIE, Calvin, of Alexandra, N. Y., m. Sarah C. **GRAHAM**, of		
Chatham, Oct. 9, 1836, by Rev. David Plumb, Witnesses		
Hervey Lounsbury & John H. Hubbard	1	64
WILLARD, Cynthia G., of Berlin, m. William **REED**, of New		
Haven, May 15, 1828, by Rev. Lucius Baldwin	1	31
Maria, of Berlin, m. Lucius **BALDWIN**, of Mereden, May 29,		
1828, by Rev. Eli Denniston	1	31
WILLIAMS Albert, m. Thurza **STEEL**, Apr. 14, 1824, by Rev.		
Newton Skinner	1	12
Cyrus, m. Charlotte C. **WHIPPLE**, b. of Berlin, July 31,		
1831, by Rev. Laban C. Cheney	1	43
Dolly, m. George **HINSDALE**, b. of Berlin, May 26, 1822,		
by Rev. Royal Robbins	1	7
Eliza, of Mass., m. Henry A. **STEEL**, of Berlin, Aug. 14,		
1831, by Rev. Amborse Edson	1	42
Emeline, of Berlin, m. Truman * **SMITH**, of Middletown,		
July 8, 1827, by Royal Robbins *(In pencil		
"**FREEMAN**"?)	1	27
Emily, m. Horace H. **CARPENTER**, Sept. 17, 1826, by Rev.		
Henry Jones	1	23
George, m. Jane M. **PENFIELD**, b. of Berlin, Aug. 28, 1842,		
by Rev. R. K. Reynolds	1	89
Hannah, of Berlin, m. Daniel **KILBEY**, of Wethersfield,		
May 31, 1821, by Elijah Willard, Elder	1	4
Henry, m. Caroline **SMITH**, June 29, 1840, by Rev. D. M.		
Seward	1	81
Jerusha, m. Avery **STEEL**, Feb. 18, 1826, by Rev. John		
Bentley	1	19
Minerva, of Berlin, m. Harvey W. **LEE**, of Montgomery,		
Mass., Aug. 8, 1841, by W. W. Brewer	1	84
Nancy, m. Asahel **ROOT**, b. of Berlin, June 7, 1821, by		

	Vol.	Page
WILLIAMS, (cont.)		
Samuel Goodrich	1	4
Nancy, of West Hartford, m. Thurolin **WILCOX,** of Suffield,		
Sept. 15, 1831, by Rev. John Nixon	1	44
Richard, m. Lucy Ann **STANLEY,** b. of Berlin, Aug. 29, 1842,		
by Rev. S. H. Clark	1	89
Warner, m. Mary **BURRET,** b. of Berlin, May 26, 1825, by		
Rev. Royal Robbins	1	16
Willis, m. Lucy **PECK,** b. of Berlin, Aug. 9, 1835, by Rev.		
William A. Stickney	1	58
WILSON, Archelaus, of Manchester, N. H., m. Julia H.		
ANDREWS, d. Prof. E. A., of Berlin, Oct. 9, 1848, by		
Rev. Samuel Rockwell	1	127
Martin, of West Springfield, Mass., m. Adaline **BELDEN,**		
of Berlin, Apr. 3, 1837, by Rev. W. A. Stickney	1	67
Moses B., of Providence, R. I., m. Emeline **STEEL,** of Berlin,		
July 1, 1832, by Rev. William Bentley	1	47
Richard, Col., m. Mrs. Betsey **SMITH,** Nov. 11, 1827, by		
Rev. Samuel Goodrich	1	28
William, of Pittsfield, Mass., m. Martha **STEEL,** of New		
Britain, Nov. 20, 1842, by Rev. R. K. Reynolds	1	90
William, of Berlin, m. Levana **CROWELL,** of Middletown,		
Jan. 5, 1847, by Rev. Royal Robbins	1	115
WINCHELL, WINCHEL, [see also **WINCHET**], Calvin, m. Lois		
PATTISON, b. of Berlin, Mary 5, 1824, by Rev. Royal		
Robbins	1	13
Eliza, of Berlin, m. John W. **MURPHY,** of Coventry, Nov.		
26, 1828, by Royal Robbins	1	34
Ellen, d. Capt. Jairus, of Berlin, m. Isaac **SMITH,** of		
New Burgh, N. Y., Oct. 2, 1848, by Rev. Royal Robbins	1	127
Lois, m. Caleb H. **AUSTIN,** b. of Berlin, Feb. 26, 1830,		
by Rev. Theron Osborn	1	38
WINCHET, [see also **WINCHELL**], Stephen, m. Irene **DUNHAM,**		
b. of Berlin, Jan. 22, 1823, by Rev. Royal Robbins	1	9
WITHERELL, Mary, Mrs., of Berlin, m. Roger **STILLMAN,** of		
Colebrook, Aug. 2, 1829, by Rev. J. Cogswell	1	36
WOOD, Hannah, m. Edwin **SAGE,** b. of Berlin, Jan. 15, 1843, by		
William W. Woodworth	1	90
Nancy, m. George **ROBINSON,** b. of Pawtucket, R. I., Jan.		
21, 1827, by Rev. E. Washburn	1	25
WOODRUFF, Almira, m. Alanson **WARREN,** Jan. 18, 1837, by		
Dwight M. Seward	1	68
Diantha, m. Gad **ANDREWS,** b. of Southington, May 1, 1833,		
by Royal Robbins	1	51
Elizabeth, m. Edmund **WARNER,** Oct. 8, 1838, by Dwight M.		
Seward	1	72
Huldah, Mrs. of Southington, m. Isaiah **SHEPARD,** of		
Litchfield, Feb. 4, 1821, by Samuel Hart, J. P.	1	4

BETHANY VITAL RECORDS
1832 - 1853

ALLEN, [see also ALLING], Athe, of Cheshire, m. Orrin TALMAGE, of Oxford, Mar. 19, 1851, by Rev. S. Howland, of Humphreysville 30

Harriet A., m. Albert DRIOR, b. of Bethany, Oct. 27, 1839, by Rev. J. H. Rouse, at the Rectory of Christ Church 15

Herman, m. Rebecca LOUNSBURY, Apr. 10, 1843, by Rev. Frederick Woodward 21

ALLING, [see also ALLEN], Charlotte E., m. Harpin H. HOTCHKISS, b. of Bethany, Feb. 15, 1852, by Rev. Henry Zell, at the house of Albert Hoadley 31

Cornelius L., of New Haven, m. Rebeckah E. SPERRY, of Bethany, Apr. 20, 1843, by Rev. Henry Townsend, of New Haven 22

George H., of Orange, m. Martha SPERRY, of Bethany, May 17, 1848, by Rev. Henry Zell 27

ANDREWS, ANDREW, Adeline F., m. Charles L. NORTHROP, , b. of Bethany, July 14, 1850, by F. Harrison, V. D. M. 26

Charlotte, of Bethany, m. Amzi WILLIAMS, of Prospect, Aug. 6, 1842, by Rev. Ebenezer O. Beers. Witnesses, Kneeland Downs, E. O. Beers 19

Mary, of Bethany, m. Samuel BASSETT, of Durham, N. Y., Sept. 28, 1832, by George F. Peck, J. P. 1

Nathan, m. Elizabeth NETTLETON, b. of Bethany, [Sept] 28, [1845], by Rev. D. B. Butts 22

ASPINWALL, George, of Mereden, m. Eliza Ann GRISWOLD, of Rocky Hill, Nov. 20, 1853, by Rev. Alex[ande]r Leadbetter 36

ATWATER, Margaret A., of Bethany, m. Ervin MIX, of Cheshire, Oct. 8, 1850, by F. Harrison, V. D. M. 27

BACON, Dwight, of Simsbury, m. Eunice SPERRY, of Bethany, Sept. 18, 1836, by Sylvester Smith 7

BAGDEN, Margaret E., m. Jonathan SIMMONS, Mar. 17, 1842, by Geo[rge] F. Peck, J. P. 20

BALDWIN, Mary E., of Bethany, m. Oliver T. BEACH, of Plymouth, [Nov.] 1, 1841, by Oliver Hopson 18

BARKER, Henrietta, m. Paul BUCKINGHAM, Apr. 2, 1843, by Rev. Frederick Woodward 21

BASSETT, John R., m. Mary A. THOMAS, Nov. 12, 1837, by Stephen W. Stebbins 10

Samuel, of Durham, N. Y., m. Mary ANDREW, of Bethany, Sept. 28, 1832, by George F. Peck, J. P. 1

BEACH, Clark, m. Mary SMITH, b. of Woodbridge, Dec. 22, 1833, by Jairus Wilcox 4

Lucy Ann, of Cheshire, m. Joseph O. HUBBILL, of Oxford, Jan. 19,

Page

BEACH, (cont.)
    1851, by Rev. Henry Zell   29
    Oliver T., of Plymouth, m. Mary E. **BALDWIN**, of Bethany, [Nov.]
      1, 1841, by Oliver Hopson   18
BEECHER, Dennis, m. Mary Jane **CLARK**, adopted d. of Nelson **CLARK**,
    Apr. 18, 1852, by Rev. Charles G. Acly, in Christ Church   32
    Enos, m. Lucy L. **RUSSELL**, of Bethany, Mar. 20, 1838, by Rev. John
      H. Rouse, at the Rectory of Christ Church   12
    Guy, m. Sarah An[n] **CHATFIELD**, b. of Bethany, Feb. 22, 1846, by
      D. Potter   24
    Lucy L., of Bethany, m. Jarvis **BRONSON**, of Derby, Nov. 14, 1852,
      by Rev. Henry Zell   34
    Mary G., of Bethany, m. William S. **PIERPOINT**, of Waterbury, Apr.
      25, [1852(?)], by Rev. Henry Zell   32
    Polly Minerva, of Bethany, m. Nelson **NEWTON**, of Woodbridge, Dec.
      16, 1832, by Jairus Wilcox   1
    Roswell, m. Adaline **BURNHAM**, Oct. 21, 1837, by Rev. John H. Rouse,
      at the Rectory of Christ Church   11
    Silvia P., d. of Beri E., of Bethany, m. John H. **SHERWOOD**, of
      Southport (Fairfield), Oct. 13, 1853, by Rev. John M. Guion   36
    William S., of Prospect, m. Mary A. **SPERREY**, of Bethany, Oct. 22,
      1851, by Rev. Henry Zell   31
BENHAM, Washington, of Southbury, m. Adaline A. **JUDD**, of Bethany, Nov.
    29, 1835, by Rev. John B. Kendall   6
BIRD, Samuel J., of Bethleham, m. Caroline F. **HARRISON**, of Bethany,
    Oct. 9, 1851, by F. Harrison, V. D. M.   31
    Theodore, of Bethleham, m. Esther E. **HARRISON**, of Bethany, Oct.
    10, 1849, by Fordis Harrison, V. D. M.   26
BRADLEY, Catharine E., m. Henry A. **SMITH**, Jan. 7, 1838, by Rev. John
    H. Rouse, at the house of Joseph Bradley   12
    Charles, m. Sarah D. **UMBERFIELD**, b. of Bethany, [Jan.] 19, [1847],
      by D. B. Butts   24
    Charry, of Bethany, m. Samuel **FRENCH**, of Waterbury, Mar. 14, 1841,
      by Rev. Isaac Jones   17
    Elizur Tomlinson, m. Juliania Lavinia **TUTTLE**, b. of Bethany, Nov.
      10, 1833, by Oliver Hopson   4
    Emma, of Middlebury, m. Stiles **CLARK**, of Bethany, Apr. 16, 1846,
      by Rev. J. D. Marshall   24
    Joseph William, m. Mary Jane **NEAL**, b. of Woodbridge, Nov. 21,
      1850, by Rev. Henry Zell   28
    Stephen, of Prospect, m. Eliza **GIBBON**, of Waterbury, Jan. 25,
      1839, by Rev. John H. Rouse, at the house of Guy Perkins   14
    Willet, of Courtlandville, N. Y., m. Har[r]i[e]t G. **HOTCHKISS**,
      of Bethany, Aug. 18, 1837, in Christ Church, by Rev. John H.
      Rouse   9
[BROCKET], **BROOCKET**, Harriet, m. James **ELIOT**, b. of Hamden, Aug.
    10, 1851, by Fosdic Harrison, V. D. M.   31
BRONSON, Jarvis, of Derby, m. Lucy L. **BEECHER**, of Bethany, Nov. 14,

Page

COE, (cont.)
    by Rev. John E. Bray   17
COLBY, Lucius H., m. Rosette F. PERKINS, Aug. 30, 1835, by John D.
    Smith   5
COLLINS, Harriette M., m. D. W. RUSSELL, Jan. 19, 1843, by Rev.
    Frederick Woodward   21
    Jeremiah, m. Nora E. LOUNSBURY, b. of Bethany, Mar. 29, 1842, by
    Rev. Isaac Jones   19
CONDY, William C., m. Ellen E. THOMAS, b. of Bethany, Mar. 23, 1851,
    by F. Harrison, V. D. M.   30
CULVER, Miles, of Oxford, m. Laura WHEELER, of Bethany, Oct. 18, 1840,
    by Rev. John E. Bray   17
DAVIS, Ann Elizabeth, of Bethany, m. Andrew JOHNSON, of
    Humphreysville, Apr. 14, 1851, by Rev. Henry Zell   29
DICKERMAN, Wales C., of Hamden, m. Celia TODD, of Bethany, Feb. 8,
    1853, by Rev. Henry Zell, in Christ Church   34
DINGIE, Fanny, of Bethany, m. Amasa BROOKS, of Prospect, Feb. 18, 1850,
    by A. A. Perkins, J. P., at the house of Philo Hotchkiss   26
DOOLITTLE, Reuben, of Hamden, m. Alma HITCHCOCK, of Woodbridge,
    Apr. 17, 1842, by G. F. Peck, J. P.   20
    Samuel J., of Wallingford, m. Hannah FRENCH, of Bethany, Aug. 19,
    1838, by Rev. David Miller   13
    Sylvia M., of Hamden, m. David A. LOUNSBURY, of Bethany, May 6,
    1852, by Rev. Henry Zell   32
    Willis, of Hamden, m. Abigail HITCHCOCK, of Woodbridge, Oct. 8,
    1837, by Rev. John H. Rouse, at the Rectory of Christ Church   11
DOWNS, Charles, m. Sarah DURANT, Aug. 24, 1847, by Reuben Downs, J.P.   25
    Emily G., of Woodbridge, m. David A. BURNHAM, of Bethany, June
    16, 1850, by Rev. Henry Zell   28
    Mary L., of Bethany, m. Orange W. RACE, of Hamden, May 4, 1851,
    by Rev. Henry Zell   30
DRIOR, Albert, m. Harriet A. ALLEN, b. of Bethany, Oct. 27, 1839, by
    Rev. J. H. Rouse, at the Rectory Christ Church   15
DURAND, [see under DURANT]
DURANT, DURAND, Return, m. Henr[i]etta PORTER, b. of Bethany, Oct.
    29, 1837, by Rev. Hershel Sanford   10
    Sarah, m. Charles DOWNS, Aug. 24, 1847, by Reuben Downs, J. P.   25
DURRIE, George Henry, of New Haven, m. Sarah Amelia PERKINS, Sept.
    14, 1841, by Rev. Isaac Jones   18
ELIOT, James, m. Harriet BROOCKET, b. of Hamden, Aug. 10, 1851, by
    Fosdic Harrison, V. D. M.   31
FORD, David, of Westville, m. Sarah M. UMBERFIELD, of Bethany, Oct. 1,
    1843, by Rev. Frederick Woodward   21
    Friend C., of New Haven, m. Mary Jane CHATFIELD, of Bethany, Dec.
    23, 1849, by Rev. Geo[rge] L. Fuller   26
FRENCH, Amey, of Prospect, m. Jared HOTCHKISS, of Bethany, Sept. 13,
    1840, by Rev. Isaac Jones, in Christ Church   16
    George W., of New Haven, m. Ellen S. SCOTT, of Naugatuck, Aug. 2,

FRENCH, (cont.)

1846, by [Rev. Dexter Potter]   24

Hannah, of Bethany, m. Samuel J. DOOLITTLE, of Wallingford, Aug. 19, 1838, by Rev. David Miller   13

Henry, m. Mary WOODING, of Bethany, Nov. 11, 1832, by Tho[ma]s J. Davis   2

Jane, of Bethany, m. Justus PECK, of Cheshire, Apr. 11, 1839, by Rev. John E. Bray   15

John, m. Margaret HOTCHKISS, d. of Spencer, last Sunday in Apr. 1852, by Harris B. Munson, J. P.   33

Samuel, of Waterbury, m. Charry BRADLEY, of Bethany, Mar. 14, 1841, by Rev. Isaac Jones   17

GAYLORD, Benjamin L., of Saymour, m. Martha L. HOTCHKISS, of Bethany, Apr. 20, 1851, by Rev. Senaca Howland, of Humphreysville   32

Harriet, of Hamden, m. Merret HITCHCOCK, of Bethany, Apr. 12, 1835, by Oliver Hopson   5

Jennett, of Hamden, m. John WOODING, Jr., of Bethany, Sept. 11, 1842, by Arch[ibal]d A. Perkins, J. P.   20

GIBBON, Eliza, of Waterbury, m. Stephen BRADLEY, of Prospect, Jan. 25, 1839, by Rev. John H. Rouse, at the house of Guy Perkins   14

GILEAD, William French, of Derby, m. Wealthy Ann HOTCHKISS, of Bethany, Oct. 11, 1840, by Rev. Isaac Jones   16

GOODYEAR, Amasa M., of Waterbury, m. Melinda HINE, of Waterbury, Jan. 31, 1836, by Rev. Oliver Hopson   7

GRISWOLD, Eliza Ann, of Rocky Hill, m. George ASPINWALL, of Mereden, Nov. 20, 1853, by Rev. Alex[ande]r Leadbetter   36

GUNN, Jobahanah E., of Waterbury, m. Rebecca A. HOTCHKISS, of Bethany, Nov. 13, 1836, by Rev. John H. Rouse, at the Rectory of Christ Church   8

HALL, Sarah F., of Bethany, m. Edwin HOPKINS, of Waterbury, [Dec.] 28, 1835, by Rev. John B. Kendall   6

HARRISON, Caroline F., of Bethany, m. Samuel J. BIRD, of Bethleham, Oct. 9, 1851, by F. Harrison, V. D. M.   31

Esther E., of Bethany, m. Theodore BIRD, of Bethleham, Oct. 10, 1849, by Fordis Harrison, V. D. M.   26

HAWLEY, Leverett, m. Mary PECK, b. of Bethany, May. 12, 1833, by Alvan Sperry, J. P.   3

HILL, Henry, of Waterbury, m. Ann D. HINE, of Bethany, Nov. 5, 1832, by Thomas J. Davis   2

HINE, Ann D., of Bethany, m. Henry HILL, of Waterbury, Nov. 5, 1832, by Thomas J. Davis   2

Bennet, of Bethany, m. Rhoda WOODING, of Oxford, Apr. 30, 1836, by Rev. Hershel Sanford   7

Melinda, m. Amasa M. GOODYEAR, b. of Waterbury, Jan. 31, 1836, by Rev. Oliver Hopson   7

Sally, of Bethany, m. Enoch NEWTON, of Woodbridge, Nov. 16, 1834, by John A. Coe, J. P.   4

HISCOX, [see also HITCHCOCK], Elizur, of Woodbridge, m. Mary C.

Page

HISCOX, (cont.)

HOTCHKISS, of Bethany, Dec. 29, 1848, by Ira H. Smith   25

HITCHCOCK, [see also **HISCOX**], Abigail, of Woodbridge, m. Willis

DOOLITTLE, of Hamden, Oct. 8, 1837, by Rev. John H. Rouse, at

the Rectory of Christ Church   11

Allen C., m. Lucy L. **THOMAS,** Sept. 5, 1843, by Jason W. Bradley, J.P.   21

Alma, of Woodbridge, m. Reuben **DOOLITTLE,** of Hamden, Apr. 17,

1842, by G. F. Peck, J. P.   20

Betsey Ann, of Bethany, m. Alva K. **MUNSON,** of Hamden, Oct. 16,

1853, by Rev. Alex[ande]r Leadbetter   36

Edmund B. W., m. Angeline **TERREL,** Jan. 21, 1838, by Rev. John H.

Rouse, at the Rectory of Christ Church   12

Enos, of Hamden, m. Ruth Ann **UMBERFIELD,** of Bethany, Dec. 20,

1832, by Jairus Wilcox   2

Harriet, m. Harris **HOTCHKISS,** b. of Prospect, Dec. 27, 1850, by

F. Harrison, V. D. M.   28

Lucinda, m. Harris **HOTCHKISS,** b. of Prospect, [Sept.] 1, 1844,

by D. B. Butts   22

Merret, of Bethany, m. Harriet **GAYLORD,** of Hamden, Apr. 12, 1835,

by Oliver Hopson   5

Orrin, m. Althea **PERKINS,** b. of Bethany, June 30, 1844, by

Arch[ibal]d A. Perkins, J. P.   22

Sarah L., of Bethany, m. Jared **SPERRY,** of Woodbridge, May 26, 1851,

by F. Harrison, V. D. M.   30

HOADLEY, Augusta A., of Salem, m. Isaac **COE,** of Bethany, Apr. 18, 1841,

by Rev. John E. Bray   17

HOPKINS, Edwin, of Waterbury, m. Sarah F. **HALL,** of Bethany, [Dec.] 28,

1835, by Rev. John B. Kendall   6

HOTCHKISS, Abigail, of Prospect, m. Stephen **HOTCHKISS,** Jr., of Bethany

Sept. 10, 1837, by Rev. John H. House, at the Rectory of Christ

Church   10

Adna, m. Elizabeth **PERKINS,** b. of Bethany, Dec. 25, 1846, by

[Rev. Dexter Potter]   24

Beecher D., m. Betsey **PERKINS,** b. of Bethany, Oct. 6, 1839, by Rev.

John H. Rouse, in Christ Church   15

Charlotte, m. Noyes **NICHOL,** b. of Waterbury, Sept. 6, 1840, by Rev.

Hershel Sanford   16

Eliza A., of Bethany, m. Eugene D. **SHARP,** of Newtown, Nov. 12,

1837, by Rev. John E. Bray   10

George m. Laura **SPERRY,** Apr. 4, 1841, by Rev. Isaac Jones   17

Harpin H., m. Charlotte E. **ALLING,** b. of Bethany, Feb. 15, 1852,

by Rev. Henry Zell, at the house of Albert Hoadley   31

Harriet, of Bethany, m. Lewis **WOODIN,** of Prospect, [Nov.] 5, [1845],

by Rev. D. B. Butts   23

Har[r]i[e]t G., of Bethany, m. Willet **BRADLEY,** of Courtlandville,

N. Y., Aug. 18, 1837, by Rev. John H. Rouse, in Christ Church   9

Harris, m. Lucinda **HITCHCOCK,** b. of Prospect, [Sept.] 1, 1844,

by D. B. Butts   22

HOTCHKISS, (cont.)

Harris, m. Harriet **HITCHCOCK**, b. of Prospect, Dec. 27, 1850, by
    F. Harrison, V. D. M.   28

Jairus B., m. Eunice **RUSSELL**, b. of Bethany, Jan. 13, 1839, by Rev.
    John H. Rouse, at the Rectory of Christ Church   14

Jared, of Bethany, m. Amey **FRENCH**, of Prospect, Sept. 13, 1840,
    by Rev. Isaac Jones, in Christ Church   16

Jesse, m. Caroline **LOUNSBURY**, b. of Bethany, Sept. 26, 1839, by
    Rev. John H. Rouse, at the Rectory of Christ Church   15

Margaret, d. of Spencer, m. John **FRENCH**, last Sunday in Apr., 1852,
    by Harris B. Munson, J. P.   33

Martha L. of Bethany, m. Benjamin L. **GAYLORD**, of Seymour, Apr.
    20, 1851, by Rev. Senaca Howland, of Humphreysville   32

Mary C., of Bethany, m. Elizur **HISCOX**, of Woodbridge, Dec. 29,
    1848, by Ira H. Smith   25

Rebecca, m. Alonzo **SPERRY**, Mar. 14, 1838, by Rev. John H. Rouse,
    at the Rectory of Christ Church   12

Rebecca A., of Bethany, m. Jobahanah E. **GUNN**, of Waterbury, Nov.
    13, 1836, by Rev. John H. Rouse, at the Rectory of Christ Church   8

Rhoda, of Granville, m. Spencer **HOTCHKISS**, of Bethany, Dec. 9,
    1832, by Prince Hawes   2

Spencer, of Bethany, m. Rhoda **HOTCHKISS**, of Granville, Dec. 9,
    1832, by Prince Hawes   2

Stephen, Jr., of Bethany, m. Abigail **HOTCHKISS**, of Prospect,
    Sept. 10, 1837, by Rev. John H. House, at the Rectory of Christ
    Church   10

Wealthy Ann, of Bethany, m. William French **GILEAD**, of Derby, Oct.
    11, 1840, by Rev. Isaac Jones   16

HUBBILL, Joseph O., of Oxford, m. Lucy Ann **BEACH**, of Cheshire, Jan. 19,
    1851, by Rev. Henry Zell   29

HUBBURT, Charlotte E., of Waterbury, m. Jacob W. **WILCOX**, of New
    Haven, Nov. 18, 1852, by Rev. Henry Zell   34

HUGHES, William A., of Humphreysville, m. Sarah **WILCOX**, of Bethany,
    Oct. 18, 1846, by Rev. Sylvester Smith   23

HUNGERFORD, Janette, Mrs., m. Navel **LOUNSBURY**, b. of Bethany, Feb.
    12, 1837, by Rev. John H. Rouse, at the house of A. A. Perkins   9

JOHNSON, Andrew, of Humphreysville, m. Ann Elizabeth **DAVIS**, of
    Bethany, Apr. 14, 1851, by Rev. Henry Zell   29

Ann, m. George **SANFORD**, b. of Bethany, Nov. 7, 1852, by Miles
    French, J. P.   33

Henry N., of Westville, m. Sylvia **NORTHROP**, of Woodbridge, Apr.
    17, 1853, by Rev. Henry Zell   35

Jarvis, m. Mariah **STRONG**, b. of Waterbury, Aug. 8, 1832, by Rev.
    Samuel Potter   1

JUDD, Adaline A., of Bethany, m. Washington **BENHAM**, of Southbury, Nov.
    29, 1835, by Rev. John B. Kendall   6

Sarah E., m. Benjamin S. **CHATFIELD**, b. of Bethany, Dec. 11,
    [1848], by Rev. Henry Zell   27

NORTHROP, (cont.)

George, of Bethany, m. Laura E. TRUESDALE, of Humphreysville, July
29, 1849, by [Rev. Henry Zell]   27

Sylvia, of Woodbridge, m. Henry N. JOHNSON, of Westville, Apr. 17,
1853, by Rev. Henry Zell   35

NORTON, Norman, of Goshen, m. Lucy TUTTLE, of Bethany, Dec. 23,
1832, by Tho[ma]s J. Davis   2

OSBORN, George, m. Cynthia BROOKS, Jan. 11, 1846, by Edwin
Buckingham, J. P.   23

Sophia A., m. Charles PERKINS, Mar. 3, 1833, by Tho[ma]s J. Davis   3

PARDEE, Edwin, of Orange, m. Caroline PRIME, of Bethany, May 14, 1835,
by Rev. John D. Smith   5

PECK, Anon B., m. Minerva NETTLETON, b. of Bethany, Sept. 2, 1837, by
Rev. John H. Rouse, at the Rectory of Christ Church   9

Justus, of Cheshire, m. Jane FRENCH, of Bethany, Apr. 11, 1839,
by Rev. John E. Bray   15

Mary, m. Leverett HAWLEY, b. of Bethany, May 12, 1833, by Alvan
Sperry, J. P.   3

PERKINS, Althea, m. Orrin HITCHCOCK, b. of Bethany, June 30, 1844, by
Arch[ibal]d A. Perkins, J. P.   22

Betsey, m. Beecher D. HOTCHKISS, b. of Bethany, Oct. 6, 1839, by
Rev. John H. Rouse, in Christ Church   15

Charles, of Bethany, m. Sophia A. OSBORN, Mar. 3, 1833, by
Tho[ma]s J. Davis   3

Charles, of Bethany, m. Mary Ann MERIAM, of Waterbury, Dec. 24,
1838, by Rev. John H. Rouse, at the Rectory of Christ Church   14

Charles C., m. Jane B. PERKINS, Mar. 20, 1853, by Rev. Henry Zell
in Christ Church   35

Elizabeth, m. Adna HOTCHKISS, b. of Bethany, Dec. 25, 1846, by
[Rev. Dexter Potter]   24

Huldah, of Bethany, m. Allen B. L. MYERS, of Auburn, N. Y., Jan.
1, 1838, by Rev. John H. Rouse, in Christ Church   11

Isaac, m. Emily TODD, b. of Bethany, Dec. 25, 1846, by [Rev.
Dexter Potter]   25

Jane B., m. Charles C. PERKINS, Mar. 20, 1853, by Rev. Henry
Zell, in Christ Church   35

Maria, of Bethany, m. John TUCKER, of New Haven, Sept. 16, 1838,
by Rev. John H. Rouse, at the house of George Hoadley   13

Rosette F., m. Lucius H. COLBY, Aug. 30, 1835, by John D. Smith   5

Sarah Amelia, m. George Henry DURRIL, of New Haven, Sept. 14,
1841, by Rev. Isaac Jones   18

Sarah M., of Woodbridge, m. Edwin ROBINSON, of Bethany, Nov. 15,
1835, by Rev. John B. Kendall   6

Wales F., m. Eliza E. TOLLES, b. of Bethany, Nov. 7, 1841, by
Rev. Isaac Jones   19

Wales T., of Bethany, m. Maria L. CLARK, of Woodbridge, Oct. 9,
[1848], by Rev. Henry Zell   27

PHELPS, Lucy, of Bethany, m. Akon TALMAGE, of Mereden, Mar. 16,

SMITH, (cont.)

Eveline, m. Edwin **TERRILL,** b. of Naugatuck, Sept. 16, [1848], by
Rev. Henry Zell   27

Henry A., m. Catharine E. **BRADLEY,** of Bethany, Jan. 7, 1838, by
Rev. John H. Rouse, at the house of Joseph Bradley   12

Lewis, of Woodbridge, m. Delia **ROBINSON,** of Bethany, Dec. 9, 1833,
by Jairus Wilcox   4

Mary, m. Clark **BEACH,** b. of Woodbridge, Dec. 22, 1833, by Jairus
Wilcox   4

SPERRY, SPERREY, Alonzo, m. Rebecca **HOTCHKISS,** Mar. 14, 1838, by
Rev. John H. Rouse, at the Rectory of Christ Church   12

Edson, of Bethany, m. Mrs. Roselinda **WHITING,** of Cornwall, Feb. 24,
1836, by Rev. John B. Kendall   7

Eunice, of Bethany, m. Dwight **BACON,** of Simsbury, Sept. 18, 1836,
by Sylvester Smith   7

Harriet Jane, of Bethany, m. John M. **SPERRY,** of Woodbridge, Nov.
11, [1849], by Rev. Henry Zell   27

Jared, of Woodbridge, m. Sarah L. **HITCHCOCK,** of Bethany, May 26,
1851, by F. Harrison, V. D. M.   30

John M., of Woodbridge, m. Harriet Jane **SPERRY,** of Bethany, Nov.
11, [1849], by Rev. Henry Zell   27

Julia E., of Bethany, m. Charles A. **SMITH,** of Orange, Oct. 21,
[1849], by Rev. Henry Zell   27

Laura, m. George **HOTCHKISS,** Apr. 4, 1841, by Rev. Isaac Jones   17

Martha, of Bethany, m. George H. **ALLING,** of Orange, May 17, 1848,
by Rev. Henry Zell   27

Mary A., m. Sidney B. **SPERRY,** b. of Woodbridge, June 7, 1835, by
Rev. John B. Kendall   5

Mary A., of Bethany, m. William S. **BEECHER,** of Prospect, Oct. 22,
1851, by Rev. Henry Zell   31

Rebeckah E., of Bethany, m. Cornelius L. **ALLING,** of New Haven,
Apr. 20, 1843, by Rev. Henry Townsend, of New Haven   22

Sidney B., m. Mary A. **SPERRY,** b. of Woodbridge, June 7, 1835, by
Rev. John B. Kendall   5

STRONG, Mariah, m. Jarvis **JOHNSON,** b. of Waterbury, Aug. 8, 1832, by
Rev. Samuel Potter   1

TALMAGE, Akon, of Mereden, m. Lucy **PHELPS,** of Bethany, Mar. 16,
1834, by Adonijah French, J. P.   3

Jason, of Oxford, m. Marietta **LINES,** of Bethany, Mar. 17, 1844,
by A. A. Perkins, J. P.   21

Orrin, of Oxford, m. Athe **ALLEN,** of Cheshire, Mar. 19, 1851, by
Rev. S. Howland, of Humphreysville   30

TERRILL, TERREL, TERRELL, TYRRELL, Almira, m. Isaac Treat
CLARK, b. of Bethany, Sept. 14, 1833, by Jairus Wilcox   3

Angeline, m. Edmund B. W. **HITCHCOCK,** Jan. 21, 1838, by Rev. John
H. Rouse, at the Rectory of Christ Church   12

Edwin, m. Eveline **SMITH,** b. of Naugatuck, Sept. 16, [1848], by
Rev. Henry Zell   27

Page

TERRILL, TERREL, TERRELL, TYRRELL, (cont.)

Elizabeth, of Bethany, m. Nathaniel Langdon PROCTER, of Woodbury,
June 16, 1850, by Rev. Henry Zell   27

THOMAS, Charles, of Prospect, m. Maranda KIMBALL, of Bethany, Nov. 3,
1835, by Rev. John B. Kendall   6

Daniel H., m. Sarah A. SACKET, b. of Bethany, Jan. 20, 1851, by
Sidney Sperry, J. P.   29

Elizabeth L., m. Lucius RUSSELL, b. of Bethany, Sept. 20, 1841,
by Rev. Isaac Jones, in Christ Church   18

Ellen E., m. William O. CONDY, b. of Bethany, Mar. 23, 1851, by
F. Harrison, V. D. M.   30

Lucy L., m. Allen C. HITCHCOCK, Sept. 5, 1843, by Jason W.
Bradley, J. P.   21

Mary A., m. John R. BASSETT, Nov. 12, 1837, by Stephen W. Stebbins   10

Miles D., of Bethany, m. Marietta M. WEBSTER, of Waterbury, July
29, 1852, by Rev. Alex[ande]r Leadbetter. Int. Pub.   33

TODD, Celia, of Bethany, m. Wales C. DICKERMAN, of Hamden, Feb. 8,
1853, by Rev. Henry Zell, in Christ Church   34

Emily, m. Isaac PERKINS, b. of Bethany, Dec. 25, 1846, by [Rev.
Dexter Potter]   25

Samuel, of North Haven, m. Pamelia J. CHATFIELD, of Bethany, Nov.
7, 1847, by Rev. D. Potter   25

William, of Hamden, m. Harriet LOUNSBURY, of Bethany, Nov. 28,
1832, by Jairus Wilcox   1

TOLLES, Eliza E., m. Wales F. PERKINS, b. of Bethany, Nov. 7, 1841, by
Rev. Isaac Jones   19

TRUESDALE, Laura E., of Humphreysville, m. George NORTHROP, of
Bethany, July 29, 1849, by [Rev. Henry Zell]   27

TUCKER, John, of New Haven, m. Maria PERKINS, of Bethany, Sept. 16,
1838, by Rev. John H. Rouse, at the house of George Hoadley   13

TUTTLE, , Charry S., m. Noyes WHEELER, b. of Bethany, Oct. 22, [1848],
by Rev. Henry Zell   27

Juliania Lavinia, m. Elizur Tomlinson BRADLEY, b. of Bethany,
Nov. 10, 1833, by Oliver Hopson   4

Lucy, of Bethany, m. Norman NORTON, of Goshen, Dec. 23, 1832, by
Tho[ma]s J. Davis   2

Phebe, of Derby, m. Charles NORMAN, of Bridgeport, Jan. 21, 1835,
by Rev. John D. Smith, of Humphreyville   4

Wooster, of Prospect, m. Betsey H. RUSSELL, of New Haven, Feb. 19,
1846, by A. A. Perkins, J. P.   23

UMBERFIELD, Ruth Ann, of Bethany, m. Enos HITCHCOCK, of Hamden,
Dec. 20, 1832, Jairus Wilcox   2

Sarah D., m. Charles BRADLEY, b. of Bethany, [Jan.] 19, [1847],
by D. B. Butts   24

Sarah M., of Bethany, m. David FORD, of Westville, Oct. 1, 1843,
by Rev. Frederick Woodward   21

WAKELEE, Eli H., of Derby, m. Eunice A. CHATFIELD, of Bethany, Jan.
10, 1853, by Rev. Henry Zell, in Christ Church   35

Page

WARNER, Alonzo, of Hamden, m. Ruth CHATFIELD, of Bethany, Dec. 4,
1836, by Rev. John H. Rouse, at the Rectory of Christ Church · · · · · 8

WEBSTER, Marietta M., of Waterbury, m. Miles D. THOMAS, of Bethany,
July 29, 1852, by Rev. Alex[ande]r Leadbetter, Int. Pub. · · · · · 33

WHEELER, Laura, of Bethany, m. Miles CULVER, of Oxford, Oct. 18, 1840,
by Rev. John E. Bray · · · · · 17

Noyes, m. Charry S. TUTTLE, b. of Bethany, Oct. 22. [1848], by
Rev. Henry Zell · · · · · 27

WHITING, Roselinda, Mrs., of Cornwall, m. Edson SPERRY, of Bethany,
Feb. 24, 1836, by Rev. John B. Kendall · · · · · 7

WILCOX, Jacob W., of New Haven, m. Charlotte E. HUBBURT, of
Waterbury, Nov. 18, 1852, by Rev. Henry Zell · · · · · 34

Sarah, of Bethany, m. William A. HUGHES, of Humphreysville, Oct.
18, 1845, by Rev. Sylvester Smith · · · · · 23

WILLIAMS, Amzi, of Prospect, m. Charlotte ANDREWS, of Bethany, Aug.
6, 1842, by Rev. Ebenezer O. Beers. Witnesses: Kneeland Downs,
E. O. Beers · · · · · 19

WOODING, WOODIN, Elizabeth M., of Bethany, m. Amasa B. BROOKS,
of Cheshire, May 9, 1852, by Rev. Henry Zell, in Christ Church · · · · · 33

John, Jr., of Bethany, m. Jennett GAYLORD, of Hamden, Sept. 11,
1842, by Arch[ibal]d A. Perkins, J. P. · · · · · 20

Lewis, of Prospect, m. Harriet HOTCHKISS, of Bethany, [Nov.] 5,
[1845], by Rev. D. B. Butts · · · · · 23

Mary, m. Henry FRENCH, Nov. 11, 1832, by Tho[ma]s J. Davis · · · · · 2

Mira, of Bethany, m. Verus CANDEE, of Naugatuck, Apr. 18, 1851,
by Rev. Henry Zell · · · · · 29

Rhoda, of Oxford, m. Bennet HINE, of Bethany, Apr. 20, 1836, by
Rev. Hershel Sanford · · · · · 7

Stephen, m. Mrs. Alice KIMBALL, b. of Bethany, Sept. 16, 1832,
by Rev. John H. Rouse, at the house of Eber Lines · · · · · 13

WOODRUFF, George L., of Woodbridge, m. Margaret BURNHAM, of
Bethany, Nov. 10, 1850, by Rev. Henry Zell · · · · · 28

BETHLEHEM VITAL RECORDS
1787 - 1851

Page

ALLEN, (cont.)

Nancy S., of Bethlem, m. Dr. E. BARNUM, of New Fairfield, Nov. 29,
1852, by Rev. A. G. Loomis   75

Noble, [s. Amos & 2nd w. [   ]], b. June 24, 1796   31

Polly, [d, Samuel], b. Sept. 16, 1795   4

Polly, m. Nathan CRANE, b. of Bethlem, Sept. 4, 1844, by Rev.
Fosdic Harrison   66

Polly E., of Bethlem, m. Truman M. JOHNSON, of Woodbury, Sept.
29, 1825, by Sturges Gilbert   44

Ruby, m. Edward COAN, Mar. 8, 1824, by David Bird, J. P.   41

Ruth, [d. Samuel], b. Feb. 28, 1778   4

Ruth, m. Carr WATSON, b. of Bethlem, Jan. 29, 1851, by Rev. J. S.
Covill   73

Samuel, Jr., [s. Samuel], b. Sept. 12, 1780   4

Samuel, m. Rosetta M. HAWLEY, b. of Bethlem, Feb. 28, 1849, by
Rev. F. Harrison   71

Sheldon, [s. Samuel], b. Mar. 3, 1793   4

Susan, of Bethleham, m. Jasper P. BREWSTER, of Cornwall, Oct.
18, 1843, by Rev. F. Harrison   64

Willian H., m. Lavinia A. MOSS, b. of Bethlem, May 12, 1844,
by Rev. Jonathan Coe, 2nd   66

AMBLER, Betsey, m. Lebbius CAMP, Mar. 25, 1799   2

Betsey T., [d. Billy & Elizabeth], b. June 15, 1802   28

Betsey T., of Bethlem, m. David C. HATCH, of New Preston, Apr. 8,
1832, by P. Couch   53

Billy, m. Elizabeth CAMP, Nov. 4, 1790   3

Charles, [s. Billy & Elizabeth], b. Mar. 17, 1799   3

Charlotte, d. David & Ruth, b. Nov. 12, 1797   3

Cynthia A., [d. Billy & Elizabeth], b. May 19, 1806   28

Cynthia A., of Bethlem, m. Chester HALL, of Bridgewater, N. Y.,
Nov. 15, 1831, by P. Couch   53

David, Jr., m. Ruth THOMPSON, Nov. 15, 1796   3

Dorcas, m. Laurens HULL, Oct. 3, 1803, by Rev. Azel Barkus   20

Joseph, [s. Billy & Elizabeth], b. Nov. 6, 1796   3

Joseph, of Bethlem, m. Eunice E. MASON, of Lebanon, Sept. 19,
[1832], by Paul Couch   54

Olive, d. Billy [& Elizabeth], b. Sept. 4, 1791; d. May 21, 1793   3

Polly, [d. Billy & Elizabeth], b. Nov. 29, 1795   3

Sally, m. William DURAND, Feb. 20, 1805   14

Selina, [d. Billy & Elizabeth], b. May 26, 1794; d. Aug. 19, 1796   3

Susan W., [d. Billy & Elizabeth], b. June 11, 1804   28

Susan W., m. J. Rollin CHURCH, Sept. 14, 1825, by Joseph E. Camp   44

AMES, W[illia]m B., of Litchfield, m. Clarissa L. ALLEN, of Bethleham,
May 3, 1848, by Rev. F. Harrison   70

ANDREWS, [see also ANDRUS], John P., of Bethleham, m. Harriet E.
BROWN, of Washington, Feb. 11, 1840, by Rev. Fosdic Harrison   60

Thomas, m. Susan E. BISHOP, b. of Bethlem, Mar. 9, 1842, by Rev.
Fosdic Harrison   62

Page

ANDREWS, (cont.)

William, of Watertown, m. Elizabeth **HUBBARD**, of Bethlem. July 20,
1825, by Rev. Stephen Mason, of Washington   44

ANDRUS, [see also **ANDREWS**], George W., m. Fanny B. **FOSTER**, b. of
Bethlem, Apr. 9, 1851, by Rev. J. S. Covill   73

ATWOOD, Adelia Matilda, of Bethlem, m. Charles **NORTON**, of Berlin, May
22, 1825, by Darius O. Griswold   43

Chauncey, of Woodbury, m. Martha **ATWOOD**, of Bethlem, Apr. 5,
1843, by Rev. I. H. Tuttle   65

Concurrance, d. [John & Concurrance], b. Aug. 10, 1779   25

Concurrance, w. John, d. Oct. 24, 1779   25

Concurrance, [d. John & Concurrance], d. June 28, 1786   25

Frank S., of Woodbury, m. Amelia **SCOTT**, of Bethlem, May 19, 1833,
by P. Couch   54

George M., of Watertown, m. Polly M. **SPENCER**, of Bethleham, Apr.
2, 1847, by Rev. F. Harrison   69

George N., m. Elizabeth **SMITH**, b. of Bethleham, Dec. 8, 1847, by
Rev. Philo R. Hurd, of Watertown   69

Hawkins, m. Irene **JUDSON**, Oct. 23, 1824, by John Langdon   42

Henry C., of Bristol, m. Hannah W. **THOMAS**, of Bethleham, Sept. 19,
1847, by Rev. William H. Frisbie   68

James, s. [John & Concurrance], b. Dec. 20, 1775   25

John, b. Mar. 19, 1749; m. Concurrance **HARD**, Aug. 29, 1770   25

John, m. Martha **HUBBARD**, wid. Joseph **FREEMAN**, Aug. 30, 1781   25

Josiah, of Bethlem, m. Jennett **MATTOON**, of Wallingford, Nov. 29,
1849, by Rev. J. S. Covell   72

Lucy, d. [John & Concurrance], b. June 10, 1771   25

Martha, d. May 5, 1807   25

Martha, of Bethlem, m. Chauncey **ATWOOD**, of Woodbury, Apr. 5,
1843, by Rev. I. H. Tuttle   65

Michael, [s. John & Concurrance], b. Oct. 9, 1777   25

Minerva, [d. John & Martha], b. Mar. 25, 1787   25

Noble, of Woodbury, m. Alma E. **HAWLEY**, of Bethlem, Mar. 16, 1851,
by Rev. J. S. Covill   73

Philo, s. [John & Marth], b. May 19, 1782   25

Polly Matilda, d.[John & Martha], b. June 2, 1785   25

Ruth Anne, d. [John & Martha], b. Nov. 6, 1783   25

Ruth Ann, m. Chauncey **HALL**, Dec. 5, 1804   11

Truman, s. [John & Concurrance], b. July 27, 1772   25

Washington Harry, of Woodbury, m. Maria **STONE**, of Bethlem, Nov. 3,
1822, by John Langdon   40

Wealthy Ann, of Bethlem, m. Milo **STARKS**, of Torrington, July 13,
1852, by Arvil Morris, J. P.   75

AVIAIL, Eliza S., of Bethlem, m. William **CHURCHILL**, of Stockbridge,
Mass., May 8, 1832, by Paul Couch   53

John, m. Caroline **PRINDLE**, b. of Bethlem, Jan. 3, 1827, by Rev.
Sturges Gilbert, of Woodbury   47

BACKUS, Albert, s. [Azel & Melecent], b. Nov. 24, 1796   3

Page

BLOSS, (cont.)

Nancy, [d. Francis & Esther], b. Aug. 29, 1790; d. Mar. 16, 1793 — 14

Nehemiah S., s. C. A. & Nancy, b. Feb. 20, 1828 — Z

Nelly, [d. Francis & Esther], b. June 9, 1785 — 14

Philena, [d. Francis & Esther], b. Jan. 13, 1773 — 14

Polly A., m. Gideon **ALLEN**, b. of Bethlehem, [   ], by
Rev. Sturges Gilbert, of Woodbury. Recorded Nov. 20, 1821 — 39

Polly Althy, [d. Capt. Samuel & Deborah], b. Jan. 8, 1801 — 10

Russell Burhrod(?), [s. Capt. Samuel & Deborah], b. Sept. 7, 1796 — 10

Ruth M., of Bethlehem, m. Reuben **MITCHELL**, Jr., of Woodbury,
[   ], by Rev. Sturges Gilbert, of Woodbury. Recorded Nov. 20,
1821 — 39

Ruth Maria, [d. Capt. Samuel & Deborah], b. July 15, 1798 — 10

Samuel, [s. Francis & Esther], b. Jan. 30, 1769 — 14

Samuel L., s. Charles A. & Nancy, b. July 1, 1820 — 37

Simeon, [s. Francis & Esther], b. May 8, 1770; d. May 1, 1773 — 14

Susan E., of Bethlem, m. Nathan **PEARCE**, of Woodbury, Nov. 5, 1834,
by Grove L. Brownel — 56

Susan Elvira, d. Capt. Samuel & Deborah, b. Nov. 16, 1815 — 37

Thomson, s. [Francis & Esther], b. June 16, 1776 — 14

BOOTH, Silas L., of Middlebury, m. Caroline **BALDWIN**, of Bethlem, Jan.
4, 1849, by Rev. F. Harrison — 70

BOSTWICK, Charlotte, m. Henry **THOMPSON**, Sept. 5, 1798 — 29a

BOTSFORD, Betsey M., d. [Samuel], b. May 9, 1807 — 24

Lyman, s. Samuel, b. Feb. 6, 1806 — 24

BOYLES, Clarinda, had s. Joseph, b. Apr. 4, 1787 — 2

Joseph, s. Clarinda, b. Apr. 4, 1787 — 2

BRACE, Lucy, m. Elezur **GREEN**, 2nd, Oct. 11, 1778 — 3

BRADFORD, James F., m. Catharine **CATLIN**, b. of Bethlem, on eve of Dec.
23, 1830, by P. Couch — 52

BREED, Joshua R., m. Sarah M. **SEYMOUR**, b. of Tolland, Mass., Nov. 27,
1828, by Rev. Henry Robinson, of Litchfield — 49

BREWSTER, Jasper P., of Cornwall, m. Susan **ALLEN**, of Bethleham, Oct.
18, 1843, by Rev. F. Harrison — 64

BRINSMADE, Lavinia, b. Dec. 24, 1770; m. John **LOUNSBURY**, Nov. 24,
1790 — 27

BRISTOL, Harriet, of Bethlem, m. Andrew **MARTIN**, late of Woodbury,
June 11, 1845, by Rev. Fosdic Harrison — 67

Harriet A., [d. Henry & Isabella], b. Aug. 2, 1814 — Z

Henry, [s. Henry & Isabella], b. Sept. 1, 1822 — Z

Henry P., b. Oct. 16, 1784 — Z

Isabella, b. Feb. 1, 1780 — Z

John M., [s. Henry & Isabella], b. June 1, 1818 — Z

Nathan P., [s. Henry & Isabella], b. Dec. 22, 1811 — Z

William C., [s. Henry & Isabella], b. Sept. 16, 1816 — Z

BROOKS, Alfred, s. Joseph & Lucy, b. Aug. 4, 1801 — 6

Beryntha, d. Joseph & Lucy, b. Oct. 14, 1788; d. Nov. 29, 1793 — 2

Berintha, d. Joseph & Lucy, b. Apr. 30, 1809 — 32

Page

BROOKS, (cont.)

Caroline, d. Joseph & Lucy, b. Dec. 9, 1794 — 2

Edwin, s. Joseph & Lucy, b. Feb. 15, 1804 — 13

Horatio, s. Joseph & Lucy, b. May 13, 1806 — 13

Joseph, m. Lucy **CHURCH,** Apr. 10 , 1788 — 20

Joshua C., s. Joseph & Lucy, b. Nov. 13, 1791; d. May 17, 1794 — 2

Maria, d. Joseph & Lucy, b. May 8, 1797 — 2

Martha, b. Feb. 20, 1752 — 25

Sophia, d. Joseph & Lucy, b. Sept. 5, 1799 — 2

BROWN, Anna, eldest d. [David & Philena], b. Dec. 10, 1768 — 1

Anna E., m. Leverett P. **JUDD,** b. of Bethleham, Sept. 12, 1842,
by Rev. Fosdic Harrison — 63

David, m. Philena **GARNSEY,** June 2, 1768 — 1

Elizabeth, of Litchfield, m. Andrew A. **FRENCH,** of Washington,
Mar. 15, 1841, by Rev. Fosdic Harrison — 61

Emily, m. George T. **BLOSS,** b. of Bethlem, Nov. 16, 1836, by
Rev. Fosdic Harrison — 57

Garret Garnsey, 2nd s. [David & Philena], b. Feb. 13, 1784 — 1

Garret Garnsey, s. David & Philena, b. Feb. 13, 1785 — 13

Harold, eldest s. [David & Philena], b. Nov. 15, 1782 — 1

Harriet, 6th d. [David & Philena], b. Jan. 3, 1780 — 1

Harriet A., of Bethlem, m. George P. **SHERMAN,** of Woodbury, July 2,
1835, by Rev. Fosdic Harrison — 58

Harriet E., of Washington, m. John P. **ANDREWS,** of Bethleham,
Feb. 11, 1840, by Rev. Fosdic Harrison — 60

Huldah M., m. Leverett P. **JUDD,** of Bethleham, Aug. 26, 1849, by
Rev. J. S. Covell — 71

Mary, m. Henry W. **PECK,** b. of Bethlem, June 4, 1845, by Rev.
Fosdic Harrison — 67

Olive, 4th d. [David & Philena], b. Mar. 4, 1775; d. Nov. 7, 1797 — 1

Philena, 2nd, d. [David & Philena], b. Oct. 8, 1770 — 1

Polly, 3rd d. [David & Philena], b. Jan. 23, 1773 — 1

Sally, 5th d. [David & Philena], b. Oct. 22, 1777 — 1

Sarah E., of Bethleham, m. Leonard A. **KELLEY,** of Goshen, Oct. 11,
1848, by Rev. J. S. Covill — 70

BROWNSON, Abigail, d. Abraham & Abigail, b. Mar. 11, 1772 — 1

Abraham, m. Abigail **HAWLEY,** Sept. 4, 1760 — 20

Abraham, s. Abraham & Abigail, b. July 17, 1767 — 1

Abraham, d. July 16, 1802 — 30

Israel, s. Abraham & Abigail, b. Mar. 19, 1777 — 1

Jedidiah, s. Abraham & Abigail, b. Nov. 16, 1761 — 1

John, s. Abraham & Abigail, b. Dec. 10, 1780; d. Oct. 31, 1782 — 1

Myer H., m. Sarah **MERWIN,** Oct. 24, 1793 — 20

Myar Hawley, s. Abraham & Abigail, b. Apr. 29, 1764 — 1

[BUNNELL], BUNNEL, Isaac A., m. Sabra **TOMPKINS,** b. of Harwinton,
Feb. 24, 1830, by Paul Couch — 51

Matilda, m. Henry **STONE,** of Litchfield, Feb. 13, 1842, by Rev.
George L. Foote — 63

Page

BURRITT, [see also BARRITT], Wilson*, of Stratford, m. Abigail CRANE,
   of Bethlem, Nov. 28, 1849, by Rev. George P. Prudden   *("Wilson
   BENNETT" in Cothren's Hist.)   72
BURTON, Daniel Willcox, s. Nathan, Jr. & Sarah, b. Dec. 6, 1822   Y
   Elam Beardsley, s. Daniel B. & Zeruiah, b. Sept. 20, 1822   38
   Henry Ludlow, [s. Nathan, Jr. & Sarah], b. Dec. 28, 1819; d.
      July 21, 1820   37
   Henry Ludlow, 2nd, [s. Nathan, Jr. & Sarah], b. Feb. 1, 1821   37
   Nancy Abia, d. Nathan, Jr. & Sarah, b. Aug. 28, 1826   Y
   Nathan, Jr., b. Aug. 5, 1780; m. Sarah FENN, of Plymouth, July 4,
      1816, by Rev. Luther Hart, of Plymouth   37
   Nathan F., d. Aug. 9, 1886, in Plymouth, Ill.   37
   Nathan Fenn, [s. Nathan, Jr. & Sarah], b. Oct. 19, 1818   37
   Rebecca Beardsley, d. Nathan, Jr. & Sarah, b. Mar. 28, 1824   Y
   Sarah, [d. Nathan, Jr. & Sarah], b. Sept. 22, 1817   37
   Sarah, w. Nathan, Sr., d. Mar. 28, 1822, ae 72   38
BUTLER, Samuel M., of Erie Cty., N. Y., m. Julia An[n] INGERSOLL,
   of Bethlem, Nov. 18, 1839, by Rev. Fosdic Harrison   60
CABLES, Irene, of Warren, m. Washington SEELEY, of Bethlem, Jan. 25,
   1852, by A. G. Loomis   74
CADY, Aug, m. Caroline TYRREL, July 3, 1842, by Rev. Isaac H. Tuttle   63
CAM, Betsey, m. George CHATFIELD, Dec. 20, 1827, b. of Bethlem, by
   Benjamin F. Stanton   48
   Catharine, of Bethlem, m. Nelson WESTON, of Derby, Sept. 30,
      1838, by Rev. N. S. Richardson, of Watertown   59
CAMP, Caroline, 2nd d. [Samuel & Mindwell], b. Nov. 2, 1802   7
   Elizabeth, m. Billy AMBLER, Nov. 4, 1790   3
   George Washington, s. [Gideon & Hannah], b. Sept. 9, 1805   27
   Gideon, m. Hannah CAMP, Nov. 22, 1802   27
   Hannah, m. Gideon CAMP, Nov. 22, 1802   27
   Lebbius, m. Betsey AMBLER, Mar. 25, 1799   2
   Sally, d. [Samuel & Mindwell], b. May 3, 1800   7
   Sally, d. [Gideon & Hannah], b. Oct. 6, 1803   27
   Samuel, m. Mindwell HOPKINS, Mar. 25, 1798   7
   Selina, m. George D. KASSON, Dec. 19, 1792   8
CANFIELD, James W., of Litchfield, m. Mary J. WILLIAMS, of Bethlem,
   Apr. 21, 1835, by R. S. Crampton, V. D. M.   56
CARRINGTON, Celestia, m. Frederick E. THOMPSON, b. of Bethlem, Mar.
   14, 1842, by Rev. I. H. Tuttle   63
CASTLE, Scovill B., of Woodbury, m. Fanny CRANE, of Bethlem, June 13,
   1830, by P. Couch   51
CATLIN, Catharine, m. James F. BRADFORD, b. of Bethlem, on eve of Dec.
   23, 1830, by P. Couch   52
   Helen A., m. John W. PAUL, b. of Bethlem, Dec. 25, 1843, by Rev.
      Fosdic Harrison   65
CHAPMAN, Esther, wid. Nathan, d. June 16, 1821, ae 88   38
   Nathan, d. Oct. 25, 1796   30
   Nathaniel, m. Ruth M. TOMPKINS, Feb. 28, 1822, by John Langdon   40

Page

CLARK, (cont.)

Page

COWLES, (cont)

Page

CUDINGTON, (cont.)

Eliphalet, m. Lois **MUNGER**, Feb. 15, 1787   30

Frederick L., [s. Eliphalet & Lois], b. May 13, 1807
  (Date conflicts with birth of "Lewis")   30

Harriet, [d. Eliphalet & Lois], b. Oct. 5, 1802   30

Lewis, s. [Eliphalet & Lois], b. Dec. 8, 1807 (Date conflicts
  with birth of "Frederick L.")   30

Polly, [d. Eliphalet & Lois], b. Aug. 21, 1799   30

CURTISS, Abigail, m. Orange **MUNGER**, Feb. 21, 1793   28

DeFOREST, Angeline, m. Abel **BENNET**, Mar. 24, 1807   29a

Augusta*, of Bethleham, m. Jackson **GANON**, of New York, Oct. 1,
  1848, by Rev. Fosdic Harrison *("August A." in Cothren's
  Hist.)   70

DEMING, Melecent, m. Azel **BACKUS**, Feb. 7, 1791   3

DeWOLF, Andrew, [s. Levi & Huldah], b. Dec. 19, 1795   10

Levi, m. Huldah **STANLEY**, June 26, 1787   10

Rufus, [s. Levi & Huldah], b. Apr. 17, 1793   10

Selina, [d. Levi & Huldah], b. Apr. 23, 1799   10

Stanley, [s. Levi & Huldah], b. June 7, 1791; d. July 27, 1792   10

Stanley, [s. Levi & Huldah], b. Mar. 8, 1801   10

DOOLITTLE, Alfred Wait, 3rd, s. [Capt. Ephraim & Polly], b. Dec. 1, 1805   21

David E., m. Mary J. **TRYON**, Apr. 21, 1851, by Rev. A. G. Loomis   73

Eleazer, eldest s. Capt. Ephraim & Polly, b. Sept. 18, 1800   21

Eleazer G., m. Ruth Ann **RIGGS**, Oct. 6, 1824, by Asahel Nettleton   42

Ephraim, m. Polly **GREEN**, Dec. 3, 1797   4

Harriet, d. Ephraim & Polly, b. June 1, 1804; d. Oct. 25, 1804   21

Mary, of Bethlem, m. Guy S. **HARD**, of Litchfield, South Farms, Jan.
  4, 1837, by Rev. Fosdic Harrison   57

Sally, d. [Ephraim & Polly], b. Jan. 3, 1799   4

Sarah, m. Sheldon **HILL**, b. of Bethlem, Dec. 3, 1851, by Rev. A.
  G. Loomis   74

Sarah L., b. Apr. 21, 1778; m. Jared **BALDWIN**, Oct. 19, 1800   19

Susan H., of Bethlem, m. David A. **NORTON**, of Washington, on eve
  of Feb. 11, [1831], by P. Couch   52

Theron, m. Hellen L. **JUDD**, b. of Bethleham, Mar. 4, 1849, by
  Rev. F. Harrison   71

Thomas, d. May 26, 1805   21

William, 2nd s. [Capt. Ephraim & Polly], b. May 17, 1802   21

DOWNS, Anna, [d. Zeri], b. May 8, 1797   17

Anna, m. Dauid **KIMBERLEY**, b. of Bethlem, Aug. 12, 1823, by John
  Langdon   42

Betsey, [d. Zeri], b. Oct. 2, 1802   17

Lewis, [s. Zeri], b. Oct. 23, 1806   17

Lucretia, [d. Zeri], b. Oct. 12, 1800   17

Lucretia, m. Frederick L. **LUDINGDON**, b. of Bethlem, Nov. 11,
  1829, by Paul Couch   50

Wealthy Maria, [d. Zeri], b. Dec. 31, 1794   17

Wyllys, [s. Zeri], b. Dec. 26, 1799   17

Page

DOWNS, (cont.)

Zeri Albert, [s. Zeri], b. Nov. 12, 1804   17

DUDLEY, Frederick, of Litchfield, m. Olive **MARTIN,** of Bethlem,

[   ], 15, [1833], by Paul Couch   54

Lucena, d. Asa & Loes, b. Apr. 20, 1796   12

DUNNING, Maria, of Litchfield, m. Horace **KIMBALL,** of Woodbridge, Sept.

3, 1826, by David Bird   46

Sarah, m. Daniel **SKIDMORE,** Nov. 27, 1800   28a

DURAND, Frances, d. [William & Sally], b. July 31, 1807   14

William, m. Sally **AMBLER,** Feb. 20, 1805   14

EDMUNDS, Nelson, m. Jennet **HILL,** b. of Bethlem, Jan, 26, 1835, by Rev.

Charles Hyde   56

EDWARDS, Charles, of Roxbury, m. Patty **FOOT,** of Bethlem, Nov. 9, 1826,

by John Langdon   47

EGGLESTONE, EGLESTON, Anne, m. Daniel Clark **SHERMAN,** Nov. 27,

1801   23

Emeline, d. Rosel & Irene, b. Feb. 9, 1805   11

Erastus, s. James & Ruth, b. Sept. 12, 1797   12

Horace, m. Susan **NORTHROP,** b. of Bethlem, Nov. 28, 1841, by Rev.

Henry Fitch, of Hamden   62

Maria, d. Roswell & Irene, b. Dec. 27, 1807   23

Polly, d. James & Ruth, b. Jan. 13, 1795   12

Rosel, m. Irene **CLARK,** May 3, 1804   11

EMORY, Julia Amanda, d. Polly, b. Apr. 1, 1795   1

Polly, had d. Julia Amanda, b. Apr. 1, 1795   1

EVERITT, EVERETT, Abner, of Warren, m. Deborah **KASSON,** of Bethlem,

[Dec.], 1, [1830], by P. Couch   52

Daniel B., m. Julia **SMITH,** b. of Bethlem, Mar. 26, [1834], by

Paul Couch   56

Harmon, m. Betsey **HULL,** June 16, 1803, by Rev. Azel Barkus   20

Henry Filghman, s. Harmon & Betsey, b. Sept. 26, 1804   11

EVERTS, David Bishop, s. David & Orpha, b. Feb. 20, 1813   38

FENN, Horace, of Bethlem, m. Mary A. **LELLARRELL*,** of Watertown, Nov.

1, 1852, by [   ]. *("**LOCKWOOD**" in Cothren's Hist.)   75

James, of Ohio, m. Mary B. **NETTLETON,** of Bethlem, Sept. 22, 1839,

by Rev. Isaac H. Tuttle   61

Sarah, of Plymouth, b. Aug. 29, 1783; m. Nathan **BURTON,** Jr., of

Bethlehem, July 4, 1816, by Rev. Luther Hart, of Plymouth   37

William, m. Phebe **BEACH,** Aug. 23, 1803; d. Mar. 15, 1804   13

FLOWERS, Eliza, m. Nelson **HAWLEY,** b. of Bethlem. May 20, 1849, by

Rev.J. C. Covill   74

FOOT, Emmeline, of Bethlem, m. John **KIRK,** of Bristol, Dec. 23, 1829,

by Paul Couch   51

Jane A., of Bethlem, m. Jeremiah **TRYON,** of Litchfield, Oct. 28,

[1832], by Paul Couch   54

Olive E., of Bethlem, m. Ashbel **MIX,** of Bristol, Mar. 4, 1829,

by David Bird, J. P.   49

Patty, of Bethlem, m. Charles **EDWARDS,** of Roxbury, Nov. 9, 1826, by

Page

FOOT, (cont.)

John Langdon   47

FORD, Polly, m. Milo KNAPP, May 20, 1822, by John Langdon   40

FORESTER, George K., of Somers, N. Y., m. Nancy E. STRONG, of
Bethlem, Dec. 14, 1836, by Rev. Fosdic Harrison   57

FOSTER, Charles, s. [   ] FOSTER, & Laura GUTHRIE, b. June 29, 1802   36

Fanny B., m. George W. ANDRUS, b. of Bethlem, Apr. 9, 1851, by
Rev. J. S. Covill   73

FOWLER, Parleman B., Dr., m. Polly LEMAN, Nov. 17, 1807   33

Polly, m. Samuel CHURCH, Jr., June 15, 1814   35

Ramulus P., d. Oct. 8, 1826, ae 17 y. 10 1/2 m.   X

Remulus, s. Dr. Parleman B. & Polly, b. Nov. 23, 1808   33

FRENCH, Andrew A., of Washington, m. Elizabeth BROWN, of Litchfield,
Mar. 15, 1841, by Rev. Fosdic Harrison   61

FRISBIE, Amos, Capt., m. Eleanor ALLEN, Jan. 26, 1791   22

Benjamin, s. Capt. Amos & Eleanor, b. May 7, 1793   22

Calvin, s. Amos & 1st w. Mary, b. Dec. 15, 1779   22

Caroline, [d. Jacob, Jr. & Thankful], b. Nov. 12, 1794   19

Jacob, Jr., m. Thankful CHAPMAN, Dec. 23, 1773   19

Jacob, Sr., d. Sept. 16, 1798, in the 72nd y. of his age   18

Jacob. d. Apr. 26, 1811, in the 61st y. of his age   34

Levi, [s. Jacob, Jr. & Thankful], b. Nov. 25, 1774; d. Sept. 16, 1795   19

Lucinda, [d. Jacob, Jr. & Thankful], b. Sept. 16, 1776   19

Nabby, [d. Jacob, Jr. & Thankful], b. June 25, 1779   19

Ruth, w. [Jacob, Sr.], d. Feb. [   ], 1794, in the 76th y. of his age   18

GALPIN, Amelia, m. Sheldon THOMSON, Dec. 9, 1807   23

Hannah, m. Norman STONE, Oct. 6, 1791   27

John, d. Oct. 27, 1801   24

Olive, m. Darius PERKINS, Oct. 19, 1804   13

Sarah, m. Nehemiah LAMBERT, June 24, 1790   5

GANON*, Jackson, of New York, m. Augusta D. FOREST, of Bethleham,
Oct. 1, 1848, by Rev. Fosdic Harrison   *("GANNER" in Cothren's
Hist.)   70

[GARNSEY], [see under GUERNSEY]

GATES, Sally, of Woodbury, m. Samuel P. TREAT, of Waterbury, June 29,
1825, by David Bird, J. P.   43

GAYLORD, Giles A., m. Emily HILL, b. of Bethlem, Aug. 7, 1825, by
Asahel Gaylord   43

Philander C., of Norfolk, m. Lucy BIRD, of Bethlem, Jan. 25, 1826,
by B. F. Stanton   44

GOLDSMITH, Polly, of Bethlem, m. Nelson PERKINS, of Goshen, Oct. 18,
1829, by David Bird, J. P.   50

GOODWIN, Edward, of Hartford, m. Susan LEAVITT, of Bethlem, Apr. 9,
1827, by Benjamin F. Stanton   47

GORDON, Alexander, m. Nancy BARRITT, Jan. 20, 1799   31

Alexander, [s. Capt. Alexander & Eleanor], b. Mar. 13, 1814   36

Charles Leonard, [s. Alexander & Nancy], b. July 7, 1806   31

Edwin Everett, s. Capt. Alexander & Eleanor, b. Jan. 15, 1811   36

Page

GORDON, (cont.)

Mary, b. Nov. 6, 1760; m. Capt. Seth MARTIN, June 6, 1788   17

Nancy, [w. Alexander], d. Aug. 25, 1808, ae 28 y.   31

Robert, [s. Capt. Alexander & Eleanor], b. July 18, 1812   36

Sophronia, [d. Alexander & Nancy], b. Dec. 30, 1799   31

Susan Anne, [d. Alexander & Nancy], b. Aug. 28, 1802   31

William Chauncey, [s. Alexander & Nancy], b. July 24, 1804   31

GREEN, Daniel, s. [Eleazer & Thankfull], b. Feb. 18, 1777   24

Darius, [s. Eleazer & Thankfull], b. Jan. 27, 17[ ]; d. Feb. 21, 1781   24

Elezur, 2nd, m. Lucy BRACE, Oct. 11, 1778   3

Eleazer, [s. Eleazer & Thankfull], b. Mar. 21, 1779; d. June 17, 1796   24

Esther, [d. Eleazer & Thankfull], b. June 21, 1789; d. Mar. 24, 1793   24

Harriet, d. [Elezur, 2nd & Lucy], b. Jan. 25, 1781   3

James, [s. Eleazer & Thankfull], b. Apr. 12, 1784   24

Jesse, [s. Eleazer & Thankfull], b. June 1, 1786   24

Lucy, [d. Elezur, 2nd & Lucy], b. Dec. 7, 1794   3

Nancy, [d. Elezur, 2nd & Lucy], b. Feb. 6, 1798   3

Nancy, d. Elezur & Lucy, d. Aug. 19, 1802   7

Polly, d. [Elezur, 2nd & Lucy], b. Mar. 24, 1779   3

Polly, m. Ephraim DOOLITTLE, Dec. 3, 1797   4

Sally, [d. Elezur, 2nd & Lucy], b. May 23, 1783   3

Seth, s. Eleazer & Thankfull, b. July 8, 1773   24

Thankful, d. [Eleazer & Thankfull], b. May 1, 1775   24

GRISWOLD, Harry, m. Lucia Ann HILL, b. of Bethlem, Mar. 24, 1845, by

Rev. Fosdic Harrison   66

Laura, m. Linus WESTOVER, b. of Bethlehem, Dec. 29, 1844, by

David Bird, J. P.   66

[GUERNSEY], GARNSEY, Eunice Polly, d. [Mylo & Ursula], b. Sept. 26,

1799   4

Mylo, m. Ursula COWLES, Sept. 19, 1796   4

Philena, m. David BROWN, June 2, 1768   1

Susan Cowles, d. [Mylo & Ursula], b. Aug. 15, 1797   4

GUTHRIE, Laura, had s. Charles FOSTER, b. June 29, 1802; f. [ ]

FOSTER   36

HALL, [see also HULL], Chauncey, s. [Ebenezer & Abigail], b. Sept. 20,

1781   10

Chauncey, m. Ruth Ann ATWOOD, Dec. 5, 1804   11

Chester, of Bridgewater, N. Y., m. Cynthia A. AMBLER, of Bethlem,

Nov. 15, 1831, by P. Couch   53

Ebenezer, b. Dec. 21, 1757; m. Abigail PARMELEE, June 8, 1779   10

Frederick Clark, s. Chauncey & Ruth Ann, b. Sept. 12, 1805   18

Sally, d. [Ebenezer & Abigail], b. Aug. 29, 1783   10

Sally, m. Rollin CHURCH, Apr. 13, 1803   7

HAMLIN, Benjamin, of Bethlehem, m. Belinda WEBSTER, of Litchfield,

Jan. 29, 1821, by John Langdon   39

William, m. Loevisa HUBBARD, b. of Litchfield, Apr. 23, 1846,

by David Bird, J. P.   68

HANNAH, Abigail, [d. David & Susanna], b. Jan, 8, 1803   15

Page

HANNAH, (cont.)

Caroline, of Bethlem, m. Lorenzo **ABBOTT**, of Reading, Hillsdale,
Cty., Mich., June 2, 1851, by Rev. A. G. Loomis   74

David, b. May 9, 1799(?)*; m. Susannah **SANFORD**, May 5, [   ]
*(1777?)   15

David Parleman, [s. David & Susannah], b. Jan. 13, 1807   15

Edwin, s. Col. Robert & Jerusha, b. Aug. 16, 1807   Y

Edwin, m. Sarah **CRANE**, Dec. 23, 1838, b. of Bethlem, by G. V. C.
Eastman   59

Eliza, [d. David & Susanna], b. Jan. 25, 1805   15

George Noble, [s. David & Susanna], b. Apr. 13, 1799   15

John, of Nelson, O., m. Susan **HANNAH**, of Bethleham, Sept. 28,
1847, by Rev. William H. Frisbie   68

Lucina, m. Alfred **PORTER**, b. of Bethlem, Nov. 1, 1826, by John
Langdon   46

Lucy, m. Robert **PORTER**, Jan. 4, 1795   6

Maria, [d. David & Susanna], b. Jan. 25, 1794   15

Maria, of Bethlem, m. Jabish **ADKINS**, of Granville, Mass., Jan. 16,
1828, by Benjamin F. Stanton   48

Myrilla, [d. David & Susanna], b. Aug. 5, 1795   15

Sanford, [s. David & Susanna], b. June 28, 1797   15

Susan, [d. David & Susanna], b. Dec. 14, 1800   15

Susan, of Bethleham, m. John **HANNAH**, of Nelson, O., Sept. 28, 1847,
by Rev. William H. Frisbie   68

Susanna (**SANFORD**), [w. of David], b. Jan. 27, 1774   15

HARD, Abijah, of Newton, m. Susan M. **LUDINGTON**, of Bethlem, Nov. 24,
1825, by Joshua Williams   44

Concurrance, b. Dec. 20, 1748; m. John **ATWOOD**, Aug. 29, 1770   25

David Brinsmade **WILLCOCKSON**, b. Aug. 14, 1807   16

Eliza, b. Oct. 16, 1803   16

Guy S., of Litchfield, South Farms, m. Mary **DOOLITTLE**, of Bethlem,
Jan. 4, 1837, by Rev. Fosdic Harrison   57

Nancy, b. Oct. 28, 1796   16

HARPER, William, m. Rene **STEEL**, Nov. 22, 1801   6

HARRISON, Betsey B., of Bethleham, m. Robert **TOWNSEND**, of
Middlebury, Aug. 29, 1837, by Rev. Fosdic Harrison   60

Susan, m. Arza A. **PARMELEE**, b. of Bethlem, Mar. 4, 1829, by
Grove L. Brownell   50

William R., m. Susan S. **KASSON**, b. of Bethlem, Mar. 25, 1846, by
Rev. Fosdic Harrison   68

HATCH, David C., of New Preston, m. Betsey T. **AMBLER**, of Bethlem,
Apr. 8, 1832, by P. Couch   53

HAWLEY, Abigail, m. Abraham **BROWNSON**, Sept. 4, 1760   20

Alma E., of Bethlem, m. Noble **ATWOOD**, of Woodbury, Mar. 16, 1851,
by Rev. J. S. Covill   73

Nathan, m. Patty **STOW**, Dec. 7, 1794   7

Nelson, m. Eliza **FLOWERS**, b. of Bethlem, May 20, 1849, by Rev. J.
C. Covill   74

HAWLEY, (cont.)

Norval(?), m. Sally **PECK**, b. of Bethlem, June 11, 1826, by
Benjamin F. Stanton   44

Rosetta M., m, Samuel **ALLEN**, b. of Bethlem, Feb. 28, 1849, by
Rev. F. Harrison   71

Susanna, m. Samuel **JACKSON**, Sept. 14, 1786   25

HAYES, Hannah, m. Abner **ALLEN**, b. of Bethleham, Oct. 5, 1846, by Rev.
F. Harrison   69

Jerial, of Bethlem, m. Lydia H. **BARNES**, of New Haven, Jan. 11,
1846, by Rev. Fosdic Harrison   68

John W., of Trunbull, m. Maria A. **THOMAS**, of Bethlem, Sept. 6,
1829, by Stephen Mason   50

HESLER, Thomas, m. Mary **NAP***, formerly of Ireland, now b. of Bethlem
Sept. 4, 1850, by Rev. A. G. Loomis *("NOSS" in Cothren's Hist.)   72

HILL, Alma J., d. [Isaac & Patty], b. Apr. 16, 1806   29

Alma J., of Bethlem, m. Curtiss J. **JUDSON**, of Woodbury, [ ],
29, [ ], by S. R. Andrews. Recorded Jan. [ ], 1843   55

Althea, m. Truman **HILL**, Oct. 2, 1802, by Rev. Azel Barkus   20

Ann Maria, m. Cephas **BEACH**, Mar. 1, 1821, by John Langdon   39

Daniel, b. Mar. 22, 1767; m. Electa **MINOR**, Oct. 1, 1790   23

Emily, 3rd, d. [Daniel & Electa], b. Sept. 11, 1799   23

Emily, m. Giles A. **GAYLORD**, b. of Bethlem, Aug. 7, 1825,
by Asahel Gaylord   43

Gilman, 3rd s. [Daniel & Electa], b. Sept. 15, 1805   23

Gilman E., m. Nancy **CRANE**, b. of Bethlem, [Mar.] 5, [1834],
by Paul Couch   55

Isaac, b. Oct. 19, 1779; m. Patty **JUDSON**, Dec. 22, 1802   29

Jane E., m. Demick S. **MONSON**, b. of Bethlem, Oct. 22, 1839, by
Rev. Fosdic Harrison   60

Jennet, m. Nelson **EDMUNDS**, b. of Bethlem, Jan. 26, 1835, by Rev.
Charles Hyde   56

Julia S., d. [Daniel & Electa], b. July 7, 1791   23

Lucia Ann, m. Harry **GRISWOLD**, b. of Bethlem, Mar. 24, 1845, by
Rev. Fosdic Harrison   66

Maria A., 2nd d. [Daniel & Electa], b. Feb. 4, 1794   23

Reuben, eldest s. [Daniel & Electa], b. Jan. 14, 1797; d. Aug. 5, 1800   23

Rollin, 2nd s. [Daniel & Electa], b. May 21, 1802   23

Rollin, of Livania, N. Y. m. Susan **KASSON**, of Bethlem, Oct. 13,
1825, by John Langdon   44

Sally, m. Ebenezer **MANSFIELD**, Feb. 7, 1805   16

Sheldon, m. Sarah **DOOLITTLE**, b. of Bethlem, Dec. 3, 1851, by
Rev. A. G. Loomis   74

Truman, m. Althea **HILL**, Oct. 2, 1802, by Rev. Azel Barkus   20

HINE, Alvin, of Watertown, m. Julia C. **COWLES**, of Bethlehem, Apr. 11,
1827, by Rev. Darius O. Griswold, of Watertown   47

Amos, [s. Dan & Abigail], b. Jan. 18, 1790   17

Charles, [s. Dan & Abigail], b. Dec. 23, 1798   17

Charlotte, [d. Dan & Abigail], b. Apr. 15, 1786   17

Page

HINE, (cont.)

Dan, b. Mar. 17, 1763; m. Abigail **COWLES**, Nov. 17, 1784   17

Dan, Jr., [s. Dan & Abigail], b. Feb. 12, 1801; d. Oct. 4, 1804   17

Dan, d. Oct. 17, 1805   17

Jared, [s. Dan & Abigail], b. Feb. 29, 1788   17

Mary m. Abel **STILSON**, Dec . 30, 1779   21

Nathaniel, [s. Dan & Abigail], b. Jan. 23, 1797   17

Pamela, [d. Dan & Abigail], b. Jan. 5, 1795   17

Sheldon, [s. Dan & Abigail], b. Apr. 3, 1792   17

HINMAN, John, d. Oct. 15, 1801   30

HITCHCOCK, Abigail, m. Usal **MANSFIELD**, Feb. 15, 1808   31

Almy, [d. Benjamin & Mary], b. Dec. 2, 1797   12

Benjamin, Jr., m. Mary **JOHNSON**, Apr. 6, 1785   12

Benjamin Rice, s. Benjamin & Mary, b. Aug. 15, 1806   29

Betsey, [d. Benjamin & Mary], b. Aug. 10, 1804   12

Daniel, of Waterbury, m. Deziah B. **TOLLES**, of Bethleham, Apr. 11,
    1842, by Rev. Fosdic Harrison   63

Delia, [d. Benjamin & Mary], b. Mar. 9, 1792   12

Edwin E., of Sharon, m. Ruth A. **WATTLES**, of Bethleham, Oct. 24,
    1849, by Rev. J. Garnsey, of Derby   72

George R., of Champlain, N. Y., m. Eliza **ALLEN**, of Bethlem,
    June 29, 1846, by Rev. Fosdic Harrison   68

Lowly, [child of Benjamin & Mary], b. Aug. 6, 1787; d. May 18, 1792   12

Lucy, [d. Benjamin & Mary], b. Apr. 23, 1790   12

Nabby, [d. Benjamin & Mary], b. Oct. 16, 1799   12

Patty, [d. Benjamin & Mary], b. Dec. 3, 1795   12

Polly, [d. Benjamin & Mary], b. Dec. 19, 1793   12

Sally, [d. Benjamin & Mary], b. Feb. 23, 1802   12

Sally, d. [Benjamin & Mary], d. May 30, 1807   29

Samuel Johnson, s. Benjamin & Mary, b. Feb. 4, 1786   12

HOLBROOK, Anna, w. Joseph, d. Sept. [ ], 1807   X

Debannah*, m. Andrew **MARTIN**, Dec. 6, 1795 *("Deborah"?)   27

HOLMES, Andrew S., of Salisbury, m. Mary E. **POTTER** of Bethlem [ ],
    by Rev. William Watson, of Plymouth *("1841" or "1842")   62

HOLT, Samuel, m. Ann **MARTIN**, May 1, 1802   29a

HOPKINS, Mindwell, m. Samuel **CAMP**, Mar. 25, 1798   7

HUBBARD, Elizabeth, of Bethlem, m. William **ANDREWS**, of Watertown,
    July 20, 1825, by Rev. Stephen Mason, of Washington   44

Joseph Freeman, s. Joseph Freeman & Martha, b. Oct. [ ], 1778   25

Loevisa, m. William **HAMLUN**, b. of Litchfield, Apr. 23, 1846, by
    David Bird, J. P.   68

Martha, wid, Joseph Freeman, m. John **ATWOOD**, Aug. 30, 1781   25

HUBBELL, HUBBEL, Amos Bird, s. Jonathan & Anna, b. Jan. 2, 1802   7

Anne, w. Jonathan, d. Oct. 1, 1807   14

Jonathan, m. Anna **BIRD**, Feb. [ ], 1801   7

Lucy, [twin with Pamela], d. Jonathan & Anna, b. Apr. 18, 1804   10

Pamela, [twin with Lucy], d. Jonathan & Anna, b. Apr. 18, 1804   10

HULL, [see also **HALL**], Andrew, [s. Titus & Olive], b. Oct. 28, 1792   4

Page

HULL, (cont.)

Betsey, m. Harmon Everitt, June 16, 1803, by Rev. Azel Barkus ... 20

Laurens, m. Dorcas **AMBLER,** Oct. 3, 1803, by Rev. Azel Barkus ... 20

Leverett, [s. Titus & Olive], b. Dec. 3, 1796 ... 4

Olive Experience, [d. Titus & Olive], b. Mar. 13, 1790 ... 4

Rufus Lewis, [s. Titus & Olive], b. Mar. 10, 1799 ... 4

Titus, had servant Phebe **ELKA,** who had s. Cambridge, b. Nov. 10,
1805; f. Peter **TREADWELL,** a freeman ... 12

HUNT, Truman, of Woodbury, m. Sarah **STONE,** of Bethlem, Dec. 16, 1829,
by Paul Couch ... 51

HURLBUT, Mary, m. Friend **CLARK,** July 10, 1781 ... 5

INGERSOLL, Eliza, 3rd d. [Jonathan & Polly], b. Jan. 19, 1803 ... 21

Eliza, m. Chester **ALLEN,** Oct. 31, [1822], by John Langdon ... 40

Jonathan, m. Polly **WADSWORTH,** Jan. 3, 1799 ... 21

Jonathan, d. Jan. 31, 1812 ... 35

Julia Ann, d. Jonathan & Polly, b. Mar. 28, 1810 ... 35

Julia An[n], of Bethlem, m. Samuel M. **BUTLER,** of Erie Cty., N. Y.,
Nov. 18, 1839, by Rev. Fosdic Harrison ... 60

Martha, of Bethlem, m. Jacob **SCOVIL,** of Cornwall, June 21, 1827,
by Benjamin F. Stanton ... 48

Mary, 2nd d. [Jonathan & Polly], b. Apr. 25, 1801 ... 21

Mary, of Bethlehem, m. Alexander **KELLOGG,** of Livania, N. Y.,
Mar. 3, 1825, by John Langdon ... 42

Patty, 4th d. [Jonathan & Polly], b. Aug. 15, 1805 ... 21

Ralph W., m. Sarah M. **JOHNSON,** b. of Bethlem, Feb. 16, 1831, by
Rev. D. O. Griswold, of Watertown ... 53

Ralph Wadsworth, s. [Jonathan & Polly], b. Dec. 28, 1807 ... 21

Semantha, d. [Jonathan & Polly], b. Jan. 1, 1800 ... 21

Semantha, m. Gideon **MARTIN,** b. of Bethlehem, Nov. 29, 1820, by
John Langdon ... 39

JACKSON, Betsey, d. [Theophilus & Elizabeth], b. May 26, 1776 ... 29

Caroline, d. [Samuel & Susanna], b. Dec. 31, 1802 ... 25

Caroline, m. Joshua **BIRD,** b. of Bethlem, Sept. 4, 1822, by John Langdon ... 40

Charles, [s. Theophilus & Elizabeth], b. Dec. 17, 1794 ... 29

Dorcas, d. [Samuel & Susanna], b. Feb. 9, 1787 ... 25

Dorcas, [d. Samuel & Susanna], b. Nov. 30, 1807 ... 25

Esther, [d. Samuel & Susanna], b. Oct. 12, 1806 ... 25

Esther D., of Bethleham, m. William **JACKSON,** of Augusta, N. Y.,
Sept. 18, 1843, by Rev. F. Harrison ... 64

Fanny, of Bethlem, m. Merit **WARNER,** of Plymouth, [Nov.] 13,
[1833], by Paul Couch ... 55

Harriet, of Bethlem, m. Gaius F. **WARNER,** of Plymouth, June 13,
1832, by Paul Couch ... 54

Harry, m. Sarah E. **SHELTON,** b. of Bethlem, Nov. 15, 1843, by Rev.
Fred Holcomb, of Northfield ... 66

Henry, m. Annis **SKIDMORE,** Mar. 13, 1803 ... 28a

Isaac, s. [Theophilus & Elizabeth], b. Sept. 2, 1778 ... 29

James, [s. Theophilus & Elizabeth], b. June 21, 1792 ... 29

Page

JACKSON, (cont.)

James, m. Fanny **CLARK**, b. of Bethlem, May 9, 1838, by Rev. Fosdic
Harrison   58

Levi, s. [Theophilus & Elizabeth], b. Dec. 1, 1780   29

Lucy, [d. Theophilus & Elizabeth], b. May 2, 1783   29

Lucyett, of Bethlem, m. William **JACKSON**, of Augusta, N. Y., Sept.
24, 1838, by Rev. Fosdic Harrison   59

Mary, [d. Samuel & Susanna], b. Oct. 27, 1804   25

Nathan, s. [Samuel & Susanna], b. Apr. 19, 1793   25

Olive, [d. Theophilus & Elisabeth], b. Aug. 3, 1785   29

Olive, m. Daniel **STRONG**, Jr., b. of Bethlem, Mar. 29, 1824, by
David Bird, J. P.   41

Patty, d. [Samuel & Susanna], b. Apr. 19, 1795   25

Patty, d. [Samuel & Susanna], d. Jan. 3, 1800   25

Polly, d. [Samuel & Susanna], b. Apr. 30, 1789   25

Polly, d. [Samuel & Susanna], b. May 30, 1805   25

Samuel, m. Susanna **HAWLEY**, Sept. 14, 1786   25

Samuel & Susanna, had twin d. [ ], s. b. Mar. 25, 1788   25

Samuel, [s. Samuel & Susanna], b. Dec. 22, 1795 [sic]   25

Sheldon, s. [Samuel & Susanna], b. Apr. 4, 1791   25

Sheldon, s. [Henry & Annis], b. July 28, 1805   28a

Susan P., d. [Samuel & Susanna], b. Mar. 26, 1801   25

Theophilus, m. Elizabeth **THOMSON**, Dec. 15, 1774   29

Theophilus, m. Ruth **MUNSON**, b. of Bethlehem, June 18, 1820, by
John Langdon   39

Truman, s. [Samuel & Susanna], b. July 17, 1799   25

William, [s. Theophilus & Elizabeth], b. Sept. 7, 1788   29

William, m. Emmeline **CRANE**, b. of Bethlem, Mar. 25, 1824, by Rev.
Grove L. Brownell, of Woodbury   41

William, of Augusta, N. Y., m. Lucyett **JACKSON**, of Bethlem, Sept.
24, 1838, by Rev. Fosdic Harrison   59

William, of Augusta, N. Y., m. Esther D. **JACKSON**, of Bethleham,
Sept. 18, 1843, by Rev. F. Harrison   64

William, of Augusta, N. Y., m. Elizabeth M. **BIRD**, of Bethlehem,
Apr. 7, 1852, by Rev. A. G. Loomis   75

JOHNSON, Henry, m. Lydia H. **WATTLES**, b. of Bethlem, Nov. 8, 1826, by
Benjamin F. Stanton   46

Mary, m. Benjamin **HITCHCOCK**, Jr., Apr. 6, 1785   12

Sarah M., m. Ralph W. **INGERSOLL**, b. of Bethlem, Feb. 16, 1831,
by Rev. D. O. Griswold, of Watertown   53

Sheldon, of Southbury, m. Keziah **WATTLES**, of Bethlem, Dec. 7,
1836, by Rev. Fosdic Harrison   57

Truman M., of Woodbury, m. Polly E. **ALLEN**, of Bethlem, Sept. 29,
1825, by Sturges Gilbert   44

JUDD, Ann, of Bethlem, m. Titus **PIERCE**, of Southbury, Sept. 24, 1838,
by Rev. Fosdic Harrison   59

Anna Charolotte, [d. Leverett & Olive Charlotte], b. Dec. 21, 1800   28

Caroline A., of Litchfield, m. Harmon **TUTTLE**, of South Canaan,

Page

KASSON, (cont.)

	Page
Couch	53
Joseph Miller, 4th s. James & Reliance, b. June 4, 1790	2
Leverett, [s. Daniel & Ruth Ann], b. May 4, 1801	18
Mary Ann, m. Chauncey STRONG, June 2, 1833, by Paul Church	54
Olive, m. Elizur WHEELER, Nov. 19, 1783	5
Polly, [d. Alexander & Comfort], b. Jan. 17, 1781	18
Reliance, Jr., 7th d. James & Reliance, b. Jan. 11, 1793	2
Samuel Steele, s. [George & Lucy], b. Apr. 26, 1801	8
Selina, [d. Alexander & Comfort], b. Sept. 26, 1776	18
Selina, w.[George D.], d. Nov. 20, 1793	8
Selina, m. Ichabod PRENTICE, Aug. 20, 1800	14
Selina Camp, d. George D. & Selina, b. Nov. 7, 1793	8
Susan, of Bethlem, m. Rollin HILL, of Livania, N. Y., Oct. 13, 1825, by John Langdon	44
Susan Margaret, d. George D. & Lucy, b. Apr. 15, 1805	12
Susan S., m. William R. HARRISON, b. of Bethlem, Mar. 25, 1846, by Rev. Fosdic Harrison	68
Theron, 5th s. James & Reliance, b. Nov. 16, 1795	2
KELLEY, Leonard A., of Goshen, m. Sarah E. BROWN, of Bethleham, Oct. 11, 1848, by Rev. J. S. Covill	70
KELLOGG, Alexander, of Livania, N. Y., m. Mary INGERSOLL, of Bethlehem, Mar. 3, 1825, by John Langdon	42
KILLBORNE, Homer, of Litchfield, m. Harriet D. WATTLES, of Bethlem, June 3, 1844, by Rev. Fosdic Harrison	65
KIMBALL, KIMBAL, Horace, of Woodbridge, m. Maria DUNNING, of Litchfield, Sept, 3, 1826, by David Bird	46
Maria O., of Bethleham, m. Anson A. PERKINS, of Waterbury, Dec. 24, 1845, by Rev. Fosdic Harrison	67
KIMBERLEY, Dauid, m. Anna DOWNS, b. of Bethlem, Aug. 12, 1823, by John Langdon	42
KING, Susan Aurelia, of Bethlem, m. Frederick WICKWIRE, of Litchfield, Apr. 3, 1830, by P. Couch	51
KIRK, John, of Bristol, m. Emmeline FOOT, of Bethlem, Dec. 23, 1829, by Paul Couch	51
KNAPP, NAP, Betsey Ann, of Bethlem, m. Seneca L. LOOMIS, of Windsor, Aug. 11, 1835, by Rev. Fosdic Harrison	58
Mary*, m. Thomas HESLER, formerly of Ireland, now b. of Bethlehem, Sept. 4, 1850, by Rev. A. G. Loomis *("Mary NOSS" in Cothren's Hist.)	72
Myso, [child of Moses], b. Apr. 22, 1775	19
Milo, m. Polly FORD, May 20, 1822, by John Langdon	40
Noble, [s. Moses], b. May 1, 1784	19
Olive, [d. Moses], b. Feb. 17, 1773	19
Seymour, [s. Moses], b. July 17, 1781	19
LAKE, Amos, m. Catharine BLACKMAN, Nov. 20, 1806	26
Mary, of Bethlem, m. Thomas C. BENNETT, of Portage, N. Y. Oct. 8, 1849, by Rev. J. S. Covell	72

LAKE, (cont.)
Norman, s. [Amos & Catharine], b. Nov. 14, 1807   26
Norman, m. Louisa M. BEACH, b. of Bethlem, Nov. 30, 1843, by Rev.
I. H. Tuttle   65
Peter, of Bethlem, m. Susan PIERCE, of Watertown, Apr. 4, 1852,
by J. D. Berry   75
LAMBERT, Clarissa, [d. Nehemiah & Sarah], b. Aug. 22, 1801   5
Clarissa, of Bethlem, m. Nicholas MOSS, of Derby, Mar. 20, 1822,
by John Langdon   40
Frederick, [s. Nehemiah & Sarah], b. Oct. 29, 1794   5
Nancy, [twin with Sally], d. [Nehemiah & Sarah], b. July 30, 1799   5
Nehemiah, m. Sarah GALPIN, June 24, 1790   5
Nehemiah & Sarah, had twin s.[ ], b. Dec. 25, 1797; d. same day   5
Sally, [twin with Nancy], d. [Nehemiah & Sarah], b. July 30, 1799   5
Treat, [s. Nehemiah & Sarah], b. July 8, 1791   5
LANGDON, Abby, m. Samuel CHURCH, b. of Bethlem, [Feb.] 11, [1834],
by P. Couch   55
LEAVENWORTH, Nancy, of Bethlem, m. Harvey SMITH, of Washington,
Nov. 23, 1836, by Rev. Fosdic Harrison   57
LEAVITT, Susan, d. David, Jr., decd. & Lucy, b. Apr. 14, 1800   13
Susan, of Bethlem, m. Edward GOODWIN, of Hartford, Apr. 9, 1827,
by Benjamin F. Stanton   47
LELLARRELL *, Mary A., of Watertown, m. Horace FENN, of Bethlem,
Nov. 1, 1852, by [ ] *("LOCKWOOD" in Cothren's Hist.)   75
LEMAN, LEMMON, Polly, m. Dr. Parleman B. FOWLER, Nov. 17, 1807   33
Sally B., m. Joseph B. BELLAMY, June 12, 1811   34
LEWIS, Adeline, d. [Martin & Sarah], b. Feb. 17, 1806   20
Edward, s. Martin & Sarah, b. Aug. 23, 1801   5
Edward, s. [Martin & Sarah], b. Aug. 23, 1801   20
Elihu T., of Huntington, m. Mary C. THOMAS, of Bethlem, June 22,
1840, by Rev. I. H. Tuttle   61
Martin, b. Apr. 16, 1767; m. Sarah WHEADON, Sept. 14, 1800   20
Martin, m. Sarah WHEADON, Sept. 14, 1800   20
LINSLEY, Abigail Joanna, d. Solomon & Irene, b. July 30, 1813   35
Edward Alonzo, s. Solomon & Irene, b. Jan. 30, 1809   32
Elizabeth, d. Solomon & Irene, b. Aug. 7, 1819   37
Eunice Stilson, d. Solomon & Irene, b. June 26, 1816   36
Irene, d. Solomon & Irene, b. Apr. 28, 1822   38
Mary Floria, d. Solomon & Irene, b. Nov. 26, 1810   33
Solomon, m. Irene STILSON, Sept. 15, 1807   14
Solomon Harvey, s. Solomon & Irene, b. Mar. 23, 1824   38
LOCKE, Joel, of Portland, Me., m. Ann Jenet STATES, of Southbury,
May 21, 1840, by Rev. I. H. Tuttle   61
LOCKWOOD*, Mary A., of Watertown, m. Horace FENN, of Bethlem, Nov.
1, 1852, by [ ] *(Arnold copy has LELLARRELL")   75
LOGAN, Samuel Mansfield, of Washington, m. Emily KASSON, of Bethlem,
May 24, 1826, by John Langdon   46
LOOMIS, , Joab, Jr., of Bloomfield, m. Martha SHELTON, of Bethlem,

Page

MANSFIELD, (cont.)

Page

MARTIN, (cont.)

Sally, [d. Capt. Seth & Mary], b. Mar. 10. 1789   17

Samuel S., b. Feb. 11, 1767; m. Olive **MINOR**, Jan. 5, 1791   29

Scovil, [s. Samuel S. & Olive], b. Mar. 14, 1797   29

Selina, d. [Samuel S. & Olive], b. Oct. 5, 1791   29

Seth, Capt., b. Mar. 8, 1763; m. Mary **GORDON**, June 6, 1788   17

Seth, [s. Capt. Seth & Mary], b. Jan. 3, 1798   17

Thankfull, w. Judson, d. July 12, 1809, ae 37 y.   32

Wealthy, [d. Capt. Seth & Mary], b. July 14, 1795   17

MASON, Eunice E., of Lebanon, m. Joseph **AMBLER**, of Bethlem, Sept. 19, [1832], by Paul Couch   54

MATTOON, Jennett, of Wallingford, m. Josiah **ATWOOD**, of Bethlem, Nov. 29, 1849, by Rev. J. S. Covell   72

MAY, Clarissa, m. James **ALLEN**, b. of Bethlehem, May 15, 1816, by Rev. John Langdon   37

MEIGS, Benjamin, [s. Phineas & Sarah], b. Aug. 9, 1789   8

Charles, [s. Phineas & Sarah], b. Oct. 25, 1793   8

David, s. Jesse & Hannah, b. Aug. 6, 1796   2

Harmon, s. Jesse & Hannah, b. Feb. 10, 1799   2

Irene, d. Jesse & Hannah, b. Apr. 27, 1791   2

Jesse, m. Hannah **PRITCHARD**, Feb. 6, 1782   20

John, [s. Phineas & Sarah], b. Oct. 26, 1787   8

John, d. Dec. 31, 1802   30

Phineas, m. Sarah **TOMLINSON**, Jan. 24, 1786   8

Phinehas, Dr., d. Aug. 12, 1805   19

Rebeckiah, d. Jesse & Hannah, b. Aug. 10, 1785   2

Samuel, [s. Phineas & Sarah], b. Apr. 27, 1791   8

Sarah, d. Jesse & Hannah, b. Sept. 12, 1793   2

Sheldon, s. Jesse & Hannah, b. May 16, 1788   2

MERRIAM, Sarah M., m. Cornelius F. **ALLEN**, b. of Bethlem, Sept. 26, 1849, by Rev. Fosdic Harrison   71

MERWIN, Sarah, m. Myer H. **BROWNSON**, Oct. 24, 1793   20

MINOR, Armila, [d. Jonas & Anna], b. Jan. 5, 1806   29a

Chloe, d. [Jonas & Anna], b. Sept. 29, 1787   29a

Electa, b. May 12, 1767; m. Daniel **HILL**, Oct. 1, 1790   23

Electa, d. [Jonas & Anna], b. Mar. 20, 1799   29a

Jonas, b. Mar. 31, 1762   29a

Jonas, m. Anna **MARTIN**, Oct. 26, 1785   29a

Olive, m. Samuel S. **MARTIN**, Jan. 5, 1791   29

MITCHELL, Reuben, Jr., of Woodbury, m. Ruth M. **BLOSS**, of Bethlehem, [   ], by Rev. Sturges Gilbert, of Woodbury. Recorded Nov. 20, 1821   39

MIX, Ashbel, of Bristol, m. Olive E. **FOOT**, of Bethlem, Mar. 4, 1829, by David Bird, J. P.   49

MORRIS, Winthrop, of Roxbury, m. Amy **MALLORY**, of Bethleham, June 6, 1840, by Rev. Fosdic Harrison   61

MORSE, [see also **MOSS**], Amos, of Litchfield, m. Betsey Priscilla **SEYMOUR**, of Bethlem, June 11, 1827, by Rev. Seth Higby, of

Page

MORSE, (cont.)

Litchfield 48

Roswell A., of Plymouth, m. Julia **SKIDMORE**, of Bethlem, Oct. 28, 1828, by Benjamin F. Stanton 49

MOSS, [see also **MORSE**], Lavinia A., m. William H. **ALLEN**, b. of Bethlem, May 12, 1844, by Rev. Jonathan Coe, 2nd 66

Nicholas, of Derby, m. Clarissa **LAMBERT**, of Bethlem, Mar. 20, 1822, by John Langdon 40

MUNGER, Amos, s. [Orange & Abigail], b. Apr. 16, 1796 28

Charles, [s. Orange & Abigail], b. Mar. 17, 1803 28

Curtiss, [s. Orange & Abigail], b. May 30, 1807 28

Harmon, s. [Orange & Abigail], b. Aug. 7, 1794 28

Lewis, d. Mar. 26, 1801 30

Lois, m. Eliphalet **CUDINGTON***, Feb. 15, 1787 *("LUDINGTON"?) 30

Luman, [s. Orange & Abigail], b. Mar. 16, 1798 28

Orange, m. Abigail **CURTISS**, Feb. 21, 1793 28

MUNN, Patty, m. Amos **STILSON**, May 10, 1812 36

MUNSON, MONSON, Alfred, [s. Miles & Elizabeth], b. Apr. 8, 1801 31

Charles, m. Lucy **PRENTICE**, b. of Bethlem, June 22, 1826, by B. F. Stanton 44

Demick S., m. Jane E. **HILL**, b. of Bethlem, Oct. 22, 1839, by Rev. Fosdic Harrison 60

Derrick, [s. Miles & Elizabeth], b. Feb. 15, 1800 31

Hannah, [d. Miles & Elizabeth], b. Mar. 31, 1797 31

Harriet E., of Bethlem, m. Albert **MANSFIELD**, of Sheffield, Mass., Dec. 3, 1850, by Rev. Frederick Munson, of North Greenwich 73

Lambert, [s. Miles & Elizabeth], b. May 6, 1806 31

Lewis, [s. Miles & Elizabeth], b. Feb. 17, 1804 31

Miles, m. Lucinda **TRYON**, b. of Bethlem, Sept. 19, 1831, by P. Couch 52

Ralph, m. Mary **CRANE**, b. of Bethlem, Sept. 22, 1844, by Rev. Fosdic Harrison 66

Ruth, m. Theophilus **JACKSON**, b. of Bethlehem, June 18, 1820, by John Langdon 39

MURRAY, Ruth, m. John **STEEL**, 3rd, Nov. 6, 1785 20

NAP, [see under **KNAPP**]

NETTLETON, , Ashley, m. Sarah **STODDARD**, b. of Woodbury, Sept. 25, 1826, by Benjamin F. Stanton 46

Mary B., of Bethlem, m. James **FENN**, of Ohio, Sept. 22, 1839, by Rev. Isaac H. Tuttle 61

NEWTON, Eunice, ae 22, m. John **PRUDDEN**, Jr., ae 29, Apr. 15, 1771, at Milford; d. Nov. 13, 1774 28

NICHOLS, Jane, m. Phinehas **CRANE**, Jan. 23, 1800 22

NORTH, Loomis, Dr., m. Betsey **BIRD**, b. of Bethlem, Sept. 6, 1841, by Rev. Fosdic Harrison 62

NORTHROP, Susan, m. Horace **EGGLESTONE**, b. of Bethlem, Nov. 28, 1841, by Rev. Henry Fitch, of Hamden 62

NORTON, Charles, of Berlin, m. Adelia Matilda **ATWOOD**, of Bethlem, May 22, 1825, by Darius O. Griswold 43

NORTON, (cont.)

David A., of Washington, m. Susan H. DOOLITTLE, of Bethlem, on
eve of Feb. 11, [1831], by P. Couch   52

NOSS*, Mary, m. Thomas HESLER, formerly of Ireland, now b. of
Bethlehem. Sept. 4, 1850, by Rev. A. G. Loomis *(Arnold copy has
"NAP")   72

OSBORN, Alecta, of Woodbury, m. Daniel PRENTICE, of Bethlem, Jan. 21,
1827, by S. R. Andrews   47

Luthena, of Bethlem, m. Luther MALLORY, of Bethel, Sullivan Cty.,
N. Y., Dec. 18, 1825, by Rev. Benjamin F. Stanton   44

PARKS, Charles, [s. Elizur], b. June 30, 1794   15

Eliphalet, [s. Elizur], b. Jan. 14, 1787; d. Oct. 29, 1789   15

Eliphalet Clark, [s. Elizur], b. Jan. 31, 1805   15

Elizur, m. [ ], Apr. [ ], 1784   15

Harmon, [s. Elizur], b. Jan. 16, 1799   15

Irene, [d. Elizur], b. Jan. 30, 1785   15

Sheldon, [s. Elizur], b. June 16, 1801   15

Truman, [s. Elizur], b. May 15, 1791   15

PARMELEE, Abigail, b. Aug. 27, 1759; m. Ebenezer HALL, June 8, 1779   10

Amos Allen, [s. Oliver & Kezia], b. Aug. 1, 1793   11

Arza A., m. Susan HARRISON, b. of Bethlem, Mar. 4, 1829, by
Grove L. Brownell   50

Betsey, d. Samuel & Nancy, b. Dec. 23, 1791   35

Cornelius C., m. Lucy E. ALLEN, b. of Bethlem, Sept. 17, 1851,
by Rev. A. G. Loomis   74

Esther, m. Samuel CHURCH, May 6, 1798   3

Frederick William, [s. Oliver & Kezia], b. May 26, 1799   11

George Edwards, [s. Oliver & Kezia], b. Mar. 12, 1797, in Sharon   11

Jedediah Clark, [s. Oliver & Kezia], b. Aug. 27, 1803   11

Lucy Maria, [d. Oliver & Kezia], b. Apr. 7, 1795   11

Mary, of Bethleham, m. Henry R. WHITTLESEY, of Litchfield, South
Farms, July 6, 1837, by Rev. Fosdic Harrison   67

Oliver, m. Kezia ALLEN, Nov. 28, 1792   11

Rebeckah, b. Apr. 21, 1756; m. Josiah STILSON, Feb. 15, 1776   18

Richard Oliver, [s. Oliver & Kezia], b. June 20, 1801   11

Samuel, m. Nancy STEELE, Oct. 25, 1781   35

PAUL, John W., m. Helen A. CATLIN, b. of Bethlem, Dec. 25, 1843, by
Rev. Fosdic Harrison   65

PECK, Henry W., m. Mary BROWN, b. of Bethlem, June 4, 1845, by Rev.
Fosdic Harrison   67

Sally, m. Norval (?) HAWLEY, b. of Bethlem, June 11, 1826, by
Benjamin F. Stanton   44

PERKINS, Anson A., of Waterbury, m. Maria O. KIMBAL, of Bethleham,
Dec. 24, 1845, by Rev. Fosdic Harrison   67

Darius, s. Ebenezer & Mercy, b. Aug. 14, 1782   24

Darius, m. Olive GALPIN, Oct. 19, 1804   13

Ebenezer & Mercy, had 5th child s. [ ], b. Jan. 4, 1792; d. Jan. 5, 1792   24

Esther, d. [Ebenezer & Mercy], b. Apr. 26, 1789   24

PERKINS, (cont.0
   Esther, [d. Ebenezer & Mercy], b. [ ], 1794; d. [ ] 1794 — 24
   John Peck, s. [Darius & Olive], b. May 12, 1807 — 13
   Melinda, d. [Ebenezer & Mercy], b. Apr. [ ], 1793 — 24
   Nelson, of Goshen, m. Polly **GOLDSMITH**, of Bethlem, Oct. 18, 1829,
     by David Bird, J. P. — 50
PERRY, Bennett, s. John C. & Esther, b. Mar. 21, 1802 — 23
   Harry, [s. John C. & Esther], b. Nov. 2, 1807 — 23
   Sally Jenet, d. [John C. & Esther], b. Feb. 10, 1805 — 23
PETTIT, Samuel, of Lagrange, m. Emeline **MARTIN**, of Bethlem, [Feb.] 12,
   [1834], by P. Couch — 55
PIERCE, PEARCE, Nathan, of Woodbury, m. Susan E. **BLOSS**, of Bethlem,
   Nov. 5, 1834, by Grove L. Brownel — 56
   Susan, of Watertown, m. Peter **LAKE**, of Bethlem, Apr. 4, 1852, by
     J. D. Berry — 75
   Titus, of Southbury, m. Ann **JUDD**, of Bethlem, Sept. 24, 1838, by
     Rev. Fosdic Harrison — 59
PLATT, Ambrose, of New York City, m. Sally **SEELEY**, of Lenox, Mass.,
   Sept. 23, 1829, by Nathan Benton, Jr. J. P. — 50
   Caroline, d. [Ebenezer & Sarah], b. May 30, 1801 — 29a
   Catharine, [d. Ebenezer & Sarah], b. Feb. 7, 1805 — 29a
   Charles Bryan, [s. Ebenezer & Sarah], b. May 11, 1807 — 29a
   Ebenezer, m. Sarah **SMITH**, Apr. 3, 1800 — 29a
   Edwin Adolphus, [s. Ebenezer & Sarah], b. Sept. 3, 1803 — 29a
   Sidney S., of Bridgewater, m. Jane E. **ALLEN**, of Bethleham,
   Oct. 28, 1847, by Rev. F. Harrison — 69
PORTER, Alfred, s. [Robert & Lucy], b. Jan. 24, 1802 — 6
   Alfred, m. Lucina **HANNAH**, b. of Bethlem, Nov. 1, 1826, by John
     Langdon — 46
   Betsey, eldest d. Robert & 1st w. Betsey, b. Apr. 17, 1794 — 6
   Curtis, eldest s. Robert & 1st w. Betsey, b. Dec. 27, 1792 — 6
   Richard W., of Farmington, m. Wealthy E. **LUDINGTON**, of Bethlem
     Nov. 3, 1828, by Benjamin F. Stanton — 49
   Robert, m. Lucy **HANNAH**, Jan. 4, 1795 — 6
POTTER, Mary E., of Bethlem, m. Andrew S. **HOLMES**, of Salisbury, [ ],
   by Rev. William Watson, of Plymouth (" 1841" or "1842") — 62
PRENTICE, Anna, [d. Sherman & Susanna], b. Jan. 5, 1800; d. [ ], ae 20 d. — 9
   Betsey, [d. John & Martha], d. Feb. 18, 1794 — 15
   Dan Sherman, [twin with Dianna Susan], s. [Sherman & Susanna], b.
     July 23, 1802 — 9
   Daniel, of Bethlem, m. Alecta **OSBORN**, of Woodbury, Jan. 21, 1827,
     by S. R. Andrews — 47
   David, [s. Sherman & Susanna], b. Sept. 7, 1787 — 9
   Dianna Susan, [twin with Dan Sherman], d. [Sherman & Susanna], b.
     July 23, 1802; d. [ ] ae 34 d. — 9
   Dotha, [d. John & Martha], b. Dec. 16, 1790 — 15
   Drake, s. [Sherman & Susanna], b. Oct. 5, 1789 — 9
   Drusilla, [d. John & Martha], d. Apr. 23, 1794 — 15

Page

SMITH, (cont.)

Lyman, of Derby, m. Elizabeth H. **CLARK**, of Woodbury, Sept. 22,
1824, by John Langdon   42

Marcia, m. John P. **WARD**, b. of Bethlehem, Sept. 11, 1842, by
David Bird, J. P.   63

Mary, d. [Jonathan, 2nd & Sally], b. Aug. 19, 1804   29a

Rebecca, [d. Jonathan & Rebecca], b. June 20, 1798   4

Sally, [d. Jonathan & Rebecca], b. Nov. 11, 1792   4

Sarah, m. Ebenezer **PLATT**, Apr. 3, 1800   29a

Sarah A., of Watertown, m. George W. **BALDWIN**, of Washington, Mar.
22, 1848, by Rev. Fosdic Harrison   69

William, [s. Jonathan, 2nd & Sally], b. Dec. 28, 1805   29a

SPAULDING, Simeon, of Litchfield, m. Charlotte **WASSON**, of Bethlem,
July 21, 1825, by Rev. Henry Robinson, of Litchfield   43

SPENCER, Lucia, m. Edwin **CLARK**, b. of Bethlem, Dec. 12, 1827, by
Benjamin F. Stanton   48

Lucius W., m. Emeline **SEELEY**, b. of Bethlem, Mar. 11, 1849, by
Rev. J. S. Covill   71

Medad G., m. Emmeline **CLARK**, Nov. 27, 1828, by Rev. Stephen
Mason, of Washington   49

Polly M., of Bethleham, m. George M. **ATWOOD**, of Watertown, Apr. 2,
1847, by Rev. F. Harrison   69

SPROULES, Robert C., of Woodbury, m. Eliza E. **CHURCHILL**, of Bethlem,
Jan. 24, 1843, by Rev. F. Harrison   64

STANLEY, Huldah, m. Levi **DeWOLF**, June 26, 1787   10

STARKS, Milo, of Torrington, m. Wealthy Ann **ATWOOD**, of Bethlem, July
13, 1852, by Arvil Morris, J. P.   75

STATES, Ann Jenet, of Southbury, m. Joel **LOCKE**, of Portland, Me., May
21, 1840, by Rev. I. H. Tuttle   61

STEELE, STEEL, Alathea, 2nd d. John, 3rd & Ruth, b. Apr. 13, 1790   1

Altha, d. [John & Rebeckah], b. May 11, 1798   8

Anne, d. [Elish & Susanna], b. Mar. 10, 1779   26

Betsey, d. [Elisha & Susanna], b. Sept 19, 1784   26

Charles, s. John 3rd & Ruth, b. Nov. 12, 1793   1

David, [s. Jonathan & Fanny], b. Feb. 27, 1798   26

Ebenezer Warner, [s. Jonathan & Fanny], b. May 24, 1807   26

Hanan, w. Samuel, d. Mar. 15, 1781   8

Harriet, d. [Jonathan & Fanny], b. June 17, 1795   26

John, 2nd, m. Rebeckah **STODDARD**, Oct. 27, 1779   8

John, 3rd, m. Ruth **MURRAY**, Nov. 6, 1785   20

John, 3rd, d. Oct. 3, 1795   30

John, s. [Jonathan & Fanny], b. July 3, 1805   26

Jonathan, m. Fanny **WARNER**, Nov. 15, 1793   26

Joseph, s. [Elisha & Susanna], b. Nov. 29, 1788   26

Julius, s. [Elisha & Susanna], b. Dec. 27, 1786   26

Lucy, d. Elisha & Susanna, b. Nov. 23, 1771   26

Lucy, m. George D. **KASSON**, May 18, 1796   8

Nancy, m. Samuel **PARMELEE**, Oct, 25, 1781   35

Page

STEELE, STEEL, (cont.)

Nancy, d. John, 3rd & Ruth, b. Aug. 31, 1786 — 1

Olive, d. [Elisha & Susanna], b. Aug. 23, 1775 — 26

Olive Charlotte, m. Leverett JUDD, Oct. 20, 1798 — 28

Polly, d. [Elisha & Susanna], b. Sept. 17, 1780 — 26

Renee, d. John & Rebeckah, b. Mar. 23, 1783 — 8

Rene, m. William HARPER, Nov. 22, 1801 — 6

Sally, d. [Jonathan & Fanny], b. Nov. 1, 1803 — 26

Samuel, d. June 16, 1801 — 8

Sheldon, s. John & Rebeckah, b. Feb. 10, 1786 — 8

Wealthy, d. [John & Rebeckah], b. May 24, 1796 — 8

William, s. [Elisha & Susanna], b. Sept. 27, 1782 — 26

STEVENS, John L., m. Charlotte A. WATROUS, May 28, 1848, by Rev.

David L. Parmelee — 70

STILSON, Abel, m. Mary HINE, Dec. 30, 1779 — 21

Amadeus, [s. Josiah & Rebeckah], b. Aug. 28, 1779 — 18

Amos, [s. Abel & Mary], b. Feb. 29, 1788 — 21

Amos, m. Patty MUNN, May 10, 1812 — 36

Asahel, [s. Josiah & Rebeckah], b. Jan. 9, 1789 — 18

Betsey, [d. Abel & Mary], b. Apr. 26, 1786; d. July 2, 1792 — 21

Betsey, [d. Abel & Mary], b. July 17, 1797 — 21

David, [s. Josiah & Rebeckah], b. Mar. 14, 1791 — 18

Eunice, [d. Abel & Mary], b. Feb. 7, 1791 — 21

Harriet C., of Bethleham, m. Richard TIBBUL, of Colebrook, Sept.

5, 1843, by Rev. F. Harrison — 64

Irene, d. [Abel & Mary], b. Mar. 23, 1782 — 21

Irene, m. Solomon LINSLEY, Sept. 15, 1807 — 14

Joseph, s. [Abel & Mary], b. Mar. 4, 1784 — 21

Joseph, 2nd, m. Laura SKINNER, b. of Bethlem, May 28, 1843, by

David Bird, J. P. — 64

Josiah, b. June 14, 1753; m. Rebeckah PARMELEE, Feb. 15, 1776 — 18

Philo, [s. Josiah & Rebeckah], b. July 2, 1777 — 18

Phinehas, [s. Josiah & Rebeckah], b. Jan. 19, 1783 — 18

Polly, [d. Josiah & Rebeckah], b. Mar. 19, 1781 — 18

Rebecca, [d. Abel & Mary], b. Oct. 25, 1793 — 21

Rebeckah Jane, d. [Amos & Patty], b. July 19, 1813 — 36

STODDARD, Billy, m. Caroline McKEAN, May 1, 1800 — 9

Hooker, s. [Billy & Caroline], b. Apr. 5, 1801 — 9

Lavina, d. [Billy & Caroline], b. Oct. 5, 1802 — 9

Philette, m. Henry ALLEN, b. of Bethleham, Nov. 26, 1843, by Rev.

Fosdic Harrison — 64

Rebeckah, m. John STEELE, 2nd, Oct. 27, 1779 — 8

Sarah, m. Ashley NETTLETON, b. of Woodbury, Sept. 25, 1826, by

Benjamin F. Stanton — 46

STONE, Almira, [d. Norman & Hannah], b. June 8, 1795 — 27

Edward, s. [Norman & Hannah], b. June 31, 1799 — 27

Henry, of Litchfield, m. Matilda BUNNEL, Feb. 13, 1842, by Rev.

George L. Foote — 63

Page

STONE, (cont.)
John, s. [Norman & Hannah], b. Feb. 15, 1804   27
Maria, d. [Norman & Hannah], b. Sept 19, 1801   27
Maria, of Bethlem, m. Washington Harry **ATWOOD**, of Woodbury, Nov.
   3, 1822, by John Langdon   40
Moses Sheldon, s. [Norman & Hannah], b. Mar. 1, 1807   27
Norman, m. Hannah **GALPIN**, Oct. 6, 1791   27
Polly, d. [Norman & Hannah], b. May 2, 1792   27
Sally, [d. Norman & Hannah], b. Sept. 2, 1797   27
Sarah, of Bethlem, m. Truman **HUNT**, of Woodbury, Dec. 16, 1829,
   by Paul Couch   51
STOW, Patty, m. Nathan **HAWLEY**, Dec. 7, 1794   7
STRONG, Chauncey, m. Mary Ann **KASSON**, June 2, 1833, by Paul Couch   54
Daniel, Jr., m. Olive **JACKSON**, b. of Bethlem, Mar. 29, 1824, by
   David Bird, J. P.   41
John L., s. Daniel. & Esther, b. Dec. 9, 1789   24
Lucy, d. [Daniel & Esther], b. Nov. 6, 1791   24
Mary, ae 27, m. John **PRUDDEN**, Jr., ae 35, Oct. 19, 1776   28
Nancy E., of Bethlem, m. George K. **FORESTER**, of Somers, N. Y.,
   Dec. 14, 1836, by Rev. Fosdic Harrison   57
[TERRILL], [see under **TYRREL**]
THOMAS, Elizabeth E., of Bethlem, m. William C. **ADAMS**, of Danbury,
   May 17, 1835, by Rev. F. Harrison, of Roxbury   56
Hannah W., of Bethleham, m. Henry C. **ATWOOD**, of Bristol Sept. 19,
   1847, by Rev. William H. Frisbie   68
Maria A., of Bethlem, m. John W. **HAYES**, of Trumbull, Sept. 6, 1829,
   by Stephen Mason   50
Mary C., of Bethlem, m. Elihu T. **LEWIS**, of Huntington, June 22,
   1840, by Rev. I. H. Tuttle   61
Mary J., of Bethlem, m. Alva M. **TYRREL**, of Reading, June 22, 1840,
   by Rev. Isaac H. Tuttle   61
THOMPSON, THOMSON, Aaron, m. Annis **MARTIN**, July 4, 1782   19
Alfred, [s. Aaron & Annis], b. Aug. 24, 1797   19
Charles, [s. Aaron & Annis], b. June 20, 1787   19
Edmund, [s. Aaron & Annis], b. Aug, 7, 1791   19
Elizabeth, m. Theophilus **JACKSON**, Dec. 15, 1774   29
Esther, m. Francis **BLOSS**, Feb. 23, 1768   14
Frederick E., m. Celestia **CARRINGTON**, b. of Bethlem, Mar. 14, 1842,
   by Rev. I. H. Tuttle   63
Hannah, d. Henry & Prudence, b. Oct. 19, 1793   X
Henry, m.Charlotte **BOSTWICK**, Sept. 5, 1798   29a
John, [s. Aaron & Annis], b. July 22, 1802   19
Mary A., of Bethlem, m.W[illia]m **LOWE**, of Woodbury, Sept. 11, 1842,
   by Rev. I. H. Tuttle   63
Polly, 2nd d. [Henry & Charlotte], b. Nov. 28, 1802   29a
Polly P., of Bethlem, m. Bennet **WARNER**, of Watertown, Dec. 13,
   [1830], by Rev. Bradley Selleck   52
Prudence, d. [Henry & Charlotte], b. Nov. 23, 1800   29a

Page

WHITTLESEY, Henry R., of Litchfield, m. Mary PARMELEE, of
    Bethleham, July 6, 1837, by Rev. Fosdic Harrison   67
WICKWIRE, Benjamin, of Litchfield, m. Cynthia CLARK, of Bethleham,
    Dec. 6, 1847, by Rev. William H. Frisbie   69
    Frederick, of Litchfield, m. Susan Aurelia KING, of Bethlem, Apr.
    3, 1830, by P. Couch   51
WILLIAMS, Mary J., of Bethlem, m. James W. CANFIELD, of Litchfield,
    Apr. 21, 1835, by R. S. Crampton, V. D. M.   56
    Sally, m. Jonathan SMITH, 2nd, Oct. 3, 1803   29a
WOODRUFF, David, of Litchfield, m. Laura SEYMOUR, of Bethlem, Mar.
    3, 1824, by Rev. Henry Robinson, of Litchfield   41
WOOSTER, Eleanor, d. Sept. 12, 1807   X
YOUNG, Andrew, [s. Hugh Murray & Ann], b. Apr. 27, 1787   X
    Clarissa, d. Hugh Murray & Ann, b. Nov. 12, 1779   X
    Edmund, Stafford, [s. Hugh Murray & Ann], b. Aug. 12, 1781   X
    Emily, [d. Hugh Murray & Ann], b. Mar. 7, 1791   X
    George, [s. Hugh Murray & Ann], b. Apr. 1, 1802   X
    James, [s. Hugh Murray & Ann], b. June 16, 1783   X
    John, [s. Hugh Murray & Ann], b. Apr. 5, 1793   X
    Joseph, [s. Hugh Murray & Ann], b. Nov. 20, 1798   X
    Lucy, [d. Hugh Murray & Ann], b. Oct. 27, 1796   X
    Sarah Ann, [d. Hugh Murray & Ann], b. Feb. 16, 1789   X
    William, [s. Hugh Murray & Ann], b. Apr. 29, 1785   X
    William M., 3rd s. Hugh M. & Anne, b. Apr. 23, 1786   36

BLOOMFIELD VITAL RECORDS
1835 - 1853

Page

BINGHAM, Henry, of Suffield, m. Mrs. Susan P. BROWN, of Bloomfield,
Feb. 1, 1852, by N. Whiting   19
BLINN, George H., of New Hartford, m. Louisa M. ENO, of Bloomfield,
Sept. 16, 1847, by Rev. J. A. Edmonds   14
BOWERS, Catharine M., of Bloomfield, m. Oscar WOOD, of Hartford, Mar.
10, 1838, by Cornelius B. Everist   4
BRAEL, Edwin, of Hartford, m. Dimmis DANIELS, of Granby, Mar. 28, 1842,
by Rev. Davis Stocking   6
BREWER, Albert F., of East Hartford, m. Emma J. EGGLESTON, Oct. 31,
1847, by Rev. N. Whiting   14
BRIDGE, Joseph A., of Simsbury, m. Jane A. HOLCOMB, of Granby, Nov.
17, 1846, by Rev. Sylvester S. Strong   13
BROWN, Almira J., of Bloomfield, m. Joseph L. BROWN, of Lansingburg,
N. Y., Oct. 5, 1852, by Niles Whiting   24
Emily, m. Elihu N. SHEPARD, b. of Bloomfield, Feb. 16, 1847,
by A. C. Raymond   14
Flavel, of Bloomfield, m. Susan B. LOOMIS, of Simsbury, June 13,
1842, by Williaam W. Backus   7
James, m. Elizabeth A. CADWELL, Sept. 10, 1837, by Cornelius B.
Everist   3
Jay H., m. Aminda K. BARNARD, b. of Bloomfield, Jan. 27, 1852, by
Francis W. Williams   21
Joseph L., of Lansingburg, N. Y., m. Almira J. BROWN, of Bloomfield,
Oct. 5, 1852, by Niles Whiting   24
Julia M., m. Lemuel d. ROBERTS, b. of Bloomfield, Oct. 30, 1839,
by Cornelius B. Everist   4
Kezia, of Bloomfield, m. William K. PARSONS, of Bennington,
Wyoming Co., N. Y., Mar. 2, 1842, by William W. Backus   6
Mary Ann, of Bloomfield, m. Rollin K. STODDARD, of Hartford, Aug.
25, 1824, by Cornelius B. Everist   4
Susan C., m. Enos H. BARRETT, b. of Bloomfield, [ ], by N. Whiting.
Recorded [ ], 1852   21
Susan P., Mrs. of Bloomfield, m. Henry BINGHAM, of Suffield, Feb.
1, 1852, by N. Whiting   20
BRUCE, Agness, m. Samuel McINTYRE, b. of Simsbury, Mar. 7, 1853, by
Rev. Ralph H. Bowles   25
BULL, Isabel, Mrs. of Simsbury, m. William SMITH, of Bloomfield, Oct.
8, 1849, by N. Whiting   18
BUMSTEAD, Harriet N., of Bloomfield, m. Levi J. HOLT, of Springfield,
May 18, 1831, by Rev. William Bentley   1
Hiram T., m. Susannah GILLET, b. of Bloomfield, May 17, 1836, by
Rev. T. H. Gallaudet   1
Jeduthan, m. Mrs. Rhoda LORD, b. of Bloomfield, Jan. 8, 1843, by
Rev. Alfred Gates   8
John, m. Julia A. CADWELL, May 30, 1846, by A. C. Raymond   13
BURNHAM, Shaylor F., m. Mrs. Elizabeth T. ROBERTS, May 31, 1837, by
Cornelius B. Everest   2
BURR, Achsah R., m. Sanders L. MOORE, b. of Bloomfield, Apr. 5, 1846,

Page

BURR, (cont.)

by William S. Knapp   12

Celia, of Bloomfield, m. Asa **GOODMAN**, of West Hartford, Nov. 25,
1847, by John A. Edmonds   15

Eliza Ann, of Bloomfield, m. Oliver N. **DANIELS**, of Hartford, Feb.
25, 1848, by John A. Edmonds   15

Lamira, of Bloomfield, m. Charles **OLDERSHAW**, of New Britain, Oct.
19, 1852, by N. Whiting   24

Martin, Jr., m. Aurelia **LAMB**, b. of Bloomfield, Jan. 3, 1838, by
David Osborn   3

Theda, m. Festus **HIGLEY**, b. of Bloomfield, July 27, 1842, by Rev.
Alfred Gates   7

BURRINGTON, Mary Ann, of Maysdose(?), Ohio, m. Albert **COMEY**, of
Foxboro, Mass., Sept. [ ], 1851, by Rev. Ralph H. Bowles   23

CADWELL, Elizabeth A., m. James **BROWN**, Sept. 10, 1837, by Cornelius B.
Everist   3

Emily, of Bloomfield, m. Chester **ELMER**, of West Hartford, Nov. 3,
1847, by John A. Edmonds   15

Flora, of Bloomfield, m. Alfred **LOOMIS**, of Windsor, Oct. 23, 1836, by
Cornelius B. Everest   2

Helen E., of Bloomfield, m. Mark N. **HUMPHREY**, of Simsbury, Aug. 8,
1849, by N. Whiting   18

Julia A., m. John **BUMSTEAD**, May 30, 1846, by A. C. Raymond   13

Mary, of Bloomfield, m. Chauncey **BEACH**, of Hartford, last evening,
[Nov. 30, 1835], by John Bartlett   1

Mary E., of Bloomfield, m. Tracy **KINGSBURY**, of East Windsor, Oct.
18, 1847, by John A. Edmonds   14

Matilda, of Bloomfield, m. Samuel **HALE**, of Guilford, Oct. 20, 1840,
by Rev. A. B. Goldsmith, of Guilford   5

Nancy A. C., m. Albert G. **NEARING**, of Granby, Feb. 20, 1838, by
Cornelius B. Everist   3

Sarah M., of Bloomfield, m. David L. **HUBBARD**, of Windsor, June 2,
1842, by William W. Backus   7

CALHOON, George, of Simsbury, m. Rosannah **SMITH**, of Boston, May 28,
1843, by W. W. Backus   8

CHAMBERLAIN, Martin, of Vermont, m. Louisa **MEACHAM**, of
Bloomfield, Jan. 14, 1849, by John A. Edmond   17

CHAPIN, A. Burdett, of Utica, N. Y., m. Clarinda P. **MILLS**, of Bloomfield,
June 27, 1852, by Niles Whiting   22

CLAPP, Amelia, of Bloomfield, m. Samuel **SMITH**, of Buffalo, July 5, 1852,
by Rev. Ralph H. Bowles   23

Samuel, of Sandisfield, Mass., m. Chloe **WATROUS**, of Bloomfield,
Nov. 24, 1836, by Rev. Augustus Bolles   2

CLARK, Edward G., of Providence, R. I., m. Jane **COOMBS**, of Bloomfield,
Apr. 7, 1843, by Rev. Alfred Gates   9

Roswell, of Bloomfield, m. Mary H. **ALBROW**, of Hartford, July 4,
1838, by Cornelius B. Everist   4

COLLINS, Anson A., of Granby, m. Mary A. **NEWBERRY**, Aug. 9, 1836, by

Page

COLLINS, (cont.)

Cornelius B. Everest   2

COMEY, Albert, of Foxboro, Mass., m. Mary Ann BURRINGTON, of
Maysdose(?), Ohio, Sept. [ ], 1851, by Rev. Ralph H. Bowles   23

COOK, Louisa, m. John F. WILSON, b. of Bloomfield, Mar. 26, 1846, by
William S. Knapp   12

COOMBES, Jane, of Bloomfield, m. Edward G. CLARK, of Providence, R. I.,
Apr. 7, 1843, by Rev. Alfred Gates   9

CORNISH, Edwin, of Simsbury, m. Ellen M. ROCKWELL, of Bloomfield,
Sept. 25, 1851, by Niles Whiting   20

CURTIS, Hezekiah P., of New Hartford, m. Welthan A. PARSONS, of
Bloomfield, Oct. 2, 1844, by Rev. Daniel Gibbs   9

DANIELS, Dimmis, of Granby, m. Edwin BRAEL, of Hartford, Mar. 28, 1842,
by Rev. Davis Stocking   6

Oliver N., of Hartford, m. Eliza Ann BURR, of Bloomfield, Feb. 25,
1848, by John A. Edmonds   15

DARROW, Asa, of Farmington, m. Mrs. Adelia S. FRANCIS, of Hartford,
Sept. 14, 1840, by Cornelius b. Everist   5

DEWEY, Watson, of Granby, m. Susan H. McLEAN, of Bloomfield, Nov. 3,
1847, by C. B. Everist   15

DICKINSON, Timothy, of New Britain, m. Ann Eliza SMITH, of Hartford,
July 13, 1848, by Rev. N. Whiting   16

DUNBAR, Paulene M., of Bloomfield, m. Gurdon BAKER, of New York, May
18, 1845, by Rev. Daniel Gibbs   11

EGGLESTON, Emma J., m Albert F. BREWER, of East Hartford, Oct. 31,
1847, by Rev. N. Whiting   14

ELMER, Chester, of West Hartford, m. Emily CADWELL, of Bloomfield,
Nov. 3, 1847, by John A. Edmonds   15

ELY, Nancy H., m. Nathan F. MILLER, Feb. 12, 1846, by A. C. Raymond   12

ENO, Elvia H., of Bloomfield, m. Enskin D. OGDEN, of Poquonock, Mar.
14, 1852, by Francis Williams   21

Louisa M., of Bloomfield, m. George H. BLINN, of New Hartford,
Sept. 16, 1847, by Rev. J. A. Edmonds   14

Salmon C., of Simsbury, m. Sarah C. GOODWIN, of Bloomfield, Oct.
29, 1845, by Allen McLean   12

ERWINS, Thomas G., m. Julia A. GRISWOLD, b. of Bloomfield, Oct. 7,
1851, by Rev. Ralph H. Bowles   22

FENNER*, Julius, m. Cecelia J. PINNEY, Oct. 13, 1850, by Rev. Ralph H.
Bowles, of Tariffville *(Perhaps "TANNER")   20

FILLEY, Catharine N., m. Willis F. ROCKWELL, b. of Bloomfield, Apr. 12,
1849, by Rev. N. Whiting   17

Emily M., m. Charles FLINN, Mar. 30, 1851, by N. Whiting   20

John E., m. Rebecca C. PHELPS, b. of Bloomfield, Mar. 6, 1843,
by Rev. Alfred Gates   8

Maria, of Bloomfield, m. Seymour H. HILLS, of Kent, Dec. 8, 1844,
by Rev. Nathaniel Kellogg   10

Rebecah C., m. Amasa H. JEROME, b. of Bloomfield, Dec. 9, 1852,
by T. P. Gillett   24

Page

GRISWOLD, (cont.)

    Sylvester S. Strong   13

HACK, John, of West Granby, m. Laura **GRISWOLD,** of Bloomfield, Nov.
30, 1851, by Rev. Ralph H. Bowles   23

HALE, Samuel, of Guilford, m. Matilda **CADWELL,** of Bloomfield, Oct. 20,
1840, by Rev. A. B. Goldsmith, of Guilford   5

HALL, John L., m. Mary M. **ADAMS,** b. of Bloomfield, Apr. 23, 1846, (in
Scotland) Bloomfield, by William S. Knapp   12

HAMBLIN, Sophronia, of Hinsdale, m. George **HUMPHREY,** of Bloomfield,
Sept. 11, 1837, by Cornelius B. Everist   3

HAYES, Elihu, of Granby, m. Mrs. Mable B. **OLDS,** of Bloomfield, Oct. 22,
1845, by William S. Knapp   11

    Mary R., of Granby, m. Hector W. **MILLER,** of Avon, Nov. 2, 1845,
by Rev. William S. Knapp   11

    Priscilla, m. Julius **HURLBURT,** b. of New Britain, Dec. 28, 1848,
by Rev. N. Whiting   17

HIGLEY, Carmi, of Windsor, m. Phebe Ann **GOULD,** of Montgomery, Mass.,
Jan. 24, 1841, by W. C. Hoyt   5

    Festus, m. Theda **BURR,** b. of Bloomfield, July 27, 1842, by Rev.
Alfred Gates   7

    Sally, m. Hiram **WEBSTER,** b. of Bloomfield, Sept. 27, 1840, by W.
C. Hoyt   5

HILLMAN, Eli D., of Mansfield, m. Helen C. **PECK,** of Bloomfield, Jan. 26,
1852, by N. Whiting   20

HILLS, Franklin F., m. Lucy C. **OSBORN,** of Windsor, Sept. 4, 1844, by
Lathrop W. Wheeler   9

    Seymour H., of Kent, m. Maria **FILLEY,** of Bloomfield, Dec. 8, 1844,
by Rev. Nathaniel Kellogg   10

HITCHCOCK, Electa, m. Albert A. **ALLYN,** Dec. 16, 1840, by Cornelius B.
Everist   5

    Gaylord, m. Achsah Angeline **PROSSER,** Feb. 5, 1845, by L. W. Wheeler   10

    Mary, m. George **STRAND,** June 26, 1849, by N. Whiting   18

    Sarah, m. John F. **PHELPS,** b. of Bloomfield, Mar. 30, 1848, by Rev.
Niles Whiting   15

HOLCOMB, Charles J., m. Cornelia **PRATT,** b. of Hartford, Aug. 6, 1848,
by Rev. N. Whiting   16

    Fanny A., m. W[illia]m W. **PIERCE,** b. of Granby, Mar. 13, 1853, by
Rev. Ralph H. Bowles   25

    Jane A., of Granby, m. Joseph A. **BRIDGE,** of Simsbury, Nov. 17, 1846,
by Rev. Sylvester S. Strong   13

    Martin B., of Windsor, m. Mary Jane **SHEPARD,** of Bloomfield, Jan.
10, 1845, by Rev. Nathaniel Kellogg   10

HOLDWICK, Anna R., of Granby, m. Jerome **NORTON,** of New Haven,
Nov. 3, 1852, by Rev. Ralph H. Bowles   25

HOLT, Levi J., of Springfield, m. Harriet N. **BUMSTEAD,** of Bloomfield,
May 18, 1831, by Rev. William Bentley   1

HOSKINS, Chloe, m. Henry **WRIGHT,** Dec. 9, 1849, by George Newberry,
J.P.   18

HOSKINS, (cont.)

Maria E., of Bloomfield, m. Jonathan **NURSE,** of Burlington, N. Y.,
June 27, 1841, by Rev. Davis Stocking 6

Thirsah A., of Bloomfield, m. James **MARSH,** Jr., of Hartford, June
29, 1841, by Rev. Davis Stocking 6

HOUSE, Clarissa Elizabeth, of Manchester, m. Henry **HUBBARD,** of
Bloomfield, June 30, 1846, in Rainbow, by William S. Knapp 13

HUBBARD, Anna, of Bloomfield, m. Benjamin **VIETS,** of Granby, Sept. 1,
1853, by Rev. Ralph H. Bowles 25

Caroline S., Mrs. of Bloomfield, m. Dea. Roger E. **ROWLEY,** of
Bennington, N. Y., Feb. 6, 1853, by Rev. William A. Smith 24

David L., of Windsor, m. Sarah M. **CADWELL,** of Bloomfield, June 2,
1842, by William W. Backus 7

Henry, of Bloomfield, m. Clarissa Elizabeth **HOUSE,** of Manchester,
June 30, 1846, in Rainbow, by William S. Knapp 13

Trumbull, of Bloomfield, m. Rhoda **BARBER,** of Windsor, Nov, 22,
1836, by Cornelius B. Everest 2

HUMPHREY, George, of Bloomfield, m. Sophronia **HAMBLIN,** of Hinsdale,
Sept. 11, 1837, by Cornelius B. Everist 3

Henrietta, of Bloomfield, m. Wilbert **REED,** of Granby, on the eve
of Nov. 27, 1845, by William S. Knapp 11

James H., of Winchester, m. Lucy H. **MILLER,** of Bloomfield, Sept.
5, 1837, by Cornelius B. Everest 3

Mark N., of Simsbury, m. Helen E. **CADWELL,** of Bloomfield, Aug. 8,
1849, by N. Whiting 18

Julius, m. Priscilla **HAYES,** b. of New Britain, Dec. 28, 1848, by
Rev. N. Whiting 17

JEROME, Amasa H., m. Rebecah C. **FILLEY,** b. of Bloomfield, Dec. 9, 1852,
by T. P. Gillett 24

JONES, Almena, of Springfield, m. Quartus **SEARL,** June 9, 1844, by
Lathrop W. Wheeler 9

KELSEY, Mary, of Bloomfield, m. Gustavus **WEST,** of New Britain, Sept. 6,
1843, by Rev. Alfred Gates 9

KENEDY, Louisa, m. Charles **LAMSON,** b. of Simsbury, Oct. 2, 1849, by N.
Whiting 18

KILBURN, Eli Dwight, m. Jane M. **PECK,** Aug. 5, 1850, by Rev. Henry H.
Bates, of Warehouse Point 19

KINGSBURY, Tracy, of East Windsor, m. Mary E. **CADWELL,** of
Bloomfield, Oct. 18, 1847, by John A. Edmonds 14

LAMB, Aurelia, m. Martin **BURR,** Jr., b. of Bloomfield, Jan. 3, 1838,
by David Osborn 3

LAMBERTON, Ruth A., of Bloomfield, m. Salmon **STEEL,** of New Britain,
Aug. 6, 1837, by Rev. D. Osborn 2

LAMSON, Charles, m. Louisa **KENEDY,** b. of Simsbury, Oct. 2, 1849, by
N. Whiting 18

LATIMER, Clarissa, m. Lester **GOODWIN,** b. of Bloomfield, Nov. 18, 1846,
by A. C. Raymond 13

Mary M., m. Stephen **GOODWIN,** of Simsbury, Oct. 13, 1841, by

Page

LATIMER, (cont.)

William Backus   6

Rebecca M., m. George W. ROWLEY, Mar. 19, 1845, by Rev. L. W.
Wheeler   10

Susan E., m. Timothy B. FILLEY, May 11, 1836, by Rev. T. H.
Gallaudet   1

LAW, Mary M., m. Alixander PATTERSON, b. of Simsbury, Dec. 12, 1852,
by Rev. Ralph H. Bowles   25

LEONARD, Lewis D., m. Mary M. GRISWOLD, b. of Bloomfield, Nov. 22,
1846, by Rev. Sylvester S. Strong   13

Mesheck W., of Millbury, Mass., m. Fanny J. LORD, of Bloomfield,
Nov. 2, 1842, by Rev. Alfred Gates   7

LOOMIS, Alfred, of Windsor, m. Flora CADWELL, of Bloomfield, Oct. 23,
1836, by Cornelius B. Everest   2

Betsey, of Bloomfield, m. Elane TUTTLE, of Hartford, Mar. 24, 1831,
by Rev. Augustus Bolles   1

Cynthia, of Bloomfield, m. Nathan STARKWEATHER, of Hartford,
Nov. 7, 1838, by Cornelius B. Everist   4

Susan B., of Simsbury, m. Flavel BROWN, of Bloomfield, June 13,
1842, by William W. Backus   7

LORD, Eliza Ann, of Bloomfield, m. Nathaniel R. ALFORD, of Windsor,
Mar. 4, 1849, by N. Whiting   17

Fanny J., of Bloomfield, m. Mesheck W. LEONARD, of Millbury, Mass.,
Nov. 2, 1842, by Rev. Alfred Gates   7

Rhoda, Mrs., m. Jeduthan BUMSTEAD, b. of Bloomfield, Jan. 8, 1843,
by Rev. Alfred Gates   8

McINTYRE, Samuel, m. Agness BRUCE, b. of Simsbury, Mar. 7, 1853, by
Rev. Ralph H. Bowles   25

MACKINTOSH, William, m. Mary RICHARDSON, b. of Bloomfield, Oct. 8,
1837, by David Osborn   3

McLEAN, Henry, m. Abigail ALLYNE, of Bloomfield, Jan. 6, 1846, by Rev.
A. C. Raymond   12

John, m. Elizabeth C. ALLYN, Nov. 17, 1842, by Cornelius B. Everist   8

Susan H., of Bloomfield, m. Watson DEWEY, of Granby, Nov. 3, 1847,
by C. B. Everist   15

MAGAN, Lewis, of Hartford, m. Janet PINNEY, of Bloomfield, Dec. 24,
1845, by Rev. E. Cushman   11

MARSH, James, Jr., of Hartford, m. Thirsah A. HOSKINS, of Bloomfield,
June 29, 1841, by Rev. Davis Stocking   6

MEACHAM, Louisa, of Bloomfield, m. Martin CHAMBERLAIN, of
Vermont, Jan. 14, 1849, by John A. Edmond   17

MERRELLS, Henry, of Hartford, m. Emily WRIGHT, of Bloomfield, Sept.
23, 1844, by Lathrop W. Wheeler   9

MILLER, Hector W., of Avon, m. Mary R. HAYES, of Granby, Nov. 2, 1845,
by Rev. William S. Knapp   11

Lucy H., of Bloomfield, m. James H. HUMPHREY, of Winchester, Sept.
5, 1837, by Cornelius B. Everest   3

Nathan F., m. Nancy H. ELY, of Bloomfield, Feb. 12, 1846, by A. C.

Page

PARSONS, (cont.)

Welthan A., of Bloomfield, m. Hezekiah P. **CURTIS**, of New Hartford,
Oct. 2, 1844, by Rev. Daniel Gibbs   9

William K., of Bennington, Wyoming Co., N. Y., m. Kezia **BROWN**, of
Bloomfield, Mar. 2, 1842, by William W. Backus   6

PATTERSON, Alixander, m. Mary M. **LAW**, b. of Simsbury, Dec. 12, 1852,
by Rev. Ralph H. Bowles   25

PECK, Helen C., of Bloomfield, m. Eli D. **HILLMAN**, of Mansfield, Jan. 26,
1852, by N. Whiting   20

Jane M., m. Eli Dwight **KILBURN**, Aug. 5, 1850, by Rev. Henry H.
Bates, of Warehouse Point   19

PERKINS, Bradley, m. Esther **THOMPSON**, b. of Granby, May 6, 1851, by
Rev. Ralph H. Bowles   23

PHELPS, Amanda, m. John **FORSYTH**, b. of Simbury, Oct. [ ], 1851, by
Rev. R. H. Bowles   23

Emma E., m. George **GAY**, b. of Bloomfield, May 25, 1852, by Niles
Whiting   21

John F., m. Sarah **HITCHCOCK**, b. of Bloomfield, Mar. 30, 1848, by
Rev. Niles Whiting   15

Rebecca C., m. John E. **FILLEY**, b. of Bloomfield, Mar. 6, 1843, by
Rev. Alfred Gates   8

PIERCE, Luther, of Amherst, Mass., m. Lavinia **GRISWOLD**, of Bloomfield,
Oct. 23, 1836, by Cornelius B. Everest   2

W[illia]m W., m. Fanny A. **HOLCOMB**, b. of Granby, Mar. 13, 1853,
by Rev. Ralph H. Bowles   25

PINNEY, Cecelia J., m. Julius **TANNER***, Oct. 13, 1850, by Rev. Ralph H.
Bowles of Tariffville   *(Perhaps **"FENNER"**)   20

Janet, of Bloomfield, m. Lewis **MAGAN**, of Hartford, Dec. 24, 1845,
by Rev. E. Cushman   11

Julia E., of Bloomfield, m. Edwin C. **GRISWOLD**, of Windsor, Feb.
16, 1852, by Rev. Pliney F. Sanborn, of East Granby   21

PRATT, Cornelia, m. Charles J. **HOLCOMB**, b. of Hartford, Aug. 6, 1848,
by Rev. N. Whiting   16

PROSSER, Achsah Angeline, m. Gaylord **HITCHCOCK**, Feb. 5, 1845, by L.
W. Wheeler   10

REED, Wilbert, of Granby, m. Henrietta **HUMPHREY**, of Bloomfield, on the
eve of Nov. 27, 1845, by William S. Knapp   11

RICHARDSON, Mary, m. William **MACKINTOSH**, b. of Bloomfield, Oct. 8,
1837, by David Osborn   3

ROBERTS, Elizabeth T., Mrs., m. Shaylor F. **BURNHAM**, May 31, 1837, by
Cornelius B. Everest   2

Lemuel D., m. Julia M. **BROWN**, b. of Bloomfield, Oct. 30, 1839, by
Cornelius B. Everist   4

Mary J., m. George **MILLS**, b. of Bloomfield, Sept. 8, 1852, by
Francis Williams   22

ROBINSON, James C., m. Anna W. **PARSONS**, Sept. 14, 1846, by Rev.
Septimus Robinson   13

ROCKWELL, Ellen M., of Bloomfield, m. Edwin **CORNISH**, of Simsbury,

ROCKWELL, (cont.)

Sept. 25, 1851, by Niles Whiting   20

Willis F., m. Catharine N. FILLEY, b. of Bloomfield, Apr. 12,
1849, by Rev. N. Whiting   17

ROGERS, Samuel, m. Mana L. SARGEANT, b. of Hartford, Nov. 13, 1848,
by Rev. N. Whiting   16

ROSE, Harriet A., of Granby, m. Chauncey NEWBURY, of Bloomfield, Dec.
17, 1848, by Rev. N. Whiting   17

ROWLEY, George W., m. Rebecca M. LATIMER, Mar. 19, 1845, by Rev.
L. W. Wheeler   10

Roger E., Dea. of Bennington, N. Y., m. Mrs. Caroline S. HUBBARD,
of Bloomfield, Feb. 6, 1853, by Rev. William A. Smith   24

SARGEANT, Mana L., m. Samuel ROGERS, b. of Hartford, Nov. 13, 1848,
by Rev. N. Whiting   16

SEARL, Quartus, m. Almena JONES, of Springfield, June 9, 1844, by
Lathrop W. Wheeler   9

SEYMOUR, Wooster C., of Hartford, m. Eliza C. ADAMS, of Bloomfield,
Dec. 20, 1849, by Rev. R. H. Main, of Tariffville   18

SHAW, W[illia]m H., of Glastonbury, m. Almira L. PARKER, of Newington,
Sept. 8, 1847, by Rev. J. A. Edmonds   14

SHEPARD, Elihu N., m. Emily BROWN, b. of Bloomfield, Feb. 16, 1847, by
A. C. Raymond   14

George L., m. Mrs. Rebecca L. MILLS, b. of Bloomfield, Jan. 13,
1851, by Rev. James C. Haughton   19

Laura C., of Bloomfield, m. Isaac BECKWITH, of New Hartford, May
25, 1840, by C. B. Everist   4

Maria A., of Bloomfield, m. Alfred L. GRIFFIN, of Windsor, Feb.
13, 1852, by Francis Williams   21

Mary Jane, of Bloomfield, m. Martin B. HOLCOMB, of Windsor, Jan.
10, 1845, by Rev. Nathaniel Kellogg   10

Melissa A., of Bloomfield, m. William H. WHITIING, of Leicester,
Mass., May 2, 1848, by Rev. A. C. Raymond   16

SMITH, Ann Eliza, of Hartford, m. Timothy DICKINSON, of New Britain,
July 13, 1848, by Rev. N. Whiting   16

Fanny, m. Warham FILLEY, Aug. 18, 1850, by Hiram Thall, J. P.   19

George E., m. Mary E. PARSONS, b. of Bloomfield, Mar. 28, 1848,
by John A. Edmonds   16

Orrin, of Hartford, m. Francis GRAHAM, of Bloomfield, Dec. 31,
1837, by D. Osborn   3

Rosannah, of Boston, m. George CALHOON, of Simsbury, May 28,
1843, by W. W. Backus   8

Samuel, of Buffalo, m. Amelia CLAPP, of Bloomfield, July 5, 1852,
by Rev. Ralph H. Bowles   23

William, of Bloomfield, m. Mrs. Isabel BULL, of Simsbury, Oct. 8,
1849, by N. Whiting   18

STARKWEATHER, Nathan, of Hartford, m. Cynthia LOOMIS, of
Bloomfield, Nov. 7, 1838, by Cornelius B. Everist   4

STATES, Adeline, m. Stephen GOODWIN, b. of Bloomfield, Aug. 26, 1852,

STATES, (cont.)
  by Francis Williams   22
STEEL, Salmon, of New Britain, m. Ruth A. LAMBERTON, of Bloomfield,
  Aug. 6, 1837, by Rev. D. Osborn   2
STODDARD, Rollin K., of Hartford, m. Mary Ann BROWN, of Bloomfield,
  Aug. 25, 1824, by Cornelius B. Everist   4
STRAND, George, m. Mary HITCHCOCK, June 26, 1849, by N. Whiting   18
TANNER*, Julius, m. Cecelia J. PINNEY, Oct. 13, 1850, by Rev. Ralph H.
  Bowles, of Tariffville *(Perhaps "FENNER")   20
TAYLOR, Elizabeth, m. William C. WOODRUFF, Apr. 18, 1852, by Hiram
  Thrall   22
TEFFT, William G., of Hartford, m. Emily G. NEARING, of Bloomfield,
  Mar. 15, 1842, by Rev. Davis Stocking   6
THOMPSON, Esther, m. Bradley PERKINS, b. of Granby, May 6, 1851, by
  Rev. Ralph H. Bowles   23
TORRELL, Frances A., of Norfolk, m. Hiram P. WAKEFIELD, of
  Colebrook, Oct. [ ], 1851, by Rev. Ralph H. Bowles   24
TUTTLE, Elane, of Hartford, m. Betsey LOOMIS, of Bloomfield, Mar. 24,
  1831, by Rev. Augustus Bolles   1
VIETS, Benjamin, of Granby, m. Anna HUBBARD, of Bloomfield, Sept. 1,
  1853, by Rev. Ralph H. Bowles   25
WAKEFIELD, Hiram P., of Colebrook, m. Frances A. TORRELL, of
  Norfolk, Oct. [ ], 1851, by Rev. Ralph H. Bowles   24
WATERS, Martha D., m. George GAY, b. of Bloomfield, Oct. 1, 1840, by
  W. C. Hoyt   5
WATROUS, Chloe, of Bloomfield, m. Samuel CLAPP, of Sandisfield, Mass.,
  Nov. 24, 1836, by Rev. Augustus Boles   2
WEBSTER, Hiram, m. Sally HIGLEY, b. of Bloomfield, Sept. 27, 1840, by
  W. C. Hoyt   5
WEST, Gustavus, of New Britain, m. Mary KELSEY, of Bloomfield, Sept.
  6, 1843, by Rev. Alfred Gates   9
WESTLAND, Chester U., m. Cordelia ALLYN, b. of Bloomfield, Feb. 28,
  1847, by William S. Knapp   14
WHITING, William H., of Leicester, Mass., m. Melissa A. SHEPARD, of
  Bloomfield, May 2, 1848, by Rev. A. C. Raymond   16
WILBUR, Aaron E., of Providence, R. I., m. Jane A. FRISBIE, of
  Bloomfield, Aug. 8, 1842, by W. W. Backus   7
WILCOX, Calista, of Simsbury, m. John F. WILSON, of Bloomfield,
  Sept. 17, 1848, by Rev. N. Whiting   16
WILSON, Amelia J., m. Allyn C. BARBER, b. of Bloomfield, Feb. 19, 1843,
  by W. W. Backus   8
  John F., m. Louisa COOK, b. of Bloomfield, Mar. 26, 1846, by
    William S. Knapp   12
  John F., of Bloomfield, m. Calista WILCOX, of Simsbury, Sept. 17,
    1848, by Rev. N. Whiting   16
WING, Sylvanus, Jr., of St. Louis, Mo., m. Harriet NEWBERRY, of
  Bloomfield, Sept. 12, 1837, by Cornelius B. Everist   3
WOOD, Oscar, of Hartford, m. Catharine M. BOWERS, of Bloomfield, Mar.

Page

WOOD, (cont.)

    10, 1838, by Cornelius B. Everist   4

WOODRUFF, William C., m. Elizabeth **TAYLOR,** Apr. 18, 1852, by Hiram
    Thrall   22

WRIGHT, Emily, of Bloomfield, m. Henry **MERRELLS,** of Hartford, Sept.
    23, 1844, by Lathrop W. Wheeler   9

    Henry, m. Chloe **HOSKINS,** Dec. 9, 1849, by George Newberry, J. P.   18

BOZRAH VITAL RECORDS
1786 - 1850

	Vol.	Page
ABEL ABELL, (cont.)		
Hezekiah, of Colchester, m. Mary Ann **BILL**, of Franklin, May 8, 1834, by John W. Salter	1	30
Jared A., soldier, single, d. June 27, 1864, ae 32; killed at Cedar Mountain, Va.	3	43
Jared Andrus, s. W[illia]m C. & Lucy H., b. Dec. 16, 1832	1	140
Jesse, m. Elizabeth **LATHROP**, b. of Bozrah, Nov. 11, 1788	1	38
John, s. Jesse & Elizabeth, b. Sept. 24, 1790	1	38
John, of Bozrah, m. Lucretia **MEECH**, of Preston, Sept. 24, 1818, by Rev. John Hyde	1	77
John Wellington, s. John & Lucretia, b. July 12, 1821	1	77
Lucretia Maria, d. John & Lucretia, b. June 20, 1819	1	77
Lucy H., m. William C. **ABELL**, Nov. 16, 1826, by Rev. David Austin	1	140
Lucy H., w. Simeon, d. Mar. 30, 1853	1	51
Lucy Huntington Leffingwell, d. Simeon, Jr. & Lucy, b. Nov. 29, 1800	1	51
Lydia, wid. Samuel, d. Aug. 15, 1786	1	38
Lydia, d. Jesse & Elizabeth, b. Jan. 24, 1796; d. Feb. 24, 1796	1	38
Lydia Huntington, d. John & Lucretia, b. July 26, 1831	1	77
Mary, d. Jesse & Elizabeth, b. Feb. 14, 1798	1	38
Mary E., d. July 4, 1856, ae 2	3	13
Mary G., of Bozrah, m. Frederick A. **PARKER**, of Ellsworth, O., Oct. 13, 1823, by Rev. D. Austin	1	44
Mindwell, w. Capt. Elijah, d. Apr. 9, 1827, ae 46 y. 6 m.	1	114
Philura, d. Gurdon & Ann Vera, b. Mar. 24, 1821	1	83
Rhoda, m. Gardiner **AVERY**, b. of Bozrah, May 25, 1813	1	69
Samuel, d. June 17, 1785	1	38
Serviah E., of Colchester, m. Clark **HOUGH**, of Bozrah, Dec. 1, 1818, by William Palmer, Elder	1	84
Simeon, Jr., of Bozrah, m. Lucy H. **LEFFINGWELL**, of Norwich, Mar. 12, 1796	1	51
Simeon, s. Elijah & Mindwell, b. Oct. 29, 1822	1	114
Simeon, s. William C. & Lucy H., b. July 25, 1829	1	140
Simeon, d. Sept. 16, 1849, ae 82	1	51
Simeon, farmer, d. Sept. 16, 1849, ae 82	2	9
Simeon, m. Fanny E. **STARK**, b. of Bozrah, Oct. 29, [ ], by Rev. W[illia]m P. Avery	1	161
Simon Lathrop, s. John & Lucretia, b. Feb. 1, 1825	1	77
Thomas Meech, s. John & Lucretia, b. May 12, 1822	1	77
William C., m. Lucy H. **ABEL**, Nov. 16, 1826, by Rev. David Austin	1	140
William Calkins, s. Jesse & Elizabeth, b. Apr. 6, 1800	1	38
William Jesse, s. William C. & Lucy H., b. Oct. 16, 1827	1	140
Zeruiah, w. Hezekiah, d. Dec. 29, 1823, ae 76	1	27
Zervia, see also Serviah		
ADAMS, Charles, Carpenter, ae 21, b. Norwich, res. Norwich, m. Olive **HALL**, ae 21, b. Bozrah, Sept. [ ], 1849, by		

	Vol.	Page
ADAMS, (cont.)		
Rev. Edward Elles	2	8
Charles B., of Greenville, Norwich, m. Olive **LORD**, of Bozrah, Sept. 10, 1849, by Rev. Edward Eells	1	156
Emeline, res. Bozrah, m. W[illia]m, P. **GARDNER**, ae 21, b. Canterbury, res. Bozrah, May 1, 1851, by Rev. W[illia]m B. Avery	2	10
Emeline A., m. William B. **GARDINER**, b. of Bozrah, May 1, 1851, by Rev. W[illia]m P. Avery	1	159
Joseph L., of Colchester, m. Fanny **PACKER**, of Salem, Sept. 25, 1836, by Rev. Benjamin G. Goff	1	139
Olive, m. Daniel **HERRICK**, b. of Canterbury, Oct. 26, 1817	1	106
Rachel, m. Elias **LOOMIS**, b. of Colchester, Oct. 8, 1850, by Rev. Benjamin G. Goff	1	158
ALBEE, Lucy, b. [ ]; m. Elijah **WATERMAN,** [ ]	1	103-4
ALLEN, [see also **ALLYN**], Ambrose, s. Jason & Sarah, b. Mar. 14, 1788	1	1
Ellen, farmer, b. Franklin, res. Bozrah, d. Dec. 7, 1852, ae 1; bd. Norwich	3	4
Eunice A., m. Samuel W. **RIPLEY**, June 18, 1832, by Rev. Erastus Ripley	1	130
Flavius, d. Feb. 16, [1871?], ae 10 m.; bd. Feb. 16, [1871?] in Baldic	3	62
James Deans, s. Jason & Sarah, b. June 27, 1792	1	1
Jason, m. Sarah **CROCKER**, b. of Bozrah, Oct. 5, 1786, by Neh[emiah] Waterman, J. P.	1	1
Lucy J., m. Rev. Joseph S. **EMERY**, b. of Bozrahville, June 24, 1832, by Salmon Cone, V. D. M.	1	130
Thomas Crocker, s. Jason & Sarah, b. Feb. 18, 1790	1	1
ALLYN, [see also **ALLEN**], Abigail, m. Daniel **RUDD**, Dec. [ ], 1780	1	73
ANDREW, Charles G., d. Oct. 20, 1854, ae 15; bd. Throop B. G.	3	7
Elizabeth, married, b. Mass., d. Nov. 7, 1861, ae 39	3	31
Gilbert, m. Eliza **MAYNARD**, b. of Bozrah, Dec. [ ], 1843, by Rev. George Perkins	1	154
ARMSTRONG, Abigail, m. William **CROCKER**, Jr., b. of Bozrah, Nov. 26, 1829, by Rev. David Austin	1	122
Albert, of Killingly, Conn., m. Anna H. **HOUGH**, of Bozrah, Sept. 6, 1843, by Rev. Bela Hicks	1	86
Charlotte E., of Bozrah, m. Samuel **VINING**, of Norwich, May 3, 1846, by Rev. W[illia]m M. Berchard	1	126
Eleanor F., m. Nelson L. **LEAMANS**, b. of Bozrah, Nov. 10, 1844, by Rev. Jesse B. Denison	1	127
George D., s. W[illia]m L., farmer, ae 30, & Sarah, ae 28, b. July 25, 1849	2	4
Joel, farmer, married, d. Apr. 19, 1864, ae 67	3	43
Julia A., m. Daniel **CAPIN**, b. of Bozrah, June 16, 1844, by Rev. George Perkins	1	52

	Vol.	Page
ARMSTRONG, (cont.)		
Laura, d. Learned, farmer, ae 39, & Desire, ae 26, b.		
Aug. 27, 1847	2	1
Lucy Ann, d. Leonard T. & Lois, b. July 19, 1823	1	115
Olive, of Bozrah, m. Cephus N. **PORTER**, of Hebron, Mar.		
4, 1841, by Rev. George Perkins	1	126
Pamela, m. Cyrus W. **MOORE**, b. of Bozrah, Mar. 24, 1839,		
by Rev. Oliver Brown	1	143
Solomon, of Lebanon, m. Orra Ann **AUSTIN**, of Bozrah, Oct.		
19, 1834, by Rev. John W. Salter	1	108
ASP, Hans D., of Norwich, m. Sarah N. **AUSTIN**, of Bozrah, Oct.		
27, 1851, by Rev. W[illia]m P. Avery	1	121
ATCHISON, Mary, housekeeper, b. Franklin, res. Bozrah, d. Jan.		
12, 1853, ae 27, bd. New Haven	3	4
AUSTIN, Alfred, m. Roba **SIMMONS**, of Bozrah, Dec. 11, 1831,		
by Rev. Jared Andrus	1	84
Anis Eliza, m. Hiram C. **MINER**, b. of Bozrah, Nov. 1, 1835,		
by Rev. Oliver Brown	1	137
Joseph, cooper, b. Foster, R. I., res. Bozrah, d. Jan.		
2, 1848, ae 63	2	3
Orra Ann, of Bozrah, m. Solomon **ARMSTRONG**, of		
Lebanon, Oct. 19, 1834, by Rev. John W. Salter	1	108
Owen J., d. [ ], 1847	2	3
Reuben E., m. Almira S. **FRINK**, Apr. 27, 1851, by Rev.		
Henry B. Whittington	1	121
Sarah N., of Bozrah, m. Hans D. **ASP**, of Norwich, Oct. 27,		
1851, by Rev. W[illia]m P. Avery	1	121
Thomas P., d. Oct. 10, 1855, ae 1 y. 5 m.	3	10
Warner, laborer, single, b. R. Island, d. Jan. 24, 1864, ae 63	3	43
AVERY, A. F., farmer, d. May 20, 1870, ae 66	3	49
Albert G., m. Hannah F. **WATERMAN**, b. of Bozrah, Feb. 3,		
1830, by Rev. Cornelius B. Everest	1	123
Albert G., m. Alice T. **ABELL**, b. of Bozrah, Apr. 14, 1839,		
by Rev. Joel R. Arnold	1	123
Albert Gallatin, s. Gardner & Rachel, b. Apr. 8, 1804	1	69
Alice S., housekeeper, married, d. Jan. 30, 1855, ae 44	3	10
Alice T., w. Albert G., d. Jan. 31, 1855	1	123
Charles, carpenter, d. May 19, 1869, ae 83	3	49
Dimis, d. Charles, laborer, ae 63, & Caroline, ae 40, b. Nov. 9,		
1847	2	1
Dimmis, d. [1848], ae 1 m.	2	3
Elisha V., m. Mary **HAMMOND**, Sept. 23, 1832, by Asa		
Wilcox, Elder	1	113
Elizabeth M., of Montville, m. Francis E. **GARDNER**, of		
Bozrah, Nov. 13, 1842, by Levi Meech, Elder	1	150
Ellenette, d. W[illia]m P., clergyman, ae 35, b. July 3, 1851	2	11
Emily, m. Uriah **GARDINER**, b. of Bozrah, Dec. 1, 1833, by		
John W. Salter	1	1

	Vol.	Page
BABCOCK, (cont.)		
the house of Capt. Chesebrough	1	73
Jona[than], of Brookfield, N. Y., m. Caroline L.		
CHESEBEROUGH, of Bozrah, Feb. 6, 1832, by Rev.		
Peter Sabin	1	95
BACKUS, BACKAS, Abel, s. Ozias & Elizabeth, b. May 10, 1805	1	32
Anna H., m. Henry **GILLET**, of Lebanon, Nov. 12, 1823, by		
Rev. David Austin	1	64
Betsey, d. Ebenezer & Phebe, b. Feb. 14, 1779	1	4
Charles. [s. Simeon & Eunice], b. [ ]	1	99
Clarrisy, d. Jabez & Hannah, b. Aug. 11, 1811	1	15
Clarissa, m. William **KELLEY**, [ ]	1	111
Deborah, m. William **FISH**, b. of Norwich, Mar. 22, 1772	1	9
Dice, d. Oliver & Dice, b. Aug. 7, 1796	1	15
Ebenezer, Jr., m. Elizabeth **WATERMAN**, b. of Norwich, Oct.		
14, 1766	1	4
Ebenezer, m. Phebe **CALKINS**, b. of Norwich, May 28, 1778	1	4
Ebenezer, m. Elizabeth **CROCKER**, b. of Bozrah, Dec. 30,		
1787	1	4
Eber, s. Ebenezer & Elizabeth, b. Oct. 10, 1767	1	4
Eliza, of Bozrah, m. Othniel **GAGER**, of Franklin, Jan. 28,		
1827, by Rev. David Austin	1	87
Elizabeth, w. Ebenezer, d. Oct. 8, 1776	1	4
Elizabeth, d. Oliver & Dice, b. Nov. 10, 1801	1	15
Elizabeth Mary, d. Jabez & Hannah, b. Mar. 10, 1813	1	15
Elizabeth Waterman, [twin with Lydia Waterman], d. Ozias		
& Elizabeth, b. May 24, 1802	1	32
Esther, d. Oliver & Dice, b. Sept. 12, 1793	1	15
Ezra, s. Ebenezer & Elizabeth, b. July 17, 1771	1	4
Harriet, d. Ozias & Elizabeth, b. Apr. 23, 1799	1	32
Harry, s. Ebenezer & Phebe, b. Apr. 21, 1784	1	4
Jabez, s. Oliver & Dice, b. Apr. 26, 1788	1	15
Jabez, m. Hannah **LATHROPE**, Nov. 25, 1810	1	15
Joshua, s. Ebenezer & Elizabeth, b. Jan. 9, 1789	1	4
Josiah, manufacturer, b. Montville, res. Bozrah, d. Dec. 19,		
[1852], ae 40; bd. T[h]roop B. G.	3	4
Josiah, [s. Simeon & Eunice], b. [ ]	1	99
Love, [d. Simeon & Eunice], b. [ ]	1	99
Lucy, d. Ebenezer & Phebe, b. Mar. 6, 1782	1	4
Lydia, d. Oliver & Dice, b. Aug. 2, 1798	1	15
Lydia Waterman, [twin with Elizabeth Waterman], d. Ozias		
& Elizabeth, b. May 24, 1802	1	32
Nabby, d. Ozias & Elizabeth, b. Mar. 10, 1789	1	32
Oliver, of Bozrah, m. Dice **HYDE**, of Franklin, May 20,		
1787, by Samuel Nott, Clerk	1	15
Ozias, of Franklin, m. Elizabeth **ABELL**, of Bozrah, Sept.		
21, 1786	1	32
Ozias, s. Ozias & Elizabeth, b. July 22, 1787	1	32

	Vol.	Page
BACKUS, BACKAS, (cont.)		
Phebe, d. Ebenezer & Phebe, b. July 21, 1780	1	4
Phebe, w. Ebenezer, d. Sept. 11, 1785	1	4
Phebe, d. Ebenezer & [Phebe], d. Sept. 19, 1785	1	4
Phebe, m. William **DURKEE**, b. of Bozrah, June 8, 1787	1	6
Sally, m. Thomas Baldwin, [ ]	1	81
Salley B., d. Jabez & Hannah, b. Dec. 9, 1814	1	15
Sarah, d. Oliver & Dice, b. June 29, 1790	1	15
Simeon, m. Eunice **WATERMAN**, Oct. 28, 1772	1	99
Simeon, d. Jan. 5, 1782, ae 25	1	100
Simeon, [s. Simeon & Eunice], b. [ ]	1	99
Tallcott, s. Eben[ezer] & Elizabeth, b. Jan. 22, 1791	1	4
------, wid., m. Silas **HARTSHORN**, [ ]	1	99
BAILEY, Charles Henry, s. Roswell & Sally, b. Dec. 9, 1827	1	107
Eliza M., of Bozrah, m. Lucius **BROWN**, of Lebanon, [Dec.]		
3, 1851, by Rev. W. P. Avery	1	151
Emily E., d. Jan. 5, 1870, ae 20	3	49
Hannah, b. Oct. 14, 1784	1	72
Hannah, m. Guy **HOUGH**, Mar. 31, 1806	1	72
Henry, d. Apr. 22, 1861, ae 67	3	24
Jabez Hough, s. Roswell & Sally, b. Oct. 3, 1824	1	107
Julia, m. John **BARSTOW**, Mar. 29, 1837, by Rev. John Hyde	1	142
Lydia, b. Norwich, res. Bozrah, d. Jan. 25, 1854, ae 57;		
bd. T[h]roop B. G.	3	7
Mary, of Bozrah, m. Oliver **FOWLER**, of Norwich, Sept. 27,		
1848, by Rev. John P. Gulliver, Norwich	1	154
Mary J., ae 24, of Bozrah, m. Oliver **FOWLER**, carpenter,		
ae 22, b. Lebanon, res. Bozrah, Sept. 27, 1848, by Rev. J.		
P. Gulliver	2	5
Otis G., Dr., of Paulet, Vt., m. Tragene A. **HILL**, of Bozrah,		
Jan. 5, 1851, by Rev. W[illia]m P. Avery	1	159
Otis G., ae 28, b. Vermont, res. Vermont, m. Aurelia **HILL**,		
ae 22, b. Saybrook, res. Bozrah, Jan. 5, 1851, by Rev.		
W[illia]m B. Avery	2	10
Phebe J., d. W[illia]m F., farmer, ae 27, & Phebe A.,		
ae 23, b. Mar. 14, 1851	2	11
Roswell, m. Sally C. **HOUGH**, Jan. 7, 1821, by Rev. William		
Palmer, at Deacon Jabez Hough's	1	107
Roswell, d. Feb. 16, 1833	1	107
Roswell Leander, s. Roswell & Sally, b. Dec. 1, 1829	1	107
Sally C., domestic, widow, d. [ ], 1864, ae 67	3	43
Sally Jane, d. Roswell & Sally, b. Mar. 1, 1833	1	107
William F., of Colchester, m. Phebe A. **JOHNSON**, of Bozrah,		
Nov. 26, 1846, by Rev. W[illia]m M. Birchard	1	147
William Francis, s. Roswell & Sally, b. Aug. 17, 1823	1	107
BAKER, Annis, of New York City, m. John Jaspers **RICKERS**, of		
Nesmeright, Provice Ostfinisland, Kingdom of Hanover,		
July 10, 1817, by Rev. Mr. Clarke. Witnesses: W[illia]m		

	Vol.	Page
BAKER, (cont.)		
Ritter, Sally Smith of New York	1	21
Elizabeth, w. Asa, d. Dec. 27, 1808	1	29
Gilbert, m. Lydia **CALKINS**, b. of Bozrah, Mar. 29, 1795, by Neh[emiah] Waterman, Jr. J. P.	1	49
BALDWIN, Andrew, s. Eliphalet & Sibel, b. May 30, 1789; d. Feb. 11, 1790	1	11
Charles B., m. Frances D. **HOUGH**, b. of Bozrah, [Feb], 19, 1840, by Tho[ma]s L. Shipman	1	146
Charles Backus, s. Thomas & Sally, b. Oct. 2, 1811	1	81
Eliphalet, m. Sibel **WOOD**, b. of Norwich, Oct. 6, 1774	1	11
Eliphalet, s. Eliphalet & Sibel, b. Apr. 13, 1787	1	11
Harriet, d. Eliphalet & Sibel, b. July 25, 1779	1	11
Hariot, m. William **GAGER**, b. of Bozrah, Mar. 21, 1799	1	57
Henry, single, d. May 2, 1859, ae 17	3	24
Jabez Backus, s. Thomas & Sally, b. Dec. 7, 1815	1	81
Marian Arabella, d. Thomas & Sally, b. Apr. 23, 1824	1	81
Mason A., single, d. Sept. 18, 1861, ae 37	3	31
Octavia, d. Eliphalet & Sibel, b. Aug. 11, 1777	1	11
Rachel, d. Eliphalet & Sibel, b. Sept. 8, 1781	1	11
Rachel, m. Gardner **AVERY**, b. of Bozrah, June 10, 1802	1	69
Sally, w. Thomas, d. Aug. 15, 1854, ae 64 y.	1	81
Sarah, d. Aug. 15, 1854, ae 64; bd. Throop B. G.	3	7
Sarah Maria, d. Thomas & Sally, b. Jan. 28, 1828	1	81
Susan B., of Bozrah, m. Thomas M. **NICHOLS**, of Yonkers, N. Y., Nov. 5, 1832, by Rev. John W. Salter	1	130
Sibel, d. Eliphalet & Sibel, b. Aug. 19, 1783	1	11
Sibel, m. Oliver **WOODWORTH**, b. of Bozrah, Feb. 7, 1809	1	68
Sybel, w. Eliphalet, d. Oct. 13, 1833, ae 76	1	11
Thomas, s. Eliphalet & Sibel, b. June 27, 1785	1	11
Thomas, farmer, widower, d. Apr. 14, 1864, ae 79	3	43
Thomas, m. Sally **BACKUS**, [ ]	1	81
BANNING, Austin, d. Sept. 19, 1864, ae 2 m.	3	38
J., laborer, d. Nov. 19, 1870, ae 42	3	49
BARKER, Lucy Cordelia, d. James & Lucy, b. May 13, 1820	1	36
------, st. b., d. Richard, carpenter, ae 21, & Mary, ae 19, June 13, 1849	2	4
BARRETT, Calvin, m. Mary **WATERMAN**, b. of Bozrah, July 17, 1785, by Nehemiah Waterman, J. P.	1	43
Mary Calvin, d. Calvin & Mary, b. Feb. 19, 1786	1	43
BARROWS, Adaline, m. Simon **CLARK**, b. of Bozrah, Oct. 14, 1832, by Rev. R. Landfear	1	130
Lucretia, of Bozrahville, m. Joseph **PRIOR**, of Plainfield, Mar. 18, 1832, by Rev. Jared Andrus	1	127
BARRY, John, ae 22, res. Norwich, m. Julia **SULLIVAN**, ae 16, Apr. 24, 1851, by Rev. C. Leffingwell	2	10
Samuel, of East Haddam, m. Mary **WOODWORTH**, of Franklin, Nov. 13, 1823, by Rev. David Austin	1	64

	Vol.	Page
BARSTOW, BARSTO, John, m. Julia **BAILEY**, Mar. 29, 1837, by Rev. John Hyde	1	142
William Kelley, s. John & Julia, b. Nov. 22, 1838; d. May 18, 1843, by drowning	1	142
BARTLETT, Mary, m. Charles H. **CHURCH**, b. of Bozrah, Aug. 31, 1851, by Rev. W[illia]m P. Avery	1	160
BASS, Elizabeth H., m. Lloyd A. **WAITE**, Oct. 24, 1830, by Rev. Leonard B. Griffing	1	58
BATES, William, of Bozrah, m. Cealia **DURFY**, of Scituate, R. I., Dec. 1, 1834, by Rev. Hiram Walden	1	91
BAYSET, Joseph, manufacturer, married, d. Aug. 18, 1857, ae 45	3	16
BECKWITH, Allen, married, d. May 5, 1859, ae 63	3	24
Cirrenus, m. Patty **INGRAHAM**, b. of Bozrah, Sept. 16, 1821, by William Palmer, Elder, at the house of Mr. Ingraham	1	108
Lemuel, of Franklin, m. Julia **BINGHAM**, of Bozrah, Jan. 30, 1842, by Rev. John W. Salter. Witnesses: Capt. Orimel Johnson, Maj. D. S. Hough, Allen Beckwith, etc.	1	144
Phebe, m. Daniel **VERGASON**, Oct. 8, 1786, by N. Waterman, J. P.	1	20
BEEBE, Abigail, d. Nov. 8, 1869, ae 71	3	49
Ardelia G., of Norwich, m. Henry W. **CAREW**, of Norwich, May 7, 1848, by Rev. Christ. Leffingwell	2	2
Amelia G., m. Henry W. **CAREW**, b. of Norwich, May 7, 1848, by Rev. Christopher Leffingwell	1	135
Elizabeth M., of Norwich, m. Chauncey A. **WILLARD**, of Madison, Nov. 24, 1850, by Rev. Christopher Leffingwell	1	158
Elizabeth M., ae 22, b. Norwich, res. Norwich, m. Chauncey A. **WILLARD**, ae 26, b. Madison, res. Madison, Nov. 24, 1850, by Rev. Christopher Leffingwell	2	10
Samuel D., farmer, b. Norwich, married, d. Dec. 13, 1856, ae 30	3	13
BENNETT, BENET, Henry, of Canterbury, m. Sarah M. **DRAKE**, of Lebanon, Sept. 8, 1851, by Rev. W[illia]m P. Avery	1	160
James, farmer, married, b. Norwich, d. Mar. 15, 1858, ae 53	3	16
BENOIT, Joseph, d. Jan. 30, [1871?], ae 9 y. 9 m.; bd. Jan. 31, [1871?] in Baltic	3	62
BERWICH, Martha, d. John, mason, ae 42, & Jane, ae 39, b. June 30, 1848	2	1
BILL, Benjamin, domestic, single, d. Mar. 17, 1855, ae 57	3	10
Hannah, single, d. Apr. 18, 1859, ae 86	3	24
Lyman E., of Lebanon, m. Maria **HOUGH**, of Bozrah, Nov. 5, 1828, by Rev. David Austin	1	119
Mary Ann, of Franklin, m. Hezekiah **ABELL**, of Colchester, May 8, 1834, by John W. Salter	1	30
Palmer, farmer, b. Ledyard, res. Bozrah, m. Mary A. **BROWN**, b. Lebanon, res. Lebanon, [, 1848?], by Rev. P. Mathewson	2	5
BINGHAM, Abiah, s. Nathan & Susannah, b. Jan. 3, 1780	1	35

	Vol.	Page
BINGHAM, (cont.)		
Adonijah, d. May 15, 1812	1	17
Alexander, s. Nathan & Zeruiah, b. Aug. 18, 1792	1	35
Charles, s. Nathan & Zeruiah, b. Oct. 18, 1784	1	35
David, d. May 31, 1794	1	17
Elizabeth, d. June 16, 1803	1	17
Eunice, d. Nathan & Zeruiah, b. July 5, 1794	1	35
Eunice R., of Norwich, m. John C. **LUCE**, of Worcester, Mass., Oct. 5, 1847, by Rev. W[illia]m M. Birchard	1	149
Ezra, s. David & Hannah, d. July 13, 1775	1	17
Ezra, s. Nathan & Susannah, b. Feb. 25, 1782	1	35
Hannah, d. David & Hannah, d. Aug. 11, 1769	1	17
Hannah, d. Nathan & Susannah, b. Jan. 22, 1778	1	35
Hannah, w. David, d. June 24, 1788	1	17
Henry, d. Aug. 28, 1863, ae 34	3	38
Henry A., of Norwich, m. Clarissa L. **PENDLETON**, of Bozrah, Dec. 9, 1845, by Rev. W[illia]m M. Birchard	1	90
Isaac, s. Nathan & Zeruiah, b. Nov. 17, 1788	1	35
Julia, of Bozrah, m. Lemuel **BECKWITH**, of Franklin, Jan. 30, 1842, by Rev. John W. Salter. Witnesses: Capt. Orimel Johnson, Maj. D. S. Hough, Allen Beckwith, etc.	1	144
Martha, d. David & Hannah, d. Sept. 2, 1750	1	17
Nathan, of Norwich, m. Susannah **STARK**, of Lebanon, Mar.		35
27, 1777, by Timothy Stone, Clerk, Lebanon	1	35
Nathan, m. Zeruiah **SABIN**, b. of Norwich, Jan. 29, 1784	1	35
Oliver, s. Nathan & Zeruiah, b. Dec. 6, 1786	1	35
Sarah, of Norwich, m. Asahel **SANGER**, of Bozrah, Dec. 27, 1789	1	36
Susan E., of Norwich, m. Charles M. **PENDLETON**, of Bozrah, Dec. 10, 1845, by Rev. W[illia]m M. Birchard	1	89
Susannah, w. Nathan, d. Mar. 15, 1782	1	35
Susannah, d. Nathan & Zeruiah, b. Oct. 28, 1790	1	35
BIRCHARD, BERCHARD, BURCHARD, Asenath, d. Nov. 24, 1850, ae 78	2	9
Edwards Metcalf, s. William M. & Mary W., b. Oct. 28, 1846	1	155
Eunice, single, d. Apr. 16, 1859, ae 75	3	24
Phebe, m. Isaac **JOHNSON**, b. of Bozrah, Apr. 5, 1795	1	67
William Edwards, s. William M. & Mary, b. Oct. 31, 1844	1	155
William M., of Bozrah, m. Mary **WHITMAN**, of Turner, Me., Dec. 8, 1843	1	155
BISHOP, Abby E., domestic, d. June 29, 1868, ae 31	3	48
Andrew, soldier, d. [ ], 1865, ae 31, in service at Andersonville	3	44
Elizabeth, d. [, 1858, ae 22	3	21
Hannah, m. Daniel **FARGO**, May 9, 1782	1	60
Jeremiah, single, d. Dec. 25, 1858, ae 26	3	21
Lewis, d. Oct. 11, 1866, ae 11 m.	3	44
Mary J., d. Dec. 18, 1866, ae 5	3	44

	Vol.	Page
BROWN, (cont.)		
29, 1849, by Rev. Christ. Leffingwell	2	5
Alice I., d. Sept. 12, 1855, ae 6 m. 11 d.	3	10
Almira, ae 18, b. Montville, res. Bozrah, m. Benj[amin]		
INGRAHAM, laborer, ae 20, b. Chatham, res. Bozrah,		
July 11, 1849, by Rev. Lyman Story	2	5
Charles F., farmer, res. Lebanon, m. B. **SPICER**, res.		
Bozrah, Sept. 9, 1849, by Rev. E. Elles	2	8
Charles L., of Lebanon, m. Eunice B. **SPICER**, of Bozrah,		
Sept. 9, 1849, by Rev. Nathan W. Miner	1	155
Clarrissa Ann, d. Daniel, farmer, ae 31, & Mary Ann, ae		
26, b. Oct. 16, 1847	2	1
Edwin, s. Edwin, laborer, & Mary, b. Dec. 3, 1849	2	7
Edwin H., m. Mary **CARROLL**, Sept. 14, 1851, by Rev.		
W[illia]m P. Avery	1	160
Harriet A., d. Dec. 31, 1847, ae 2	2	3
Julette A., d. Dec. 8, 1847, ae 4	2	3
Julia Abby, d. Dec. 17, 1847, ae 4	2	3
Lucius, of Lebanon, m. Eliza M. **BAILEY**, of Bozrah, [Dec.] 3,		
1851, by Rev. W. P. Avery	1	151
Mary A., of Bozrah, m. Henry **LATHROP**, of Lebanon, Apr.		
1, 1841, by Rev. Benjamin G. Goff	1	124
Mary A., b. Lebanon, res. Lebanon, m. Palmer **BILL**, farmer,		
b. Ledyard, res. Bozrah, [1848?], by Rev. P.		
Mathewson	2	5
Mary Eny, d. George, farmer, ae 48, & Rachal, ae 32, by		
July 6, 1848	2	1
Paul H., of Bozrah, m. Esther P. **MAINE**, of Norwich, June		
26, 1847, by Rev. Christopher Leffingwell	1	114
Stephen A., carpenter, res. Bozrah, m. Mary E. **MARE**, res.		
Bozrah, Nov. 19, 1849, by Rev. E. Elles	2	8
Stephen A., m. Angeline **MOORE**, Nov. 29, 1849, by Rev.		
Edward Eells	1	156
W[illia]m, of Lisbon, m. Lucy **PARTELO**, of Bozrah, July		
4, 1847, by John W. Houghton, J. P.	1	122
W[illia]m J., married, d. [ ], 1863, ae 27	3	38
W[illia]m J., mechanic, d. Feb. 15, 1865, ae 63	3	44
William W., of Norwich, m. Nancy **POST**, of Bozrah, Jan.		
3, 1822, by Rev. Reuben Palmer, at Mr. Stephen Post's	1	55
BRUMLEY, Charles Newton, s. Stephen D. & Julia, b. July 25,		
1844; d. Oct. 4, 1844	1	70
Elizabeth H., ae 23, b. Chester, Mass., m. Henry **DEWEY**,		
farmer, ae 26, b. Westfield, Mass., res. Westfield, Mass.,		
May 11, 1851, by Rev. C. Leffingwell	2	10
Elizabeth W., of Chester, Mass., m. Henry **DEWEY**, of		
Westfield, Mass., May 11, 1851, by Rev. Christopher		
Leffingwell	1	160
Jane, d. Mar. 28, 1855, ae 70	3	10

	Vol.	Page
BRUMLEY, (cont.)		
Mary, m. Jedediah **VERGASON**, Jr., [ ]	1	47
Reuben L., of Norwich, m. Mary **LEFFINGWELL**, of Bozrah, Dec. 5, 1821, by Reuben Palmer, Jr., Adm., at the house of Gurdon Leffingwell	1	16
BUCK, Matilda, ae 18, worker in cotton mill, b. East Haddam, res. Bozrahville, m. Erastus A. **MINER**, spinner, ae 23, b. Bozrah, res. Bozrahville, Dec. 17, 1847, by Rev. Stephen Hays	2	2
BUDDER, ------, d. Carl, laborer, b. Feb. 17, 1850	2	7
BUELL, Freedom, of Lebanon, m. Caleb **GARDINER**, of Bozrah, Jan. 4, 1795	2	7
BULKEY, M., domestic, d. Mar. 7, 1870, ae 55	3	49
BUMP, Ebenezer, of Lyme, m. Mary Ann **ROSE**, of Bozrah, Apr. 5, 1835, by Gardner Avery, J. P.	1	121
BUMSTEAD, Mary R., of Munson, Mass., m. Benjamin N. C. **PEIRCE**, of North Kingston, R. I. Dec. 27, 1835, by Rev. Oliver Brown	1	137
BURDICK, Fanny M., of Bozrah, m. William L. **WEAVER**, of Windham, May 26, 1847, by Rev. W[illia]m M. Burchard	1	122
BURKLEE, Patrick, married, b. Ireland, d. Mar. 26, 1862, ae 54	3	32
BUSHNELL, Chauncey H., of Norwich, m. Mary A. **POST**, of Bozrah, Mar. 29, 1840, by Rev. John Paine	1	77
Lucy, domestic, d. [ ], 1867, ae 88	3	48
BUSWICH, [see also **BERWICH**], Martha, d. Mar. 22, 1862, ae 12	3	32
BUTTERS, ----, girl, d. Apr. 13, 1855	3	10
-----, girl, d. Apr. 14, 1855	3	10
-----, Mrs., d. May 5, 1855, ae 40	3	10
CALKINS, CALKIN, Betsey, m. Thomas **CROCKER**, Jr., b. of Bozrah, Apr. 15, 1792	1	43
Hannah, m. Samuel **GAGER**, July 29, 1773, by Benj[amin] Throop, Clerk	1	2
Lydia, m. Gilbert **BAKER**, b. of Bozrah, Mar. 29, 1795, by Neh[emiah] Waterman, Jr., J. P.	1	49
Naomi, m. Steyphen **PALMER**, of Franklin, Nov. 4, 1792	1	19
Phebe, m. Ebenezer **BACKUS**, b. of Norwich, May 28, 1778	1	4
CAMADA, Mariettenee, of Bozrah, m. John **HUMES**, of Norwich, July 1, 1849, by Rev. James Mather	1	133
CAPIN, Almond Adelbert, [d. Philip A. & Temperance C.], b. Mar. 17, 1845	1	116
Cyrus Randall, s. Randall, b. July 5, 1845	1	135
Daniel, m. Julia A. **ARMSTRONG**, b. of Bozrah, June 16, 1844, by Rev. George Perkins	1	52
Erastus S., [s. Philip A. & Temperance C.], b. Apr. 6, 1848	1	116
Erastus S., s. Philip A., manufacturer, ae 30, & Temperance, ae 29, b. Apr. 6, 1848	2	1
Henry Dwight, [s. Philip A. & Temperance C.], b. Mar. 16, 1843	1	116

	Vol.	Page

CAPIN, (cont.)

Philip A., m. Temperance C. **SERRIL**, Apr. 25, 1841 — 1 — 116

CARDWELL, Ann Vera, m. Gurdon **ABEL**, May 30, 1820, by Rev.
Abishia Auldin — 1 — 83

Belinda West, d. Uriah & Jemima, b. July 13, 1816 — 1 — 25

Edmund Augustus, s. Uriah & Jemima, b. Apr. 2, 1811 — 1 — 25

Julia Ann, d. Uriah & Jemima, b. May 24, 1814 — 1 — 25

Nancy, m. Stedman **WOODWORTH**, Dec. 26, 1811 — 1 — 64

Uriah, m. Jemima **HOUGH**, b. of Bozrah, Oct. [ ], 1810 — 1 — 25

William S., s. Samuel & Aphiah, b. Nov. 27, 1780 — 1 — 37

CAREW, Henry W., m. Amelia G. **BEEBE**, b. of Norwich, May 7,
1848, by Rev. Christopher Leffingwell — 1 — 135

Henry W., of Norwich, m. Ardelia G. **BEEBE**, of Norwich,
May 7, 1848, by Rev. Christ. Leffingwell — 2 — 2

CAREY, Abby, d. Jan. 15, 1860, ae 1 — 3 — 24

CARROLL, Catharine, ae 20, m. John **McMAHON**, ae 28, res.
Norwich, Mar. 27, 1851, by Rev. C. Leffingwell — 2 — 10

Mary, m. Edwin H. **BROWN**, Sept. 14, 1851, by Rev.
W[illia]m P. Avery — 1 — 160

CARTTONELLO, -----, stillborn child of Oliebe, Jan. 19, [1871];
bd. Jan. 20, [1871], in Baltic — 3 — 62

CARVIN, Mary, d. Sept. 17, 1861, ae 1 — 3 — 31

CENTER, William, d. July 28, 1865, ae 1 — 3 — 44

CHAFFUT, Lydia, res. Bozrah, m. Asa **GRAVES**, res. Colchester,
Mar. 11, 1851, by Rev. W[illiam] B. Avery — 2 — 10

CHALFORD, Lydia, of Bozrah, m. Asa **GRAVES**, of Colchester,
Mar. 11, 1851, by Rev. W[illia]m P. Avery — 1 — 159

CHAPMAN, B. F., farmer, res. Norwich, m. Mary E. **GATES**, res.
Salem, Nov. 25, 1848, by Rev. Christ. Leffingwell — 2 — 2

Benjamin F., of Norwich, m. Mary E. **GATES**, of Salem, Nov.
25, 1847, by Rev. Christopher Leffingwell — 1 — 78

Charles, farmer, d. Aug. 27, 1853, ae 66; bd. T[h]roop B. G. — 3 — 4

Harriot, m. Valentine **WIGHTMAN**, b. of Bozrah, Oct. 27,
1828, by William Whiting, J. P. — 1 — 80

Harriet G., of Bozrahville, m. Edward G. **EMMONS**, of
Colchester, [Sept], 4, 1836, by Oliver Brown, Elder — 1 — 138a

Phebe, d. Nov. 30, 1848, ae 74 — 2 — 3

Silas, m. Oliva **PEABODY**, b. of Salem, Feb. 7, 1827, by
James Lam, J. P. — 1 — 86

[CHAPPEL], CHAPEL, Alfred S., of Montville, m. Almira
DANIELS, of Bozrah, Mar. 3, 1850, by Rev. Edward
Eells — 1 — 156

Alfred S., farmer, res. Montville, m. Almira **DANIELS**,
res. Bozrah, Mar. 5, 1850, by Rev. E. Elles — 2 — 8

Alfred S., carpenter, married, b. Montville, d. Sept.
17, 1863, ae 39, at Philadelphia in service of U. S. A. — 3 — 38

CHEIL, John, manufacturer, single, b. Ireland, d. Feb. 10,
1858, ae 18 — 3 — 21

	Vol.	Page
CHESEBROUGH, CHESEBEROUGH, Caroline L., of Bozrah, m. Jona[than] BABCOCK, of Brookfield, N. Y., Feb. 6, 1832, by Rev. Peter Sabin	1	95
Julia, of Bozrah, m. Jonathan BABCOCK, of Brookfield, N. Y., Aug. 12, 1821, by Rev. Reuben Palmer, Jr., at the house of Capt. Chesebrough	1	73
CHURCH, Charles H., m. Mary BARTLETT, b. of Bozrah, Aug. 31, 1851, by Rev. W[illia]m P. Avery	1	160
Peleg, farmer, widower, b. Montville, d. Oct. 29, 1856, ae 64	3	13
Sally, b. Montville, res. Bozrah, d. Nov. [ ], 1850, ae 54	2	9
CLARE, Rosanna, d. June 19, 1857, ae 4	3	16
CLARK, CLARKE, Arabella, single, b. Preston, d. Mar. 22, 1862, ae 54	3	32
Edward, of Montville, m. Hannah POWERS, of Bozrah, May 12, 1839, by John W. Houghton, J. P.	1	98
Elizabeth, of New London, m. Daniel GARDINER, of Norwich, July 6, 1763	1	26
Ephraim W., of Lebanon, m. Susan Maria WOODWORTH, of Bozrah, Mar. 6, 1834, by Rev. John W. Salter	1	82
Hannah, of Lebanon, m. Erastus HYDE, of Bozrah, Sept. 28, 1835, by Rev. John Hyde	1	135
Isaac, m. Julia A. WILLEY, b. of Bozrah, Nov. 11, 1832, by Rev. R. Landfear	1	129
Julia Ann, of Lebanon, m. Orlando LEE, of Colchester, Oct. 29, 1846, by Rev. Paunel (Powel?) Mathewson	1	94
Lavinda, m. Asa L. ROGERS, July 4, 1847, by Rev. Perciville Mathewson	1	124
Mercy, domestic, married, b. Ireland, d. Dec. 9, 1855, ae 26	3	10
Olive, d. Thomas & Fanny, b. June 13, 1795	1	42
Sarah, d. July 12, 1860, ae 85	3	24
Sarah d. Mar. 15, 1870, ae 3	3	49
Simon, m. Adaline BARROWS, b. of Bozrah, Oct. 14, 1832, by Rev. R. Landfear	1	130
Thomas, s. Thomas & Fanny, b. Apr. 1, 1793	1	42
CLEMENT, Emily Parlee, d. John M. & Eunice, b. Feb. 1, 1795	1	47
Eunice, of Norwich, m. Jabez HOUGH, Jr., of Bozrah, Oct. 28, 1790	1	41
John M., of Norwich, m. Eunice TYLER, of Brooklyn, Jan. 1, 1792	1	47
CLEVELAND, William N., of Windham, m. Pamelia T. STANDISH, of Bozrah, Mar. 14, 1841, by Tho[ma]s L. Shipman	1	139
COALMAN, Oliver, of Marlborough, m. Susannah JOHNSON, of Bozrah, Jan. 21, 1838, by Roderick Gardner, J. P.	1	109
COLE, Erastus, of Norwich, m. Prudence M. BITGOOD, of Bozrah, Dec. 25, 1843, by Rev. William M. Birchard	1	150
COLLINS, Daniel P., of Stonington, m. Sarah R. QUIN[N], of Bozrah, Dec. 25, 1843, by Rev. Bela Hicks	1	44

	Vol.	Page
COLLINS, (cont.)		
Hannah, wid., d. Nov. 19, 1803	1	57
COLVERT, Fanny L., wid., of Bozrah, m. Winthrop **HURLBURT**,		
of Lyme, Mar. 7, 1847, by Rev. W[illia]m M. Birchard	1	134
COMSTOCK, Ellen, cotton-manufacturer, single, d. Dec. 5, 1856,		
ae 14	3	13
John K., b. Montville, d. Dec. 15, 1857, ae 4	3	16
Sarah A., b. Salem, res. Bozrah, d. Sept. 23, 1854, ae		
39; bd. Throop B. G.	3	7
CONDALL, Melora, of Bozrah, m. Cha[rle]s L. **DRINKWATER**,		
of Hebron, Sept. 24, 1848, by W[illia]m Palmer, V.D.M	1	93
CONGDON, Elisha, of Norwich, m. Eliza **STANDISH**, of Lebanon,		
Apr. 8, 1827, by Rev. David Austin	1	87
Louisa, m. James **FALES**, b. of Norwich, Jan. 28, 1849, by		
Rev. Christopher Leffingwell	1	93
Loiza, ae 27, b. Montville, m. James **FALE[S]**, mechanic,		
ae 30, b. Millbury, Mass., res. Norwich, her 2d h., July		
28, 1849, by Rev. C. Leffingwell	2	5
COOK, Sarah T., m. Hazard **WELLS**, b. of Colchester, Nov. 19,		
1843, by Rev. Benjamin G. Goff	1	86
CORRIGAN, -----, st. b. male, Jan. 23, 1857	3	16
CRANDALL, Julia A., of Colchester, m. Robert A. **PATRIDGE**, of		
Baltimore, Jan. 10, 1842, by Rev. Benjamin G. Goff	1	126
Lodowick B., m. Maria L. **TRACY**, Nov. 11, 1844, by Rev.		
W[illia]m M. Burchard	1	98
Maria L., domestic, b. Franklin, married, d. Nov. 21,		
1855, ae 31	3	10
CRESTEY, Chauncey F., d. Dec. 31, 1847, ae 5	2	3
CROCKER, Abby L., m. Dyer **HARRIS**, b. of Bozrah, Apr. 15,		
1825, by Rev. David Austin	1	53
Abby Lyon, d. George W. & Polly b. Sept. 3, 1832	1	82
Abigail Lyon, d. William & Sibyl b. July 13, 1797	1	12
Ammi, s. Jabez & Elizabeth, b. Sept. 30, 1783	1	48
Andrew M., m. Eunice **FRINK**, Nov. 3, 1834, by Rev. John		
W. Salter	1	127
Andrew Metcalf, s. W[illia]m L. & Philena, b. Jan. 1,		
1814; d. Oct. 23, 1857	1	85
Anna, m. Daniel **GARDNER**, Jr., b. of Bozrah, July 1, 1787	1	27
Asa, m. Lois **CROCKER**, of Franklin, May 20, 1791, by		
Samuel Nott, Clerk		50
Betty, m. William **SMITH**, b. of Norwich, Nov. 15, 1781	1	20
Charlotte, d. Asa, Jr. & Lois, b. Sept. 27, 1791	1	50
Elizabeth, m. Ebenezer **BACKUS**, b. of Bozrah, Dec. 30, 1787	1	4
Elizabeth, w. Asa, d. Oct. 24, 1788, in the 56 y. of her age	1	40
Eunice, m. William **HARRIS** b. of Bozrah, Nov. 23, 1786	1	8
Ezekiel Lathrop, s. William & Sybyl, b. Aug. 7, 1792; d.		
Sept. 8, 1818	1	12
George W., m. Polly **HUNTLEY**, Mar. 17, 1825, by Gardner		

	Vol.	Page
CROCKER, (cont.)		
Avery, J. P.	1	82
George Washington, s. William & Sibyl, b. Aug. 31, 1799	1	12
Hyde, s. Thomas, Jr. & Betsey, b. Jan. 25, 1793	1	43
Jabez, Jr., of Norwich, m. Elizabeth TALCOTT, of Bolton, Oct. 5, 1773	1	48
Jabez, s. Jabez, Jr. & Elizabeth, b. Sept. 26, 1776	1	48
Jabez, d. June 29, 1785	1	48
Lois, of Franklin, m. Asa CROCKER, May 20, 1791, by Samuel Nott, Clerk	1	50
Mary, m. Arunah HACKLEY, b. of Norwich, Nov. 27, 1783	1	22
Mary, d. George W. & Polly, b. Aug, 28, 1825	1	82
Oliver, s. Jabez & Elizabeth, b. July 20, 1781	1	48
Phebe, pauper, d. Jan. 24, 1849, ae 73	2	6
Philena, w. W[illia]m L., d. Feb. 25, 1843; ae 55 y. 10 m. 12 d.	1	85
Rozamon, d. Asa, Jr. & Lois, b. June 17, 1795	1	50
Ruth, d. Jabez, Jr. & Elizabeth, b. Sept. 12, 1774	1	48
Samuel C., carriage maker, ae 24, b. Montville, res. Bozrah, m. Fanny E. HERRICK, ae 27, of Bozrah, Oct. 25, 1848, by Rev. W[illia]m M. Birchard	2	2
Sarah, m. Jason ALLEN, b. of Bozrah, Oct. 5, 1786, by Neh[emiah] Waterman, J. P.	1	1
Sarah, w. Thomas, d. Feb. 17, 1823, ae 80	1	12
Sophia, d. William & Sybel, b. Oct. 18, 1794	1	12
Sophia, m. Cyrus STEWARD, Oct. 24, 1816	1	75
Thomas, Jr., m. Betsey CALKINS, b. of Bozrah, Apr. 15, 1792	1	43
Thomas, d. Apr. 2, 1811, ae 80	1	12
Vilate, d. William & Sibyl, b. Feb. 28, 1788	1	12
Vilatee, m. John GARDNER, Jr., Feb. 18, 1808	1	59
William, of Bozrah, m. Sibyl LATHROP, of Franklin, May 17, 1787, by Samuel Nott, Clerk	1	12
William, s. William & Sibyl, b. Mar. 14, 1790; d. June 28, 1802	1	12
William, s. William & Sybel, d. Oct. [ ], 1803	1	12
William, Jr., m. Abigail ARMSTRONG, b. of Bozrah, Nov. 26, 1829, by Rev. David Austin	1	122
William, d. Oct. 18, 1833	1	12
William L., m. Philena WOODWORTH, b. of Bozrah, Feb. 3, 1811	1	85
William L., d. July 9, 1846, ae 62	1	85
CROUCH, Ogden, m. Mary WELLS, Mar. 26, 1837, by Rev. Benjamin G. Goff	1	139
CROWLEY, Frances, m. Lucinda FOX, June 16, 1825, by Gardner Avery, J. P.	1	42
CRUBE, W[illia]m, b. Scotland, res. Bozrah, d. Jan. 10, 1851, ae 70	2	9
CRUFT, William Smith, of New York, m. Sophia Ingraham FITCH, of Fitchville, Bozrah, Nov. 22, 1842, by Rev. S. B. Paddock	1	90

	Vol.	Page
CULVER, Lucy, of German Flats, m. Christopher **HUNTINGTON,**		
Jr., May 20, 1794, by Jeremiah Snow, J. P.	1	33
Hannah H., of Bozrah, m. Samuel **LINCOLN**, of Hampton,		
Apr. 17, 1822, by Rev. William Palmer, at Wid. M.		
Baldwin's Colchester	1	43
Sally S. m. Gershom R. **GARDNER**, b. of Bozrah, [Aug.] 28,		
1822, by Rev. William Palmer, at Wid. Culver's,		
Colchester	1	113
CUTTER, Ammi G., Capt., of Portland, Me., m. Elizabeth		
GREELEY, of Turner, Me., Apr. 6, 1847, by Rev.		
W[illia]m M. Burchard	1	85
DANIELS, Abby, of Bozrahville, m. Ira F. **MINSON**, Oct. 3, 1847,		
by Rev. Stephen Hays	1	153
Abby, ae 46, b. Preston, res. Bozrahville, m. Ira H.		
MINER, carpenter, ae 49, b. Groton, res. Bozrahville,		
Oct. 3, 1847, by Rev. Stephen Hays	2	2
Almira, of Bozrah, m. Alfred S. **CHAPEL**, of Montville, Mar.		
3, 1850, by Rev. Edward Eells	1	156
Almira, res. Bozrah, m. Alfred s. **CHAPEL**, farmer, res.		
Montville, Mar. 5, 1850, by Rev. E. Elles	2	8
Charles, mill operator, ae 25, b. Colchester, res. Bozrahville, m.		
Eliza **READ**, ae 18, b. Ireland, res. Bozrahville, Mar. 26,		
1848, by Rev. Stephen Hays	2	2
George, of Farmington, m. Susannah **JOHNSON**, of Bozrah,		
May 6, 1834, by Ezra Lathrop, J. P.	1	6
Lucy A., of Bozrah, m. Edward D. **HOLDREDGE**, of		
Colchester, Aug. 23, 1846, by Rev. W[illia]m M.		
Burchard	1	92
Owen, d. Aug. 3, 1848, ae 30	2	3
DARROW, Ann, laborer, d. Jan. 27, 1863, ae 70	3	38
DART, Albert, s. Moses F. & Mahaleth, b. Feb. 22, 1822	1	75
DAVIS, Aphea S., child of Samuel, manufacturer, ae 37, &		
Aphea W., ae 29, b. Apr. 25, 1848	2	1
Apha S., d. June 25, 1848, ae 3 m.	2	3
Thomas, m. Maria G. **NORTHAM**, b. of Bozrah, July 20,		
1834, by John W. Salter	1	81
DAY, Hammerville, black, d. [1854], ae 100; bd. Norwich Town	3	7
Johanna, single, b. Lebanon, d. July 8, 1864, ae 8	3	43
DEAN, DEANS, Amanda, d. James & Anna, b. Dec. 29, 1797	1	40
Amanda, m. William **RIDER**, Nov. 27, 1823, by Rev. David		
Austin	1	64
Sarah, see under Eliza E. **HALL**	2	7
W[illia]m Robert, manufacturer, widower, b. England, d.		
July 9, 1855, ae 78	3	10
DENNETT, Lucretia, b. New Bedford, res. Bozrah, d. July 8, 1854,		
ae 38; bd. Throop B. G.	3	7
DEWEY, Henry, of Westfield, Mass., m. Elizabeth W. **BRUMLEY**,		
of Chester, Mass., May 11, 1851, by Rev. Christopher		

	Vol.	Page
DEWEY, (cont.)		
Leffingwell	1	160
DICKINSON, DICKENSON, Eliza Lincoln, d. Rufus W. & Nancy		
B. L., b. Jan. 10, 1838	1	153
Emeline Corbett, d. Rufus W. & Nancy B. L., b. Oct. 17, 1834	1	153
Lucy Ashley, d. Rufus W. & Nancy B. L., b. Nov. 24, 1839	1	153
Mary Fitch, d. Rufus W. & Nancy B. L., b. May 11, 1843	1	153
Nancy Bicknel, d. Rufus Wells & Nancy Bicknell Lincoln,		
b. Mar. 16, 1829	1	153
Rufus Wells, s. Rufus W. & Nancy B. L., b. Oct. 1, 1830	1	153
Sally Adams, d. Rufus W. & Nancy B. L., b. Aug. 22, 1832	1	153
William Greene, s. Rufus W. & Nancy B. L., b. June 10, 1836	1	153
DODGE, Eliza, d. William & Mary, b. Jan. 31, 1815	1	73
William, m. Mary **WARD**, Nov. 22, 1813	1	73
DOLBEAR, Margaret, of Montville, m. Azariah **WRIGHT**, of		
Colchester, Sept. 30, 1823, by Gardner Avery, J. P.	1	65
DOWD, Benj[amin] B., laborer, d. Mar. 10, 1849, ae 63	2	6
DOWNER, Annice, d. Uriah & Desire, b. Jan. 20, 1789	1	7
David Hough, s. Uriah & Desire, b. Oct. 30, 1799	1	7
Desire, d. Uriah & Desire, b. Oct. 30, 1797	1	7
Desire, w. Capt. Uriah, d. Mar. 12, 1816	1	7
Ebenezer Parker, s. Uriah & Permelia, b. May 31, 1838	1	96
Edwin Uriah, s. Uriah & Permelia, b. Feb. 28, 1836	1	96
Elizabeth, d. Uriah & Desire, b. July 22, 1794	1	7
Elizabeth Ann, d. Uriah & Permelia, b. Dec. 1, 1833	1	96
Eunice, d. Uriah & Desire, b. Oct. 17, 1791	1	7
Frances Manerva, d. Uriah & Permelia, b. Oct. 11, 1827	1	96
Hannah, d. Uriah & Desire, b. Aug. 11, 1790	1	7
Hannah, [d. Uriah & Desire], d. Sept. 1, 1836	1	7
Henry Avery, s. Uriah & Permelia, b. June 16, 1832	1	96
John, d. Sept. 21, 1859, ae 79	1	96
Mariah Ant[o]inette, d. Uriah & Permelia, b. Apr. 29, 1830	1	96
Mary M., m. Seth **WHITING**, b. of Bozrah, May 18, 1828, by		
Rev. David Austin	1	90
Mary Wightman, d. Uriah & Permelia, b. Oct. 24, 1828	1	96
Permelia Parker, d. Uriah & Permelia, b. June 3, 1831	1	96
Sibyl, m. Andrew **LATHROP**, 3d, b. of Bozrah, June 1, 1797	1	53
Uriah, m. Desire **HOUGH**, b. of Bozrah, Nov, 15, 1787	1	7
Uriah, s. Uriah & Desire, b. July 13, 1796	1	7
Uriah, Capt., d. Nov. 17, 1825	1	7
Uriah, of Bozrah, m. Permelia **PARKER**, of Saleme, Nov. 5,		
1826, by Tubal Wakefield, Elder	1	96
DRAKE, Lizzie, b. Franklin, d. June 26, 1862, ae 7	3	32
Sarah M., of Lebanon, m. Henry **BENNETT**, of Canterbury,		
Sept. 8, 1851, by Rev. W[illia]m P. Avery	1	160
DRAPER, Elizabeth, b. R. I., res. Bozrah, d. Sept. 9, 1848, ae 46	2	6
Ellen, domestic, married, b. N. Y. City, d. June 22, 1863, ae 30	3	38
Harriet, of Lebanon, m. Moses J. **GREEN**, of Bozrah, June 28,		

	Vol.	Page
FARGO, (cont.)		
Elizabeth Williams, d. Daniel & Hannah, b. Apr. 23, 1803	1	60
Frances Ann. d. Gurdon & Deborah, b. Aug. 4, 1802	1	61
Gurdon, s. Gurdon & Deborah, b. Nov. 21, 1804	1	61
Gurdon, m. Deborah **LOOMER**, [ ]	1	61
Hannah, b. Waterford, res. Bozrah, d. Apr. 8, 1854, ae 93; bd. N[orwich] Town	3	7
Henry Leonard, s. Alvin L. & Mary, b. Mar. 25, 1824	1	133
Hiram, s. Gurdon & Deborah, b. Oct. 14, 1811	1	61
Jason, s. Daniel & Hannah, b. Jan. 11, 1791	1	60
John Bishop, s. Alvin L. & Mary, b. Sept. 12, 1833	1	133
Joseph Chester, s. Gurdon & Deborah, b. June 26, 1809	1	61
Lovina Palmer, d. Gurdon & Deborah, b. Apr. 28, 1815	1	61
Lucy, d. Daniel & Hannah, b. Apr. 13, 1795	1	60
Mary Ann, twin with Ann Maria, d. Alvin L. & Mary, b. Mar. 5, 1831	1	133
Rebecca, d. Daniel & Hannah, b. Feb. 3, 1783	1	60
William D., of Lebanon, m. Mary A. **STANDISH**, of Bozrah, Oct. 10, 1831, by Rev. Reuben Ranson	1	30
William Dwight, s. Gurdon & Deborah, b. July 12, 1807	1	61
FAVOR, Joseph B., farmer, d. Nov. 20, 1867, ae 87	3	48
FILLMORE, May, d. John L., book-keeper, ae 34, & Mary A., ae 38, b. Oct. 18, 1850	2	11
FINTON, Patrick, laborer, d. Jan. 15, 1866, ae 22, widower	3	44
FISH, Backus, s. William & Deborah, b. Nov. 30, 1781; d. July 23, 1782	1	9
Backus, s. William & Deborah, b. June 29, 1783	1	9
Electa, d. John & Lydia, b. Apr. 23, 1793	1	18
Elizabeth, w. William, d. Sept. 20, 1771	1	9
Elizabeth, d. William & Deborah, b. Jan. 11, 1775	1	9
Fanny, d. William & Deborah, b. Nov. 30, 1776; d. Dec. 17, 1776	1	9
Fanny, d. William & Deborah, b. Nov. 2, 1777	1	9
John, m. Lydia **LATHROP**, b. of Bozrah, Apr. 2, 1786	1	18
John, s. John & Lydia, b. Sept. 25, 1788	1	18
Lodowich, s. William & Deborah, b. Oct. 17, 1779	1	9
Lydia, d. William & Deborah, b. Mar. 16, 1773	1	9
Lydia, d. John & Lydia, b. Aug. 6, 1796	1	18
Marg[a]ret, d. John & Lydia, b. Nov. 17, 1799	1	18
Mary A., b. Plainfield, d. June 22, 1863, ae 7 m.	3	38
Miller, s. John & Lydia, b. June 5, 1791	1	18
Moley, d. William & Elizabeth, b. Oct. 3, 1763	1	9
Nancy, twin with Sally, d. Nathaniel, Jr. & Mary, b. Aug. 14, 1786	1	5
Nancy, d. Nathaniel & Mary, d. July 20, 1795	1	5
Nathaniel, d. June 27, 1787	1	5
Polly, d. Nathaniel, Jr. & Mary, b. Jan. 11, 1782	1	5
Rebeckah, d. Nathaniel, Jr. & Mary, b. Feb. 15, 1784	1	5

	Vol.	Page
FISH, (cont.)		
Sally, twin with Nancy, d. Nathaniel, Jr. & Mary, b. Aug. 14, 1786	1	5
Sarah, d. William & Elizebeth, b. Feb. 10, 1765	1	9
Sidney, s. William & Deborah, b. Feb. 8, 1787	1	9
Simeon, s. John & Lydia, b. Feb. 1, 1787	1	18
Sophy, d. William & Deborah, b. Nov. 10, 1788	1	9
William, m. Deborah **BACKAS**, b. of Norwich, Mar. 22, 1772	1	9
FITCH, Ammi, m. Lois **WATERMAN**, Oct. 25, 1767	1	99
Andrew, [s. Ammi & Lois], b. [ ]	1	99
Asa, b. Feb. 14, 1755	1	62
Asa, m. Susanna **FITCH**, Feb. 1, 1781	1	62
Asa, s. Asa & Susanna, b. May 6, 1787	1	62
Asa, m. Mary **HOUSE**, Jan. [ ], 1816	1	62
Asa, d. Aug. 19, 1844, ae 89 y. 6 m. 5 d.	1	62
Asa, farmer, d. Oct. 30, 1865, ae 78	3	44
Clarissa, d. Asa & Susanna, b. Feb. 28, 1785; d. Apr. 3, 1785, ae 5 w.	1	62
Clarissa, 2d. d. Asa & Susanna, b. June 5, 1802	1	62
Clarissy, [d. Ammi & Lois], b. [ ]	1	99
David Gardner, s. Edwin & Lucy, b. Oct. 11, 1837	1	95
D[o]uglass, s. Asa & Susanna, b. Feb. 18, 1799	1	62
Elijah, [s. Ammi & Lois], b. [ ]	1	99
Eliza, of Bozrah, m. William **HIL[L]HOUSE**, of Montville, Apr. 19, 1825, by Rev. David Austin	1	65
Elizabeth L., of Bozrah, m. Jeremiah N. **PEABODY**, of Buffalo, N. Y., [Mar.] 6, 1839, by Rev. Tho[ma]s L. Shipman, Newark	1	143
Fanny, d. Asa & Susanna, b. Mar. 22, 1793	1	62
Fanny, of Bozrah, m. Sherwood **RAYMOND**, of Montville, on or about the year 1820-21, by Rev. David Austin, Bozrah. Recorded May 9, 1821	1	65
Harriet Walbridge, d. Edwin & Lucy b. May 8, 1835	1	95
James Billings, s. Edwin & Lucy, b. May 10, 1833	1	95
Joel, [s. Ammi & Lois], b. [ ]	1	99
Lathrop, [s. Ammi & Lois], b. [ ]	1	99
Lois, d. Asa & Susanna, b. Dec. 7, 1783 d. Aug. 27, 1803, ae 20 y.	1	62
Lucy Maria, d. Edwin & Lucy, b. Sept. 1, 1827	1	95
Maria, [d. Ammi & Lois], b. [ ]	1	99
Mary, w. Asa, d. June 23, 1836, ae 74	1	62
Mary Ann, d. Nehemiah H. & Mary, b. Jan. 6, 1809	1	69
Nehemiah Huntington, s. Asa & Susanna, b. Oct. 2, 1781	1	62
Nehemiah Huntington, of Bozrah, m. Mary **ABBEY**, of Windham, Mar. 30, 1808	1	69
Rufus, s. Edwin & Lucy, b. June 12, 1831	1	95
Sarah, [d. Ammi & Lois], b. [ ]	1	99
Simeon, [s. Ammi & Lois], b. [ ]	1	99

	Vol.	Page
FITCH, (cont.)		
Sophia Ingraham, of Fitchville, Bozrah, m. William Smith		
CRUFT, of New York, Nov. 22, 1842, by Rev. S. B.		
Paddock	1	90
Stephen, s. Asa & Susannah, b. Aug. 21, 1790	1	62
Stephen, farmer, d. Oct. 6, 1868, ae 78	3	48
Stephen Edwin, s. Edwin & Lucy, b. Sept. 14, 1825	1	95
Susanna, b. June 4, 1757	1	62
Susanna, m. Asa **FITCH**, Feb. 1, 1781	1	62
Susanna, d. Asa & Susanna, b. Nov. 15, 1788	1	62
Susannah, w. Asa, d. Apr. 22, 1814, ae 57	1	62
Susannah Lee, d. Asa & Susan, d. May [ ], 1819, ae 17	1	62
William, s. Asa & Susanna, b. Oct. 27, 1800	1	62
FOOT, Alfred, [s. Stephen & Hannah], b. Dec. 8, 1787	1	101
Daniel, [s. Stephen & Hannah], b. Sept. 23, 1789	1	101
Eli, [s. Stephen & Hannah], b. May 7, 1793	1	101
Henry, [s. Stephen & Hannah], b. Dec. 20, 1795	1	101
Sarah, [d. Stephen & Hannah], b. May 4, 1791	1	101
Stephen, m. Hannah **WATERMAN**, Nov. 16, 1786	1	101
Susy, [d. Stephen & Hannah], b. Aug. 18, 1797	1	101
FORCE, Henry G., d. Dec. 31, 1866, ae 29	3	44
Sarah, domestic, married, b. Montville, d. Aug. 24, 1863, ae 67	3	38
FORD, Alvin, s. John & Lucy, b. Oct. 15, 1799	1	74
Anna, d. Charles & Anna, b. Jan. 11, 1792	1	44
Calvin, s. John & Lucy, b. Aug. 26, 1801	1	74
Charles, s. John & Lucy, b. Apr. 1, 1787; d. Sept. 10, 1789	1	74
Charles, m. Anna **HARRIS**, b. of Bozrah, Feb. 11, 1790	1	44
Clarissa, d. Charles & Anna, b. Sept. 8, 1790	1	44
Daniel, s. John & Lucy, b. Aug. 29, 1803	1	74
Jane R., m. James E. **AVERY**, Sept. 21, 1851, by Rev. Henry		
B. Whittington	1	122
John, m. Lucy **HARRIS**, Aug. 14, 1786	1	74
John, twin with Lucy, s. Joh[n] & Lucy, b. June 22, 1794	1	74
Joseph B., m. Apama **LATHROP**, Apr. 15, 1830, by Asa		
Wilcox, Elder	1	105
Lucy, twin with John, d. John & Lucy, b. June 22, 1794	1	74
Mary, d. John & Lucy, b. Aug. 30, 1797	1	74
Mary A., of Bozrah, m. Joseph R. **KINGSLEY**, of Norwich,		
Feb. 21, 1847, by Rev. W[illia]m, M. Berchard	1	134
Matilda, d. Charles & Anna, b. Apr. 5, 1794	1	44
Prudence, d. John & Lucy, b. Jan. 20, 1792	1	74
Prudence, m. Alfred **WELTCH**, [Mar.] 27, 1812	1	42
Sarah, m. Asa **WOODWORTH**, Jr., b. of Norwich, Jan. 12,		
1769	1	23
FOSTER, Eline J., d. July 25, 1866, ae 4	3	44
FOWLER, Oliver, of Norwich, m. Mary **BAILEY**, of Bozrah, Sept.		
27, 1848, by Rev. John P. Gulliver, Norwich	1	154
Oliver, carpenter, ae 22, b. Lebanon, res. Bozrah, m. Mary		

	Vol.	Page
FOWLER, (cont.)		
J. **BAILEY**, ae 24, of Bozrah, Sept. 27, 1848, by Rev.		
J. P. Gulliver	2	5
FOX, Adelaide M., d. Aaron, farmer, & Olive, of Norwich, b.		
May 28, 1848	2	1
Allis, m. Asa **LATHROP**, b. of Norwich, Sept. 17, 1782	1	33
Charles, s. Roswell & Phebe, b. May 9, 1794	1	7
David A., m. Sally **WATERMAN**, of Bozrah, Oct. 19, 1830,		
by Cornelius b. Everest	1	125
David Austin, s. Rosewell & Phebe, b. Dec. 28, 1804	1	7
Goerge, s. Roswell & Phebe, b. Nov. 9, 1791	1	7
George, farmer, d. [ ], 1867, ae 75	3	48
Jabez, s. Roswell & Phebe, b. Nov. 6, 1786	1	7
Jerusha Perkins, d. Roswell & Phebe, b. June 26, 1797	1	7
Joel, of Hampton, m. Lydia M. **MINER**, of Bozrahville, Nov.		
28, 1839, by Rev. Nathan Wildman	1	144
Lucinda, m. Frances **CROWLEY**, June 16, 1825, by Gardner		
Avery, J. P.	1	42
Marvin Witherell, s. Roswell & Phebe, b. Jan. 14, 1800	1	7
Nehemiah Waterman, s. David A. & Sally, b. Dec. 15, 1832	1	125
Phebe, d. Roswell & Phebe, b. Sept. 17, 1788	1	7
Phebe, wid. Capt. Roswell, d. Mar. 20, 1841	1	7
Roswell, m. Phebe **HOUGH**, b. of Norwich, Dec. 11, 1785,		
by Rev. Levi Hart	1	7
Roswell, Capt. d. [ ], 1825	1	7
Roswell, physician, ae 23, b. Bozrah, res. Wethersfield,		
m. Ann M. **GAGER**, ae 19, of Bozrah, May 1, 1848, by		
[ ]	2	2
Russell, M. D., of Withersfield, m. Ann Maria **GAGER**, d.		
of Sam[ue]l A., of Bozrah, May 1, 1848, by Rev. Henry		
Brumley	1	146
W[illia]m H., b. East Haddam, single, d. Aug. 25, 1855, ae 12	3	10
FRANKLIN, Phebe L., d. Sept. 11, 1857, ae 10 m.	3	16
FREEMAN, Providence, m. Azuba **RAU**, Sept. 22, 1806, by Asa		
Woodworth, J. P.	1	60
FRINK, Almira S., m. Reuben E. **AUSTIN**, Apr. 27, 1851, by Rev.		
Henry B. Whittington	1	121
Douglass, s. Silas, carpenter, ae 31, & Almira, ae 33, b. May		
29, 1849	2	4
Ellen, b. New Haven, res. Bozrah, d. Feb. 27, 1853, ae 5 m. bd.		
Hough Burying Ground	3	4
Eunice, m. Andrew M. **CROCKER**, Nov. 3, 1834, by Rev.		
John W. Salter	1	127
FRY, Angeline M., domestic, d. Mar. 5, 1868, ae 24	3	48
FULLER, Henry, of Colchester, m. Philena H. **JOHNSON**, Jan. 9,		
1848, by Rev. W[illia]m N. Birchard	1	94
Henry, farmer, ae 28, b. Montville, res. Colchester, m. Philena		
H. **JOHNSON**, ae 28, b. Montville, res. Montville, Jan.		

	Vol.	Page
FULLER, (cont.)		
[ ],1848, by Rev. W[illia]m M. Birchard	2	2
Miner, d. Oct. 12, 1866, ae 2	3	44
GAGER, Ann M., ae 19, of Bozrah, m. Roswell **FOX**, physician,		
ae 23, b. Bozrah, res. Wethersfield, May 1, 1848	2	2
Ann Maria, d. Samuel A. & Wealthy Ann, b. Sept. 15, 1828	1	89
Ann Maria, d. Sam[ue]l A., of Bozrah, m. Russell **FOX**, M. D.		
of Withersfield, May 1, 1848, by Rev. Henry Brumley	1	146
Charles, s. Samuel & Cinthea, b. Mar. 8, 1801	1	3
Charles, s. Samuel & Cynthea, d. Mar. 11, 1806	1	3
Charles A, s. Samuel A. & Wealthy Ann, b. June 15, 1837	1	89
Charles Alonzo, s. Samuel & Cynthea, b. Mar. 15, 1814	1	3
Charles Alonzo, s. Samuel & Cynthia, d. Nov. 16, 1841,		
in Cairo, Egypt	1	148
Cynthia, domestic, widow, b. Preston, d. Jan. 13, 1864, ae 86	3	43
Cynthia M., m. Dr. Samuel **JOHNSON**, Oct. 30, 1836, by Rev.		
Oliver Brown	1	141
Cynthia Maria, d. Samuel & Cinthea, b. Oct. 12, 1807	1	3
Cynthia Maria, d. Samuel & Cynthia, d. Dec. 10, 1814	1	3
Cynthia Maria, d. Samuel & Cynthia, b. Feb. 3, 1816	1	3
Esther N., m. Ezra **HUNTLEY**, b. of Bozrah, May 5, 1822,		
by Rev. David Austin	1	109
Esther Wood, d. William & Hariot, b. Mar. 15, 1802	1	57
Eunice Isham, d. William & Harriot, b. July 16, 1809	1	57
Frances Octava Throop, d. William & Harriot, b. Aug. 1, 1811	1	57
Hannah, d. Samuel & Cinthea, b. Apr. 13, 1799	1	3
Hannah, m. Jedediah L. **STARK**, b. of Bozrah, on or about		
the year 1820-21, by Rev. David Austin, Bozrah.		
Recorded May 9, 1821	1	65
Har[r]iot, d. Will[ia]m & Har[r]iot, b. Apr. 5, 1806;		
d. Apr. 21, 1806	1	57
Harriot, d. William & Harriot, b. July 12, 1807	1	57
Harriet E., d. Sept. 7, 1864, ae 1 m.	3	43
Jerusha, d. William & Harriot, b. July 27, 1813	1	57
John Jay, s. Samuel & Cynthia, b. June 8, 1818	1	3
John Jay, s. Samuel & Cynthia, d. Dec. 31, 1821	1	3
John Jay, s. Samuel A. & Wealthy A., b. Aug. 14, 1831	1	89
Lydia Eliza, d. Samuel A. & Wealthy Ann, b. June 16, 1834	1	89
Mary, m. Dan **THROOP**, b. of Bozrah, Nov. 12, 1788	1	8
Othniel, of Franklin, m. Eliza **BACKUS**, of Bozrah, Jan.		
28, 1827, by Rev. David Austin	1	87
Rebecca, d. William & Harriot, b. Feb. 22, 1800	1	57
Samuel, m. Hannah **CALKIN**, July 29, 1773, by Benj[amin]		
Throop, Clerk	1	2
Samuel, s. Samuel & Hannah, b. Aug. 3, 1775	1	2
Samuel, d. Aug. 11, 1783	1	2
Samuel, m. Cinthea **MEACH**, Apr. 12, 1798, by Lemuel		
Tiler, Clerk	1	3

	Vol.	Page
GAGER, (cont.)		
Samuel, Capt., farmer, married, d. Oct. 4, 1855, ae 80	3	10
Samuel A., m. Wealthy Ann **HUNTINGTON,** b. of Bozrah,		
Sept. 28, 1827, by Rev. David Austin	1	89
Samuel A., d. June 26, 1846, ae 43	1	89
Samuel Austin, s. Samuel & Cynthia, b. May 18, 1803	1	3
Wealthy Ann, w. Samuel A., d. June 15, 1844, ae 37	1	89
William, s. Samuel & Hannah, b. May 25, 1777	1	2
William, m. Har[r]iot **BALDWIN,** b. of Bozrah, Mar. 21, 1799	1	57
William Tarfish, s. Will[ia]m & Har[r]iot, b. May 14, 1804	1	57
GALLUP, Jabez, of Cleveland, O., m. Lucy S. **MEECH,** of Bozrah,		
Mar. 13, 1823, by Rev. D. Austin	1	44
Orrin, of Sterling, m. Harriet J. **AVERY,** of Bozrah, Mar.		
26, 1844, by Rev. Christopher Leffingwell	1	81
GARDINER, GARDNER, Abba Ann, d. John & Vilatee, b. Mar. 7,		
1815	1	59
Abigail, m. Samuel **WOODWORTH,** Sept. 23, 1790	1	42
Adolphus Morgan, s. Broderich & Emma, b. Aug. 10, 1817	1	26
Albert Avery, s. Broderich & Emma, b. Aug. 26, 1831	1	26
Amy, d. [ ], 1866, ae 79	3	44
Amey J., ae 27, b. Bozrah, m. Elisha **AYRES,** farmer, ae		
26, b. Montville, res. Montville, Apr. 18, 1850, by Rev.		
John W. Salter	2	8
Amy S., of Bozrah, m. Elisha M. **ROGERS,** of Montville,		
[Apr] 14, 1850, by Rev. John W. Salter, Montville	1	158
Andrew Jackson, s. Broderich & Emma, b. Feb. 20, 1819	1	26
Anson, s. Broderich & Emma, b. May 19, 1829	1	26
Anstress, m. John **GARDNER,** Oct. 1, 1823, by William		
Whiting, J. P.	1	31
Austin, s. Broderich & Emma, b. July 2, 1826	1	26
Azel, laborer, married, d. Nov. 4, 1863, ae 84	3	38
Broderich, m. Emma **MINER,** May 23, 1813, by Asa Wilcox,		
Elder	1	26
Broderick, d. Jan. 1, 1849	1	26
Caleb, s. Caleb & Mary, b. Nov. 11, 1778	1	2
Caleb, of Bozrah, m. Freedom **BUELL,** of Lebanon, Jan. 4,		
1795	1	2
Celina, m. William P. **ROSE,** b. of Bozrah, Dec. 6, 1821,		
by William Palmer, Elder	1	48
Champlain, b. Oct. 13, 1791	1	78
Champlain, m. Avalina Samantha **ABELL,** [ ], 1812	1	78
Charles, s. Daniel & Elizabeth, b. Mar. 2, 1777	1	26
Charles Avery, s. Salman L. & Mary H., b. Mar. 9, 1828	1	79
Clara Crocker, d. John, Jr. & Vilatee, b. Sept, 3, 1821	1	59
Clark, s. Daniel & Elizabeth, b. Mar. 12, 1766	1	26
Daniel, of Norwich, m. Elizabeth **CLARK,** of New London,		
July 6, 1763	1	26
Daniel, s. Daniel & Elizabeth, b. May 10, 1764	1	27

	Vol.	Page
GARDINER, GARDNER, (cont.)		
Daniel, Jr., m. Anna **CROCKER**, b. of Bozrah, July 1, 1787	1	27
Daniel, Jr., d. Sept, 25, 1789	1	27
Daniel, s. Daniel, Jr. & Anna, b. Oct. 11, 1789	1	27
Daniel Wolcott, s. John Jr. & Vilatee, b. June 29, 1817	1	59
David, Jr., m. Polly **HAMMOND**, Feb. 17, 1800	1	65
David, m. Frances **MINER**, b. of Bozrah, Sept. 13, 1824, by Rev. John Whittlesey	1	74
David H., farmer, married, b. Manchester, d. Apr. [ ], 1863, ae 84 y. 7 m.	3	38
Deborah, m. Jabez **GARDNER**, Nov. 24, 1825, by Rev. Tubal Wakefield	1	56
Dimis Holmes, d. Rebeckah, b. Apr. 9, 1804	1	31
Dyer Hyde, s. Broderich & Emma, b. Feb. 11, 1814	1	26
Ebenezer, s. Daniel & Elizabeth, b. Apr. 17, 1768	1	26
Edward, s. Caleb & Mary, b. Sept. 27, 1782	1	2
Edwin B., m. Eunice E. **POST**, b. of Bozrah, Nov. 19, 1834, by Levi Meech, Elder	1	134
Elisha Miner, s. Broderick & Emma, b. July 13, 1836	1	26
Elizabeth, d. Daniel & Elizabeth, b. Aug. 29, 1772	1	26
Emeline Sarah, d. John & Vilatee, b. Sept. 28, 1811	1	59
Emma, d. [ ], 1866, ae 73	3	44
Emma Elizabeth, d. Broderich & Emma, b. Aug. 24, 1833	1	26
Erastus, Dea., of Montville, m. Eunice **HYDE**, of Bozrah, Sept. 16, 1832, by Asa Wilcox, Elder	1	128
Eunice E., w. Edwin B., d. Feb. 14, 1846, at Norwich, ae 32	1	134
Fanny, d. Sept. 30, 1860, ae 38	3	24
Francis E., of Bozrah, m. Elizabeth M. **AVERY**, of Montville, Nov. 13, 1842, by Levi Meech, Elder	1	150
George C., s. Russell S., farmer, ae 29, & Lucy, ae 27, b. Feb. 26, 1850	2	7
Gershom R., m. Sally S. **CULVER**, b. of Bozrah, [Aug.] 28, 1822, by Rev. William Palmer, at Wid. Culver's, Colchester	1	113
Gilles, s. Daniel, Jr. & Anna, b. Jan. 31, 1788	1	27
Hartley Boone, s. David, Jr. & Polly, b. Jan. 17, 1807	1	65
Henry R., m. Sarah Ann **GARDNER**, b. of Bozrah, Mar. 19, 1845, by Rev. Christopher Leffingwell	1	149
Jabez, s. Daniel & Elizabeth, b. Sept. 2, 1770	1	26
Jabez, m. Deborah **GARDNER**, Nov. 24, 1825, by Rev. Tubal Wakefield	1	56
Jacob Buell, s. Caleb & Freedom, b. May 19, 1796	1	2
James, s. John & Phebe, b. June 27, 1788	1	31
James Maderson, s. John, Jr. & Vilatee, b. Mar. 18, 1809	1	59
Jedediah Lathrop, s. John & Phebe, b. Sept. 4, 1793	1	31
Jemima, d. John & Phebe, b. July 22, 1791	1	31
Jerusha, d. Jona[than], Jr. & Jerusha, b. Nov. 24, 1783	1	40
Jerusha, w. Jonathan, d. May 6, 1847, ae 88	1	40

	Vol.	Page
GIFFORD, (cont.)		
1849, by Rev. Christopher Leffingwell	1	155
GILLET, Henry, of Lebanon, m. Anna H. **BACKUS**, Nov. 12,		
1823, by Rev. David Austin	1	64
GODFREY, Mary, operative, b. Lisbon, res. Bozrah, d. Oct. 29,		
1853, ae 19; bd. Coventry	3	4
GRACE, Virginia, d. John, carpenter, ae 25, & Emily, ae 19,		
b. Apr. 17, 1851	2	11
GRAVES, Asa, of Colchester, m. Lydia **CHALFORD**, of Bozrah,		
Mar. 11, 1851, by Rev. W[illia]m P. Avery	1	159
Asa, res. Colchester, m. Lydia **CHAFFUT**, res. Bozrah,		
Mar. 11, 1851, by Rev. W[illia]m B. Avery	2	10
GRAY, Timothy, m. Sarah **ROBESON**, Dec. 4, 1825, by Rev. Allen		
Hewitt	1	16
GREELEY, Elizabeth, of Turner, Me., m. Capt. Ammi G.		
CUTTER, of Portland, Me., Apr. 6, 1847, by Rev.		
W[illia]m M. Burchard	1	85
GREEN, Moses J., of Bozrah, m. Harriet **DRAPER**, of Lebanon,		
June 28, 1847, by John W. Houghton, J. P.	1	121
Nathaniel W., of Bozrah, m. Charlotte **SCOVILLE**, of East		
Haddam, Aug. 29, 1846, by Rev. W[illia]m M. Berchard	1	92
GREINER, Rosina, m. David F. **SEVIN**, May 1, 1836, by Rev. F.		
W. Gussenhaimer, in New York	1	157
HACKLEY, Arunah, m. Mary **CROCKER**, b. of Norwich, Nov. 27,		
1783	1	22
Martin, s. Arunah & Mary, b. Sept. 29, 1784	1	22
William, s. Marshall & Sarah, b. Mar. 21, 1762	1	6
HACKS, Richard, of Preston, m. Zerviah **FANNING**, of Bozrah,		
Nov. 4, 1827, by Rev. William Palmer, at Mr. Salmon		
Gardner's, Norwich	1	117
HALL, Eliza E., d. Eliehu, farmer, ae 40, & Sarah Dean, ae 37,		
b. July 3, 1850	2	7
Emily, d. Mar. 18, 1860, ae 6	3	24
Emma, ae 27, b. Bozrah, res. Bozrah, m. W[illia]m **KINEY**,		
ae 36, b. Norwich, res. Norwich, Apr. 16, 1850, by Rev.		
Stephen Hays	2	8
Eunice D., of Bozrah, m. William **PINNEY**, of Norwich,		
Apr. 16, 1850, by Rev. Stephen Hays	1	158
Olive, ae 21, b. Bozrah, m. Charles **ADAMS**, carpenter,		
ae 21, b. Norwich, res. Norwich, Sept. [ ], 1849, by Rev.		
Edward Elles	2	8
Susan G., ae 29, of Norwich, m. 2d h. John **HUMES**,		
manufacturer, ae 29, b. Norwich, res. Norwich, May 4,		
1851, by Rev. C. Leffingwell	2	10
HALLYKO, Harriet*, res. Bozrah, m. Justin **WELLES**, res.		
Colchester, Jan. 20, 1850, by Rev. E. Elles (*Her 2d		
marriage)	2	8
HAMILTON, [see under **HAUNTTON**]		

	Vol.	Page
HAMMOND, L., domestic, d. Feb. 20, 1869, ae 71	3	49
Mary, m. Elisha V. AVERY, Sept. 23, 1832, by Asa Wilcox, Elder	1	113
Mary Ann, domestic, d. July 25, 1865, ae 55	3	44
Polly, m. David GARDNER, Jr., Feb. 17, 1800	1	65
William, merchant, married, b. Newport, R. I., d. Oct. 17, 1855, ae 65	3	10
William A., m. Mary Ann AVERY, b. of Bozrah, Jan. 1, 1838, by Rev. Benjamin G. Goff	1	109
HARDY, Enoch, m. Hannah ROBINSON, Aug. 4, 1825, by Rev. Tubal Wakefield	1	16
HARRINGTON, George, of Essex, m. Eunice H. KELLEY, of Bozrah, Mar. 26, 1834, by John W. Salter	1	77
Giles, farmer, ae 20, b. Montville, res. Norwich, m. Malvina M. VERGASON, ae 21, b. Bozrah, Mar. 4, 1849, by Rev. C. Leffingwell	2	5
Issabelle, domestic, widow, b. Montville, d. Jan. 2, 1857, ae 64	3	16
Mehetable, m. Salman WILLIAMS, of Norwich, May 10, 1830, by Joseph Kingsley, J. P.	1	87
W[illia]m E., d. Sept. 8, 1858	3	21
HARRIS, Abby L., w. Dyer, d. Sept 22, 1829	1	53
Abigail, of Lebanon, m. Zabdiel LATHROP, of Bozrah, June 6, 1785, by Timothy Stone, Clerk	1	16
Anna, m. Zerubabel WIGHTMAN, May 2, 1779	1	64
Anna, m. Charles FORD, b. of Bozrah, Feb. 11, 1790	1	44
Daniel, m. Sarah HUNT, Dec. 24, 1795, by Jonathan Murdock, Clerk	1	31
Dyer, m. Abby L. CROCKER, b. of Bozrah, Apr. 15, 1825, by Rev. David Austin	1	53
Dyer, s. Dyer & Abby L, b. Sept. 19, 1829	1	53
Dyer, s. Dyer & Abby L., d. Nov. 14, 1829	1	53
Edwin Hazen, s. John R. & Laura, b. July 3, 1810	1	28
Eunice, w. William, d. July 18, 1791	1	8
John R., m. Laura HAZEN, Sept. 24, 1809	1	28
Laura Maria, d. John & Laura, b. Oct. 25, 1812	1	28
Lucy, m. John FORD, Aug. 14, 1786	1	74
Mary, m. Elisha WOODWORTH, Aug. 17, 1794	1	59
Mary A., m. John L. LATHROP, b. of Bozrah, Apr. 20, 1842, by Rev. Tho[ma]s L. Shipman	1	147
Prudence, m. Josiah OSGOOD, b. of Norwich, Nov. 23, 1784, by Neh[emiah] Waterman, J. P.	1	6
Sarah, d. Daniel & Sarah, b. Feb. 27, 1798	1	31
Walter, s. William & Eunice, b. Oct. 10, 1789	1	8
William, m. Eunice CROCKER, b. of Bozrah, Nov. 23, 1786	1	8
William, s. William & Eunice, b. Mar. 21, 1788	1	8
HARTLEY, Abel, s. Arunah & Mary, b. Dec. [ ], 1786	1	22
HARTSHORN, Anna, [d. Silas], b. [ ]	1	99
Eunice, [d. Silas], b. [ ]	1	99

	Vol.	Page
HARTSHORN, (cont.)		
Silas, m. Wid. **BACKUS,** [ ]	1	99
HARVEY, Elijah Benjamin, s. Levi & Lucy, b. Aug. 3, 1812, in		
Norwich	1	56
Jerusha, d. Levi & Lucy, b. Dec. 24, 1809	1	56
Levi, s. Levi & Lucy, b. Apr. 8, 1805	1	56
Levina, d. Levi & Lucy, b. June 4, 1807	1	56
Lucy, d. Levi & Lucy, b. Mar. 29, 1803	1	56
HASTINGS, Benjamin S., of Franklin, m. Nancy **KINGSLEY,** of		
Bozrah, Mar. 5, 1822, by Samuel Nott, Pastor	1	74
HATCH, Abby, m. William P. **MINER,** b. of Bozrah, Apr. 17,		
1842, by Rev. John Paine	1	126
Maria S., d. Elisha, ae 23, & Anna, as 20, b. June 16, 1849	2	4
Samuel, alias Perkins, of Lisbon, m. Philena **MINER,** of		
Bozrah, Mar. 10, 1850, by Rev. Edward Eells	1	118
HAUGHTON,[see under **HOUGHTON**]		
HAUNTTON(?), Tho[ma]s, farmer, b. Norwich, res. Norwich, d.		
June 29, 1849, ae 23 (Perhaps **HAMILTON?**)	2	6
HAWLEY, Mary, ae 27, b. East Lyme, m. 2d h. Daniel A.		
JOHNSON, farmer, ae 27, of Bozrah, Feb. 19, 1850, by		
Rev. C. Leffingwell	2	8
HAZEN, Laura, m. John R. **HARRIS,** Sept. 24, 1809	1	28
HEME (?), Lydia, d. James A., blacksmith, ae 40, & Lydia, b.		
Sept. 8, 1850	2	11
HERRICK, HERRIK, Alonzo, s. Daniel & Olive, b. Sept. 30, 1827	1	106
Daniel, m. Olive **ADAMS,** b. of Canterbury, Oct. 26, 1817	1	106
Daniel, mechanic, married, b. Canterbury, d. Aug. 19,		
1864, ae 72	3	43
Daniel Augustus, s. Daniel & Olive, b. Feb. 26, 1844	1	106
Delas, s. Daniel & Olive, b. Sept. 21, 1819; d. Sept. 26, 1820	1	106
Fanny E., ae 27, of Bozrah, m. Samuel C. **CROCKER,**		
carriage maker, ae 24, b. Montville, res. Bozrah, Oct. 25,		
1848, by Rev. W[illia]m M. Birchard	2	2
Fanny Eliza, d. Daniel & Olive, b. Sept. 25, 1821	1	106
Fanny Eliza, of Bozrah, m. Samuel C. **PARKER,** of Franklin,		
Oct. 27, 1847, by Rev. W[illia]m M. Berchard	1	148
Milan, s. Daniel & Olive, b. Dec. 10, 1834; d. Sept. 21, 1835	1	106
Olive, domestic, d. Nov. 26, 1870, ae 72	3	49
HILL, Aurelia, ae 22, b. Saybrook, res. Bozrah, m. Otis G.		
BAILEY, ae 28, b. Vermont, res. Vermont, Jan. 5, 1851,		
by Rev. W[illia]m B. Avery	2	10
Hattie L., d. Joseph, b. Jan. 26, 1850, res. Norwich	2	7
Tragene A., of Bozrah, m. Dr. Otis G. **BAILEY,** of Paulet,		
Vt., Jan. 5, 1851, by Rev. W[illia]m P. Avery	1	159
HIL[L]HOUSE, William, of Montville, m. Eliza **FITCH,** of Bozrah,		
Apr. 19, 1825, by Rev. David Austin	1	65
HILLIARD, HILYARD, Delight, m. George **LANPHEAR,** May 2,		
1782, by Neh[emiah] Waterman, Jr., J. P. Norwich	1	30

	Vol.	Page

HILLIARD, HILYARD, (cont.)

Jonathan, of Salem, m. Phebe **HOUGH,** of Bozrah, [   ],
1826, by Rev. David Austin — 1 — 75

HINCKLEY, Lois, m. Uriah **LATHROP,** b. of Norwich, Dec. 30,
1784 — 1 — 29

HINSON, John, s. William & Azubah, b. May 19, 1775 — 1 — 34

Lucindia, d. William & Azubah, b. Sept. 26, 1778 — 1 — 34

Lucretia, d. William & Azubah, b. Dec. 7, 1780 — 1 — 34

Martha, d. William & Azubah, b. May 24, 1766 — 1 — 34

Samuel, s. William & Azubah, b. Aug. 1, 1769 — 1 — 34

Sands, s. William & Azubah, b. Jan. 19, 1772 — 1 — 34

Sarah, d. William & Azubah, b. Apr. 19, 1764 . — 1 — 34

William, s. William & Azubah, b. Mar. 8, 1762 — 1 — 34

William, Jr., m. Mary **PLUMB,** Nov. 15, 1787, by Neh[emiah]
Waterman, Jr., J. P. — 1 — 21

William, s. William, Jr. & Mary, b. Nov. 14, 1789 — 1 — 21

HOLDREDGE, HOLDRIDGE, Amos, farmer, b. Norwich, res.
Bozrah, d. [1853], ae 73; bd. Huntington ground — 3 — 4

Edward D., of Colchester, m. Lucy A. **DANIELS,** of Bozrah,
Aug. 23, 1846, by Rev. W[illia]m M. Burchard — 1 — 92

-----, Mrs., d. Feb. [ ], 1854, ae 69; bd. Norwich Town — 3 — 7

HOLLESTER, Harriet, of Bozrah, m. Justin **WELLES,** of
Colchester, Jan. 20, 1850, by Rev. Edward Eells   (See
under **HALLYKO)** — 1 — 118

HOLMES, Franklin, of Stonington, m. Nancy H. **HUNTLEY,** of
Bozrah, Apr. 26, 1835, by Gardner Avery, J. P. — 1 — 122

J. H., m. Delia **WHUM,** b. of Norwich, Oct. 1, 1848, by Rev.
Benjamin G. Goff — 1 — 135

J. H., of Norwich, m. Delia **ISHAM,** of Norwich, Oct. 1,
1848, by Rev. B. G. Goff — 2 — 5

HOOK, Olive, m. Elijah **HUNTINGTON,** June 13, 1821 — 1 — 58

HOSFORD, Mindwell, of Marlborough, m. Elijah **ABELL,** of
Bozrah, Sept. 24, 1814 — 1 — 114

HOUGH, Alanson H., m. Mary A. **LATHROP,** b. of Bozrah, May
13, 1832, by Rev. Joseph Hough — 1 — 128

Alanson Hodges, s. Jabez, Jr. & Eunice, b. Oct. 26, 1803 — 1 — 41

Albert Avery, s. Clark & Serviah E., b. Apr. 12, 1827 — 1 — 84

Andrew Jackson, s. William & Philene, b. Mar. 29, 1815 — 1 — 68

Ann H., m. Nehemiah **HUNTINGTON,** b. of Bozrah, Dec. 21,
1841, by Rev. John W. Salter. Witnesses; Eben[eze]r
Hough, Guy Hough, Geo[rge] Hough, and others — 1 — 54

Anna H., of Bozrah, m. Albert **ARMSTRONG,** of Killingly,
Ct., Sept. 6, 1843, by Rev. Bela Hicks — 1 — 86

Anna Harris, d. William & Philene, b. Feb. 6, 1821 — 1 — 68

Anthony Benezett Cleveland, s. Jabez, Jr. & Eunice, b.
Dec. 17, 1808 — 1 — 41

Bernice, m. Ebenezer **HOUGH,** May 9, 1786, by Nehemiah
Waterman, J. P., Norwich. May 12, 1786 recorded — 1 — 14

	Vol.	Page
HOUGH, (cont.)		
Bernice, d. William & Philene, b. Nov. 19, 1817; d. Oct.		
12, 1848, ae 29	1	68
Bernice, w. Capt. Eben[eze]r, d. May 11, 1845, ae 78	1	14
Bernice, milliner, d. Oct. [ ], 1848, ae 29	2	3
Catharine Westcot, d. William & Philena, b. May 14, 1825	1	68
Charles, s. John & Susannah, b. Nov. 4, 1792	1	13
Charles, d. Oct. 12, 1861, ae 1	3	31
Clarissa, d. Walter K. & Nancy B., b. Apr. 13, 1834	1	97
Clark, of Bozrah, m. Serviah E. **ABELL**, of Colchester, Dec. 1,		
1818, by William Palmer, Elder	1	84
Clark, s. John & Susannah, d. Dec. 5, 1854, in New York	1	13
Clement, s. Jabez, Jr. & Eunice, b. Dec. 26, 1791	1	41
Daniel, s. John & Susannah, b. Mar. 22, 1803	1	13
Daniel Alanson, s. Guy & Hannah, b. Aug. 30, 1827; d.		
Oct. 28, 1852, ae 25 y., in Murayville, Cal.	1	72
David, s. John & Susannah, b. Sept. 23, 1796; d. Sept.		
28, 1796	1	13
David, s. John & Susannah, b. Aug. 12, 1798	1	13
David Austin, s. Guy & Hannah, b. Sept. 15, 1818	1	72
Desire, m. Uriah **DOWNER**, b. of Bozrah, Nov. 15, 1787	1	7
Ebenezer, m. Bernice HOUGH, May 9, 1786, by Nehemiah		
Waterman, J. P., Norwich. May 12, 1786	1	14
Ebenezer, s. Eben[eze]r & Bernice, b. Jan. 28, 1805	1	14
Ebenezer, Jr., m. Lucy B. **KELLEY**, b. of Bozrah, Dec. 21,		
1830, by Rev. Andrew Reid	1	98
Ebenezer, Capt., d. July 5, 1846, ae 84	1	14
Edward, s. Jabez, Jr. & Eunice, b. Feb. 18, 1807	1	41
Edward Albert, s. Edward H. & Mary Ann, b. Mar. 24, 1834	1	97
Edward H., of Bozrah, m. Mary Ann **PRENTICE**, of Lebanon,		
Dec. 27, 1832, by Elder Brown	1	97
Eunice, d. Jabez, Jr. & Eunice, b. July 14, 1802; d.		
Sept. 22, 1802	1	41
Eunice, d. Walter K. & Nancy B., b. Mar. 24, 1832	1	97
Frances D., m. Charles B. **BALDWIN**, b. of Bozrah, [Feb.]		
19, 1840, by Tho[ma]s L. Shipman	1	146
Frances Desire, d. Guy & Hannah, b. July 12, 1813	1	72
George, s. Eben[eze]r & Bernice, b. Nov. 28, 1802	1	14
George, farmer, d. Apr. 21, 1869, ae 66	3	49
George A., b. Bozrah, res. Colchester, d. Apr. 10, 1854,		
ae 2; bd. Throop B. G.	3	7
George E., d. [ ], 1868	3	48
Guy, b. Oct. 22, 1779	1	72
Guy, m. Hannah **BAILEY**, Mar. 31, 1806	1	72
Hannah, d. John, Jr. & Susannah, b. Oct. 5, 1783	1	13
Hannah, m. Isaac **JOHNSON**, Nov. 25, 1846, by Rev.		
W[illia]m M. Birchard	1	138
Hannah, d. Mar. 17, 1869, ae 84, domestic	3	49

	Vol.	Page
HOUGH, (cont.)		
Hannah, d. John & Susannah, d. [ ] , in New York	1	13
Hannah Jemima, d. Guy & Hannah, b. Aug. 29, 1824	1	72
Hannah McAll, d. John & Susannah, d. Nov. [ ], 1855	1	13
Harriet Tracy, d. Jabez, Jr. & Eunice, b. May 3, 1794	1	41
Henry W., m. Hannah D. **HUNTINGTON,** June 6, 1837, by Rev. Benjamin G. Goff	1	142
Henry Wightman, s. William & Philene, b. Feb. 6, 1810	1	68
J. P., d. Feb. 27, 1869	3	49
Jabez, Jr., of Bozrah, m. Eunice **CLEMENT,** of Norwich, Oct. 28, 1790	1	41
Jabez, s. Jabez, Jr. & Eunice, b. May 14, 1799	1	41
Jane, d. Ebenezer, Jr. & Lucy, b. May 10, 1834	1	98
Jedidiah, s. Eben[ezer] & Bernice, b. Feb. 11, 1792	1	14
Jedediah Stark, s. Guy & Hannah, b. June 29, 1815	1	72
Jemima, d. Eben[eze]r & Bernice, b. May 14, 1794	1	14
Jemima, m. Uriah **CARDWELL,** b. of Bozrah, Oct. [ ], 1810	1	25
Jirah I., m. Belinda **WEST,** b. of Bozrah, Nov. 14, 1811	1	58
Jirah Isham, s. Eben[ezer] & Bernice, b. Mar. 22, 1790	1	14
John, Jr., m. Susannah **JOHNSON,** b. of Norwich, Nov. 18, 1782	1	13
John, s. John & Susannah, b. Aug. 13, 1791	1	13
John, d. Nov. 19, 1832, in New York	1	13
John, s. John & Susannah, d. [ ], in Georgia	1	13
John B., m. Sarah S. **PALMER,** [Dec.] 18, 1833, by John W. Salter	1	24
John Bailey, s. Guy & Hannah, b. Apr. 14, 1809	1	72
Joseph, s. Jabez, Jr. & Eunice, b. Jan. 6, 1793	1	41
Joseph, m. Levina P. **WIGHTMAN,** b. of Bozrah, May 23, 1822, by Rev. William Palmer, at the house of Mr. Elijah Wightman, Colchester	1	110
Lorana, d. John & Susannah, b. Feb. 8, 1785	1	13
Larana, m. Alvin **WOODWORTH,** Jan. 30, 1803, by Rev. Jonathan Murdock	1	61
Lydia, d. Ebenezer, Jr. & Lucy, b. Oct. 13, 1831	1	98
Mariah, d. Guy & Han[n]ah, b. May 17, 1807	1	72
Maria, of Bozrah, m. Lyman E. **BILL,** of Lebanon, Nov. 5, 1828, by Rev. David Austin	1	119
Martha A., ae 19, b. Norwich, m. Charles D. **MARK,** farmer, ae 20, b. Norwich, Mar. 24, 1850, in Willimantic	2	8
Mary A., of Bozrah, m. Charles A. **KINGSLEY,** of Franklin, Nov. 26, 1850, by Rev. William P. Avery	1	159
Mary A., ae 21, of Bozrah, m. Charles A. **KINGSLEY,** ae 22, b. Franklin, res. Franklin, Nov. 26, 1850, by Rev. W[illia]m B. Avery	2	10
Mary H., domestic, d. Apr. 26, 1869, ae 64	3	49
Mary Moosely, d. Jabez, Jr. & Eunice, b. Sept. 14, 1795	1	41
Mercy, wid. Jabez, Sr., d. Oct. 16, 1833, ae 83 y.	1	27

	Vol.	Page
HOUGH, (cont.)		
Nancy, d. Ebenezer & Bernice, b. May 20, 1788	1	14
Nancy, m. Artemus **WOODWORTH**, Nov. 24, 1808	1	106
Phebe, m. Roswell **FOX**, b. of Norwich, Dec. 11, 1785, by		
Rev. Levi Hart	1	7
Phebe, d. Eben[eze]r & Bernice, b. Apr. 8, 1796; d. Apr. 25,		
1797	1	14
Phebe, d. Eben[eze]r & Bernice, b. July 25, 1798	1	14
Phebe, of Bozrah, m. Jonathan **HILLIARD**, of Salem, [ ],		
1826, by Rev. David Austin	1	75
Philena, domestic, married, d. Dec. 17, 1856, ae 72	3	13
Sally C., m. Roswell **BAILEY**, Jan, 7, 1821, by Rev. William		
Palmer, at Deacon Jabez Hough's	1	107
Sally Clement, d. Jabez, Jr. & Eunice, b. Dec. 5, 1796	1	41
Sarah, b. May 27, 1775	1	103-4
Sarah, m. Nehemiah **WATERMAN**, Jr., Oct. 25, 1795, by		
Nehemiah Waterman, J. P.	1	103-4
Sophia, d. John & Susannah, b. Apr. 30, 1794	1	13
Susan Sophia, d. Clark & Serviah E., b. Sept. 5, 1819	1	84
Susannah, d. John & Susannah, b. Jan. 31, 1787	1	13
Susannah, w. John, d. [ ], in New York	1	13
Thomas Hyde, s. Guy & Hannah, b. May 28, 1811	1	72
Urban, s. Jabez, Jr. & Eunice, b. Oct. 4, 1800	1	41
Wade, s. John & Susannah, b. June 10, 1788	1	13
Walter K., m. Nancy B. **KELLEY**, b. of Bozrah, Apr. 14,		
1831, by William Palmer, Elder	1	97
Walter King, s. Jabez, Jr. & Eunice, b. Jan. 23, 1805	1	41
William, s. Ebenezer & Bernice, b. Aug. 9, 1786	1	14
William, m. Filene **WIGHTMAN**, b. of Bozrah, Feb. 15, 1809	1	68
William, farmer, widower, d. Apr. 10, 1864, ae 77	3	43
W[illia]m M., s. Andrew J., farmer, ae 34, & Charlotte,		
ae 32, b. June 9, 1849	2	4
Witherell, s. Eben[eze]r & Hough, b. June 6, 1800	1	14
-----, child of J. S., farmer, ae 36, & Amelia, ae 28,		
b. [1851?]	2	11
HOUGHTON, John W., farmer, d. July 31, 1871, ae 73	3	58
Samuel Wells, s. John W. & Clarissy, b. Sept. 30, 1831	1	152
HOUSE, Henry D., single, d. Sept. 1, 1864, ae 1 1/2	3	43
Mary, m. Asa **FITCH**, Jan. [ ], 1816	1	62
HOW, Abigail M., of Canterbury, m. George **WILLARD**, of		
Bozrahville, Feb. 12, 1837, by Rev. Oliver Brown	1	138a
HULBERT, [see also **HURLBURT**], Sarah C., of Bozrah, m.		
Erastus M. **WILCOX**, of Groton, Mar. 10, 1828, by Rev.		
David Austin	1	119
Susan S., of Lebanon, m. William F. **TRACY**, of Lisbon, Oct.		
5, 1828, by Rev. David B. Ripley	1	91
HULL, Lucy H., farmer's wife, b. Norwich, res. Bozrah, d.		
Mar. 27, 1853, ae 84; bd. T[h]roop Burying Ground	3	4

	Vol.	Page
HUNTLEY, (cont.)		
William Asher, s. Ezekiel & Ruth, b. July 19, 1804	1	75
HURLBURT, [see also **HULBERT**], Winthrop, of Lyme, m. Wid.		
Fanny L. **COLVERT**, of Bozrah, Mar. 7, 1847, by Rev.		
W[illia]m Birchard	1	134
HUTCHINS, Leonora, d. Mar. 8, 1862, ae 1	3	32
HYDE, Anna, [d. Love], d. May [ ], 1799	1	100
Dice, of Franklin, m. Oliver **BACKUS**, of Bozrah, May 20,		
1787, by Samuel Nott, Clerk	1	15
Elisha, d. July 29, 1838, ae 86	1	47
Erastus, s. Elisha & Hannah, b. July 5, 1808	1	47
Erastus, of Bozrah, m. Hannah **CLARKE**, of Lebanon, Sept.		
28, 1835, by Rev. John Hyde	1	135
Eunice, d. [Joseph & Susannah, 2d], b. Feb. 20, 1781	1	101
Eunice, [d. Joseph & Susannah, 2d], d. June 2, 1795, of		
Canker Rash, sick 8 d.	1	102
Eunice, d. Elisha & Hannah, b. Sept. 4, 1797	1	47
Eunice, 2d. [d. Joseph & Susannah, 2d], b. June 17, 179[ ]	1	101
Eunice, of Bozrah, m. Dea. Erastus **GARDNER**, of Montville,		
Sept. 16, 1832, by Asa Wilcox, Elder	1	128
Hannah, [d. Joseph & Susannah, 2d], b. Aug. 11, 1789	1	101
Hannah, w. Elisha, d. Mar. 19, 1848, ae 74	1	47
Hannah, b. Norwich, res. Bozrah, d. Mar. 19, 1848, ae 78	2	3
Horatio, [s. Joseph & Susannah, 2d], b. Feb. 23, 1792	1	101
Horatio, [s. Joseph & Susannah, 2d], d. May 17, 1793 of		
Canker rash	1	102
John Lathrop, [s. Joseph & Susannah, 2d], b. Oct. 10, 1794	1	101
Joseph, ae 25, m. Susannah **WATERMAN**, 2d, ae 19, Sept. 6,		
1780	1	101
Joseph, [s. Joseph & Susannah, 2d], b. Jan. 20, 1783	1	101
Joseph, d. May 31, 1795, sick 4 d.	1	102
Joseph, 2d, [s. Joseph & Susannah, 2d], b. Feb. 9, 1797	1	101
Lois, d. Elisha & Hannah, b. Nov. 30, 1794	1	47
Love, d. Mar. 1, 1800	1	100
Mary, d. Elisha & Hannah, b. Sept. 30, 1800	1	47
Mary, m. Isaac B. **AVERY**, Oct. 2, 1831, by Rev. Jared		
Andrus	1	112
Phebe, d. Nov. 27, 1852, ae 61	1	47
Phebe, farmer, d. Nov. 27, [1852], ae 61; bd. Doth (?) Hill	3	4
Simeon, [s. Joseph & Susannah, 2d], b. Mar. 12, 1785	1	101
Susannah, [d. Joseph & Susannah, 2d], b. July 3, 1787	1	101
W. B., b. Norwich, d. June 25, 1861, ae 2	3	31
INGRAHAM, Benjamin, of Chatham, Conn., m. Almira		
BRIAM, of Bozrah, Feb. 11, 1849, by Rev. Lyman		
Strange	1	93
Benj[amin], laborer, ae 20, b. Chatham, res. Bozrah, m.		
Almira **BROWN**, ae 18, b. Montville, res. Bozrah, July		
11, 1849, by Rev. Lyman Story	2	5

	Vol.	Page
INGRAHAM, (cont.)		
Patty, m. Cirrenus **BECKWITH,** b. of Bozrah, Sept. 16, 1821, by William Palmer, Elder, at the house of Mr. Ingraham	1	108
ISHAM, Delia, of Norwich, m. J. H. **HOLMES,** of Norwich, Oct. 1, 1848, by Rev. B. G. Goff	2	5
Susannah, 2d, d. Joseph & Susannah, of Colchester, b. Feb. 15, 1738. Entered Jan. 1, 1800	1	102
Susannah, 2d, d. Joseph & Susannah, of Colchester, b. Feb. 15, 1738; m. [ ], Dec. 24, 1760	1	102
Susannah, m. Nehemiah **WATERMAN,** Dec. 24, 1760	1	99
JAMES, Frances C., of Bozrah, m. Roswell G. **LAMB,** of Ledyard, Mar. 23, 1841, by Tho[ma]s L. Shipman	1	141
Giles, ae 26, b. Groton, res. Montville, m. Hannah E. **RATHBUN,** ae 29, b. Salem, Mar. 3, 1851, by Rev. Christopher Leffingwell	2	10
Henrietta, domestic, single, b. N. Y., d. July 14, 1855, ae 13	3	10
Sarah E., m. William P. **GARDNER,** b. of Bozrah, July 5, 1836, by Jonathan Miner, Elder	1	138a
JANES, Aurelia E., of East Haddam, m. Larien **PIERCE,** Rev., of Montville, Feb. 24, 1839, by Rev. A. W. Swetherton	1	48
JILLSON, David, m. Mary M. **WATROUS,** Aug. 15, 1826, by Rev. Tubal Wakefield	1	67
JOHNSON, Andrew, s. Samuel, laborer, ae 60, & Lucretia, ae 45, b. Aug. 5, 1847	2	1
Ann Jerusha, d. Jehiel & Jerusha, b. Dec. 2, 1826	1	115
Anna, d. Ebenezer & Anna, b. Feb. 15, 1765	1	10
Anna, wid. Eben[ezer], d. Dec. 31, 1809	1	10
Antionette, domestic, married, b. Lebanon, d. Feb. 9, 1865, ae 64	3	44
Benjamin, Jr., m. Susan **JOHNSON,** b. of Bozrah, Apr. 25, 1840, by William L. Crocker, J. P.	1	144
Benjamin Tracy, s. Isaac & Phebe, b. Aug. 29, 1807; d. Mar. 4, 1880	1	67
Burgess M., s. Burgess, Jr., laborer, ae 24 & Susan, ae 25, b. Mar. 29, 1848	2	1
Charles, d. Apr. 10, *1758 or 1858. (The 7 & 8 were typed over each other)	3	21
Charles Augustus, s. Jehiel & Jerusha, b. Dec. 6, 1841	1	115
Christina Rickers, d. Jehiel & Jerusha, b. Aug. 8, 1846	1	115
Cromel, farmer, d. May 15, 1869, ae 75 y. 3 m. 7 d.	3	49
Daniel A., farmer, ae 27, of Bozrah, m. Mary **HAWLEY,** ae 27, b. East Lyme, Feb. 19, 1850, by Rev. C. Leffingwell	2	8
Delia E., d. May 5, 1860, ae 8 m.	3	24
Ebenezer, m. Anna **MILLS,** b. of Norwich, Nov. 7, 1759	1	10
Ebenezer, s. Ebenezer & Anna, b. June 24, 1767	1	10
Ebenezer, d. Dec. 11, 1804, in the 74th y. of his age	1	10
Ebenezer, d. Dec. 11, 1804, in the 74th y. of his age	1	67
Edward, s. Samuel & Cynthia, b. Jan. 9, 1854	1	141

	Vol.	Page
JOHNSON, (cont.)		
Edward B., d. June 19, 1849, ae 24	2	6
George W., s. Benjamin, laborer, ae 31, & Susan, ae 29,		
b. [1851?]	2	11
Hannah, d. Ebenezer & Anna, b. Oct. 4, 1770	1	10
Hannah, d. Isaac & Phebe, b. Dec. 21, 1810	1	67
Isaac, s. Ebenezer & Anna, b. July 24, 1773	1	10
Isaac, m. Phebe **BIRCHARD,** b. of Bozrah, Apr. 5, 1795	1	67
Isaac, s. Orimel & Artemissa, b. Jan. 20, 1823	1	138
Isaac, m. Hannah **HOUGH,** Nov. 25, 1846, by Rev. W[illia]m		
M. Birchard	1	138
Jane Maria, [d. Dr. Samuel & Cynthia M.], b. Mar. 1, 1846	1	141
Jehial, s. Ebenezer & Anna, b. Sept. 16, 1762	1	10
Jeheil, s. Isaac & Phebe, b. Mar. 19, 1802	1	67
Jehiel, m. Jerusha **WHITING,** b. of Bozrah, Jan. 1, 1826,		
by Rev. David Austin	1	115
Jehiel, Col., d. July 29, 1861, ae 59	1	115
Jehiel, d. Mar. 21, 1862, ae 1 m. 10 d.	3	32
Jahiel, married, d. July 29, 1862, ae 59	3	32
Jehiel Lathrop, twin with William Whiting, s. Jehiel &		
Jerusha, b. Aug. 22, 1828	1	115
Jerusha, d. Isaac & Phebe, b. May 16, 1800; d. May 29, 1801	1	67
Jerusha Lathrop, d. Isaac & Phebe, b. Dec. 16, 1812	1	67
Marah C., ae 17, b. Bozrah, m. Alfred **VERGASON,** farmer,		
ae 24, b. Bozrah, res. Montville, Aug. 26, 1849, by Rev.		
C. Leffingwell	2	8
Mary Lauretta, d. Jehiel & Jerusha, b. Jan. 16, 1831; d.		
Apr. 26, 1833	1	115
Mary Lauretta, 2d. d. Jehiel & Jerusha, b. June 16, 1833	1	115
Nathan, s. Jehiel & Jerusha, b. Sept. 15, 1837; d. Nov. 30, 1843	1	115
Nathan, [s. Dr. Samuel & Cynthia M.], b. Apr. 19, 1851	1	141
Olive, d. Orimel & Artemissa, b. Aug. 25, 1828	1	138
Oramil, s. Isaac & Phebe, b. Feb. 8, 1796	1	67
Orimel, s. Isaac & Hannah, b. Oct. 20, 1848	1	138
Orimel A., s. Isaac, farmer, ae 27, & Hannah A., ae 25,		
b. Oct. 20, 1848	2	4
Patience, m. John **MORRISON,** Nov. 3, 1805, by Elisha Hyde,		
J. P.	1	60
Permela, d. Patience, b. May 3, 1799	1	60
Phebe A., of Bozrah, m. William F. **BAILEY,** of Colchester,		
Nov. 26, 1846, by Rev. W[illia]m M. Birchard	1	147
Phebe Artemissa, d. Orimel & Artemissa, b. Oct. 23, 1826	1	138
Philena H., of Bozrah, m. Henry **FULLER,** of Colchester,		
Jan. 9, 1848, by Rev. W[illia]m M. Birchard	1	94
Philena H., ae 28, b. Montville, res. Montville, m. Henry		
FULLER, farmer, ae 28, b. Montville, res. Colchester,		
Jan. [ ], 1848, by Rev. W[illia]m M. Birchard	2	2
Rachel, d. Patience, b. June 17, 1803	1	60

	Vol.	Page
KELLEY, (cont.)		
David Austin	1	120
John B., d. June 1, 1832	1	120
Lucy B., m. Ebenezer HOUGH, Jr., b. of Bozrah, Dec. 21,		
1830, by Rev. Andrew Reid	1	98
Lucy Brown, d. William & Lydia, b. Jan. 28, 1810	1	111
Lydia, w. William, d. May 9, 1844	1	111
Nancy, d. William & Clarissa, b. Oct. 28, 1804	1	111
Nancy B., m. Walter K. HOUGH, b. of Bozrah, Apr. 14, 1831,		
by William Palmer, Elder	1	97
William, m. Lydia STILLMAN, Oct. 29, 1808, by Asa		
Woodworth, J. P.	1	111
William, m. Clarissa BACKUS, [ ]	1	111
William Sanford, S. William & Lydia, b. Jan. 14, 1813;		
d. Mar. 8, 1838	1	111
KELSO, Joseph, farmer, ae 30, b. Chester, Mass., res. Chester,		
Mass., m. Harriet LEFFINGWELL, ae 31, b. Bozrah,		
May 11, 1851, by Rev. C. Leffingwell	2	10
Joseph C., of Chester, Mass., m. Harriet LEFFINGWELL,		
of Bozrah, May 11, 1851, by Rev. Christopher		
Leffingwell	1	160
KENNEY, Mary, d. Mar. 1, 1868, ae 2 2/3 m.	3	48
KEY, Mary E., ae 21, b. Mansfield, res. Bozrah, m. George		
SYMONS, millwright, ae 28, b. E. Hartford, res. E.		
Hartford, June 11, 1848, by Rev. W[illia]m Palmer (See		
also Mary E. **KING**)	2	2
KIMBALL, John, m. Nancy LOOMIS, Oct. 30, 1817, by Rev.		
Daniel Putman	1	42
Rebecca, of Stonington, m. Silvester GARDNER, of Bozrah,		
Feb. 24, 1803, by Samuel Nott, J. P.	1	55
KINEK, Allice, d. Nov. 24, 1857, ae 6	3	16
KINEY, W[illia]m, ae 36, b. Norwich, res. Norwich, m. Emma		
HALL, ae 27, b. Bozrah, res. Bozrah, Apr. 16, 1850, by		
Rev. Stephen Hays	2	8
KING, Mary E., of Bozrah, m. George SIMMONDS, of East		
Hartford, June 11, 1848, by Rev. W[illia]m Palmer (See		
also Mary E. **KEY**)	1	140
KINGBERGER, **KINBERGER**, Charles, mechanic, married, d.		
May 4, 1866, ae 40	3	44
John, b. New York, d. Feb. 6, 1856, ae 19 m.	3	13
KINGSLEY, Charles A., of Franklin, m. Mary A. HOUGH, of		
Bozrah, Nov.. 26, 1850, by Rev. William P. Avery	1	159
Charles A., ae 22, b. Franklin, res. Franklin, m. Mary		
A. HOUGH, ae 21, of Bozrah, Nov. 26, 1850, by Rev.		
W[illia]m B. Avery	2	10
Joseph R., of Norwich, m. Mary A. FORD, of Bozrah, Feb.		
21, 1847, by Rev. W[illia]m M. Berchard	1	134
Mary Ann, w. Charles A., d. Aug. [ ], 1852	1	159

	Vol.	Page
KINGSLEY, (cont.)		
Nancy, of Bozrah, m. Benjamin S. **HASTINGS** of Franklin, Mar. 5, 1822, by Rev. Samuel Nott	1	74
Nancy C., d. Simeon L. & Dolly Ann Elizabeth, b. Feb. 3, 1827	1	117
KIPP, John, blacksmith, d. Sept. 17, 1849, ae 74	2	9
KNIGHT, Earl, s. Earl & Jerusha, b. Jan. 24, 1827	1	116
Earl, Dr., f. of Mary & Earl, d. Apr. 24, 1832	1	116
Mary, d. Earl & Jerusha P., b. Mar. 16, 1825	1	116
KOONSLEY, Charles, d. June 1, 1864, ae 10 m.	3	38
KUNDLE, Ann, widow, b. Norwich, d. Jan. 23, 1858, ae 38	3	16
LAD[D], Hannah, domestic, d. Aug. 7, 1853, ae 70; bd. Hough Burying Ground	3	4
Samuel S., laborer, d. July 20, 1850, ae 54	2	9
LAMANJS, Gilbert, single, d. Apr. 30, 1859, ae 22	3	24
LAMB, Esther, of Lebanon, m. Dr. John **SCOTT**, of Bozrah, Jan. 27, 1828, by James Lam, J. P.	1	87
Roswell G., of Ledyard, m. Frances C. **JAMES**, of Bozrah, Mar. 23, 1841, by Tho[ma]s L. Shipman	1	141
LANPHEAR, LAMPHEAR, LAMPHERE, Dan[iel], s. George & Delight, b. Dec. 16, 1791	1	30
David, s. George & Delight, b. July 29, 1785	1	30
Dicey, d. Mar. 4, 1851, ae 64	2	9
Erastus, s. George & Delight, b. Aug. 28, 1789	1	30
George, m. Delight **HILYARD**, May 2, 1782, by Neh[emiah] Waterman, Jr., J. P., Norwich	1	30
George, s. George & Delight, b. Sept. 6, 1787	1	30
Hernando Alvers, d. [sic] Theophilus & Elizabeth Savery, Aug. 17, 1801	1	49
Jane C., domestic, d. Jan. 16, 1869, ae 24	3	49
Jesse, s. George & Delight, b. Apr. 29, 1783	1	30
Lodice, w. Oliver, d. Mar. 4, 1851, ae 64	1	93
Lois, m. Caleb **WINCHESTER**, Sept. 7, 1800	1	49
Oliver, m. Lodice **LEFFINGWELL**, b. of Bozrah, Nov. 10, 1831, by Rev. Joseph Hough	1	93
Oliver, d. Sept. 4, 1854, ae 80	1	93
Oliver, b. Westerly, R. I., res. Bozrah, d. Sept. 4, 1854, ae 80; bd. Hough B. G.	3	7
LANSIE, Joshua, painter, d. Apr. 17, 1869, ae 35	3	49
LaPOINT, Matilda, d. Dec. 16, [1871?], ae 18; bd. Dec. 18, [1871?], in Baltic	3	62
LATHROP, A. P., d. [ ], 1867, ae 41	3	48
Abigail, d. Asa & Allis, b. Feb. 8, 1783	1	33
Abigail, d. Asa & Allis, b. June 10, 1793	1	33
Alanson Peckham, s. Simeon & Phebe, b. July 21, 1826	1	136
Alford, s. Zabdiel & Abigail, b. Nov. 5, 1786	1	16
Allis, d. Asa & Allis, b. Jan. 2, 1795	1	33
Andrew, 2d, of Bozrah, m. Lucretia **SMITH**, of Franklin,		

	Vol.	Page
LATHROP, (cont.)		
Jan. 22, 1789, by Samuel Nott, clerk	1	19
Andrew, 3d, m. Sibyl DOWNER, b. of Bozrah, June 1, 1797	1	53
Andrew, 2d, m. Zerviah POLLY, May 30, 1802	1	19
Andrew, Capt., d. July 9, 1803	1	29
Andrew, s. Simeon & Phebe, b. Mar. 10, 1822	1	136
Ann, d. Simeon & Phebe, b. Mar. 20, 1834	1	136
Anne, of Lebanon, m. William WHITING, of Bozrah, Apr. 6, 1797	1	71
Apeme, d. Andrew, 2d, & Lucretia, b. July 25, 1794	1	19
Apama, m. Joseph B. FORD, Apr. 15, 1830, by Asa Wilcox, Elder	1	105
Asa, m. Allis FOX, b. of Norwich, Sept. 17, 1782	1	33
Asa, s. Asa & Allis, b. Mar. 2, 1799	1	33
Azariah, s. Andrew, 2d, & Lucretia, b. Feb. 25, 1796	1	19
Calvin, s. Andrew & Sibyl, b. Mar. 15, 1804	1	53
Caroline, d. Zabdiel & Abigail, b. Sept. 2, 1788	1	16
Charles, s. Uriah & Lois, b. Sept. 22, 1785	1	29
Charlotte, d. Elisha, laborer, & Charlotte, b. [1847?]	2	1
Christopher L., of Norwich, m. Philura L. HUNTINGTON, of Bozrah, Mar. 22, 1832, by Rev. Jared Andrus	1	128
Clarissa, d. Uriah & Lois, b. June 6, 1789	1	29
David Austin, twin with Lydia Zerviah, s. Simeon & Phebe, b. Apr. 23, 1832	1	136
Dyce, d. Andrew, 2d, & Lucretia, b. Dec. 3, 1789	1	19
Elisha, farmer, married, d. Aug. 22, 1855, ae 52	3	10
Elizabeth, m. Jesse ABELL, b. of Bozrah, Nov. 11, 1788	1	38
Eunice, m. Elderkin SPICER, b. of Bozrah, Sept. 3, 1789	1	24
Eunice, d. Capt. Andrew & Abigail, d. Dec. 30, 1792, in the 25th y. of her age	1	29
Eunice, d. Andrew, 2d, & Lucretia, b. June 14, 1799	1	19
Eunice H., m. John B. KELLEY, Jan. 1, 1829, by Rev. David Austin	1	120
Gad, twin with Guy, s. Andres & Sibyl, b. June 4, 1800; d. June 20, 1800	1	53
Guy, twin with Gad, s. Andrew & Sibyl, b. June 4, 1800; d. June 23, 1800	1	53
Hannah, w. Deac. Simeon, d. Sept. 17, 1802	1	55
Hannah, m. Jabez BACKUS, Nov. 25, 1810	1	15
Henry, of Lebanon, m. Mary A. BROWN, of Bozrah, Apr. 1, 1841, by Rev. Benjamin G. Goff	1	124
Henry L., s. Daniel, of Norwich, & [Desire?], b. Nov. 21, 1849	2	7
Jabez Smith, s. Simeon & Phebe, b. May 28, 1824	1	136
James, s. Asa & Allis, b. June 17, 1785	1	33
Jane, d. Simeon & Phebe, b. Oct. 25, 1828	1	136
Jedidiah, d. June 9, 1792	1	17
Jemima, w. Jedidiah, d. Sept. 1, 1789	1	17
John L., m. Mary A. HARRIS, b. of Bozrah, Apr. 20, 1842, by		

	Vol.	Page
LATHROP, (cont.)		
by Rev. Tho[ma]s L. Shipman	1	147
Lois, d. Uriah & Lois, b. May 10, 1791	1	29
Lucretia, w. Andrew, 2d, d. Oct. 9, 1801	1	19
Lucy, m. Dyer **McCALL**, May 26, 1791, by Joseph Strong, Clerk, Norwich, Oct. 8, 1791	1	18
Lucy, d. Andrew, 2nd, & Lucretia, b. Mar. 8, 1798	1	19
Lucy, d. Simeon & Phebe, b. May 22, 1823	1	136
Lydia, m. John **FISH**, b. of Bozrah, Apr. 2, 1786	1	18
Lydia Z., of Bozrah, m. Henry N. **SMITH**, of Franklin, Jan. 20, 1852, by Rev. William P. Avery	1	140
Lydia Zerviah, twin with David Austin, d. Simeon & Phebe, b. Apr. 23, 1832	1	136
Mary, domestic, single, b. Plainfield, d. Mar. 8, 1863, ae 80	3	38
Mary A., m. Alanson H. **HOUGH**, b. of Bozrah, May 13, 1832, by Rev. Joseph Hough	1	128
Phebe, m. John **GARDNER**, b. of Norwich, Dec. 13, 1780	1	31
Phebe, w. Simeon, d. Aug. [ ], 1848, ae 48	1	136
Phebe, d. Oct. [ ], 1848, ae 48	2	3
Phebe C., single, b. Manchester, d. May 9, 1863, ae 36	3	38
Philena, d. Andrew, 2d, & Lucretia, b. Apr. 10, 1791	1	19
Philena, domestic, single, d. Sept. 5, 1864, ae 73	3	43
Simeon, s. Andrew, 2d, & Lucretia, b. Nov. 25, 1792	1	19
Sophia, d. Uriah & Lois, b. June 19, 1787	1	29
Sophronia, d. Andrew & Sibyl, b. July 6, 1802	1	53
Suke, d. Asa & Allis, b. Nov. 7, 1787	1	33
Sibyl, of Franklin, m. William **CROCKER**, of Bozrah, May 17, 1787, by Samuel Nott, Clerk	1	12
Uriah, m. Lois **HINCKLEY**, b. of Norwich, Dec. 30, 1784	1	29
Walter, s. Asa & Allis b. May 12, 1790	1	33
William, s. Andrew, 3d, & Sibyl, b. Mar. 10, 1798	1	53
William, s. Simeon & Abigail, b. Apr. 17, 1817	1	136
Zabdiel, of Bozrah, m. Abigail **HARRIS**, of Lebanon, June 6, 1785, by Timothy Stone, Clerk	1	16
Zabdiel, s. Zabdiel & Abigail, b. June 2, 1791	1	16
----, s. Elisha, farmer, & Charlotte H. b. Jan. 22, 1850	2	7
LAY, ----, of Montville, m. Cynthia **WIGHTMAN**, of Bozrah, Jan. 21, 1827, by Rev. David Austin (Probably W[illia]m Ray)	1	65
LEAMANS, Nelson L., m. Eleanor F. **ARMSTRONG**, b. of Bozrah, Nov. 10, 1844, by Rev. Jesse B. Denison	1	127
LEE, Ira, m. Olivenza **SLOCUM**, of Lebanon, Jan. 1, 1829, by Rev. David B. Ripley	1	119
Orlando, of Colchester, m. Julia Ann **CLARK**, of Lebanon, Oct. 29, 1846, by Rev. Paunel Mathewson	1	94
Susan, married, d. May 14, 1859, ae 75	3	24
Uriah, m. Abigail **HUNTINGTON**, Sept. 19, 1836, by Rev. Oliver Brown	1	138a

	Vol.	Page
LOOMER, (cont.)		
Lois, d. Eben[eze]r & Ednah, b. June 7, 1776	1	45
Samuel, d. Dec. 9, 1786	1	9
Stephen, s. Eben[eze]r & Ednah, b. July 13, 1768	1	45
LOOMIS, Elias, m. Rachel **ADAMS**, b. of Colchester, Oct. 8,		
1850, by Rev. Benjamin G. Goff	1	158
Nancy, m. John **KIMBALL**, Oct. 30, 1817, by Rev. Daniel		
Putnam	1	42
LORD, Adelaide M., b. Norwich, res. Norwich, d. Aug. 17,		
1849, ae 3 m.	2	6
Olive, of Bozrah, m. Charles B. **ADAMS**, of Greenville,		
Norwich, Sept. 10, 1849, by Rev. Edward Eells	1	156
LOW, Samuel H., of Cleveland, Ohio, m. Jemima A.		
WATERMAN, of Bozrah, June 17, 1850, by Rev.		
Tho[ma]s J. Waterman	1	159
LUCCA, Dorcas, domestic, d. May 20, 1868, ae 38	3	48
LUCE, John C., of Worcester, Mass., m. Eunice R. **BINGHAM**, of		
Norwich, Oct. 5, 1847, by Rev. W[illia]m M. Birchard	1	149
LYNCH, Anna, domestic, single, b. Ireland, d. Feb. 22, 1858, ae 24	3	21
MAINE, Esther P., of Norwich, m. Paul H. **BROWN**, of Bozrah,		
June 26, 1847, by Rev. Christopher Leffingwell	1	114
MALCHER, Almira, d. Apr. 12, 1860, ae 1	3	24
MANNEY, Charles B., d. Apr. 11, 1871, ae 21 d.	3	58
MAPLES, Benj[amin], farmer, b. Montville, res. Bozrah, d. Aug.		
20, 1849, ae 61	2	9
Betsey, farmer's wife, b. Norwich, d. Aug. 18, 1847, ae 59	2	3
Betsey H., of Bozrah, m. Nelson **VERGASON**, of Norwich,		
Mar. 20, 1842, by Rev. John Paine	1	134
Charles, of Norwich, m. Sally M. **POST**, of Bozrah, Feb.		
15, 1846, by Rev. Christopher Leffingwell	1	132
Hannah, of Norwich, m. Isaac **HUNTINGTON**, of Bozrah,		
Nov. 27, 1806	1	63
Joshua, single, b. Norwich, d. Jan. 25, 1862, ae 77	3	32
Nellie, d. Feb. 11, 1868, ae 11	3	48
MARCY, John C., cotton manufacturer, d. July 28, 1869, ae 31	3	49
MARE, Mary E., res. Bozrah, m. Stephen A. **BROWN**, carpenter,		
res. Bozrah, Nov. 19, 1849, by Rev. E. Elles	2	8
MARK, Charles D., farmer, ae 20, b. Norwich, m. Martha A.		
HOUGH, ae 19, b. Norwich, Mar. 24, 1850, in		
Willimantic	2	8
MASON, Alexander T., m. Mary **MINER**, of Bozrah, Nov. 27,		
1842, by John W. Houghton, J. P.	1	150
Charles, soldier, married, b. Germany, d. [ ], 1863, ae 27	3	38
MATHER, Alonzo T., of Deep River, m. Matilda B. **BROCKWAY**,		
of Bozrah, [Sept.] 19, 1852, by Rev. W[illia]m P. Avery	1	155
Edward, market, res. Norwich, m. Henrietta **WELCH**, b.		
Salem, res. Bozrah, Apr. [ ], 1850, by Rev. Stephen Hays	2	8
MATHEWSON, Darius R., of Franklin, m. Laura E. **WIGHTMAN**,		

	Vol.	Page
MATHEWSON, (cont.)		
of Bozrah, Oct. 24, 1833, by John W. Salter	1	20
Mary, m. Ansel **RUSSELL,** Nov. 24, 1823, by Rev. David		
Austin	1	64
MAYNARD, Belinda, of Lyme, m. James **MITCHELL,** of Bozrah,		
Aug. 20, 1826, by Ezra Lathrop, J. P.	1	112
Charles, d. Nov. 20, 1856, ae 1/2 y.	3	13
Eliza, m. Gilbert **ANDREW,** b. of Bozrah, Dec. [ ], 1843,		
by Rev. George Perkins	1	154
McCALL, Dyer, m. Lucy **LATHROP,** May 26, 1791, by Joseph		
Strong, Clerk, Norwich; Oct. 8, 1791 recorded.	1	18
Joseph, of Lebanon, m. Rhoda T. **SPICER,** of Bozrah, Nov.		
13, 1828, by Rev. David Austin	1	120
Luke, d. [ ], 1867	3	48
Orliver, domestic, married, d. Oct. 28, 1864, ae 62	3	38
W[illia]m, soldier, d. [ ], 1864, ae 21	3	43
McGRATH, Catharine, d. Dec. 5, 1868, ae 2 y. 9 m.	3	48
McMAHON, John, ae 28, res. Norwich, m. Catharine **CARROLL,**		
ae 20, Mar. 27, 1851, by Rev. C. Leffingwell	2	10
MEECH, MEACH, Abigail Randall, d. Gurdon & Lucy, b. Sept.		
14, 1807	1	66
Adam Swan, s. Gurdon & Lucy, b. July 8, 1805	1	66
Angeline B., of Bozrah, m. Calvin **PARKER,** of Montville,		
Jan. 15, 1829, by Rev. David Austin	1	119
Cinthea, m. Samuel **GAGER,** Apr. 12, 1798, by Lemuel Tiler,		
Clerk	1	3
Esther, m. Alexander S. **ROGERS,** of Preston, Nov. 17, 1824,		
by Rev. D. Austin	1	49
Gurdon, m. Lucy **SWAN,** Feb. 6, 1800	1	66
Gurdon, s. Gurdon & Lucy, b. Dec. 26, 1800; d. July 15, 1802	1	66
Lucretia, of Preston, m. John **ABELL,** of Bozrah, Sept. 24,		
1818, by Rev. John Hyde	1	77
Lucy S., of Bozrah, m. Jabez **GALLUP,** of Cleveland, O.,		
Mar. 13, 1823, by Rev. D. Austin	1	44
Lucy Swan, d. Gurdon & Lucy, b. Oct. 26, 1802	1	66
METCALF, Charlotte, of Bozrah, m. Cranston **BIDGOOD,** of		
Voluntown, Nov. 1, 1837, by Rev. Oliver Brown	1	139
Eunice, married, d. May 14, 1859, ae 36	3	24
Hannah Hyde, d. Andrew & Hannah, b. June 8, 1774	1	66
Hannah Hyde, m. Chandler **WOODWORTH,** Feb. 22, 1797	1	66
John G., of Lebanon, m. Eunice **DUNBAR,** of Franklin, Mar.		
13, 1842, by Rev. Benjamin G. Goff	1	82
MILLS, Anna, m. Ebenezer **JOHNSON,** b. of Norwich, Nov. 7,		
1759	1	10
MINER, Abby, w. W[illia]m P., d. Jan. 20, 1855	1	126
Abby, housekeeper, married, d. Jan. 8, 1855, ae 35	3	10
Abby E., d. John, farmer, ae 52, & Abby, ae 28, b. Nov.		
28, 1848	2	4

	Vol.	Page
MINER, (cont.)		
1839, by Rev. Nathan Wildman	1	144
Lydia Maples, d. Daniel & Susanna, b. Nov. 6, 1818	1	151
Mary, of Bozrah, m. Alexander T. **MASON**, Nov. 27, 1842,		
by John W. Houghton, J. P.	1	150
Mary Ann, d. Daniel & Susanna, b. Aug. 25, 1822	1	151
Mary E., d. Nov. [ ], 1847, ae 2	2	3
Nancy, d. Thomas & Freelove, b. May 26, 1824	1	118
Nancy, m. Oliver **VERGASON**, Jr., b. of Bozrah, May 9,		
1842, by Rev. Benjamin G. Goff	1	145
Orrin, mechanic, d. Dec. 1, 1869, ae 19	3	49
Phebe Maria, d. John & Phebe Esther, b. Sept. 9, 1840	1	145
Philena, of Bozrah, m. Samuel **PERKINS**, alias Hatch, of		
Lisbon, Mar. 10, 1850, by Rev. Edward Eells	1	118
Philena, b. Bozrah, m. Samuel **PERKINS**, farmer, b. Lisbon,		
res. Bozrah, [1849?], by Rev. Edward Elles	2	8
Philura, d. Thomas & Freelove, b. June 14, 1826	1	118
Sarah Emma, d. Daniel & Susanna, b. June 13, 1828	1	151
Sylvester, s. Thomas & Freelove, b. June 8, 1822	1	118
Sylvester P., soldier, married, d. June 5, 1864, ae 43,		
from wounds in a battle	3	43
Talitha Anne, d. Daniel & Susanna, b. Sept. 27, 1820	1	151
Thomas, m. Freelove **VERGASON**, [ ]	1	118
William P., m. Abby **HATCH**, b. of Bozrah, Apr. 17, 1842,		
by Rev. John Paine	1	126
William P., laborer, married, d. Oct. 21, 1864, ae 44 y. 8 m.	3	38
William Palmer, s. Thomas & Freelove, b. Feb. 25, 1817	1	118
----, d. Andrew, farmer, ae 34, & Eliza, b. Oct. [ ], 1849	2	4
----, s. Charles S., butcher, ae 35, & Caroline, b. Oct. [ ], 1850	2	11
MINSON, Ira F., m. Abby **DANIELS**, of Bozrahville, Oct. 3, 1847,		
by Rev. Stephen Hays	1	153
MITCHELL, Albert H., farmer, ae 26, b. Bozrah, res. Montville,		
m. Almira **GETCHELL**, ae 18, b. Waterford, Nov. 4,		
1849, by Rev. C. Leffingwell	2	8
Hannah, of Bozrah, m. George **PATTERSON**, of Edmiston,		
Nov. 10, 1831, by Rev. Joseph Hough	1	94
James, of Bozrah, m. Belinda **MAYNARD**, of Lyme, Aug. 20,		
1826, by Ezra Lathrop, J. P.	1	112
Mary, m. Oliver **VERGASON**, b. of Bozrah, Sept. 28, 1845,		
by Rev. Christopher Leffingwell	1	94
Sarah, m. Marvin **VERGASON**, b. of Bozrah, Jan. 20, 1825,		
by Rev. John Whittlesey, Salem	1	18
Wiiliam, of Bozrah, m. Sarah **WILLIAMS**, of Montville, Apr.		
8, 1832, by Rev. Joseph Hough	1	129
MONROE, Charles Henry, of Lebanon, m. Mary Ellen **NILES**, of		
Stonington, Nov. 4, 1851, by Rev. Henry B. Whittington	1	121
MOORE, MORE, Angeline, m. Stephen A. **BROWN**, Nov. 29,		
1849, by Rev. Edward Eells	1	156

	Vol.	Page

MOORE, MORE, (cont.)

Cyrus W., m. Pamela **ARMSTRONG**, b. of Bozrah, Mar. 24, 1839, by Rev. Oliver Brown — 1 — 143

David, of Lebanon, m. Martha A. **STEWART**, of Bozrah, May 29, 1842, by John W. Haughton, J. P., at the home of Amasa Ramson — 1 — 80

MORAN, John, d. Jan. 15, 1869, ae 10 m. — 3 — 49

MORRISON, John, m. Patience **JOHNSON**, Nov. 3, 1805, by Elisha Hyde, J. P. — 1 — 60

MORRITY, Bridget, d. Nov. 14, 1870, ae 16 — 3 — 49

MOTT, Gershom, farmer, widower, b. Stonington, d. Jan. 15, 1856, ae 84 — 3 — 13

Hannah, single, b. Preston, d. Jan. 9, 1862, ae 51 — 3 — 32

Willard, m. Eleanor **PERKINSON**, b. of Norwich, Sept. 14, 1852, by Rev. Henry B. Whitington — 1 — 152

MURGATORY, Michael, d. [ ], 1859, ae 13 — 3 — 21

MURPHY, James, s. Phineas, laborer, ae 30, & Ann, ae 24, b. June 26, 1851 — 2 — 11

Joseph, farmer, d. Jan. 2, 1870, ae 30 — 3 — 49

Mary, d. Feb. 2, 1868, ae 12 — 3 — 48

----, d. Matthew, laborer, & Joanna, b. May 26, 1850 — 2 — 7

MURRAY, MURREY, Minnie, d. Jan. 3, 1869, ae 2 y. 5 m. — 3 — 49

-----, d. Apr. 30, 1870, ae 2 hr. — 3 — 49

NEY, Oratio N., of New York, m. Sarah E. **RICH**, of Bozrah, Oct. 25, 1832, by Rev. R. Landfear — 1 — 129

NICHOLS, Thomas M., of Yonkers, N. Y., m. Susan B. **BALDWIN**, of Bozrah, Nov. 5, 1832, by Rev. John W. Salter — 1 — 130

NILES, Mary Ellen, of Stonington, m. Charles Henry **MONROE**, of Lebanon, Nov. 4, 1851, by Rev. Henry B. Whittington — 1 — 121

NORTHAM, Maria G., m. Thomas **DAVIS**, b. of Bozrah, July 20, 1834, by John W. Salter — 1 — 81

OSGOOD, Betsey, d. Josiah & Prudence, b. Mar. 2, 1788 — 1 — 6

Daniel, s. Josiah & Prudence, b. Mar. 18, 1793 — 1 — 6

Josiah, m. Prudence **HARRIS**, b. of Norwich, Nov. 23, 1784, by Neh[emiah] Waterman, Jr., J. P. — 1 — 6

Lebbeus, s. Josiah & Prudence, b. Apr. 24, 1786 — 1 — 6

OTIS, Charles H., clerk in store, b. Colchester, d. July 26, 1865, ae 17 — 3 — 44

PACKER, Fanny, of Salem, m. Joseph L. **ADAMS**, of Colchester, Sept. 25, 1836, by Rev. Benjamin G. Goff — 1 — 139

PALMER, Charles, s. Steyphen & Naomi, b. Aug. 22, 1799 — 1 — 19

Chasey, s. Steyphen & Naomi, b. Feb. 28, 1797 — 1 — 19

Sarah S., m. John b. **HOUGH**, [Dec] 18, 1833, by John W. Salter — 1 — 24

Sophia, d. Steyphen & Naomi, b. Jan. 12, 1795 — 1 — 19

Steyphen, of Franklin, m. Naomi **CALKINS**, Nov. 4, 1792 — 1 — 19

Steyphen, d. Sept. 18, 1800 — 1 — 19

Vol.   Page

PALMER, (cont.)

W[illia]m (?)*, d. Nov. [ ], 1854 (*Entry Says "female")   3   7

PARKER, Calvin, of Montville, m. Angeline B. MEECH, of
Bozrah, Jan. 15, 1829, by Rev. David Austin   1   119

Frederick A., of Ellsworth, O., m. Mary G. ABELL, of
Bozrah, Oct. 13, 1823, by Rev. D. Austin   1   44

Olive Fidelia, d. Samuel C. & Fanny Eliza, b. July 19, 1848   1   148

Olive Fidelia, d. Samuel C. carriage maker, ae 24, & Fanny
E., ae 27, b. July 19, 1848   2   1

Permelia, of Saleme, m. Uriah DOWNER, of Bozrah, Nov. 5,
1826, by Tubal Wakefield, Elder   1   96

Samuel C., of Franklin, m. Fanny Eliza HERRICK, of Bozrah,
Oct. 27, 1847, by Rev. W[illia]m M. Berchard   1   148

PARTELO, Lucy, of Bozrah, m. W[illia]m BROWN, of Lisbon,
July 4, 1847, by John W. Haughton, J. P.   1   122

PASSMORE, Johanna, seamstress, b. Smithfield, R. I., single,
d. Feb. 20, 1856, ae 48   3   13

PATRIDGE, George H., of Lisbon, m. Sarah Ann SWEET, of
Providence, June 11, 1848, by Rev. E. A. Shatterk   1   146

George H., farmer, ae 27, res. Lisbon, m. Sarah Ann SWEET,
res. Providence, R. I., June 11, 1848, by Rev. E. A.
Standish   2   2

Robert A., of Baltimore, m. Julia A. CRANDALL, of
Colchester, Jan. 10, 1842, by Rev. Benjamin G. Goff   1   126

PATTERSON, George, of Edmiston, m. Hannah MITCHELL, of
Bozrah, Nov. 10, 1831, by Rev. Joseph Hough   1   94

PAYNE, Abby Bingham, d. Harry & Cynthia, b. Dec. 5, 1824   1   110

Lydia Gilbert, d. Harry & Cynthia, b. Nov. 30, 1827; d.
Dec. [ ], 1828   1   110

Lydia Maria, d. Harry & Cynthia, b. Oct. 28, 1829   1   110

PEABODY, Jeremiah N., of Buffalo, N. Y., m. Elizabeth L.
FITCH, of Bozrah, [Mar.] 6, 1839, by Rev. Tho[ma]s L.
Shipman, Newark   1   143

Oliva, m. Silas CHAPMAN, b. of Salem, Feb. 7, 1827, by
James Lam, J. P.   1   86

PEASE, Ralph, laborer, d. Nov. 20, 1870, ae 46   3   49

PECK, Edward, d. Sept. 22, 1869, ae 4   3   49

Gilbert M., m. Sarah B. THOMPSON, June 15, 1837, by Rev.
Anson Gleason, of Mohegan, at the house of Burrel
Thompson   1   139

PENDLETON, Alexander Bingham, s. Charles & Susan, b. [ ]   1   89

Charles M., of Bozrah, m. Susan E. BINGHAM, of Norwich,
Dec. 10, 1845, by Rev. W[illia]m M. Birchard   1   89

Clarissa L., of Bozrah, m. Henry A. BINGHAM, of Norwich,
Dec. 9, 1845, by Rev. W[illia]m M. Birchard   1   90

Dimmis, of Westerly, R. I., m. Isreal WIGHTMAN, of Bozrah,
Aug. 4, 1790   1   28

PERKINS, Samuel, farmer, b. Lisbon, res. Bozrah, m. Philena

	Vol.	Page
PERKINS, (cont.)		
MINER, b. Bozrah, [1849?], by Rev. Edward Elles	2	8
Samuel, alias Hatch, of Lisbon, m. Philena **MINER,** of Bozrah,		
Mar. 10, 1850, by Rev. Edward Eells	1	118
PERKINSON, Eleanor, m. Willard **MOTT,** b. of Norwich, Sept. 14,		
1852, by Rev. Henry B. Whitington	1	152
PHELPS, Betsey, b. Aug. 21, 1773; m. Elijah **WIGHTMAN,** [ ]	1	76
Norman A., single, b. Preston, d. [ ], 1863, ae 19; d.		
from a wound received at the attack on Fort Hatteras,		
June 17, 1863	3	38
PHILLIPS, Oliver W., of Lisbon, m. Thankful C. **SMITH,** of		
Bozrahville, May 23, 1847, by Rev. Stephen Hays	1	145
Sarah, single, b. Preston, d. Aug. 28, 1861, ae 22	3	31
----, domestic, d. June 2, 1870, ae 65	3	49
PIERCE, PEIRCE, Benjamin W. C., of North Kingston, R. I., m.		
Mary R. **BUMSTEAD,** of Munson, Mass. Dec. 27, 1835,		
by Rev. Oliver Brown	1	137
Elizabeth, d. Sept. 29, 1855, ae 2	3	10
Larien, Rev., of Montville, m. Aurelia E. **JANES,** of East		
Haddam, Feb. 24, 1839, by Rev. A. W. Swetherton	1	48
Seth, of Woodstock, alias Pomfret, m. Elizabeth Ann		
STARK, of Colchester, alias Bozrah, Feb. 17, 1834, by		
John W. Salter	1	113
PINNEY, William, of Norwich, m. Eunice D. **HALL,** of Bozrah,		
Apr. 16, 1850, by Rev. Stephen Hays	1	158
PLUMB, Mary, m. William **HINSON,** Jr., Nov. 15, 1787, by		
Neh[emiah] Waterman, Jr., J. P.	1	21
Peter, m. Zipporah **WOODWORTH,** b. of Bozrah, Aug. 31,		
1786	1	28
POLLY, Zerviah, m. Andrew **LATHROP,** 2d, May 30, 1802	1	19
PORTER, Cephus N., of Hebron, m. Olive **ARMSTRONG,** of		
Bozrah, Mar. 4, 1841, by Rev. George Perkins	1	126
Mary J., d. Benj[ami]n, manufacturer, ae 36, & Mary S.,		
ae 19, b. Feb. 4, 1849	2	4
POST, Amy A., d. Elisha & Sally, b. June 13, 1828	1	132
Amey A., of Bozrah, m. Stephen **GIFFORD,** of Norwich, Mar.		
25, 1849, by Rev. Christopher Leffingwell	1	155
Dianthy F., d. Elisha & Sally, b. Sept. 2, 1807	1	132
Dianthy F., m. Christopher **LEFFINGWELL,** Jr., b. of Bozrah,		
Oct. 4, 1829, by Levi Meech, Elder	1	121
Elisha, s. Elisha & Sally, b. Oct. 11, 1811; d. July 6,		
1853, ae 41 y.	1	132
Elisha, Jr., farmer, d. July 6, 1853, ae 41; bd. Leffingwell Town	3	4
Elisha, Sr., d. Dec. 8, 1854, ae 80	1	132
Elisha, farmer, d. Dec. 8, 1854, ae 80, ; bd. Leffingwell farm	3	7
Eunice E., d. Elisha & Sally, b. Nov. 6, 1814	1	132
Eunice E., m. Edwin B. **GARDINER,** b. of Bozrah, Nov. 19,		
1834, by Levi Meech, Elder	1	134

	Vol.	Page
RANDALL, (cont.)		
RANDALL, b. Jan. 27, 1784	1	39
Calvin, of Colchester, m. Ann E. **LESTER,** of Bozrah, May		
6, 1849, by Rev. Christopher Leffingwell	1	154
Calvin, farmer, ae 45, b. Colchester, res. Colchester,		
m. 2d w. Eliza A. **LESTER,** ae 29, b. Norwich, May 6,		
1849, by Rev. C. Leffingwell	2	5
Esther, see under Esther **VERGESON**	1	39
Richard, ship carpenter, widower, b. New Bedford, Mass.,		
d. Mar. 27, 1856, ae 87	3	13
Triphene, illeg. d. Esther **VERGESON,** & Benaiah		
RANDALL, b. Dec. 17, 1780	1	39
RANSON, Luther Foster Azubah, a black boy, b. Feb. 24, 1799	1	57
RATHBUN, Hannah E., ae 29, b. Salem, m. Giles **JAMES,** ae 26,		
b. Groton, res. Montville, Mar. 3, 1851, by Rev.		
Christopher Leffingwell	2	10
William m. Edna **LOOMER,** June 3, 1802, by Asa Wilcox,		
Elder	1	39
William, s. William & Edna, b. May 1, 1803	1	39
RAU, Azuba, m. Providence **FREEMAN,** Sept. 22, 1806, by Asa		
Woodworth, J. P.	1	60
RAY, W[illia]m, of Montville, m. Cynthia **WIGHTMAN,** of		
Bozrah, Jan. 21, 1827, by Rev. David Austin (Possibly		
"Mr. **LAY**")	1	65
RAYMOND, Richard, m. Julia P. **GARDINER,** b. of Montville,		
Aug. 7, 1836, by Rev. Benjamin G. Goff	1	137
Sherwood, of Montville, m. Fanny **FITCH,** of Bozrah, on		
or about the year 1820-21, by Rev. David Austin.		
Bozrah, May 9, 1821, recorded	1	65
READ, Anna, d. Samuel & Charity, b. Nov. 3, 1783	1	46
Charity, d. Samuel & Charity, b. Mar. 7, 1785	1	46
Darius Boom, s. Samuel & Charity, b. Mar. 1, 1797	1	46
Eliza, ae 18, b. Ireland, res. Bozrahville, m. Charles		
DANIELS, mill operator, ae 25, b. Colchester, res.		
Bozrahville, Mar. 26, 1848, by Rev. Stephen Hays	2	2
Elizabeth, d. Samuel & Charity, b. Jan. 15, 1782	1	46
Jared, s. Samuel & Charity, b. Dec. 4, 1786; d. Aug. 15, 1787	1	46
Jared, s. Samuel & Charity, b. Feb. 29, 1788	1	46
Mary, d. Samuel & Charity, b. Sept. 12, 1779	1	46
Phebe, d. Samuel & Charity, b. Dec. 20, 1791	1	46
Samuel, s. Samuel & Charity, b. Nov. 25, 1780	1	46
Sarah, d. Samuel & Charity, b. Mar. 7, 1790	1	46
RIVILLE, John, single, d. July 5, 1862, ae 18	3	32
RICH, Sarah E., of Bozrah, m. Oratio N. **NEY,** of New York,		
Oct. 25, 1832, by Rev. R. Landfear	1	129
RICKERS, Annis Baker, d. John J. & Annis, b. Dec. 30, 1834	1	21
Anson Baker, s. John J. & Annis, b. Feb. 27, 1837; d.		
Oct. 11, 1840	1	21

RICKERS, (cont),
    Elizabeth Baker, d. John J. & Annis, b. Apr. 8, 1821;   1   21
        bp. Aug. 12, 1821, by Rev. David Austin   1   21
    Faith Christina Juliana, d. John J. & Annis, b. Oct. 10, 1825   1   21
    Fanny Raymond, d. John J. & Annis, b. Apr. 3, 1830   1   21
    Frederic Henry, s. John J. & Annis, b. Oct. 21, 1827   1   21
    Gilbert Baker, s. John J. & Annis, b. May 12, 1839
    Henry Frederic, s. John J. & Annis, b. Feb. 1823; d.   1   21
        Oct. 24, 1824
    John, s. John J. & Annis, b. Aug. 1, 1819; bp. by Rev.   1   21
        David Austin
    John Jaspers, of Nesmeright, Province Ostfinisland, Kingdom
        of Hanover, m. Annis BAKER, of New York City, July
        10, 1817, by Rev. Mr. Clarke. Witnesses: W[illia]m,
        Ritter, Sally Smith, of New York   1   21
RICKNEY, Henry, mechanic, single, d. Sept. 16, 1857, ae 22   3   16
RIDER, illiam, m. Amanda DEAN, Nov. 27, 1823 by David Austin   1   64
RIPLEY, Desire, weaver single, b. Westport, d. Oct. 4, 1863, ae 84   3   38
    Samuel W., m. Eunice A. ALLEN, June 18, 1832, by Rev.
        Erastus Ripley   1   130
ROBESON, Sarah, m. Timothy GRAY, Dec. 4, 1825, by Rev. Allen
        Hewitt   1   16
ROBINSON, Betsey E., domestic, d. Oct. 22, 1870, ae 21   3   49
    Hannah, m. Enoch HARDY, Aug. 4, 1825, by Rev. Tubal
        Wakefield   1   16
    W[illia]m, manufacturer, d. Aug. 5, 1865, ae 57   3   44
    Zerviah, m. George S. KELLEY, b. of Bozrah, Jan. 23,
        1833, by Rev. John W. Salter   1   120
ROGERS, Alexander S., of Preston, m. Esther MEECH, Nov. 17,
        1824, by Rev. D. Austin   1   49
    Alfred, m. Amanda LEFFINGWELL, Jan. 1, 1826, by Rev.
        Reuben Palmer   1   46
    Asa L., m. Lavinda CLARK, July 4, 1847, by Rev. Perciville
        Mathewson   1   124
    Christopher B., single, b. Montville, d. July 27, 1861, ae 70   3   31
    Elisha M., of Montville, m. Amy S. GARDNER, of Bozrah,
        [Apr] 14, 1850, by Rev. John W. Salter, Montville   1   158
    Henry C., farmer, d. Oct. 21, 1865, ae 61   3   44
    Jabez P., d. Feb. 6, 1865, ae 26   3   44
ROSE, Amos, s. Palmer, farmer, & Matilda, b. June 19, 1848   2   1
    George H., of Salem, m. Ellen S. BOTTOM, of Norwich
        Greeneville, Nov. 25, 1817, by Rev. Christopher
        Leffingwell (Probably 1847)   1   78
    George M., mechanic, res. Salem, m. Ellen S. BOTTOM, res.
        Norwich, [1848], by Rev. Christ. Leffingwell   2   2
    John L., m. Jerusha VERGASON, b. of Bozrah, Dec. 9, 1823,
        by Rev. Reuben Palmer   1   80

	Vol.	Page

ROSE, (cont.)

Mary Ann, of Bozrah, m. Ebenezer **BUMP**, of Lyme, Apr. 5,
1835, by Gardner Avery, J. P. — 1 — 121

William P., m. Celina **GARDNER**, b. of Bozrah, Dec. 6, 1821,
by William Palmer, Elder — 1 — 48

ROSS, Albert G., s. Enos C., mechanic, ae 30, & Mary A., ae
29, b. Apr. 1, 1850 — 2 — 7

Enos C., farmer, d. Mar. 24, 1867, ae 48 — 3 — 48

Sidney, s. Enoch C., shoemaker, & Mary M., b. July 15, 1848 — 2 — 1

ROUSE, -----, child of Henry, ae 25, b. July [ ], 1849 — 2 — 4

RUDD, Abigail, domestic, widow, b. New London, d. Jan. 20,
1857, ae 98 — 3 — 16

Charlotte, d. Daniel & Abigail, b. Apr. 16, 1785 — 1 — 73

Daniel, m. Abigail **ALLYN**, Dec. [ ], 1780 — 1 — 73

Daniel, s. Daniel & Abigail, b. Mar. 16, 1794 — 1 — 73

George, s. Daniel & Abigail, b. Oct. 8, 1786 — 1 — 73

Lucy, d. Daniel & Abigail, b. Aug. 9, 1783 — 1 — 73

Thomas, s. Daniel & Abigail, b. Oct. 29, 1788 — 1 — 73

William, farmer, married, b. R. Island, d. Jan. 6, 1865, ae 74 — 3 — 44

RUSSELL, Ansel, m. Mary **MATHEWSON**, Nov. 24, 1823, by
Rev. David Austin — 1 — 64

Rosan[n]a, d. Mar. 14, [1871?], ae 9 m.; bd. Mar. 15,
[1871?], in Baltic — 3 — 62

SABIN, Maribah, d. Jan. 23, 1803 — 1 — 57

Permelia, d. Feb. 15, 1862, ae 18 y. 8 m. — 3 — 32

Zeruiah, m. Nathan **BINGHAM**, b. of Norwich, Jan. 29, 1784 — 1 — 35

SANDFORD, Almira, domestic, d. Apr. 10, 1870, ae 35 — 3 — 49

SANGER, Asahel, of Bozrah, m. Sarah **BINGHAM**, of Norwich,
Dec. 27, 1789 — 1 — 36

Betsey, d. Asahel & Sarah, b. May 7, 1795 — 1 — 36

Eunice, d. Asahel & Sarah, b. Jan. 8, 1794 — 1 — 36

Fanny, d. Asahel & Sarah, b. July 27, 1797 — 1 — 36

Polley, d. Asahel & Sarah, b. Dec. 26, 1790 — 1 — 36

Sarah, d. Asahel & Sarah, b. Aug. 14, 1792 — 1 — 36

SANTO, A., laborer, d. Oct. 6, 1870, ae 62 — 3 — 49

Charles, d. Nov. 20, 1856, ae 6 m. — 3 — 13

SCOTT, John, Dr., of Bozrah, m. Esther **LAMB**, of Lebanon, Jan.
27, 1828, by James Lam, J. P. — 1 — 87

John, Dr. d. Feb. 3, 1834, ae 88 — 1 — 87

SCOVILLE, Charlotte, of East Haddam, m. Nathaniel W. **GREEN**,
of Bozrah, Aug. 29, 1846, by Rev. W[illia]m M. Berchard — 1 — 92

SERRIL, Temperance C., m. Philip A. **CAPIN**, Apr. 25, 1841 — 1 — 116

SEVIN, Charles H., s. David F., tailor, ae 41, & Rosina E.,
ae 33, b. Apr. 3, 1848 — 2 — 1

Charlotte Josephine Sophia, [d. David F. & Rosina], b.
Dec. 4, 1845 — 1 — 157

D. F., d. Mar. 22, 1851, ae 8 m. — 2 — 9

David F., m. Rosina **GREINER**, May 1, 1836, by Rev. F. W.

	Vol.	Page
SEVIN, (cont.)		
Gussenhainer, in New York	1	157
John Jacob Frederick, [s. David F. & Rosina], b. Aug. 20, 1838	1	157
Nathan Douglass, [s. David F. & Rosina], b. June 1, 1842	1	157
Rosina Elizabeth, [d. David F. & Rosina], b. May 3, 1837	1	157
W[illia]m W., d. June 30, 1865, ae 3 m. 3 d.	3	44
----, s. D. S., tailor, & Rosina, b. July 16, 1850	2	7
SHARPMAN, Sarah, d. Jan. 25, 1866, ae 87	3	44
SHAY, Nelly, d. Nov. 7, 1862, ae 9	3	32
SHEA, Elias, d. Nov. 10, 1861, ae 11 m.	3	31
Ellen, d. Nov. 17, 1870, ae 5	3	49
SIMMONDS, SYMONS, SIMMONS, George, of East Hartford, m. Mary E. **KING,** of Bozrah, June 11, 1848, by Rev. W[illia]m Palmer	1	140
George, millwright, ae 28, b. E. Hartford, res. E. Hartford, m. Mary E. **KEY,** ae 21, b. Mansfield, res. Bozrah, June 11, 1848, by Rev. W[illia]m Palmer	2	2
Roba, of Bozrah, m. Alfred **AUSTIN,** Dec. 11, 1831, by Rev. Jared Andrus	1	84
----, s. Nelson, laborer, ae 39, & Eleanor, ae 33, b. Jan. [ ], 1851?	2	11
SISSON, Martha Eliza, d. Noyes & Rachel B., b. Feb. 12, 1838	1	131
Noyes, m. Rachel B. **AVERY,** b. of Bozrah, Aug. 28, 1832, by Rev. John W. Salter	1	131
Rachel B., w. Noyes, d. Jan. 23, 1841	1	131
Rhoda Desire, d. Noyes & Rachel B., b. Apr. 23, 1840	1	131
William, of Lebanon, m. Hannah G. **MINER,** of Bozrah, Apr. 14, 1836, by Rev. Oliver Brown	1	137
SLOCUM, Olivenza, of Lebanon, m. Ira **LEE,** Jan. 1, 1829, by Rev. David B. Ripley	1	119
SMITH, Ann, d. W[illia]m, manufacturer, ae 25, & Mary, ae 22, b. Mar. 4, [1847]	2	1
Charles, s. William & Betty, b. Nov. 17, 1791	1	20
Elizabeth B., of Bozrah, m. Thomas H. **SMITH,** of Norwich, Feb. 3, 1834, by Rev. John W. Salter	1	32
Erastus M., m. Harriet A. **THOMAS,** b. of Colchester, July 24, 1842, by Rev. Benjamin G. Goff	1	141
Harry, s. William & Betty, b. Mar. 8, 1787	1	20
Henrietta, b. Stonington, res. Bozrah, d. Oct. 24, 1853, ae 5; bd, Griswold	3	4
Henry N., of Franklin, m. Lydia Z. **LATHROP,** of Bozrah, Jan. 20, 1852, by Rev. William P. Avery	1	140
John, laborer, black, b. N. Y., res. Bozrah, d. Feb. [ ], 1850, ae 70	2	9
Larenda, d. William & Betty, b. Apr. 5, 1789	1	20
Lois Ann, domestic, b. Conn., married, d. May 22, 1858, ae 41	3	21
Lucretia, of Franklin, m. Andrew **LATHROP,** 2d, of Bozrah, Jan. 22, 1789, by Samuel Nott, Clerk	1	19

	Vol.	Page
SMITH, (cont.)		
Marvin, s. William & Betty, b. Sept. 26, 1784	1	20
Mary L., d. July 27, 1864, ae 3 m.	3	43
Philip, manufacturer, married, d. Oct. 12, 1856, ae 65	3	13
Rebecca, domestic, d. May 25, 1870, ae 70	3	49
Robert, d. Aug. 19, 1855, ae 10	3	10
Shubail, of Colchester, m. Hannah [**WATERMAN**], June 10, 1760	1	99
Shubael, d. May 14, 1761	1	100
Thankful C., of Bozrahville, m. Oliver W. **PHILLIPS**, of Lisbon, May 23, 1847, by Rev. Stephen Hays	1	145
Theresy, d. William & Betty, b. Dec. 13, 1782	1	20
Thomas H., of Norwich, m. Elizabeth B. **SMITH**, of Bozrah, Feb. 3, 1834, by Rev. John W. Salter	1	32
William, m. Betty **CROCKER**, b. of Norwich, Nov. 15, 1781	1	20
William Jr., m. Emily **STARK**, b. of Bozrah, Mar. 24, 1822, by Rev. William Palmer, at Mr. Zopher Stark's, Colchester	1	108
William, Jr., m. Mary **WHITING**, b. of Bozrah, Mar. 28, 1830, by Asa Wilcox, Elder	1	108
----, male, d. Jan. 8, 1863, ae 13 d.	3	38
----, st. b. child of Shubail & Hannah, [ ]	1	99
SPEAR, Isaac, b. Colchester, d. Jan. 7, 1862, ae 32	3	32
SPENCER, John, laborer, single, b. Canada, d. Oct. 15, 1863, ae 20	3	38
SPICER, Avery D., s. Elderkin & Eunice, b. Sept. 24, 1790; d. Nov. [ ], 1826, at New York	1	24
B., res. Bozrah, m. Charles F. **BROWN**, farmer, res. Lebanon, Sept. 9, 1849, by Rev. E. Elles	2	8
Claricy, d. Elderkin & Eunice, b. Sept. 5, 1792	1	24
Elderkin, m. Eunice **LATHROP**, b. of Bozrah, Sept. 3, 1789	1	24
Eunice, d. July [ ], 1851, ae 88	2	9
Eunice B., of Bozrah, m. Charles L. **BROWN**, of Lebanon, Sept. 9, 1849, by Rev. Nathan W. Miner	1	155
Isaac, d. Jan. 7, 1861, ae 4	3	24
Lois, d. Elderkin & Eunice, b. Mar. 2, 1794	1	24
Rhoda T., of Bozrah, m. Joseph **McCALL**, of Lebanon, Nov. 13, 1828, by Rev. David Austin	1	120
Simeon A., m. Fanny H. **WATERMAN**, Oct. 30, 1821, by Rev. David Austin	1	50
SQUIRE, Hannah C., of Bozrah, m. George W. **WINCHESTER**, Nov. 29, 1831, by Rev. Jared Andrus	1	84
STANDISH, Amos, miller, b. Preston, res. Bozrah, d. Sept. 26, 1849, ae 63	2	6
Cynthia F., of Bozrah, m. Walter **BISHOP**, of Andover, Mar. 22, 1852, by Rev. W[illia]m P. Avery	1	147
Eliza, of Lebanon, m. Elisha **CONGDON**, of Norwich, Apr. 8, 1827, by Rev. David Austin	1	87
Elizabeth Belper, d. Ezra & Mary, b. Mar. 31, 1812	1	22
Erastus, farmer, d. Apr. 28, 1870, ae 87	3	49

	Vol.	Page
STEWARD, (cont.)		
Oct. 24, 1816	1	75
Ezekiel Lathrop, s. Cyrus & Sophia, b. Feb. 18, 1819	1	75
George Henry, s. Cyrus & Sophia, b. Jan. 24, 1833	1	75
STEWART, [see also **STEWARD**], Martha A., of Bozrah, m. David MORE, of Lebanon, May 29, 1842, by John W. Haughton, J. P., at the home of Amasa Ramson	1	80
STILLMAN, Lydia, m. William **KELLEY**, Oct. 29, 1808, by Asa Woodworth, J. P.	1	111
STILLWELL, Lydia, domestic, widow, d. [ ], 1865	3	44
STRONG, Robert, d. [ ], 1866, ae 63	3	44
SULLIVAN, Dennis, d. July 24, 1864, ae 9 m.	3	43
Jeremiah, d. Oct. 22, 1860, ae 28	3	24
Jeremiah, married, d. Oct. 25, 1860, ae 33	3	21
Jeremiah, single, d. Oct. 22, 1861, ae 28	3	31
Julia, ae 16, m. John **BARRY**, ae 22, res. Norwich, Apr. 24, 1851, by Rev. C. Leffingwell	2	10
Julia, d. Mar. 28, 1861, ae 1 y. 10 m.	3	31
Michael, married, b. Lebanon, d. May 16, 1864, ae 24	3	43
Timothy, d. May 16, 1860, ae 16	3	24
SWAN, Gilbert, m. Rhoda **TRASS**, Jan. 3, 1832, by Rev. Jared Andrus	1	50
Lucy, m. Gurdon **MEECH**, Feb. 6, 1800	1	66
SWEET, Sarah Ann, of Providence, m. George H. **PATRIDGE**, of Lisbon, June 11, 1848, by Rev. E. A. Shatterk	1	146
Sarah Ann, res. Providence, R. I., m. George H. **PATRIDGE**, farmer, ae 27, res. Lisbon, June 11, 1848, by Rev. E. A. Standish	2	2
SWETT, Esther, of Lebanon, m. Isaac **HUNTINGTON**, of Bozrah, Apr. 30, 1834, by Rev. Benjamin C. Goff	1	63
TALCOTT, Elizabeth, of Bolton, m. Jabez **CROCKER**, Jr., of Norwich, Oct. 5, 1773	1	48
TAYLOR, Joseph, m. Sally **THAYER**, July 7, 1827, by Gardner Avery, J. P.	1	86
THAYER, Betsey, domestic, d. Oct. 27, 1871, ae 64	3	58
Sally, m. Joseph **TAYLOR**, July 7, 1827, by Gardner Avery, J. P.	1	86
THOMAS, Harriet A., m. Erastus M. **SMITH**, b. of Colchester, July 24, 1842, by Rev. Benjamin G. Goff	1	141
Samuel, illeg. s. Esther **VERGESON** & Samuel **THOMAS**, b. Oct. 23, 1788	1	39
THOMPSON, Abby C., of Norwich, m. Nancy L. **HUNTINGTON**, of Bozrah, Oct. 24, 1841, by Rev. John W. Salter	1	142
David H., d. Nov. 7, [1852], ae 11 1/2 m.; bd. T[h]roop B. G.	3	4
James O., of Salem, m. Betsey E. **WIGHTMAN**, of Bozrah, Sept. 4, 1823, by Rev. D. Austin	1	44
Lydia L., b. Hebron, d. June 3, 1855, ae 2 y. 11 m.	3	10
Nancy, m. John D. **MINER**, b. of Bozrah, Aug. 14, 1835, by		

	Vol.	Page
THOMPSON, (cont.)		
John W. Haughton, J. P.	1	130
Sarah B., m. Gilbert M. **PECK,** June 15, 1837, by Rev. Anson		
Gleason, of Mohegan, at the house of Burrel Thompson	1	139
THROOP, Benjamin, Jr., of Norwich, m. Susannah **THROOP,** of		
Lebanon, Dec. 4, 1766	1	3
Benjamin, s. Benjamin, Jr. & Susannah, b. Oct. 19, 1778	1	3
Clariessa, d. Benjamin, Jr. & Susannah, b. May 5, 1770	1	3
Dan, s. Benjamin, Jr. & Susannah, b. Apr. 27, 1768	1	3
Dan, m. Mary **GAGER,** b. of Bozrah, Nov. 12, 1788	1	8
Dyer, s. Benjamin, Jr. & Susannah, b. Aug. 18, 1774	1	3
John, s. Benjamin, Jr. & Susannah, b. Mar. 31, 1772	1	3
Simon Gager, s. Dan & Mary, b. Jan. 4, 1790	1	8
Susannah, of Lebanon, m. Benjamin **THROOP,** Jr., of		
Norwich, Dec. 4, 1766	1	3
Susannah, d. Benjamin, Jr. & Susannah, b. Jan. 29, 1784	1	3
TOPLEFF, John S., of Mansfield, m. Sophia F. **STANDISH,** of		
Bozrah, June 2, 1851, by Rev. W[illia]m P. Avery	1	160
John S., res. Mansfield, m. Sophia F. **STANDISH,** b. Preston,		
res. Bozrah, June 2, 1851, by Rev. W[illia]m B. Avery	2	10
TRACY, John H., carpenter, d. June 11, 1871, ae 40	3	58
Maria L., m. Lodowick B. **CRANDALL,** Nov. 11, 1844, by		
Rev. W[illia]m M. Burchard	1	98
Matthew A., d. June 11, 1866, ae 66	3	44
William F., of Lisbon, m. Susan S. **HU[R]LBERT,** of		
Lebanon, Oct. 5, 1828, by Rev. David B. Ripley	1	91
TRAIN, George, mechanic, married, d. Sept. 17, 1857, ae 39	3	16
TRASS, Rhoda, m. Gilbert **SWAN,** Jan. 3, 1832, by Rev. Jared		
Andrus	1	50
TROLLAND, Anna, d. [ ], 1858, ae 22	3	21
John, mechanic, single, d. Nov. 22, 1858, ae 23	3	21
TRYSKAM, Charles B., s. Benj[ami]n, laborer, ae 21, & Almira,		
ae 19, b. Aug. 3, 1850	2	11
TUBBS, Mary, of New London, m. Elijah **ABELL,** of Bozrah, Oct.		
5, 1829, by Rev. Abel McEwen	1	114
TYLER, Eunice, of Brooklyn, m. John M. **CLEMENT,** of Norwich,		
Jan. 1, 1792	1	47
UNDERWOOD, Franklin, d. Nov. 8, 1866, ae 1 m. 7 d.	3	44
VERGASON, VERGESON, Alfred, farmer, ae 24, b. Bozrah, res.		
Montville, m. Marah C. **JOHNSON,** ae 17, b. Bozrah,		
Aug. 26, 1849, by Rev. C. Leffingwell	2	8
Asa, s. Jed[edia]h & Susanna, b. Aug. 1, 1793	1	45
Charles Morgan, s. Jedediah, Jr. & Mary, b. June 1, 1816	1	47
Daniel, m. Phebe **BECKWITH,** Oct. 8, 1786, by N. Waterman,		
J. P.	1	20
Elijah, d. Apr. 27, 1821	1	70
Esther, alias Esther **RANDALL** had illeg, children Triphene		
RANDALL, Azariah **RANDALL,** Samuel **THOMAS**		

	Vol.	Page
WAITE, Lloyd A., m. Elizabeth H. BASS, Oct. 24, 1830, by Rev. Leonard B. Griffing	1	58
WALWORTH, WALLWORTH, Benjamin, s. Benjamin & Aphia, b. Oct. 12, 1792	1	37
James, s. Benjamin & Aphia, b. Mar. 5, 1787	1	37
John, s. Benjamin & Aphia, b. Nov. 21, 1784	1	37
Reuben H., s. Benjamin & Aphia, b. Oct. 26, 1788	1	37
Rosamond B., d. Benjamin & Aphia, b. Feb. 27, 1783	1	37
Sarah, d. Benjamin & Aphia, b. Sept. 22, 1790	1	37
WARD, Mary, m. William DODGE, Nov. 22, 1813	1	73
WARDOCK, Nancy W., of Bozrah, m. Edwin C. WHEELER, of Montville, Sept. 17, 1851, by Rev. W[illia]m P. Avery	1	160
WATERMAN, Elijah, [s. Nehemiah, Jr. & Sarah], b. Jan. 8, 1733	1	99
Elijah, [s. Nehemiah, Sr. & Sarah], d. May 27, 1736, by Being scalded	1	100
Elijah, [s. Nehemiah, Jr.], b. Nov. 28, 1769	1	101
Elijah, b. Nov. 28, 1769	1	103-4
Elijah, s. Nehemiah & Susannah], b. [ ]	1	99
Elijah, m. Lucy ALBEE, [ ]	1	103-4
Elizabeth, m. Ebenezer BACKUS, Jr., b. of Norwich, Oct. 14, 1766	1	4
Eunice, [d. Nehemiah, Jr. & Sarah], Aug. 20, 1744	1	99
Eunice, d. May 13, 1749, with Canker	1	100
Eunice, [d. Nehemiah, Jr. & Sarah], b. Dec. 13, 1750	1	99
Eunice, m. Simeon BACKUS, Oct. 28, 1772	1	99
Eunice, [d. Nehemiah, Jr.], b. Mar. 14, 1774	1	101
Eunice, [d. Nehemiah, Jr.], d. Oct. 5, 1775	1	102
Eunice, [d. Nehemiah, Jr. & Sarah], b. May 28, 1796	1	103-4
Eunice, [d. Nehemiah & Susannah], b. [ ]	1	99
Fanna, [d. Nehemiah, Jr. & Sarah], b. Aug. 25, 1801	1	103-4
Fanny H., m. Simeon A. SPICER, Oct. 30, 1821, by Rev. David Austin	1	50
Gardner, farmer, married, d. July 10, 1866, ae 70	3	44
Hannah, [d. Nehemiah, Jr. & Sarah], b. Mar. 9, 1742	1	99
Hannah, m. Shubail SMITH, of Colchester, June 10, 1760	1	99
Hannah, [d. Nehemiah, Sr. & Sarah], d. Sept. 18, 1763, of consumption	1	100
Hannah, [d. Nehemiah, Jr.], b. Aug. 18, 1765; bp.	1	101
Hannah, m. Stephen FOOT, Nov. 16, 1786	1	101
Hannah, [d. Nehemiah & Susannah, b. [ ]	1	99
Hannah F., m. Aibert G. AVERY, b. of Bozrah, Feb. 3, 1830, by Rev. Cornelia B. Everest	1	123
Hannah F., b. Hyde Park, single, d. Feb. 17, 1858, ae 23	3	16
Jemima A., of Bozrah, m. Samuel H. LOW, of Cleveland, Ohio, June 17, 1850, by Rev. Tho[ma]s J. Waterman	1	159
Julia, [d. Elijah & Lucy], b. [ ]	1	103-4
Lois, [d. Nehemiah, Jr. & Sarah], b. May 29, 1748	1	99
Lois, m. Ammi FITCH, Oct. 25, 1767	1	99

	Vol.	Page
WATERMAN, (cont.)		
Mary, m. Calvin **BARRETT**, b. of Bozrah, July 17, 1785,		
by Nehemiah Waterman, J. P.	1	43
Mary, [d. Elijah & Lucy], b. Apr. 5, 1797	1	103-4
Mary D., d. Albert, farmer, ae 30, & Desire M., ae 28,		
b. May 13, 1849	2	4
Nehemiah, Sr., b. Aug. 17, 1708; d. Oct. 27, 1796 ae 88	1	100
Nehemiah, [s. Nehemiah, Jr. & Sarah], b. Oct. 24, 1736	1	99
Nehemiah, Jr., s. Nehemiah, Sr. & Sarah, b. Oct. 24, 1736	1	101
Nehemiah, m. Susannah **ISHAM**, Dec. 24, 1760	1	99
Nehemiah, 3d, [s. Nehemiah, Jr.], b. Aug. 17, 1767; bp.	1	101
Nehemiah, Jr., b. Aug. 17, 1767	1	103-4
Nehemiah, Jr., m. Sarah **HOUGH**, Oct. 25, 1795, by Nehemiah		
Waterman, J. P.	1	103-4
Nehemiah, 3rd, [s. Nehemiah, Jr. & Sarah], b. Oct. 12, 1799	1	103-4
Nehemiah, [s. Nehemiah & Susannah], b. [ ]	1	99
Nehemiah, Jr., m. [ ], by Rev. Thomas Skinner, of Colchester	1	101
Sally, of Bozrah, m. David A. **FOX**, Oct. 19, 1830, by		
Cornelius B. Everest	1	125
Sarah, w. Nehemiah, Sr., b. Aug. 21, 1712	1	99
Sarah, [d. Nehemiah, Jr. & Sarah], b. July 22, 1739	1	99
Sarah, m. Stephen **GIFFORD**, 3d, Apr. 20, 1762	1	99
Sarah, w. Nehemiah, Sr., d. Jan. 21, 1795, ae 83 y.	1	99
Sarah, d. June 29, 1848, ae 74	2	3
Sarah, d. Mar. 30, 1852, ae 2 y.; bd. Scott Buryiing Ground	3	4
Sarah A., d. Albert, farmer, ae 32 & Dimis, ae 30, b.		
Feb. 3, 1851	2	11
Susannah, 2d, [d. Nehemiah, Jr.], b. Jan. 19, 1762; bp.	1	101
Susannah, 2d, ae 19, m. Joseph **HYDE**, ae 25, Sept. 6, 1780	1	101
Susannah, [d. Nehemiah, Jr. & Sarah], b. Jan. 19, 1798	1	103-4
Susannah, [d. Nehemiah & Susannah], b. [ ]	1	99
----, s. [Nehemiah, Jr. & Sarah], b. Aug. 15, 1853; d.		
in a few hours	1	99
WATROUS, Mary M, m. David **JILLSON**, Aug. 15, 1826, by		
Rev. Tubal Wakefield	1	67
WATSON, ----, s. W[illia]m, laborer, & Betsey, b. Feb. 28, 1850	2	7
WAY, Eliza, Indian, single, d. Mar. 20, 1855, ae 50	3	10
WEAVER, William L., of Windham, m. Fanny M. **BURDICK**, of		
Bozrah, May 26, 1847, by Rev. W[illia]m M. Burchard	1	122
----, d. Nov. 23, 1855, ae 1	3	10
WELCH, WELTCH, Alfred, m. Prudence **FORD**, [Mar.] 27, 1812	1	42
Alford, s. Alford & Prudence, b. Feb. 18, 1813	1	42
Henrietta, b. Salem, res. Bozrah, m. Edward **MATHER**,		
market, res. Norwich, Apr. [ ], 1850, by Rev. Stephen		
Hays	2	8
WELLS, WELLES, Harriet, m. Collins G. **KEENY**, b. of		
Colchester, Sept. 20, 1840, by Rev. Benjamin Goff	1	120
Hazard, m. Sarah T. **COOK**, b. of Colchester, Nov. 19, 1843,		

	Vol.	Page
WELLS, WELLES, (cont.)		
by Rev. Benjamin G. Goff	1	86
Justin, of Colchester, m. Harriet **HOLLESTER**, of Bozrah,		
Jan. 20, 1850, by Rev. Edward Eells	1	118
Justin, res. Colchester, m. Harriet **HALLYKO**, res. Bozrah,		
Jan. 20, 1850, by Rev. E. Elles	2	8
Mary, m. Ogden **CROUCH**, Mar. 26, 1837, by Rev. Benjamin		
C. Goff	1	139
WEST, Azel, m. Sally **WIGHTMAN**, Jan. 14, 1790, by Rev.		
Jonathan Murdock	1	53
Belinda, d. Azel & Sally, b. Mar. 11, 1791	1	53
Belinda, m. Jirah I. **HOUGH**, b. of Bozrah, Nov. 14, 1811	1	58
Sally, w. Azel, d. May 29, 1791	1	53
WHEELER, Charles, carpenter, ae 21, b. Colchester, res.		
Providence, m. Lucy **STANDISH**, ae 26, b. Norwich,		
Dec. 25, 1849, by Rev. Edward Elles	2	8
Charles E., of Colchester, m. Lucy **STANDISH**, of Bozrah,		
Dec. 23, 1849, by Rev. Edward Eells	1	156
Edwin C., of Montville, m. Nancy W. **WARDOCK**, of Bozrah,		
Sept. 17, 1851, by Rev. W[illia]m P. Avery	1	160
Nancy W., housekeeper, d. Oct. 27, 1871, ae 43	3	58
WHIPPLE, Edwin H., b. Norwich, res. Bozrah, d. June 22, 1851,		
ae 2	2	9
Lucretia, m. Amos **WIGHTMAN**, b. of Bozrah, June 14, 1789	1	25
Lucretia, of New London, m. Capt. Josiah **EAMES**, of Bozrah,		
Mar. 4, 1790	1	17
Molly, illeg. d. Esther **VERGESON**, & Joseph **WHIPPLE**, b.		
Dec. 27, 1790	1	39
WHITELEY, Abell P., of Lebanon, m. Mary **POTTER**, of Bozrah,		
Oct. 2, 1831, by Rev. Joseph Hough	1	92
WHITING, Anne, w. William, d. June 21, 1807	1	71
Cypron Lathrop, s. William & Anne, b. June 16, 1807	1	71
Jerusha, d. William & Anne, b. Nov. 8, 1802	1	71
Jerusha, m. Jehiel **JOHNSON**, b. of Bozrah, Jan. 1, 1826,		
by Rev. David Austin	1	115
Lois, w. Caleb, d. Sept. 22, 1786	1	5
Mary, d. W[illia]m & Anne, b. May 22, 1804	1	71
Mary, m. William **SMITH**, Jr., b. of Bozrah, Mar. 28, 1830,		
by Asa Wilcox, Elder	1	108
Mary, domestic, married, d. July 21, 1855, ae 50	3	10
Nathan, s. William & Anne, b. Mar. 31, 1798	1	71
Seth, s. William & Anne, b. Oct. 26, 1799	1	71
Seth, m. Mary M. **DOWNER**, b. of Bozrah, May 18, 1828, by		
Rev. David Austin	1	90
William, Col., d. May 25, 1787	1	5
William, of Bozrah, m. Anne **LATHROP**, of Lebanon, Apr. 6,		
1797	1	71
W[illiam, d. Jan. 27, 1848, ae 78 y.	1	71